The Works of Gilles Deleuze I: 1953-1969

Anamnesis

Anamnesis means remembrance or reminiscence, the collection and re-collection of what has been lost, forgotten, or effaced. It is therefore a matter of the very old, of what has made us who we are. But *anamnesis* is also a work that transforms its subject, always producing something new. To recollect the old, to produce the new: that is the task of *Anamnesis*.

a re.press series

The Works of Gilles Deleuze I: 1953-1969

Jon Roffe

re.press Melbourne 2020

re.press

http://www.re-press.org
© re.press 2020

The moral rights of the author are automatically asserted and recognized under Australian law (Copyright Amendment [Moral Rights] Act 2000).

This work is 'Open Access', published under a creative commons license which means that you are free to copy, distribute, display, and perform the work as long as you clearly attribute the work to the authors, that you do not use this work for any commercial gain in any form whatsoever and that you in no way alter, transform or build on the work outside of its use in normal academic scholarship without express permission of the author (or their executors) *and* the publisher of this volume. For any reuse or distribution, you must make clear to others the license terms of this work. For more information see the details of the creative commons licence at this website: http://creativecommons.org/licenses/by-nc-nd/2.5/

ISBN: 9780992373481 (paperback)
ISBN: 9780992373498 (hardback)

A catalogue record for this book is available from the National Library of Australia

The use of philosophy is to *sadden*. A philosophy that saddens no one, that annoys no one, is not a philosophy. It is useful for harming stupidity, for turning stupidity into something shameful.

Gilles Deleuze, *Nietzsche and Philosophy*

Contents

Abbreviations	page xi
Acknowledgements	xiii
Introduction	1
Three formal constants in Deleuze's work	2
About this book	4
1. Empiricism and Subjectivity	7
Two Humes, two empiricisms	8
Belief, illusion and reason	14
Fiction and madness in the understanding	18
The moral world	21
The genesis of subjectivity	29
2. Nietzsche and Philosophy	33
Nietzsche as philosopher	33
Structural account I: force and quality	38
Structural account II: the will to power	41
The doctrine of the eternal return	45
Genealogical account I: from consciousness to bad conscience	47
Genealogical account II: nihilism and transformation	52
3. Kant's Critical Philosophy	57
The doctrine of the faculties and the transcendental method	57
The doctrine of the faculties in the Critique of Pure Reason	60
The doctrine of the faculties in the Critique of Practical Reason	65
The doctrine of the faculties in the Critique of the Power of Judgement	70
History and 'the ruse of nature'	75
4. Bergsonism	77
Two kinds of multiplicity and their confusion	78
The method of intuition	80

Memory as virtual co-existence	*85*
The actualisation of virtual memory in experience	*89*
Space and time in science and metaphysics	*91*
The élan vital	*95*

5. Coldness and Cruelty — 103

'Are Sade and Masoch complementary?'	*103*
The language of Masoch and Sade	*107*
From the drives to disavowal with Freud	*111*
Five problems with Freud's account of masochism	*115*
Fathers and mothers	*116*
Contracts and institutions, humour and irony	*119*
Perversion and repetition	*124*

6. Proust and Signs — 131

The spider, the sign, the apprenticeship	*132*
First regime: the empty worldly signs	*134*
Second regime: the signs of love	*136*
Third regime: sensuous signs	*138*
Fourth regime: the signs of art	*140*
Essence: singularity, commonality, series, groups	*143*
The plurality of time	*144*
The nature of the search	*147*
The subject of the search	*153*

7. Difference and Repetition — 157

Difference and repetition reconsidered	*158*
CRITIQUE	*159*
Objective and subjective misrecognitions of difference	*159*
The objective misrecognition of difference in the history of philosophy	*160*
Univocity	*173*
The subjective misrecognition of difference	*176*
CONSTRUCTION	*190*
What is Deleuze's positive project in Difference and Repetition?	*190*
The virtual I: Kant and Maimon	*191*
The virtual II: differential calculus	*197*
The virtual III: defining the virtual	*203*
Intensity	*204*
The intensive individual	*213*
Temporal synthesis: identity and change over time	*218*
Human being	*231*
Indi-drama-different/ciation	*242*

Introduction   ix

8. Logic of Sense   245

The three guiding questions of the Logic of Sense   *247*
Two events   *248*
The Stoic distinction between bodies and events   *252*
Five propositions on the event   *258*
Language and sense   *268*
Sense and nonsense   *275*
Elements of psychoanalysis   *279*
First genetic moment: simulacra in the schizophrenic depths   *285*
Second genetic moment: the Icon in the heights   *287*
Third genetic moment: the bodily surface and the image of the phallus   *288*
Castration and the phantasm   *291*
Fourth genetic moment: thought and sense   *299*
An ethics of the event   *304*

Works of Gilles Deleuze   315

Other Works Cited   317

Postscript   325

Abbreviations

ABC	Deleuze from A to Z (video interview)
B	Bergsonism
DI	Desert Islands and Other Texts
DR	Difference and Repetition
ES	Empiricism and Subjectivity
LAT	Lettres et autres textes
LS	The Logic of Sense
M	'Coldness and Cruelty' in Masochism
N	Negotiations
NP	Nietzsche and Philosophy
PS	Proust and Signs
TRM	Two Regimes of Madness and Other Texts
WP	What is Philosophy?

Acknowledgements

This book originated in the Deleuze seminar that I have given, over the course of more than a decade now, at the Melbourne School of Continental Philosophy. I would, consequently, like to thank all of the students who attended to labour alongside me, but also all of the School's other members who made this seminar possible, particularly AJ Bartlett, Bryan Cooke, and James Garrett. The volume would not have been possible without Paul Ashton and Justin Clemens at re.press, and their capacity to temper their incredulity.

While it would be impossible to list all the scholars who work on Deleuze that have been formative in this effort, the idea of not recalling the most important of them is equally unthinkable: Ron Bogue, Gregg Flaxman, Gene Holland, Christian Kerslake, Anne Sauvagnargues, Daniel W. Smith, and James Williams.

I would also like to thank Marg Horwell, who drew two excellent diagrams for the book, one biological (p. 216) and one topological (p.266). John Cleary, Justin Clemens, Bryan Cooke, Simon Lumsden, Craig Lundy and Mairead Phillips read and commented on parts the book, saving me from numerous errors. Graham Jones read the whole manuscript, and, years before all of this, introduced me to Maimon's philosophy and in doing so opened my narrow rhizomism onto Deleuze's thought as such. Reviewers of the text for re.press also picked up a number of embarrassing errors that I am pleased will no longer be attributed to me. What remains is the result of my own intransigence.

For numerous other reasons, let me recall with gratitude Alex, Bartlett, Bellla, Ben, Cat, Charlotte, Dean, Georgia, Isabelle, Jack, James, Joe, Joeri, Mark, Mathilda, Marg, Nathan, Steve, Sophie, and Virginia.

Introduction

This book is an introduction, not to 'the philosophy' or 'the work' of Gilles Deleuze, but to each of his individual works.

A number of general introductions already exist. The synoptic approach that they tend to adopt, however, make an assumption that carries a strong risk, particularly in the case of Deleuze. They assume, in short, that the body of works under consideration are fundamentally homogenous.

It is true of course that the synthetic mode of summary sometimes gives rise to insightful and even daring portraits of Deleuze; more frequently it has led to the production of inaccurate and unhelpful caricatures. Some are only correct about some aspects of Deleuze's thought while belittling or ignoring others; some do not manage to systematically think through these concepts and their difficult and often obscure connections; others yet again are formed too heavily in the image of the author's investments. Given that there is no simple and apparent unity to Deleuze's work, the synoptic vision too easily distorts its object in one or other fashion: the interpretive assumption becomes a Procrustean bed, leading to the lopping off of some parts that don't easily fit and the bloating of those that remain.

This is why the aim of the current book is not to be an introduction to Deleuze, but to each of Deleuze's books on their own terms. In this way, I hope to avoid the dangers of the synoptic approach by resisting the urge—often provoked by perplexity—to rise up from the particular work under examination to the level of Deleuze's *oeuvre* as a whole. I would like simply to summarise what Deleuze says on the pages of each of his books. It is my conviction that we must read Deleuze, at least initially, in the mode of a Dostoyevskian idiot that he invokes in *Difference and Repetition*; we must be willing to maintain the position of ignorance for long enough to see what is on the page in front of us, rather than much too quickly insisting on what 'everyone already knows' about Deleuze.

THREE FORMAL CONSTANTS IN DELEUZE'S WORK

Now, while the content of Deleuze's works varies in numerous ways, it possesses a number of formal invariants. This is to say that while *what* Deleuze says varies to some degree, *how* he says it remains largely consistent. There are three of these important formal constants, structural features that are in some cases so ubiquitous as to be all but overlooked by many of Deleuze's readers. Being important, they must be kept in mind; being invariant, they fall outside of the proper content of this book. Consequently, I would like to briefly enumerate them here.

The first is the seemingly banal fact that every one of Deleuze's books unfolds through a complex dialogue with other thinkers. Not one makes its claims in a vacuum. As has been remarked almost *ad nauseam*, it is often difficult to precisely locate the position of the author in Deleuze: is he writing *about* Nietzsche? With the goal of integrating his own position with Nietzsche's? Is Nietzsche's name just a mask for Deleuze's own philosophy? And so on. While these questions can sometimes be resolved, often it appears impossible to say. Consider, for example, *Difference and Repetition*, which makes contact with almost every well-known philosopher in the Western canon, along with a large number of more obscure figures. So it is essential to note that Deleuze's own position is a garment stitched out of the full variety of these different fabrics. He may be the one who puts these moments together in the way that he does, but the product would be inconceivable without reference to them. So a good deal of what is involved in reading Deleuze's various works is the reading of the work of others that underlies, informs and directs Deleuze himself.

Deleuze's works are also, from beginning to end, systematic in form and ambition. While Deleuze will engage in a series of important reflections on what constitutes a system as such, his works manifest a perennial drive to elaborate a systematically coherent vision of the material under discussion. There is a certain dogmatic vision of Deleuze that has likely arisen on the basis of a slavish reading of the concept of the rhizome in *A Thousand Plateaus*, according to which Deleuze is an anti-systematic thinker. But it is very clear at the level of his own discourse that Deleuze moves in the opposite direction. He says it himself: 'Today it is said that systems are bankrupt, but it is only the concept of system that has changed'. (WP 9)

Deleuze's reading of Nietzsche, for example, itself runs counter to the widespread view that he is a kind of poetic, elusive writer, in which the aphoristic form functions to undermine systematicity in thought. For Deleuze, nothing is further from the truth. Likewise, and despite how strange this seems, Deleuze will present Lewis Carroll's fiction in terms of a systematic investigation, alongside a different but analogous reading of Artaud, in *The Logic of Sense*—where even Humpty Dumpty is presented as a philosopher of language. Elsewhere, Maurice Blanchot, Francis Bacon and Hollywood musicals are considered in the same way. It is this drive to systematize that is the real reason we must take Deleuze at his word and read him as a classical philosopher, even when his theory of system or structure is decidedly unorthodox. This makes Deleuze's way of reading other thinkers an inversion of a certain view of deconstructive reading. For the latter, the goal is to find those symptomatic weaknesses and lacunae at the systematic level—to show, for example, how Edmund Husserl's rigorous and intricately structured phenomenology relies upon a disavowed privileging of self-presence. For Deleuze, as Graham Jones once memorably put it, the goal is the opposite: to show that, however fragmentary they may seem, the works of great thinkers always manifest a nascent systematicity.

Third, Deleuze's systematic vision is metaphysical in nature. His effort is always to engage his topic on the grounds of the fundamental questions that have never ceased to exercise philosophy from its Platonic and pre-Socratic beginning. Thus, in his hands, the art of Francis Bacon is treated neither on the basis of any existential concerns nor a psychoanalytic account, nor any form of linguistic analysis (elements of a painting taken as signifiers). Colour, line, even art itself are conceived of in strong, metaphysical terms. The same holds for the infamous pair capitalism and schizophrenia: in the end, these are not social, economic or psychological terms in *Anti-Oedipus*, but metaphysical categories that speak of being as such. *Proust and Signs* invokes at its heart the category of essence, that archetypal metaphysical concept. Again, the precise *content* of Deleuze's metaphysics changes in a variety of ways, some quite fundamental, but the *form* of every one of his investigations has the status of foundational investigations. This is equally why we must always recall the philosophical register of his work, even when the books in question appear very far removed from philosophy in a traditional sense. It's all philosophy, 'nothing but philosophy, in the traditional sense of the word'. (TRM 176)

ABOUT THIS BOOK

Due to the approach I have adopted, each of the chapters to follow are independent entities, each devoted to a summary explication of one of Deleuze's books on its own terms.

I have not attempted to be comprehensive. Aside from the fact that not one of his works is exhaustively comprehended by anyone—something that is a positive feature of any good work of philosophy as much as it is a thorn in the side of its readers—any attempt to do justice to any book in a scant handful of pages would be doomed to failure. This said, I have nevertheless striven to present *definitive* accounts of Deleuze's works. Each of the chapters that follows should provide a skeletal overlay, delineating the spine and major structural bones of the book in question. The more delicate ossature, muscle tissues and other microstructures should then be able to be fit into place.

It may go without saying that to strive to give a definitive account is not necessarily to have done so; I am not the one who will have grasped these books in their totality, if this was even possible. But, contrary to the view espoused by some who have taken too many hits on the rhizome, elucidation and explanation of Deleuze's work remains a valuable endeavor.

A glance at the contents page may have alerted you to the fact that Deleuze's complementary thesis, *Expressionism in Philosophy: Spinoza*, is not discussed. While many of Deleuze's works are studies of other philosophers, thereby giving any effort of summary an occasionally awkward tertiary character, this book is an extreme case (the *Kant* volume is a close second). So much exposition of Spinoza's thought is required in order to explain what is novel in Deleuze's reading that the goal of skeletal summary simply became impossible. If you come to the current volume looking for a summary of his reading of Spinoza, and are already in possession of an understanding of the latter's work, then let me simply say: read Deleuze's book itself.

On a related note, I have made use of *Negotiations*, and the two posthumous collections *Desert Islands and Other Texts*, and *Two Regimes of Madness*, only in passing, and only where what Deleuze says or writes there reflects directly on the book under discussion.

The abbreviations I will use to refer to Deleuze's texts are fairly self-evident; a list can be found at the front of this volume. Thanks to the capitalist vigour of the academic publishing industry, there are now two and as many as five editions of each of Deleuze's books, which makes the clear use of pagination increasingly difficult. We await a proper critical edition of his work. Here I have elected to cite the first version of the English text that appeared.

I have often modified the existing translation, but I will only make an issue of it when it concerns the content of Deleuze's argument. For the most part, errors in the existing versions are the result of the translator's zeal for the book exceeding their grasp of the intellectual context within which Deleuze is working. I have otherwise dispensed with much of the usual academic cutlery of citations. This includes, after some oscillation, the absenting of page references to the original French.

Where I cite other works, it is almost exclusively to clarify the source of Deleuze's argument. In these cases, I use only their title and the form of appropriate page reference: for instance, references to both editions of Kant's *Critique of Pure Reason* (e.g., A297/B354), or the essay number and section of Nietzsche's *On the Genealogy of Morality*. Full bibliographic details for all works cited can be found at the end of the book.

Gone too are any references to the secondary literature on Deleuze, which constitutes an ever-growing and increasingly unmanageable corpus. I do not mean to pretend that all of this material is pointless, or that this book replaces them. I am simply interested in giving to readers of Deleuze's works a considered vantage point that—in its presentation, if not my interminable labour to understand it, which has always been fed by many fine secondary works—relies upon extrinsic material as little as possible.

I

Empiricism and Subjectivity

Before being published in 1953, *Empiricism and Subjectivity: An Essay on Hume's Theory of Human Nature* was Deleuze's *diplôme d'études supérieures*, the rough equivalent of a masters degree, submitted the year before and supervised by the great Hegelian Jean Hyppolite. The thesis itself was typed up by Deleuze's friend Michel Tournier; Deleuze inscribed his copy of the book with the words 'For Michel, the book that he typed and criticized, roundly protested, and may have even shortened since I'm sure that it was longer'. (Dosse, *Intersecting Lives*, 111)

Deleuze had come into contact with Hume's thought and empiricism more generally in a number of ways. He had attended a course on Hume given by Hyppolite (to whom *Empiricism and Subjectivity* is dedicated) in the 1946-47 academic year; but it is certainly Jean Wahl who was a more significant influence. Wahl's own principal PhD thesis was entitled *Les Philosophies pluralists d'Angleterre et d'Amérique* [The pluralist philosophies of England and America], and this material was the subject he taught between 1944 and 1948 at the Sorbonne, classes attended by Deleuze. Wahl himself is less than keen about Hume's philosophy, but it seems all but certain that he was the inspiration for Deleuze working on the latter's thought.

It is also worth noting that Deleuze, along with his friend André Cresson, published another text on Hume the year prior to the appearance of *Empiricism and Subjectivity*. *David Hume, sa Vie, son Oeuvre avec un Exposé de sa Philosophie* [David Hume, his Life and Thought, with an Exposition of his Philosophy] is composed of a selection of Hume's writings, along with a biography and general summary of his thought. Though the latter is co-signed by Deleuze and Cresson, it bears all of the hallmarks of Deleuze's own take on Hume; he was doubtless the author of the text.

TWO HUMES, TWO EMPIRICISMS

The best way to introduce Deleuze's reading of Hume is to contrast it to the famous reading offered by Immanuel Kant. This contrast, offered by Deleuze himself, also allows us to distinguish between two conceptions of empiricism, and, beyond this, to make sense of the definition of philosophy that Deleuze advances in *Empiricism and Subjectivity*.

Schematically speaking—and here I'm following the opening moments of Hume's precocious masterpiece *Treatise of Human Nature* (1739)—the traditional Kantian reading emphasises the following points:

1. Because the search for knowledge is undertaken by human beings, the claims of science are bounded by human nature. What can be known with certainty is limited by what human beings can know with certainty.
2. Consequently, the first and most fundamental science has to be the science of human nature. Discovering what this nature is will tell us what we can know.
3. As a result, the science of human nature must be based in 'a cautious observation of human life'. (Treatise, Introduction.10)
4. All knowledge is drawn from experience. To be more precise, all of our ideas—our mental images of things, which constitute the substance of 'thinking'—have their source in impressions, the name we can give to sensing or 'feeling', as we do when we see or touch something, or feel pleasure or pain.
5. Most knowledge, however, involves more than just simple ideas that correspond to single impressions. They are, rather, complex ideas, which are composed of a number of simple ideas.
6. Complex ideas are formed according to certain tendencies that we can observe at work in thinking. These are the principles of association. I tend to associate ideas—I habitually associate ideas—that are similar to each other (principle of *resemblance*); I tend to associate ideas whose impressions arise in temporal proximity (principle of *contiguity*); I tend to associate ideas in terms of cause and effect (principle of *cause and effect*)

Hume as epistemologist

The reading of Hume advanced by Kant and the interpretive tradition that comes in his wake focusses on point 4, its presuppositions and its consequences. It does so in the context of a very specific belief: the belief in the reality of causality. It is unsurprising that the following example of billiards from the *Enquiry Concerning Human Understanding* is among Hume's most well-known texts:

> When I see, for instance, a Billiard-ball moving in a straight line towards another; [...] may I not conceive, that a hundred different events might as well follow from the cause? May not both these balls remain at absolute rest? May not the first ball return in a straight line, or leap off from the second in any line or direction? All these suppositions are consistent and conceivable. Why then should we give the preference to one, which is no more consistent or conceivable than the rest? All our reasonings *a priori* will never be able to show us any foundation for this preference. (Hume, *Enquiry*, 4.25)

The discussion is famous. There is no logical contradiction involved in claiming that the second billiard ball could doing anything whatsoever after coming into contact with the first. Any motion or lack of motion is easily conceivable. But, we might respond, causality is not a logical structure but a real, physical one—physics can give us certitude where thought cannot. It is here that the primary consequence of point 4 appears. Our only knowledge of physics, of the laws supposed to govern the movement of bodies, is drawn from experience. But this knowledge is not gained by any kind of direct intellectual intuition of the structure of nature. Indeed, we have *no direct access* to nature—if we have any at all. What do we know about billiards? Only that, in the cases we happen to have seen, a certain set of outcomes have taken place. But, we can reply again, haven't we always seen the white ball causing the red ball to move in a certain predictable fashion? Aren't there pool sharks who make a living on it? What we certainly haven't directly experienced are *causes*. I am in the habit of associating two ideas that commonly occur one after the other—smoke from my cigarette in the wake of the argument. This is what Hume calls 'constant conjunction', (*Treatise* 1.1.8) and it is the real kernel of beliefs about cause and effect.

While he provides his own transcendental solution to this problem, Kant thought that, despite his skepticism, Hume had discovered something essential:

> The famous David Hume was one of these geographers of human reason [...] He dwelt primarily on the principle of causality, and quite rightly remarked about that that one could not base its truth (Indeed not even the objective validity of the concept of an efficient cause in general) on any Insight **at** all... (Kant, *Critique of Pure Reason* A761/B789)

This is the negative or critical facet of Hume's argument. It is doubled by a second positive, or constructive moment. Hume's 'sceptical solution' (*Enquiry* 5.1) to this apparent impasse is grounded not in *nature*—which we have no direct access to—but, as point 6 of the summary indicates, in the principles of association, and therefore in *human nature*. Our grasp of billiards is not a result of the operation of the balls themselves, but the result of the habitual association of ideas.

So, on the one hand, we have no reason to think that real causation exists or does not; on the other, we have good reason to think that all causality is a matter of habit in thought. This problem, Hume's problem of induction, is taken by the Kantian tradition to be emblematic. The more general perspective has the same double character. On the one hand, no belief about the world itself is either justified or falsified by direct access to the world—because we have no such access. On the other hand, the legitimacy of belief is conveyed by factors internal to human thought. Thus, from this Kantian perspective, then, empiricism appears as a fundamentally epistemological affair. It is a philosophical doctrine concerned above all with ascertaining the reliability of our beliefs. This is a first version of Hume, and a first vision of empiricism to go along with it.

Hume as a social and political thinker

Notice that the very idea of knowledge itself is undone by this line of analysis. We cannot *know* anything about how the world itself is, and the alleged objects of our experience are not present to thought. In its place, Hume advances a certain conception of *belief*. What the minimalist epistemological Hume appears to provide us with—though, as we will see, things are more complicated than they appear—is a rule for distinguishing legitimate from illegitimate beliefs, and not truth and falsity or knowledge and opinion.

Now, Deleuze is certainly impressed with this line of argument. In the preface to the English translation of *Empiricism and Subjectivity*, he writes that Hume 'established the concept of *belief* and put it in the place of knowledge. He laicized belief, turning knowledge into a legitimate belief'. (ES ix) What he will not sanction is the idea that this argument, and the concept of belief, are anything like the main points of Hume's thought.

> The classical definition of empiricism proposed by the Kantian tradition is this: empiricism is the theory according to which knowledge not only begins with experience but is derived from it. But *why* would the empiricist say that? And as the result of which question? [...] The definition is in no way satisfactory: first of all, because knowledge is not the

most important thing for empiricism, but only the means to some practical activity. (ES 107)

The first reason, then, why Deleuze wishes to break with the Kantian reading of Hume is that it gives pride of place to a secondary, subordinate element. By giving pride of place to the epistemological register, this reading has located the centre of gravity of Hume's empiricism in the wrong place. What is essential, instead, is social reality, and knowledge or belief is only properly understood if we adopt this perspective.

Before arriving at these topics, Deleuze makes three central claims. The first of these finesses point two on our numbered summary above:

> Hume proposes the creation of a science of humanity, but what is really his fundamental project? [...] Hume's project entails the *substitution of a psychology of the mind with a psychology of the mind's affections*. The constitution of a psychology of the mind is not at all possible, since this psychology cannot find in its object the required constancy or universality; only a psychology of affections will be capable of constituting the true science of humanity. (ES 21)

We cannot avoid starting with human nature, but, Hume tells us, when we ask what this is exactly, the answer is not an encouraging one: 'when I enter most intimately into what I call myself, I always stumble on some particular perception or other, of heat or cold, light or shade, love or hatred, pain or pleasure. I never can catch myself at any time without a perception, and never can observe any thing but the perception. (Hume, *Treatise*, 1.4.6.3) According to another famous passage, my mind is fundamentally 'nothing but a bundle or collection of different perceptions, which succeed each other with an inconceivable rapidity, and are in a perpetual flux and movement [...] The mind is a kind of theatre, where several perceptions successively make their appearance; pass, repass, glide away, and mingle in an infinite variety of postures and situations. (Hume, *Treatise*, 1.4.6.4) This is what Deleuze means when he says that a psychology of the mind does not find enough constancy or universality in its object (the mind itself) to study it.

Obviously this is a problem! If Hume wants to ground all the sciences in the science of the mind, but the mind appears to be nothing more than a fleeting succession of impressions or images, then the prospects for the whole operation look grim. But we do not need to identify this project with Hume's. Another path lies open, and that is to consider how it is that, despite this being the mind in its basic state, our lives and thoughts in fact possess order and systematicity: I *can* predict what will happen in a game of pool.

From this point of view—and here is Deleuze's second opening move—the question of human nature shifts. Instead of asking 'what is it?', as if it was a fixed thing, identifiable with the mind, we now ask how is it that stability in this flux of images comes about? This is precisely what he calls *Hume's question*. It is presented in a variety of forms throughout the book:

> *how does the mind become human nature?* (ES 2)
>
> How does a collection become a system? (ES 3)
>
> How does the imagination become a faculty? (ES 23)
>
> How does the imagination become human nature? (ES 23)
>
> How is the subject constituted inside the given? (ES 109)

From these, let's emphasise the equivalences: by *imagination*, Deleuze does not mean any kind of active capacity that human beings possess, but just this primary state of the mind, which is just a collection of images. The question around which Deleuze's whole reading turns is thus how this *constitution* takes place. Given that the mind itself is a chaos of images, we need to study the means by which a passage to systematicity is effected—from nature to human nature, or subjectivity.

So, Deleuze's third initial point will have to concern what exactly affects the mind in order to give rise to human nature. His answer: 'the two forms under which the mind is *affected* are essentially the *passional* and the *social*'. (ES 21) Though we will need to define these terms more carefully in the pages to come, the point is straightforward: at its core, human existence is characterized by the throes of pleasure and pain, and all of the more complex passions drawn from them. But these passions or affects are never played out in a pure interiority. Our passional existence is always already caught up in the social world, which not only evokes certain passions and represses others, but much more provides means for their expression and satisfaction. This explains one of the more striking passages in the opening chapter of *Empiricism and Subjectivity*: 'the option of the psychologist may be expressed paradoxically as follows: one must be a moralist, sociologist, or historian *before* being a psychologist, *in order* to be a psychologist'. (ES 22) The theory of human nature Hume is after has to be a theory of the formation of the subject, but this formation cannot be explained without beginning with the social context in which the formation takes place.

The goal of the rest of this chapter will be to work through these points in more detail—to traverse Deleuze's argument in *Empiricism and Subjectivity* to show precisely how belief and the passions are integrated in a form of social subjectivity. We will do this in a sort of reverse order. First, we will work through the full trajectory of Hume's epistemology (abbreviated above) in order to reveal the insurmountable problems that *believing* and *reasoning* confront on their own terms. Second, we will see how the more elementary affective investment in the social world not only resolves these problems but provide believing and reasoning with the orientation that they require. And finally, we will turn explicitly to the topic of subjectivity, and see how the passage from the constitution of stable beliefs and affects is doubled by a passage from the passive imagination to the active self of Hume's thought.

What is philosophy?

But before turning to this broader task, we are already in a position to appreciate the unusual definition of philosophy that Deleuze presents in *Empiricism and Subjectivity*. As we have just seen, Deleuze in part rejects the Kantian reading of Humean empiricism because it does not manage to properly locate *which question* it is asking. In this light, his definition of philosophy is not surprising: 'A philosophical theory is an elaborately developed question, and nothing else; by itself and in itself, it is not the resolution to a problem, but the elaboration, *to the very end*, of the necessary implications of a formulated question'. (ES 106)

As Deleuze goes on to emphasise, this has a profound consequence for any attempt to critique a philosophy. There is literally no sense in claiming that a philosopher does not provide good answers to questions—Deleuze says here that the answering of questions is the domain of science. He quickly invokes four legitimate critical approaches: to object that 'the question raised by a philosopher is not a good one', to object that 'we should raise it in a better way', to object that 'we should raise a different question. The fourth is the most tantalising: we can object that a philosophy 'does not force the nature of things enough'. (ES 107) A good philosophy or a significant philosophical development therefore involves 'subordinating and subjecting things to the question, intending, through this constrained and forced subsumption, that they reveal an essence or a nature.' (ES 106) This is tantalising—the guiding pair for philosophy is not question and answer, but question and essence. The question should force something to expose what is essential about it; it constitutes a demand. This is an image of philosophy as an involuntary interrogation of things.

But what then to make of the other definition he provides, on the closing page of the book: 'Philosophy must constitute itself as a theory of what we are doing, not as a theory of what there is'? (ES 133) In fact, this is the same definition, now inflected with Hume's concerns. When we pose the question 'how is the subject constituted within the given?' in its full generality and rigour, the essential stands out: epistemology is of no concern, only practical existence, the social and moral dimension of human being.

BELIEF, ILLUSION AND REASON

The entire affair of belief in Hume takes place in the context of the *imagination*. Deleuze takes his goal to be that of isolating the two basic states of the imagination—*collection* and *faculty*—and explaining how the *qualification* of the former is what constitutes the latter.

On the one hand, the imagination is quite simply a mess, a collection of disparate elements, an inconsistent multiplicity. This is why he writes that

> Hume never ceases to affirm the identity between the mind, the imagination, and the idea. The mind is not nature, nor does it have a nature [...] The collection of ideas is called 'imagination' insofar as this term designates not a faculty but rather a set, a set of things in the vaguest sense of the term, which are as they appear—a collection without an album, a play without a stage, a flux of perceptions. (ES 23)

Following Hume, Deleuze calls this state of the imagination the *fancy*. As I have indicated, this is primarily an organisational category rather than a power or faculty. But in this disorganisation, there remains an organisation without principle. This is what explains the fact that the imagination as fancy is constantly presenting the most demented images on its own terms: 'it moves through the universe, engendering fire dragons, winged horses, and monstrous giants. The depth of the mind is indeed delirium or—the same thing from another point of view—change and indifference'. (ES 23)

On the other hand, the imagination is an active capacity to believe, which is to say, to *transcend the given*, the collection of ideas or the fancy (Deleuze's French is *dépasser*—exceed, overcome, transcend). The active capacity borne by the imagination is the capacity to 'affirm more than I know'. (ES 26) Hume's point is that we *do* transcend the given. This is what is most obvious about our beliefs. So the entire issue, to reiterate, is to explain how a qualification of an unrelated set of ideas could possibly give rise to a *believing subject*. Now, while this project has obvious developmental resonances, Deleuze repeatedly warns us against conceiving of Hume's account in *genetic* terms. The difference between the imagination as fancy and as faculty is a difference in perspective, not two discrete moments in a process ('as an infant, we have simple ideas, but how do we come to later have beliefs?'). Or, to be more precise—since Deleuze too speaks of the development of the subject—the fancy is not to be conceived of as a crude material that is used up in the formation of the subject, but a permanent stratum of the subject that is qualified in numerous and complex ways.

Very well. This is the general framework of Deleuze's account of belief in Hume. But now we need to see exactly how beliefs themselves are formed, and to what extent we are capable of discriminating between legitimate and illegitimate beliefs. Later we will turn to the question of the active imagination, or the subject *who* believes.

The principles of association

The qualification of the fancy is the effect of the principles of association. We have already seen what these are—the habitual tendency, within the mind, to associate ideas in terms of contiguity, resemblance, and the cause and effect relation. What are these principles, though? Unfortunately, we can know nothing of them in themselves, according to Hume, neither their origin, nor the reason why they function in human thought. We can only infer that the principles are at work on the basis of a careful attention to the forms of constancy in thought that they produce.

What exactly do the principles do? They do not produce beliefs as such. Instead, they constitute certain habitual tendencies in the mind. Since Hume himself encourages us to consider his work as a 'mental geography' (Hume, *Enquiry*, 1.12), let's consider a geographical metaphor. At the level of the fancy, the mind is a flat plain, without any structure at all. Any organisation of ideas on this plain would be indifferent and chaotic. The role of the principles of association is to wear certain grooves into this plain, the way that herds of animals, by dint of habit, wear paths to and from a river or water hole. In the last chapter of *Empiricism and Subjectivity*, Deleuze makes use of a related metaphor (including a reference to the idea of reason we'll come back to shortly):

> The principles of association establish natural relations among ideas, forming an entire network similar to a system of channels inside the mind. No longer do we move accidentally from one idea to another. One idea naturally introduces another on the basis of a principle; ideas naturally follow one another. In short, under the influence of association, imagination becomes reason and the fancy finds constancy. (ES 123)

Beliefs, in turn, are complex ideas formed in accordance with these habitual associations. To say 'I'm sure the sun will rise on your birthday with the same gross incandescence it always does', or 'what is mine today will be mine tomorrow', or 'hit that red ball on the corner with a little spin and it'll go in the back left pocket' is for ideas to move, according to habit, into complexes of belief.

Illegitimate beliefs and the role of reason

We encounter at this point a first, arresting problem. The principles of association give an habituated structure to the mind. But some of these are *bad habits*. Consider the example of my lucky shirt. Whenever I wear this otherwise run of the mill blue shirt, good things happen—I get the energy together to finish a book chapter, can stomach looking in the mirror, or find money on the ground. And my belief in the power of my lucky shirt is formed through the association of cause and effect—in other words, in exactly the same way that I form the belief that putting the kettle on the stove will boil the water inside of it.

A more troubling example: many people hold the belief that owning a gun will make them safe. This belief can arise in a wide range of ways, but let's say that it arises in a given case from a nexus of connections between ideas of family, raising livestock, childhood happiness, and the omnipresence of firearms in everyday life. The example is so troubling here not because it is obviously wrong, but because it is formed in exactly the same way as the belief in a convincing piece of scientific argumentation.

In a word, habitual association is *ungrounded*. The beliefs that arise from it cannot be relied upon simply because they are associated. Neither can beliefs be relied upon by virtue of the ideas they are composed of. This is what Deleuze is getting at when he invokes the externality of relations: 'Relations are external to their terms. This means that ideas do not account for the nature of the operations that we perform on them, and especially of the relations that we establish among them'. (ES 101)

What is required, clearly, is a means for distinguishing between legitimate and illegitimate beliefs, but one that can derive its force from neither the content of the associated ideas or the principles of association themselves in their primary operation. This means is what Hume calls *reason*. Reason here is neither an independent faculty or power, as it is in Kant, nor the quintessential character of thinking, as it is in Descartes or Spinoza. It is closer to what we mean when we think of the hunch of a detective; the declaration of reason in Hume is not Leibniz's 'for everything there is a reason!' but 'something seems wrong here'. As Deleuze puts it, reason is 'a kind of feeling', (ES 30) a feeling for incongruity in the set of beliefs that I hold. And like association in general, reason is habitual: 'experimental reason is born of habit—and not vice versa. Habit is the root of reason, and indeed the principle from which reason stems as an effect'. (ES 62)

Deleuze emphasises that reason in Hume is fundamentally *comparative, corrective* and *probabilistic*. Indeed, reason is corrective in function by virtue of being comparative: it feels out beliefs that, when compared to the broader range of my other beliefs, are out of place. A legitimate belief, therefore, will be consistent with the 'repetitions observed in experience'. (ES 72) My belief in the powers of the lucky shirt are undermined when I put it in the context of my other beliefs about shirts, about the nature of the physical world, and about magical powers. The belief that 'Irishmen cannot have wit' (Hume, *Treatise*, 1.3.13.7) can be tested by spending more time with the Irish. The belief in the saining power of guns, though it also engages profound social investments, can be undermined by considering this belief in the context of the other beliefs we have about safety and violence. It is no surprise, therefore, that the infamous National Rifle Association does everything it can to stop any research into gun violence. Without a broader body of beliefs to compare the 'guns are for safety' belief to, there is no way to determine its legitimacy. In Humean terms, then, the activities of the NRA are the very definition of irrationality.

But reason is also, importantly, *probabilistic*: because none of my beliefs attains to the level of true knowledge, any of them might have arisen through excessive and illegitimate use of association. Consequently, reason affirms the likelihood of correctness. The well-known Latin phrase *ceteris paribus* suits Humean reason perfectly: *all other things being equal*, this belief is legitimate.

Reason, therefore, limits the degree to which we confuse legitimate and illegitimate beliefs. This limitative function has a particular significance with respect to language—the problem here is that the repetition of claims about something come to be confused with knowledge of these things. More precisely, at issue are '*fictitious causalities*. Language, by itself, produces belief, as it substitutes observed repetition with spoken repetition, and the impression of a present object with the hearing of a specific word which allows us to conceive ideas vividly'. (ES 70) In this situation—and philosophers in particular are the target here, with our talk of monads, agents, reasons ...—reason functions to test the beliefs engendered by language against their prominence in direct experience.

Reason is thus, in sum, a comparative habit of thinking that corrects for the threat of excess borne by the principles of association.

FICTION AND MADNESS IN THE UNDERSTANDING

A kind of bucolic, conservative naturalism is thus attained. We grant that reason is only a secondary, corrective power, but it is one that it gives us more or less stable guidelines for distinguishing between legitimate and illegitimate beliefs. We keep an eye on language in particular as a source of illusions. And, despite the fact that some people are going to go on believing that possession of firearms is the guarantee and emblem of any true social compact, overall, legitimate belief will win the day.

But, Deleuze emphasises, the problem of fiction is a much more serious and profound one for Hume than this first stage of the argument conveys. My belief in the powers of my lucky shirt can be defused by situating it in the broader context of my beliefs about shirts in general, and the grimy, self-serving way the fantasy of luck is peddled. But there are some beliefs which cannot be subject to the comparative work of reason *at all*. This is the particular focus of the 'God and the World' chapter, although it is a topic returned to throughout *Empiricism and Subjectivity*; Deleuze considers four decisive uncorrectable beliefs.

The idea of *the world*—as the totality of what exists—is the first case. Notice first that I never encounter the world in experience, which is to say that even if I was to somehow total up all of my impressions, I would never arrive at the 'all' that characterises the idea of the world (in the first *Critique*, Kant will make decisive use of this in the Antinomies). It seems like a hallmark case of an illegitimate belief. The problem here concerns the fact that, as we have seen, the corrective work of reason is *comparative* ('compared to my beliefs about shirts in general ...'). But as Deleuze points out, 'The world as such is essentially the Unique' (ES 75)—there is nothing to compare it to. Worse again, the idea of the world seems embedded as a presupposition in all of my other ideas: after all, 'there are no physical objects or objects of repetition except in the world'. (ES 75) Already in this first example, we confront the general problem: I possess a belief that I can neither validate nor invalidate, and that at the same time is presupposed by all of my other beliefs.

The second case is the idea of God. In his *Dialogues concerning Natural Religion*, Hume subjects the claim that belief in God and science are compatible to penetrating criticisms. And yet, famously, as the book draws to a close, Hume (in the guise of Philo) seems to reverse tack and affirm the belief in God's existence. We cannot discuss the details of this point here, but suffice to say Deleuze sees no reversal in play. It is rather that the belief in God cannot in the end be subject to a rational criticism and rejection—

not because God is ineffable, but because of the character of rational critique itself.

The formation of a belief in God can take place in a variety of ways. For instance, recalling the capacity for repetitions in language to be taken as repetitions in experience, social practices like attending church and speaking the liturgy can achieve this end. If reason attempts to delegitimate this belief, though—as Hume does in the *Dialogues*—it confronts a problem: as even 'the most stupid thinker' recognizes, the world appears to have 'a purpose, an intention, a design'. (Hume, *Dialogues* 12.2). Deleuze puts the point like this: 'we can always think of God negatively, as the cause of the principles' (ES 77); we can always posit God as the reason why the world is the way that it is. This belief cannot be corrected, though, because (once again) we have no access to how the world is in itself. If reason functions against the background of the whole set of other beliefs that I have, then it would seem that the belief in God *does* hold weight—after all, my experience of the world *is* orderly and meaningful, as the theist claims. Even though it corresponds to no direct evidence (no impressions correspond to the ideas I have of God), then, this belief is both ungrounded and unquestionable.

The third case is the idea of the object. The situation here is, if anything, more troubling. The idea of any object involves two component fictions, produced by two different illegitimate uses of association. On the one hand, I have no experience of an object subsisting over time, but only a flux of perceptions that (like Monet's haystacks) are perpetually changing. Association allows me to form the idea of the object such that it possesses an identity beneath these changes: 'the imagination [...] feigns continuous existence in order to overcome the opposition between the identity of resembling perceptions and the discontinuity of appearances' (ES 79). The problem here is that I have no idea at all whether the haystack is one object or many different ones, or whether, to misuse Quine's celebrated example, what I just experienced was a rabbit (one object) running in front of me, or rather an ensemble of different, rabbity parts, I nevertheless habitually make this confusion.

On the other hand, the idea of the object makes illegitimate use of the causal association. Remember that, for Hume, we must remain agnostic about the status of real causality because we never have any direct experience of it. Causality, in Hume's sense, is and can only be a relation between ideas. But this distinction is exactly the one that I perpetually confuse whenever I say even innocuous things, like 'that orange was bitter'—I am claiming that the orange *itself* gives rise to certain effects. More generally, my beliefs are not beliefs about the association of my ideas, but beliefs about objects as they are in themselves. The kicker is that we *cannot* do without this belief in the subsistent unity and causal efficacy of objects. If I am not receiving facts from the real orange, then experience is not experience at all, but an hallucination. Every single belief that we have engages, explicitly or otherwise, in this confusion of the in-itself and the for-me.

The fourth uncorrectable belief concerns what Deleuze, drawing from Kant, calls *purposiveness* (*Zweckmässigkeit*) or *finality*. At issue is the relationship between nature itself and human nature, the world and human being—a primitive harmony. While the idea of the object illegitimately presupposes a causal relationship that cannot be falsified, the idea of purposiveness is that the effects of God and the object on me *are not misleading*. Just as I cannot avoid believing that it is the orange *itself* that is responsible for my belief that it is bitter, I cannot avoid believing that it is the orange itself that *really is* bitter. We must believe—we cannot avoid believing—in 'a kind of pre-established harmony between the course of nature and the succession of our ideas', *even though* 'the powers and forces by which the former is governed, be wholly unknown to us'. (Hume, *Enquiry* 2.44) While, as Deleuze notes, this pre-established harmony between self and world corresponds to no particular experience, and is 'undoubtedly the weakest and emptiest of thoughts', (ES 133) we nevertheless affirm it implicitly at each moment. We are simply not in a position to question the belief that there is a 'fit' between the world and our experience of it, despite the fact that there is no way at all to justify or rationally examine it.

Fiction as principle of human nature

The significance of these beliefs is as obvious as is their absolute precarity. The entire work of association is cast into question, for no matter how hard we strive to distinguish between the legitimate and the illegitimate in particular cases, we are unable to do so in the most important cases.

Even the most legitimate beliefs—according to a careful comparative rational examination—are in the end founded on others that are completely ungrounded. In other words, fiction itself—a fictionalising of foundational beliefs—*is a principle of human nature*. We simply cannot do without it. The entire downstream production of beliefs is, as a result, a delirium. The problem is not one, two, or four particular fictions, but the general state of affairs; the apparent 'order' of the structured mind is *madness*:

> From the point of view of philosophy, the mind is no longer anything but delirium and madness. [...] With the belief in the existence of bodies, fiction itself as a principle is opposed to the principles of association: the latter are *principally*, not *subsequently* excessive [...] Fantasy triumphs. [...] Here, the most insane is still nature. The system is a mad delirium. (ES 83)

Our earlier bucolic naturalism has now appears unnatural and terrifying, like the farmhouse in a horror film after the fall of dusk. Thought appears trapped in a hall of mirrors, where everything that is natural, reliable and true suddenly appears indiscernible from its uncanny, demented reflection. What then to do?

> The intense view of these manifold contradictions and imperfections in human reason has so wrought upon me, and heated my brain, that I am ready to reject all belief and reasoning, and can look upon no opinion even as more probable or likely than another. Where am I, or what? From what causes do I derive my existence, and to what condition shall I return? Whose favour shall I court, and whose anger must I dread? What beings surround me? and on whom have, I any influence, or who have any influence on me? I am confounded with all these questions, and begin to fancy myself in the most deplorable condition imaginable, invironed with the deepest darkness, and utterly deprived of the use of every member and faculty.
>
> Most fortunately it happens, that since reason is incapable of dispelling these clouds, nature herself suffices to that purpose, and cures me of this philosophical melancholy and delirium, either by relaxing this bent of mind, or by some avocation, and lively impression of my senses, which obliterate all these chimeras. I dine, I play a game of backgammon, I converse, and am merry with my friends; and when after three or four hours' amusement, I would return to these speculations, they appear so cold, and strained, and ridiculous, that I cannot find in my heart to enter into them any farther. (Hume, *Treatise* 1.4.7.7-8)

THE MORAL WORLD

There are two ways of summarising the problem confronting belief. We have just seen the first: legitimate beliefs and fictions are both produced in the mind by the same operation, and we have no fundamental criteria to distinguish between them. Mad delirium. From this point of view, the 'backgammon solution' looks a lot like giving up—'When there's no way out, the only way out is to give in'—a kind of defeatist quietism that would lead away from critical thinking in the name of some kind of life untroubled by thought. But Deleuze also makes the point in a slightly more promising register: belief is unable to properly orient itself *on its own terms*. The actual response to the threat of fictional beliefs is to see that the real criteria for belief and the application of reason is not found at the level of belief or reason itself. It is instead found in the practical context of social life. From this second perspective, the backgammon game with which Hume finishes the first book of the *Treatise* serves to dramatize the actual subordination of belief to practical social existence on the other.

That is: no matter how extensive my battery of habituated cause and effect associations concerning a hammer, or a television remote, I *need a reason to use it*. No one effect is good on its own terms. Consider again the critical function of reason, which is a comparative habit of mind. Why would I ever develop or employ this habit? As we well know from the shameful history of human political life, the fact that I *can* work to distinguish between legitimate and illegitimate beliefs in no way ensures that I *will*. More generally, there must be a reason why the principles of association function the particular ways that they do: as an *end* which is no longer just one logically consistent possible outcome among others. The troubling aspects of the fiction of belief are the result of the practical indifference of belief (or an hypothetical version of this fiction), and can therefore be remedied by practical engagement: 'reason can always be brought to bear, but it is brought to bear on a pre-existing world and presupposes an antecedent morality and an order of ends'. (ES 33)

Some of Hume's most celebrated claims relate to this point, for instance, this one: 'Reason is, and ought only to be the slave of the passions, and can never pretend to any other office than to serve and obey them'. (Hume, *Treatise*, 3.3.3.4) Deleuze has his own favourite line: 'the principal sentence of the *Treatise* is this: "'Tis not contrary to reason to prefer the destruction of the whole world to the scratching of my finger"' (ES 33; Hume, *Treatise*, 2.3.3.6). So, precisely how does all of this fit together?

The nature of the passions and the limits of sympathy

Hume's moral philosophy begins with what he takes to be the two most important impressions of sensation involved in motivating action: pleasure and pain. These impressions give rise to ideas of course, but what makes them particularly important is that they also have a further effect. Right at the beginning of the *Treatise*, this is how Hume explains it:

> An impression first strikes upon the senses, and makes us perceive heat or cold, thirst or hunger, pleasure or pain, of some kind or other. Of

this impression there is a copy taken by the mind, which remains after the impression ceases; and this we call an idea. This idea of pleasure or pain, when it returns upon the soul, produces the new impressions of desire and aversion, hope and fear, which may properly be called impressions of reflection, because derived from it. (T 1.1.2.2)

Impressions of reflection play a key role in Deleuze's account of subjectivity in Hume, as we will see in the next section. For now, the takeaway is specific: these are secondary impressions that arise not in relation to encounters in sensation, but as the result of ideas. While Hume's account is more complex than this might appear—since the passions are either direct or indirect, either the immediate result of an idea of pain or pleasure, or caught up in other ideas as well—for our purposes this elementary structure will be adequate.

As Hume's examples show, a passion is an *emotion* or *affect*. Deleuze will also use the term *drive* in this context, in recognition of the fact that, for Hume, passions are the source of motivation. Notice what this means: we are motivated to act by neither pleasure and pain themselves, nor by rational considerations. The sphere of agency is the sphere of the passions, impressions that arise *from* pleasure and pain and reflected *in* the mind through the imagination, while exceeding both. And it is this definition, in effect, that the coming pages will explicate.

The other elementary component of Hume's moral theory—it's a famous one—is the idea of sympathy. Whereas the passions are like drives, sympathy is an *instinct*, a *habit* of the mind. It is the habit to be concerned for those who are like us and nearest to us. The pleasure and pain that affect us are not strictly speaking identified only with our selves, but with our 'inner circle'. Here is Hume:

> Whoever is united to us by any connexion is always sure of a share of our love, proportioned to the connexion, without enquiring into his other qualities. Thus the relation of blood produces the strongest tie the mind is capable of in the love of parents to their children, and a lesser degree of the same affection, as the relation lessens. (Hume, *Treatise*, 2.2.4.2)

When I see my brother clearly relishing a taco, I also feel the affect of pleasure. Human beings are for Hume loci of resonance. Like wine glasses standing near each other, making one ring out will also cause the second to do the same.

Deleuze emphasises how strongly this differentiates Hume from egoist philosophers like Hobbes and de Mandeville. We are not naturally selfish—we are naturally *partial*, partial to our own. But this partiality is its own problem. There is, Deleuze suggests, a kind of 'paradox of sympathy': 'it opens up for us a moral space and a generality, but this space is without extension, a generality without quantity'. (ES 37) In a nutshell, sympathy might be the natural barrier to selfishness, but is also a natural barrier to society, which cannot flourish if a 'clan mentality' is predominant. Consequently, 'The moral and social problem is how to go from real sympathies which exclude one another to a real whole which would include these sympathies. The problem is how *to extend* sympathy'. (ES 40)

Notice, incidentally, that morality confronts the opposite problem confronted by belief. In the latter case, the problem was that we believed *too many* things; in morality, the problem is that we don't care *enough*—too many people are naturally excluded from our sympathies. In other words, 'the problem of society is not a problem of limitation, but rather a problem of integration. To integrate sympathies is to make sympathy transcend its contradiction and natural partiality. Such an integration implies a positive moral world, and is bought about by the positive invention of such a world'. (ES 39–40)

General rules

Hume resolves this problem with a novel account of what he calls general rules. Far from being a purely rational matter, general rules are conventionalised social practices or *institutions*. Marriage is a general rule, but so too is a literary genre, adoption, taxation, and good taste in art. The function of general rules is to extend natural sympathy through a confected, artificial sociality. For Deleuze, the hallmark feature of this account is that it is *positive*. Society functions not to constrain selfishness (Hobbes), or stunt natural human freedom (Rousseau), but to create new means by which what it means to be human can expand.

On Deleuze's account, far and away the most important general rule for Hume is that of *property*. I take what is currently in my possession to be mine—and I expect to keep it—and, because of my natural sympathies, I care that nobody snatches the taco from my brother's hands before he gets to eat it. The possessions of other people, though, are less my concern. And in fact, if I found out that my brother had swiped that taco from someone else's order at the food truck, I might even find it amusing. This degree of unequal concern is a general problem though—my own possessions could equally appear to be a part of a Mexican food heist by other people. What is therefore required is a conventional social practice that extends my investment in the continued possession of certain objects to society as a whole.

As Deleuze presents it, the institution of property provides a basic lingua franca for social relations—a kind of inter-objectivity that supports the flourishing of intersubjectivity more generally:

> The convention of property is the artifice by means of which the actions of each one are related to those of the others. It is the establishment of a scheme and the institution of a symbolic aggregate or of the whole. Hume thus finds property to be a phenomenon which is essentially political—in fact, the political phenomenon par excellence. (ES 42)

In Hume's own words, 'By this means, every one knows what he may safely possess'. (*Treatise* 3.2.2.9)

The extension and correction of general rules

Now notice, Deleuze says, the peculiar way in which practical social existence has transformed the role of fiction. In belief, fictions are the ultimate threat. But general rules themselves are literally *made up*. There is nothing necessary about any particular institution or general rule—they are creative responses to tensions that arise because of the parochial character of sympathy. Unfortunately, though, these confected social institutions are not, on their own terms, sufficient. General rules can extend—indeed, *generalise*—the claims we make on behalf of ourselves and our own, but they are incapable of generalising the vivacity of our feelings. In being generalised, our passions are weakened: 'sympathy, through general rules, has won the constancy, distance and uniformity of true moral judgment but has lost in vividness what it has gained in extension'. (ES 50)

Another parallel appears here between morality and belief: a second, corrective moment is required. But again, the problem has been inverted. We need to further extend and strengthen the passionate investment in the general rules rather than, under the aegis of reason, restricting what it is we believe. Indeed, what any general rule calls for, on Deleuze's reading, are *more general rules*, whose role will be increasing specification and invigoration of the first. He makes two sets of remarks on this front.

On the one hand, we can identify the existence of *complementary rules*. His main example (on the way to slyly putting together a summary of Hume's political economy) is the institution of government, which is a corrective for the institution of property. This passage from the *Treatise* explains the corrective mechanism:

> There are the persons, whom we call civil magistrates, kings and their ministers, our governors and rulers, who being indifferent persons to the greatest part of the state, have no interest, or but a remote one, in

any act of injustice; and being satisfied with their present condition, and with their part in society, have an immediate interest in every execution of justice, which is so necessary to the upholding of society. (Hume, *Treatise* 3.2.7.7)

Members of the institution of government are, first of all, invested in 'their present condition', that is, the lives to which they have habitually become accustomed. They will consequently do what they must to maintain this situation, which, in the case of government, is maintaining the laws of the land. Correlatively, the subjects of the government have a direct and personal interest in not being on the wrong end of an encounter with the law. The legal notion of property ownership is, as a result, charged with an immediacy and force that it lacked on its own terms.

Now notice that the corrective rule of government has its own limitations. Because it reinforces the bond between owner and property, it has the tendency to produce dynasties—property 'remains in the family'. Systemic inequality now threatens. As a result, the institution of government itself must be corrected, through for instance the institution of commerce, which encourages the circulation of property. But then, there's the danger that commercial monopolies might form and repeat the problem, so a further correction is required—and so on. As Deleuze reads Hume, we must not conceive of society as defined by a fixed set of institutions, but as the ongoing production of new general rules to refine and redirect those that already exist: the creative resolution of excessive tendencies in society.

On the other hand, Deleuze points out that, really, there isn't *one* institution of property ownership. We only need to think about the different ways in which someone 'comes into possession' of something, as we say: inheritance, gift giving, occupation, 'finder's keepers', at the shops, and so on. At the same time, these all achieve property ownership, so there must be a first general rule to work from. There must be, consequently, a range of secondary rules that *determine* the first (and of course these in turn will need correction, and so on). By determining the first rule, these other institutions allow it to broaden its role in society, to engage in increasingly specific ways that further strengthen our particular affective investment in it.

General rules and the imagination

Now we arrive at a further, key question: where do these new general rules come from exactly? What capacity do we have as human beings to come up with new models that have no relationship to what currently exists? Of course, I'm telegraphing the answer: it is the imagination. We are about to rescue it from its pariah status.

On its own terms, the imagination drifts in the void. Belief, constituted in the mind, was not able to legitimate itself, or at least was unable to avoid embracing fiction as its very foundation. Moreover, we saw that even the most rational beliefs were, literally, practically useless. We can claim that something is the effect of a given cause, but without this *effect* being a desired *end*, it came to nothing. Deleuze now presents two lines of argument in order to resituate belief *within* social reality.

First, he shows that the demented character of belief is ameliorated to the degree that the beliefs are integrated into social life. The idea of God, for instance, loses its ungrounded character once we see that, like all beliefs, its sense is provided not by its (alleged) real referent, but by the social practices in which it flourishes and by which is framed. Hume reverses the familiar view here: it is not that the church serves and supports the belief in God, but that the belief in God only gains its true meaning as an element in the socialising function of the church as an institution. The example of belief in the object is even more to the point: it finds its stability and significance in the institution of property. The object is not first of all *res cogitatum* but *property*—and later, under certain circumstances, *goods*. Or, as Deleuze summarises the point:

> association links ideas in the imagination; the passions give a sense to these relations, and thus they provide the imagination with a tendency. It follows, therefore, that the passions somehow need the association of ideas, and conversely, that association presupposes the passions. Ideas are associated in view of a goal, an intention, or a purpose which only the passions can confer upon human activity. We associate our ideas because we have passions. (ES 63)

Second, Deleuze will insist upon the fact that, while we do indeed 'associate our ideas because we have passions,' (ES 63) the institutions that flourish in order to extend and ramify these passions draw upon the fabulating capacity of the imagination. Earlier I pointed to the fact that fiction appears to have inverse roles in belief and moral life. Now we can see that in fact it is one and the same role—the imagination produces new complex ideas without grounding them—taken first in an abstract state, and then in its true form, as a fabulation bounded and motivated by social reality. This is to say:

> The imagination is revealed as a veritable production of extremely diverse *models*: when drives are reflected in an imagination submitted to

the principles of association, institutions are determined by the figures traced by the drives according to the circumstances. (ES 48)

So the true power of the imagination is to produce images of possible worlds. This is, after all, what a complex idea really is: an internally coherent structure built from the materials provided in our encounters with the world. When such an image is charged by the drives, or passions, it begins to affect the institutional fabric of society—at least insofar as these charged images comprehend the particularities of the circumstances (which passions? Which institutions? Which beliefs?)

All of this can also be put in more concrete terms. New types of socialised behaviour are always possible—we can imagine them. Those that come into being are the ones that actually catch hold of passions which are not addressed by the current ensemble of institutions. In an interview with the weekly *Gai Pied*, Michel Foucault provides an excellent example. Asked about his experience as young gay man, he responds:

> As far back as I remember, to want guys was to want relations with guys. That has always been important for me. Not necessarily in the form of a couple but as a matter of existence: how is it possible for men to be together? To live together, to share their time, their meals, their room, their leisure, their grief, their knowledge, their confidences? What is it to be "naked" among men, outside of institutional relations, family, profession, and obligatory camaraderie? It's a desire, an uneasiness, a desire-in-uneasiness that exists among a lot of people. (Foucault, 'Friendship as a Way of Life,' 136)

He goes on to note that the institution of heterosexual marriage resolves these questions in advance for relations between men and women, but that men 'have to invent, from A to Z, a relationship that is still formless, which is friendship: that is to say, the sum of everything through which they can give each other pleasure'. (Foucault, 'Friendship,' 136) But what institutional forms could friendship defined in this manner take? His biographer David Macey notes that Foucault had discussed the possibility of *adopting* his lover, Daniel Defert. This is a very precise example of a model for a new institution, a new general rule that would allow for the formation of new kinds of social relationships. In another text from *Gai Pied* during the same period, Foucault also considers another, more challenging case: a new kind of hotel that you could go to in order to commit suicide, a place where one could have 'a chance to die without any identity'. (Foucault, 'Un plaisir si simple', 10)

Now, while a modified institution of adoption of the kind that Foucault dreams of never arose, the recent transformations in the institution of marriage to include same-sex couples provides an excellent example of what the correction and modification of institutions in Humean terms would look like. On the other hand, the proposal for a way to integrate the desire for suicide into social practice remains an image without social realisation. This would have troubled Hume himself, who, in his posthumously published 'Of Suicide,' insisted in a Stoic vein that suicide 'preserve[s] to everyone his chance for happiness in life, and would effectually free him from all danger of misery'. (Hume, 323)

THE GENESIS OF SUBJECTIVITY

Now, at this point, it might seem that we have gone about answering every question except for the question that, in all of its variations, animates the whole of *Empiricism and Subjectivity*:

how does a collection become a system? (ES 22)

how does the mind become a subject? How does the imagination become a faculty? (ES 23)

how can a subject that transcends the given be constituted in the given? (ES 86)

In fact we are closer than it may seem; we have all of the materials we need to define subjectivity in Humean terms. But first a caveat—we must take care to avoid looking for a certain kind of answer to these questions. The subject that Deleuze will draw from Hume's work is decidedly not the disaffected, sovereign subject of rational action theory, nor the slightly less pallid subject of political liberalism. It shares nothing with either the formal unity of apperception in Kant's first *Critique*, nor the agent that enjoys noumenal freedom in the second. As we will see in what follows, the passage from collection to system is not a magic act that would somehow mysteriously produce Howard Roark from the disarray of the fancy. Going forward, the following claim will be our guide: 'Isn't this the answer to the question "what are we?" We are habits, nothing but habits—the habit of saying "I"'. (ES x)

Impressions of reflection

We need to begin here by returning to the basic elements of Hume's account: the first components of the mind are *impressions of sensation*. How these arise within us, and in relation to what, we cannot say. On the basis of these impressions, *ideas* are formed, as copies. And from this point, under the influence of the principles of association—tendencies that allow ideas to be grouped together—beliefs, or complex ideas, are produced. However, there is another result from the formation of ideas. They give rise to secondary impressions, what Hume calls *impressions of reflection*. We have already seen the importance of impressions of reflection in the context of moral life: from the initial impressions of pleasure and pain, and the ideas that these give rise to, joy and sadness, blame, praise, and so on, arise as secondary impressions.

It is this latter moment that is central in the formation of the subject. Here is Deleuze, in a particularly useful summary passage that also functions as something of a rebuke to the Kantian reading of Hume:

> The impressions of sensation are only the origin of the mind; as for the impressions of reflection, they are the qualification of the mind and the effect of principles in it. The point of view of the origin, according to which every idea derives from a preexisting impression and represents it, does not have the importance that people attribute to it: it merely gives the mind a simple origin and frees the ideas from the obligation of having to represent *things,* and also from the corresponding difficulty of having to understand the resemblance of ideas. The real importance is on the side of the impressions of reflection, because they are the ones which qualify the mind as subject. (ES 31)

The way in which Deleuze develops this point involves what is perhaps the most interesting interpretive move in *Empiricism and Subjectivity*. Hume appears, especially early in the *Treatise*, to identify impressions of reflection solely with the refraction of pleasure and pain through the principles of association. This would mean that the only impressions of reflection are those that directly relate to the passions. But as this passage above indicates, Deleuze insists that *every* impression of sensation is reflected in the imagination. Moreover, it is precisely this claim that undergirds his account of subjectivity. The Humean subject is the reflection in the imagination of the impressions of sensation.

From passive to active

How could this possibly furnish us with an account of subjectivity? We need to recall here that the principles of association function in the mind as *tendencies*. At one level, then, the only structure that characterises thought is the structure given to it by the principles. But, as we have just seen, the principles have two orders of effect. If the first effect is to give rise to beliefs, the second is to make the imagination itself a field of tendencies. Impressions of reflections, therefore, are not produced in the same was that complex ideas are produced. They are produced by the mind *as* tendential. Here is Deleuze:

> there are two ways of defining the principles: within the collection, the principle elects, chooses, designates and invites certain impressions of sensation among others; having done this, it constitutes impressions of reflection in connection with these elected impressions. Thus, it has two roles *at the same time*: a selective role and a constitutive role. (ES 113)

So, the principles of association are, at one level, the only agencies in the mind. But in the course of their selective qualification of the ideas in the mind ('this is the cause of that'), they 'ingrain' this tendency into the mind itself. At the second level, then, the predominant agencies in the mind are the mind's habits, which are the reflections, in the mind, of the principles of association. It is from these habits in turn that the impressions of reflection truly arise. Ultimately then, Hume proposes a theory, not of personal identity, but of personal *indentity*.

Here's another passage that takes a particular principle as an example to make the same point:

> the principle of resemblance designates certain ideas that are similar, and makes it possible to group them together under the same name. Based on this name and in conjunction with a certain idea taken from the group—for example, a particular idea awakened by the name—the principle produces a habit, a strength, and a power to evoke any other particular idea of the same group; it produces an impression of reflection. (ES 114)

Key here is the term *power*. A habit is a power of selection and contraction. To say that I have a habit of looking for gerbera in every flower store I pass is to say that I filter my experience of the world in a certain way; I polarise it. This is not the direct result of the principles of association, but the indirect result or imprint of their functioning in the mind. Consequently, it is as though the role of selection is 'handed over' to the mind's new habits from the principles of association. And *the subject is*, to recall our emblematic quote, *the ensemble of these habits*. No longer just an atomistic collection, it is a machine for organising the collection.

But now, a final point. The way I have just reconstructed the argument might give the sense that subjectivity in Hume belongs to the side of belief—especially since it is the principles of association that bring about impressions of reflection. If we think this, though, we have missed the historical, political and moral kernel of Hume's thought. The habits that compose me in the imagination do not run along tracks internal to my mind, but traverse the vast, interconnected circuitry of social life. Some ideas are only mine, since they don't have a place in social life; others end up finding a corner of the world in which to be expressed and to flourish; others again are so caught up in the music of sympathy and intersubjective life it's hard to distinguish what is mine, or yours, or everyone's. The subject, however eccentric its particular habits of thought, is formed in the image of the passionate investments of the social world.

2

Nietzsche and Philosophy

Deleuze's second book, *Nietzsche et la philosophie* appeared in 1962, nine years after his first. Reflecting on this gap in a late interview, he describes it as a hole in his life during which he "produced nothing." (N 138) This is hardly true. A series of articles, including important texts that presage later books, were published in these years. But during these same years, Deleuze was also engaged in a number of initiatives around the thought of Friedrich Nietzsche. He was, for starters, an inaugural member of the French Society for Nietzsche Studies, which began in 1946 and remained active until the mid-1960s. Somewhat later, Deleuze was a part of the editorial team for the French edition of Colli-Montinari translation of Nietzsche's collected works, along with Michel Foucault and Maurice de Gandillac.

While Deleuze was neither the first nor only figure of importance in the reception of Nietzsche in Twentieth century France—Georges Bataille's name must be mentioned here, whose role in refuting the Nazified caricature of Nietzscheanism should not be underestimated—*Nietzsche and Philosophy* was essential in reviving a specifically *philosophical* reading of Nietzsche's work in that context.

NIETZSCHE AS PHILOSOPHER

To treat Nietzsche as a philosopher is one thing, even if it is already controversial to some of his readers, who would rather cast him as a critic of philosophy in its systematic and metaphysical guise. But in fact Deleuze goes much further, completely overturning such readings of Nietzsche. First of all, he does so by presenting his work as a system, and Nietzsche as a systematic thinker. *Nietzsche and Philosophy* is in turn, a systematic reading of Nietzche's work. Second, and this is the hallmark of *Nietzsche and Philosophy*, Nietzsche is not for Deleuze a *critic of metaphysics*, but the author of a *critical metaphysics*.

On the first page of the book, Deleuze makes clear that he reads Nietzsche as the rightful heir of Kantian metaphysics, and the one who took it to its completion: 'there is, in Nietzsche, not only a Kantian heritage, but a half-avowed, half-hidden, rivalry.' (NP 52) Nietzsche therefore presents a new, completed *critical metaphysics*.

Evaluating Kant

What does this heritage amount to? For Deleuze, Kant's critical philosophy constitutes a genuine achievement. Kant conceives of his critique as an *immanent* critique. If we ask what the limits of reason are, and what role it plays in knowledge, we must remain on the terrain of reason itself, and not invoke criteria that arise from other sources. To the degree that we proceed in this kind of way, we will never know what reason is capable of on its own terms. So Kant, like Nietzsche, explicitly rejects any recourse to transcendent criteria of evaluation.

Consequently, if we ask what justifies particular kinds of knowledge claims—for example, those of science—we must always look for their immanent conditions, that is, their conditions within the subject who knows.

But Kant's success is also marred by a series of serious problems. In *Nietzsche and Philosophy*, Deleuze emphasizes three points on this front:

1. Kant presumes that thoughts we happen to or habitually have are correct, and have value in and of themselves. He does not pose the important question 'what is the value of knowledge, or truth?', and this is because he presupposes its intrinsic value, which is of course the same thing as presuming its value-neutrality. His philosophy therefore 'moves in the *indifferent* element of the valuable in itself or the valuable for all.' (NP 2) He fails to go as far as asking, as Nietzsche famously does at the start of *Beyond Good and Evil*, 'Given that we want truth: *why do we not prefer* untruth? And uncertainty? Even ignorance?' ('On the Prejudices of Philosophers,' §1) The category of truth cannot itself be the object of Kant's critique, though by presupposing it, he remains as dogmatic as the thinkers he critiques.

2. For Kant, the critical project aims to map the boundary of the legitimate uses of reason in the service of knowledge (but also morality, aesthetics and politics). But in fact, current values and

modes of evaluation are neither natural nor static. What is required instead is a search for the conditions of the *transformation* of values— precisely what Nietzsche means, for Deleuze, by the term *genealogy*.

3. Correlatively, Kant's search for immanent conditions is a search for the universal and the necessary. But if values are not themselves natural or fixed, neither are the conditions that explain their genesis. Consider the famous example of good and evil that we'll return to below. Not only does the meaning of the word 'good' change because of a shifting set of evaluations that constitute the kernel of human history, the reason these evaluations shift is due to a change in the conditions of contemporary values themselves. The belief in an eternal and unchanging set of structural rules for the constitution of experience—Kant's transcendental conditions—is just as unwarranted as the belief that contemporary values are naturally correct because they currently come to bear.

In what follows, we will see the way in which Deleuze takes some of Nietzsche's most difficult concepts as the means to adequately complete Kant's critical project: 'Nietzsche seems to have sought (and to have found in the "eternal return" and the "will to power") a radical transformation of Kantianism, a re-invention of the critique which Kant betrayed at the same time as he conceived it.' (NP 52)

The dogmatic image of thought

But we first need to recognize that this problem is not unique to Kant, who is in this respect just 'the last of the classical philosophers,' (NP 94) in this regard. Like the bulk of Western thought that came before him, Kant falls prey to what Deleuze calls 'the dogmatic image of thought.' (NP 103) This image is a set of presuppositions about what thought is, how it is oriented, and what it is capable of doing, one belonging not just to philosophers but to modern human experience in general.

The essential character of this image is its abstraction. As Deleuze puts it, 'The most curious thing about this image of thought is the way in which it conceives of truth as an abstract universal. We are never referred to the real forces that *form* thought, thought itself is never related to the real forces that it presupposes *as thought*.' (NP 97) Thought is supposed to naturally seek the truth, and we thinkers—assuming no external obstacles are put in our way—will always seek it out. But what the image forecloses is both its own origin and the real origin and structure of thinking.

Consequently, 'what the dogmatic image of thought conceals [is] the work of established forces.' (NP 104) By framing thought as the natural, value-neutral search for the truth, it hides the historically determined and value-motivated origins of thought. 'Clearly thought cannot think by itself,' (NP 104) Deleuze notes, so what we really should be asking is what it is that really and in fact causes us to think, and not tarrying with an opaque fiction that hides the sense of this question.

So we can, from this point of view, engage in a genealogical analysis of Kant's philosophy itself. We can ask, for instance, 'what is the evaluative framework that underpins Kant's conceptual edifice? By which values is it oriented?' But then we can also ask 'what are the conditions that gave rise to these values which are expressed through Kant's thought? What established powers were invested in this set of evaluations?'

This line of attack is pursued most forcefully by Deleuze in *Nietzsche and Philosophy* with respect, not to Kant, but to one of the other great modern philosophers: Hegel. In the conclusion we read the following, perhaps most well-known passage of the book: 'There is no possible compromise between Hegel and Nietzsche. Nietzsche's philosophy has a great polemical range; it forms an absolute anti-dialectics and sets out to expose all the mystifications that find a final refuge in the dialectic.' (NP 195) Now, it is unlikely that Nietzsche was as intimately familiar with Hegel's work as Deleuze suggests. But, as we will see, Nietzsche's genealogy of modern human existence uncovers the very structure of the Hegelian dialectic, not as a philosophical position but as a very specific organization of (slavish, resentful and life-denying) values.

'Nietzsche's most general project'

We are in a position now to reframe all of these points in a positive way, as Deleuze does right at the start of the book when he writes that 'Nietzsche's most general project is the introduction of the concepts of sense and value into philosophy.' (NP 1) Quite often, Deleuze uses 'sense and value' together, without distinguishing the two different concepts. We will return to their difference shortly, but for now take them both as terms for the dynamic play of evaluation that constitutes reality.

To say then that this is Nietzsche's aim is to treat everything—every statement, every phenomenon, every body—as the expression of an evaluative point of view. Nothing is neutral, and nothing is natural. So in the case of the category of truth we have been discussing, what is essential is that 'We always have the truths we deserve as a function of the sense of what we conceive, of the value of what we believe.' (NP 104)

For Deleuze, this philosophy is therefore unavoidably *interpretive* in character; philosophy is always a 'symptomatology.' (NP 3) It is this genealogical perspective that leads Nietzsche to displace the famous 'what is … ?' of philosophy since Plato, and to ask instead 'which one?' (the phrase with which Deleuze's translator Hugh Tomlinson renders the French '*Qui?*'). Every question that appears in its more traditional guise—like 'what is truth?'—is really in fact a swarm, which can be summarized under this emblematic question: 'for whom is this the truth?' As he writes:

> when we ask the question "what is it?" we not only fall into the worst metaphysics but in fact we merely ask the question "which one?" in a blind, unconscious and confused way. The question "what is it?" is a way of establishing a sense seen from another point of view. Essence, being, is a perspectival reality and presupposes a plurality. Fundamentally it is always the question "What is it *for me?*" (for us, for everyone that sees etc.) […] When we ask what beauty is we ask from what standpoint things appear beautiful: and something which does not appear beautiful to us, from what standpoint would it become so? (NP 77)

This symptomatological perspective dominates every important discussion in *Nietzsche and Philosophy*. Deleuze himself will return to it over and over again, when considering—to take only the most prominent examples—the concept of tragedy (chapter one), the concepts of force and power (chapter two), the nature of truth as we have already seen (chapter three), morality (chapter four), and nihilism and the overman (chapter five). In each case, he argues, we miss the singularity and importance of Nietzsche's philosophy if we do not grasp the life-affirming, positive and vital evaluative perspective that these concepts embody. And more, we mutilate his thought if we take these concepts to be equal to others bearing the same names.

But now, it is important to emphasise the irreducibility of this Nietzschean perspectivalism to any simple relativism of the true. Nietzsche is not, Deleuze insists, simply telling us that all truths are equal. Not only is there no such equality (for reasons we'll see in a moment), it is a mistake to think that perspective is a matter of knowledge. It is not that Nietzsche is abandoning any idea of essence or reality, by which a truth could be justified or to which it refers. Instead, as the enigmatic sentence in the passage cited above says, being itself is irreducibly plural. This is why all truths express a perspective.

The completion of Kant

Now we are in a better position to see in what sense Nietzsche completes the critical project. Recall that, on Deleuze's view, the positive part of Kant's legacy was its double emphasis on immanence: he conceived of critique as an immanent critique that rejected all transcendent or extrinsic criteria, and he conceived of the conditions of thought as immanent to thought.

Nietzsche too is a thinker of immanence for Deleuze. But he completes this Kantian effort, on the one hand, by making critique always turn around values, dispensing with the lingering transcendence of a value-free conception of truth. On the other, he transforms the notion of immanent conditions of thought by grasping them in their plurality and historicity. At issue is no longer the conditions for the possibility of knowledge or morality, but the conditions of all things, all phenomena, and all experience, in their historical actuality.

So far, we have summarily examined chapters one and three of *Nietzsche and Philosophy*, which frame everything that Deleuze considers to be essential in Nietzsche's thought. The rest of the book pursues two further complementary lines of argument. The first of these, advanced in chapter three, is *structural*. It gives us an outline of Nietzsche's positive metaphysics, linking together the concepts of the body and force, the will-to-power and the eternal return. It is these concepts that will allow us to understand more fully how value might be an immanent condition. The second is *genealogical*, and occupies Deleuze in the final two chapters. Here the goal is to show how the structural account undergirds Nietzsche's history of the advent of modern human existence, its arrival at the apparent terminus of contemporary nihilism, and the passage through which this nihilism can be overcome. We will discuss each of these now in turn.

STRUCTURAL ACCOUNT I: FORCE AND QUALITY

In famous passages like the following from the *Gay Science*, Nietzsche emphasizes the primacy of the body and the secondary character of conscious thought.

> The problem of consciousness (or rather, of becoming conscious of something) first confronts us when we begin to realize how much we can do without it; and now we are brought to this initial realization by physiology and natural history [...] For we could think, feel, will, remember, and also 'act' in every sense of the term, and yet none of all this would have to 'enter our consciousness' (as one says figuratively). All of life would be possible without, as it were, seeing itself in the mirror. (*The Gay Science* §354)

Later we will see Nietzsche's resolution of this problem, but for Deleuze the point that must be emphasized first is that consciousness is necessarily secondary, a secondary product. What comes first is *the body*, or rather bodies plural, whether 'chemical, biological, social or political.' (NP 37)

In turn, if we ask what constitutes a body—that is, anything at all—we must say that it is composed of *forces*. Here, force can be understood as a synonym for two other terms, *capacity* and *drive*, both of which capture the same sense of dynamic activity. Now, as a composite of forces, bodies are organized hierarchically, and are always structured according to a (contingent) 'unity of domination'. (NP 40)

Now, implicit in this notion of domination is the heterogeneity of forces. If there was one force, or one kind of force (a kind of monism of force), then domination would itself be the secondary product. On the other hand, because forces are necessarily plural, there can be no question that any one force is 'equal' to any other. This idea is, for Deleuze, 'a statistical dream,' (NP 43) one that idealises reality and abstracts from the real play of force. Reality is a dynamic, irreducibly heterogeneous and hierarchical play of forces.

Forces are thus necessarily characterised by being either *dominant* or *dominated* in relation to another force or other forces. The following example Nietzsche gives in *Daybreak* shows very clearly what is at stake here and will serve as a useful reference point as we complicate the analysis:

> Suppose we were in the market place one day and we noticed someone laughing at us as we went by: this event will signify this or that to us according to whether this or that drive happens at that moment to be at its height in us—and it will be a quite different event according to the kind of person we are. One person will absorb it like a drop of rain, another will shake it from him like an insect, another will try to pick a quarrel, another will examine his clothing to see if there is anything about it that might give rise to laughter, another will be led to reflect on the nature of laughter as such, another will be glad to have involuntarily augmented the amount of cheerfulness and sunshine in the world—and in each case a drive has gratified itself whether it be the drive to annoyance or to combativeness or to reflection or to benevolence. This drive seized the event as its prey: why precisely this one? Because, thirsty and hungry, it was lying in wait. (*Daybreak* §119)

Active and reactive: from quantity to quality

What makes one drive—to annoyance, to reflection, etc.—the dominant one is the fact that it is the strongest. Every drive or force pushes to its limit, and strives to dominate, at all times, but it is the strongest that comes to orient the others. This, however, cannot be the full account of how bodies are organized. Deleuze insists that for Nietzsche this quantitative point of view must be supplemented with the qualitative perspective. The two qualities that can belong to differences in quantities of force are the *active* and the *reactive*.

For Deleuze, active force is '1) plastic, dominant and subjugating; 2) force which goes to the limit of what it can do; 3) force which affirms its difference, which makes its difference an object of enjoyment and affirmation'. The reactive, conversely describes the 1) utilitarian force of adaptation and partial limitation; 2) force which separates active force from what it can do, which denies active force (triumph of the weak or the slaves); 3) force separated from what it can do, which denies or turns against itself (reign of the weak or of slaves)'. (NP 61) Several of these characteristics will have to be returned to in what follows, particularly this unusual notion of a force separated from what it can do. The key point here is found in the latter text, since it is not necessarily the case that to dominate is to be active: 'inferior forces can prevail without ceasing to be inferior in quantity'. (NP 58)

In fact, the whole of Nietzsche's diagnosis of the contemporary human condition turns around this point: sometimes the weak triumphs. As a consequence, as Deleuze will say, 'One of the finest remarks in *The Will to Power* is: "The strong will always have to be defended against the weak."'. (NP 54)

To return to the example of laughter in the marketplace: there will always be some drive that dominates my response. However, the crucial difference lies between an active response that affirms the situation, drawing enjoyment from it, and a reason for active contemplation; and the reactive response that finds in the situation only self-doubt, resentment, a reason to parade around one or all of the panoply of everyday neurotic miseries.

Sense and value

Now we're in a position to see the specific difference between sense and value. Deleuze writes of 'the progression from sense to value, from interpretation to evaluation as tasks for genealogy. The sense of something is its relation to the force which takes possession of it, the value of something is the hierarchy of forces which are expressed in it as a complex phenomenon.' (NP 8)

So genealogy, as a new kind of critical analysis, will involve two moments. The first leads us from the body to the relations between forces that constitute it, while the second goes from these forces to the qualities that characterize them. When I interpret my disposition in response to the laughter in the marketplace, I ask about the force or drive which dominates the unconscious organization of my experience (quantitative disposition). The evaluation which follows concerns the quality of the hierarchical relations that this domination involves, its active or reactive character (qualitative disposition). What we must keep in mind here is that the genealogical act is not itself a neutral one, since it always proceeds from a particular perspective; it is itself the expression of certain dominant forces and their attendant qualities. This is as true of my response to the marketplace laughter as it is for the scholar interpreting a poem or aphorism (NP 31).

STRUCTURAL ACCOUNT II: THE WILL TO POWER

Now Deleuze introduces one of Nietzsche's most infamous concepts, one which provides us with a third level to this structural analysis of what there is: the will to power.

He begins here by clearly rejecting the kinds of misinterpretations of that the concept has fallen prey to, which he traces back to a central root, the idea that the will to power is a hunger for power, '*as if power were what the will wanted*'. (NP 80) This misunderstanding is the most common, and famously made of Nietzsche the purported prophet of National Socialism. What this reading misunderstands is the nature of the relationship between will and power. Here is Deleuze, citing Nietzsche's *Zarathustra*: 'The expression "desiring power" is no less absurd than "willing to live". "He who shot the doctrine of 'will to live' at truth certainly did not hit the truth: this will does not exist! For what does not exist cannot will; but that which is alive, how could it still will to live?"' (NP 79)

To misunderstand power in this way is to take it as a certain kind of pre-existent *object* that one can aim to possess, but as Nietzsche here insists, the will to power is rather a condition for the existence of an individual, not something that an existing individual might desire. This is why Deleuze writes that 'Will to power does not imply any anthropomorphism in its origin, signification or essence'. (NP 85)

The will to power as genetic condition

What then is the relationship between will and power? Why is the concept of the will to power important? Deleuze's answer is that the will to power is what explains how qualified hierarchies of forces can come into being and—most importantly—come to change.

In sum, for Deleuze the will to power is what comes to replace Kant's transcendental conditions of possibility in Nietzsche's critical thought, with all the differences that we noted above. It will be a genetic condition for the constitution of real beings rather than a condition of possibility for epistemological judgments. When we ask 'why this particular truth, this particular person, this particular society?' we are asking a genetic question. How is it that this set of forces entered into this relationship and not some other one? *What accounts for this*? How to explain the *quality* of active or passivity? How to explain, for example, that the more powerful can be mastered by the less powerful? How to explain how a force can be cut off from what it can do, made potential? How to explain *reaction*? Resistance? The advent of complexity from simple systems?

The will to power is the genetic element (what explains the genesis) of any given relation that answers these questions. It is not apparent on its own terms: "The will to power is, indeed, never separable from particular determined forces, from their quantities, qualities and directions (NP 50) But without reference to it, the advent and modification of these forces will be impossible to explain. So now we can read the following key passage with some insight:

> Nietzsche calls the genealogical element of force the will to power. Genealogical means differential and genetic. The will to power is the differential element of forces, that is to say the element that produces the differences in quantity between two or more forces whose relation is presupposed. The will to power is the genetic element of force, that is to say the element that produces the quality due to each force in this relation. (NP 50)

The will to power as differential condition

All of this still remains a bit unclear, though, without the explanation of the term 'differential'. Perhaps surprisingly, Deleuze's point of reference here is the branch of mathematics created by Leibniz and Newton in the eighteenth century. It is the differential calculus that allows us to think through the structure of the relationship between two forces and the qualities that belong to it. Deleuze's reference to mathematics is brief and rather elusive, and embedded in these scant pages is a complicated engagement with the history of the reception of the calculus in mathematics, and unfolds in unusual proximity to Leibniz himself. All of this cannot be discussed here, but one point—the point where Leibniz and the nineteenth century treatment of the calculus in mathematics coincide—is essential.

Contrary to the high school exposition of calculus, Deleuze insists on the genetic significance of the differential relation. The former conception involves starting with an equation of some kind, for instance $y = -x^2 + 5$ which gives us the following graph:

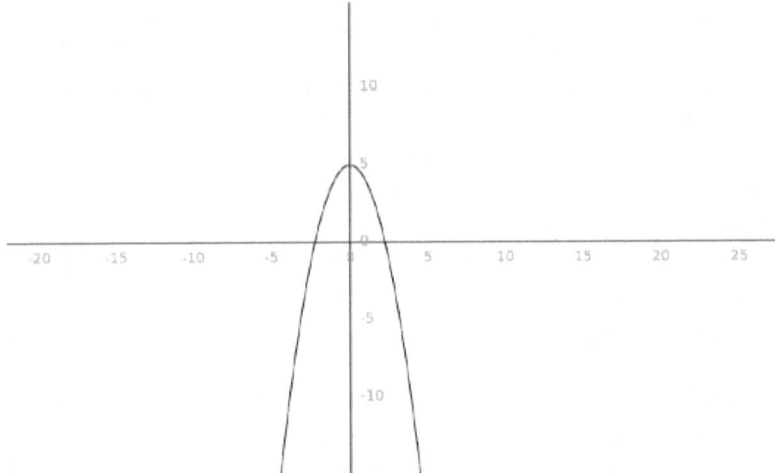

We would then differentiate the equation in order to find the distinctive points of the curve. But grasping the calculus this way makes the differential relation a secondary product, a kind of heuristic addition to our understanding of the equation. Deleuze will insist on the second approach, which makes the differential relation primary in relation to the so-called 'primitive' function. If we have the differential relation, which describes the turning point in the graph, the integral event of the function, and its relationship to the ordinary points that populate the rest of the curve, we can produce the equation itself as the product. The differential relation becomes primitive and generative—that is, *genetic*.

Two other things should be noted here. The first is that what the differential calculus allows to identify are the *singularities* of a function—here, for instance, the point of inflection. It is specific rather than general, marking what is distinctive about this function. The second is that the point of inflection is not somehow in excess of the curve, something transcendent or separate. It is immanent to the curve. Nevertheless, as Deleuze is very careful to insist, 'Inseparable does not mean identical'. (NP 50) The immanent difference between singular and ordinary points must never be overlooked, because it is this that explains the phenomenon of the function itself. Correlatively, it is only by distinguishing between forces and their qualities on the one hand, and the will to power that explains them, on the other, that we grasp the sense of Nietzsche's metaphysics for Deleuze.

The qualities of the will to power

We see now that genealogy must attend to a third category beyond sense and value. The examination of the sense of a phenomenon involves grasping the hierarchy of forces that constitute it, and the evaluation of a phenomenon concerns the way these forces are qualified (as active or reactive). But both of these moments open onto a third, which is concerned with the modality of the will to power which accounts for the genesis of both relations between forces and their qualities. It is only by examining phenomena in terms of the will to power that we will be able to answer the most puzzling question that all of the previous categories lead to. Force, by its nature, is dominating, 'victorious' (NP 51), as Deleuze says. But if this is so, how is it possible for forces to be stripped of their activity—how are reactive forces to be accounted for?

The will to power itself, Deleuze argues, must also be thought in qualitative terms. Whereas the qualities of force relations are *active* and *passive*, Nietzsche will give to the will to power two qualities of its own: *affirmative* and *negative*. However, we already know that the will to power is the dynamic, plastic and genetic kernel of phenomenon, so we can characterize them in an even more direct way, as *becoming-active* and *becoming-reactive*: the affirmative modality of the will to power is what explains the passage to greater activity, and the negative modality the inverse. 'Affirmation is not action but the power of becoming active, *becoming active* personified. Negation is not simple reaction but *becoming reactive*'. (NP 54) If, when I hear laughter at the market, I turn dour, bitter and short-tempered, what has happened? What accounts for the passage of my affects in this direction? The answer is that the will to power expressed by the body that I am is characterized by a becoming-reactive that inclines all interactions between forces with a reactive quality.

We should note one final point before we move on. While the will to power can be qualified as negative, and a play of forces can be qualified as reactive, it is crucial to see that the active, dominating characteristic of force itself seems to resist at its root both qualifications. So the problem we posed just before remains in play: how in fact is the becoming-reactive of forces really to be accounted for on the basis of Nietzsche's concepts? For Deleuze, this difficult tension and its resolution is the object of Nietzsche's genealogy of modern human existence, which will turn to shortly.

THE DOCTRINE OF THE ETERNAL RETURN

At this point in his discussion, though, Deleuze introduces a second famously complicated Nietzschean concept, the eternal return. As we will see, he thinks that there are three aspects to this concept, but in each case, we find the same admonishment, one that runs in parallel with his attack on the anthropomorphic acceptation of the will to power. The admonishment is this: the eternal return does not involve identity. In fact, a renovation of the idea of repetition is in play here. Deleuze's point is that if we examine what repetition means in Nietzsche, we will see that it cannot leave the object of repetition unchanged.

Cosmological sense of the eternal return

This is very clear in the first sense of the eternal return that he finds in Nietzsche, as a cosmological doctrine, that is, a claim about the nature of reality at large. Deleuze's best formulation of this aspect is also both allusive and elusive: '*Returning is the being of that which becomes*'. (NP 48) His point is that, for Nietzsche, it is not being, a fixed state of reality, but becoming and transformation that are fundamental. The fundamental fact about reality is that it changes. It has no natural state. The eternal return in this first sense thus guarantees the inequality of forces, precisely because it rules out any natural 'being' or final state of harmony.

So, we can be more precise, and say that the cosmological sense of the eternal return on Deleuze's account is a claim about the fundamental character of *time*. If there was no passage of time, a form of identity would be fundamental and eternal. But the fact that there is time is what the doctrine of the eternal return turns around. 'In other words, identity in the eternal return does not describe the nature of that which returns but, on the contrary, the fact of returning for that which differs. This is why the eternal return must be thought of as a synthesis; a synthesis of time and its dimensions'. (NP 48)

Ethical sense of the eternal return

The second, ethical sense of the eternal return that Deleuze emphasizes also bears this out. It is expressed in the following famous and entirely remarkable text:

> **The Greatest Weight**.—What, if some day or night a demon were to steal after you into your loneliest loneliness and say to you: "This life as you now live it and have lived it, you will have to live once more and innumerable times more; and there will be nothing new in it, but every

> pain and every joy and every thought and sigh and everything unutterably small or great in your life will have to return to you, all in the same succession and sequence—even this spider and this moonlight between the trees, and even this moment and I myself. The eternal hourglass of existence is turned upside down again and again, and you with it, speck of dust!"
>
> Would you not throw yourself down and gnash your teeth and curse the demon who spoke thus? Or have you once experienced a tremendous moment when you would have answered him: "You are a god and never have I heard anything more divine." If this thought gained possession of you, it would change you as you are or perhaps crush you. The question in each and every thing, "Do you desire this once more and innumerable times more?" would lie upon your actions as the greatest weight. Or how well disposed would you have to become to yourself and to life to crave nothing more fervently than this ultimate eternal confirmation and seal? (Nietzsche, *The Gay Science* §341)

What we find here, Deleuze argues, is a radical ethical thought, a principle opposed (once more) to Kant's famous categorical imperative, which is why he paraphrases this aspect of the eternal return by writing '*Whatever you will, will it in such a way that you also will its eternal return.*' (NP 68)

How does this function as an ethical maxim though? Nietzsche's key insight here for Deleuze is that any decision made from the point of view of its eternal affirmation transforms the object of the decision. Any 'laziness, stupidity, baseness, cowardice or spitefulness that would will its own eternal return would no longer be the same laziness [or] stupidity'. (NP 63-4)

We can see therefore what Deleuze means when he says that the eternal return is necessarily *selective* in character. Boredom or laziness as they used to exist are subtracted from my experience, selected out thanks to the transformation effected by the thought of the eternal return. To embrace this act of spite as the expression not just of a passing whim but of my whole being, not once as if over and over again eternally is to transform it from a petty, passing moment into a profound and positive act.

The becoming-reactive of forces and the limits of selection

Put another way, we can say that the eternal return as a thought selects out all those forces that do not go to the limit of their capacity, everything affirmed half-heartedly. However, we have already seen a class of forces qualified in just this way—reactive forces—and the corresponding modality of the will to power—becoming-reactive—that accounts for it. And far from being the exception, reactive forces have for Nietzsche triumphed in a profound way. The name Nietzsche gives to this situation—our situation—is *nihilism*. In nihilism, the becoming-reactive of the will to power is everywhere dominant.

In light of all of this, the eternal return in both the cosmological and ethical sense appears to be inconsequential. This is of course not what Nietzsche will come to argue, but from the point of view of this structural account of his metaphysics, we seem unable to move beyond it. More specifically, there are two questions that the structural account cannot answer on its own: 1) how in fact do forces become reactive, that is, become cut off from what they can do? and 2) is there any way in which nihilism, this generalized becoming-reactive, can be overturned? The answer to both questions is to be found by following the trajectory of a complementary genealogical analysis of contemporary human existence.

GENEALOGICAL ACCOUNT I: FROM CONSCIOUSNESS TO BAD CONSCIENCE

Our first goal is to explain the mechanism through which reactive forces could possibly triumph. Before this, though, we must see that there are always reactions in play in any phenomenon. We already know that everything involves a plurality of forces organized hierarchically, so there will always be forces made to respond in certain ways to what is encountered in keeping with the drive that is dominant. In these situations, reactions are *acted*—as Deleuze glosses it, 're-acted'. (NP 111)

The other key feature and guarantor of this active reaction to external stimuli is that it is forgotten; the encounter does not linger in conscious thought. This is the result of a faculty of forgetting. As Deleuze points out, for Nietzsche this is 'no mere *vis inertiae* as the superficial imagine, it is rather an active and in the strictest sense positive faculty of repression'. (*Genealogy*, Essay II, §1; cited at NP 113) Deleuze often refers to Freud in this conjunction, pointing out that both he and Nietzsche insist on the fact that unless the traces of the present encounter pass into the unconscious, nothing new will be able to take place in the experiencing subject, who will instead be haunted by the undying spectres of the past. This is what Freud calls neurosis, and Nietzsche *ressentiment*.

The advent of ressentiment

This last point finally gives us the means to explain how reactive forces might emerge in the human being—the failure of the repressive faculty of forgetting. I encounter something, but instead of reacting directly to it, the encounter gives rise to a memory that becomes entangled with the stimulus. But now, I have *felt* the encounter instead of reacting to it; I have become *passive*. To the degree that traces of past activity become conscious, they come to dominate the organization of experience, and to the same degree we cease to be active. As Deleuze notes, 'The consequences of this are immense: no longer being able to act a reaction, active forces are deprived of the material conditions of their functioning, they no longer have the opportunity to do their job, *they are separated from what they can do.*' (NP 114)

This is the essential point, and the means that Nietzsche will use to account for everything else that follows. Because forces can be cut off from reacting to stimuli directly, instead being caught in the loop of conscious thought and memory, they are cut off from acting at all. In this hall of mirrors, activity consists of contemplating reflections. This is why, later on the same page, Deleuze offers the following definition: "*ressentiment* is a reaction which simultaneously becomes perceptible and ceases to be acted." (NP 114)

The resentful type

Deleuze discusses a great range of different features that characterize the resentful type, but before we note some of these, two additional points need to be made. First of all, the use of the term 'type' is important here. Nietzsche's goal is not to present an orthodox historical argument about particular people and their responsibility for introducing reactive forces, demeaning life in the name of passivity, and so on. The mechanism is more general than that, and so too are its effects: the leader of a student socialist group on campus can be as reactive and passive as any office drone.

The second point concerns the notion of *ressentiment* itself: why and in what way is the reactive type resentful exactly? The key to the answer is this: everything that the resentful person encounters *forces* them to feel something. Something happens *to* me, not *because* of me, and even if this something is a pleasurable affect of some kind, it is interwoven with my having *suffered* it rather than engendered it. Consequently, as Deleuze notes, 'This reaction therefore blames its object', (NP 115) and that as a result 'The man of *ressentiment* experiences every being and every object as an offence in exact proportion to its effect on him.' (NP 116)

This is the meaning of pain for the resentful person—everything is painful. But it is at the same time a perverse response to suffering in general, since it always propels the resentful type to look for someone or something to *blame* for it. There are many great passages in *Nietzsche and Philosophy*, but this is surely one of them, bristling with anger:

> What is most striking in the man of *ressentiment* is not his nastiness but his disgusting malevolence, his capacity for disparagement. Nothing can resist it. He does not even respect his friends or even his enemies [...] he must recriminate and distribute blame: look at his inclination to play down the value of causes, to make misfortune 'someone else's fault'. (NP 110)

The other traits of the resentful type that Deleuze discusses all flow from this. For instance, the resentful type is characterized by the inability to forget anything: 'One cannot get rid of anything, one cannot get over anything, one cannot repel anything—everything hurts. Men and things obtrude too closely; experiences strike one too deeply; memory becomes a festering wound.' (NP 108, quoting *Ecce Homo* I.6) This is what leads Nietzsche to the memorable claim that 'The German *drags* his soul, he drags everything he experiences. He digests his events badly, he is never "done" with them'. (*Beyond Good and Evil*, §244) Equally, the resentful type cannot 'admire, respect, or love': 'The man of *ressentiment* does not know how to and does not want to love, but wants to be loved. He wants to be loved, fed, watered, caressed and put to sleep.' (NP 117) In place of any affirmation of something or someone that is good, and makes me stronger and better, there is only the desire to never be troubled; your lover becomes your anaesthetic.

In all of this, we can see why Deleuze will say in summary that 'If we ask what the man of *ressentiment* is, we must not forget this principle: he does not re-act'. (NP 111) To the degree that anything happens, it is internal to the resentful person, and consists in this downwards spiral.

The birth of evil and the weakening of the strong

In the first essay of the *Genealogy of Morality*, Nietzsche famously characterizes this difference between the affirmative and the resentful through the allegorical counterposing of the bird of prey and the lamb. The bird of prey does not judge its own actions, because it *is* these actions. To the bird's keen gaze, the lamb looks like nothing so much as a delicious meal.

If it is meaningful to use the word 'good' here, it is to describe the bird itself in its fierce power, its delirious attacking fall and the fullness of its life. Correlatively, if we can call the lamb 'bad' it can only mean 'weaker', 'capable of less'. In truth, to describe the two figures in terms that even hint at morality is to miss the point. Nevertheless, it is the lamb that develops the moral perspective, or more precisely, the category of *evil*. In turn, as Nietzsche puts it, what has to be explained is 'the *other* origin of "good", of good as thought up by the man of *ressentiment*.' (*Genealogy*, First Essay, § 13).

How does the lamb see this situation? 'There is nothing strange about the fact that lambs bear a grudge towards large birds of prey,' as Nietzsche points out, 'but that is no reason to blame the large birds of prey for carrying off the little lambs.' (§13) But what this allegorical lamb proposes is precisely such a judgment. Imagine, Deleuze says, that this lamb is a logician, one that proposes a classical syllogism:

> Premise 1: You, the bird of prey, are evil.
>
> Premise 2: I am the opposite of you.
>
> Conclusion: Therefore I am good.

The first premise, and indeed the whole argument, is motivated purely and simply by the *ressentiment* that the lamb feels; to pass from this primary negation of the bird of prey to the positive assertion, a second negation is required. '*Ressentiment* needs negative premises, two negations, in order to produce a phantom of affirmation.' (NP 196)

I said earlier that Deleuze takes Hegel to be the true enemy of Nietzsche's metaphysics, and now we can see why. It is not merely that the two philosophers have opposed visions of reason, let's say, or of the State, but that Hegel's metaphysics is itself the integral expression of resentment. The answer to the Nietzschean question 'who, what kind of thinker, advances the dialectic, which requires two negations to attain an affirmation, as the motor of history and the key to reality?' is Hegel. Deleuze is insistent: Hegel's philosophy is literally slave morality, *ressentiment*, in its most refined form, an apology for the diminishment of life and the abnegation of everything strong and good in it.

Deleuze calls the lamb's argument a *paralogism*—an argument that appears logically sound but is not. In what sense is this the case? What the lamb illegitimately presupposes is a separation of the *agent* from the *act*, accusing the eagle of doing something that it could have refrained from doing. In fact, as we have already seen, there is no distinction between the forces that compose a body and what that body does—a force is what it does. The logical lamb insists on the opposite, that forces *can* remain inactive, and moreover that it is in this inactivity that they remain virtuous. This assertion is therefore far from a neutral description of reality. The passivity that *ressentiment* craves has now been treated as *the* moral good.

The bird of prey is the victim of this fiction. Accused of 'evil acts'—a phrase which is for the lamb a secret pleonasm—it becomes an increasingly contemplative animal. It now *feels* its encounters with the world rather than reacting to them in its immediate strength. The sight of the lamb is no longer the opportunity for a meal but the invitation to moral self-examination. This is why Nietzsche tells us we must protect the strong from the weak, Deleuze emphasises. The unique 'power' of the resentful is found in this moral fiction of a passive agent, and it is one that the strong are susceptible to, in and despite their strength.

The priestly type and bad conscience

At this point, we have still yet to step into history with Nietzsche. We possess an understanding of the nature of *ressentiment* but not how it in fact played out. As Deleuze puts it, *ressentiment* is (to a certain significant degree) the *content* of human subjectivity, but human existence does not have any one necessary *form*. The sequence we have just described belongs to every human being, but its concrete reality has differed a great deal over history. What is it that gives form to this generalised content?

The first and crucial development, and the one that sets human being on the path to contemporary nihilism, is the advent of what Nietzsche calls *the priestly type*. Without the priest, Deleuze writes, 'the slave would never have known how to raise himself above the brute state of *ressentiment*'. (NP 126) The priestly type 'extends *ressentiment*, leads us further into a domain in which the contagion has spread. Active force becomes reactive, the master becomes slave'. (NP 120)

What precisely does the priestly type bring about? Nietzsche calls it *bad conscience*. *Ressentiment* transforms the healthy hierarchy of active and passive into an essential passivity revolving around the black star of moral accusation. It is directed to other parties, who are judged in their actions to be 'evil'. But the first truly creative moment in the history of human existence, given the reality of *ressentiment*, was the advent of a socio-techical means for the *introjection* of blame. Deleuze cites what is arguably Nietzsche's key definition on this front: 'If one wanted to express the value of the priestly existence in the briefest formula it would be: the priest *alters the direction of ressentiment*'. (*Genealogy*, Third Essay, §15; NP 131).

In the wake of this creative intervention, it will no longer simply be a matter of the moral perversion of the strong, but the judgment of one's own drives as the source of wrong-doing. The forces that were once deployed in reaction to stimuli—which 'do not evaporate' (NP 120)—are now directed within. It is no longer just '*You are to blame*', but '*I am to blame, I am guilty.'* We saw the profound relationship between *ressentiment* and pain before, but this moment of internalization gives it a new depth: '*A new sense is invented for pain, an internal sense, an inward sense*: pain is made the consequence of a sin, a fault'. (NP 129)

We know, however—all too well—this internalisation does *not* get rid of the hatred directed at others, but is fed by it, as if symbiotically. The guilty, children of resentment, still hunger to blame: 'how ready they themselves are at bottom to *make* one pay; how they crave to be *hangmen*'. (*Genealogy*, Third Essay, §13, quoted NP 143) Nietzsche traces this sociotechnics to the historical advent of Christianity, but before that to Judaism. As Deleuze points out, this genealogical claim allowed for some of the most egregious misreadings of Nietzsche—and Deleuze makes quick work of them (NP 126-7)—as an anti-semitic precursor to National Socialism. Deleuze emphasizes that the nature of the analysis, though, is not racial but *typological*. The priestly type is found at the intersection of a great many historical developments, and cannot be derived from any simple source.

In a sense then, at least for Deleuze, the analysis of the priestly type is the first truly genealogical element of Nietzsche's analysis. This explains one of the more enigmatic summary remarks that Deleuze makes: 'Nietzsche's greatness was to know how to separate these two plants, *ressentiment* and bad conscience'. (NP 197) Isolating the first is an act of psychological topology, one that grasps the structure of action and reaction in conscious human being. Isolating the second is an act of historical or genealogical typology, and concerns the discovery of the 'artist' of *ressentiment*, the priestly type.

GENEALOGICAL ACCOUNT II: NIHILISM AND TRANSFORMATION

We have looked at the individual triumph of reactive forces, and the interpersonal triumph, that is, the means by which the reactive type can come to dominate the active type. This analysis is completed at the level of culture itself. As Deleuze notes, the activity of culture is meant to be 'exercised on reactive forces, it gives them habits and imposes models on them in order to make them suitable for being acted'. (NP 134) Principally—and famously—for Nietzsche this involves the formation of memory, or rather a second kind of memory, one added to the memory of traces that characterizes human subjectivity more generally.

The first form of memory, let's recall, involves the recording of encounters in the unconscious. The return of these traces to conscious experience characterizes the resentful type, since they turn encounters with the environment into the passive recollection of the past rather than an engagement with the future. What the second, socialized, memory gives me is a means to make and keep promises. Unlike the first form, then, it is oriented towards the future rather than the past, putting it under my control to a certain degree: I can act towards it rather than remaining passive in the face of those encounters greater than me.

More generally, the goal of culture is to produce active individuals: 'The finished product of species activity is *not* the responsible man himself, or the moral man, but the autonomous and supramoral man, that is to say the one who actually acts his reactive forces and in whom all reactive forces are acted'. (NP 137) But in truth, and as a matter of bitter and blatant historical record, this is exactly not what culture has achieved. It is true that the means of culture—laws, institutions, memory—have been deployed in order to manifest a hierarchy, but it is a reactive and resentful one:

> The most stupid laws, the most limited communities, still want to train man and make use of his reactive forces. But to make use of them for what? To carry out what training, what selection? Training procedures are used but in order to turn man into a gregarious, docile and domesticated animal. Training procedures are used but in order to break the strong, to sort out the weak, the suffering or the slaves. (NP 129)

To be even more direct: the problem is that culture itself has grown the disease of *ressentiment*, to the degree that it begins to sicken human existence itself.

Nihilism and the will to power

We have seen that the first moment of this downwards spiral is the advent of the priestly type, which brings about the heightening and introversion of *ressentiment* and with it the creation of subjective interiority. But for Nietzsche, Deleuze emphasizes, things do not stop there. To the degree that the denegation of activity proceeds, it gradually degrades not only actions done in the name of a particular value, but in the name of any value whatsoever. This is the situation Nietzsche calls *nihilism*, the modern state of human existence. Resentment turns on life itself, hollows it out and takes it as essentially worthless, meaningless, unredeemable in any way: the triumph of reactive forces.

The real problem, though, is that nihilism, far from being some purely exterior and contingent historical fact, is belongs to the will to power itself. Here is Deleuze: 'In the word nihilism *nihil* does not signify non-being but primarily a value of nil. Life takes on a value of nil insofar as it is denied and depreciated [...] Nihil *in 'nihilism' means negation as quality of the will to power*'. (NP 139) This is the sense of the decisive final passage of the *Genealogy*, which describes:

> this hatred of the human, and even more of the animalistic, even more of the material, this horror of the senses, of reason itself, this fear of happiness and beauty, this longing to get away from appearance, transience, growth, death, wishing, longing itself—all that means, let us dare to grasp it, a *will to nothingness*, an aversion to life, a rebellion against the most fundamental prerequisites of life, but it is and remains a *will*! [...] man still prefers to *will nothingness*, than *not* will ... (Third Essay, §28)

'Is man essentially "reactive"'?

It is in light of this situation of nihilism that we need to consider to what degree human existence is free or capable of freeing itself from the triumph of reactive forces. The answer is, first of all, that to be human is to be a creature of *ressentiment* and reaction through and through. Here is Deleuze, alluding to the 'Of Great Events' passage in *Thus Spoke Zarathustra*:

> Man's essence is the becoming-reactive of forces, this becoming as universal becoming. The essence of man and of the world occupied by man is the becoming reactive of all forces, nihilism and nothing but nihilism. Man and his generic activity—these are the two skin diseases of the earth. (NP 159)

Even the strongest of human beings—in Nietzsche's sense—are plagued by this negative quality of the will to power: 'The strong man can oppose the weak, but not his own becoming-weak, which is bound to him by a subtle attraction'. (NP 158)

But what of the infamous Nietzschean thematic of the Übermensch, the Overman? For Deleuze, it is crucial to see that the Übermensch is precisely *not* some kind of superior human being, a particularly strong instance that could overthrow resentment. This is already implied in the fact that human being as such is a reactive type of being. For Deleuze, the Übermensch can only signify a *post-human* type, and if there is hope for an exit from nihilism, it is a hope that the human form will pass away and something else will arise. But how could this be possible?

The irreducibility of affirmation, and the genealogical sense of the eternal return

In an enigmatic handful of pages near the end of *Nietzsche and Philosophy*, Deleuze gives us a striking answer to this question, one that follows from his analysis of the nature of force and the will to power.

We know that the will to power is increasingly expressed in terms of a becoming-reactive—or more precisely, that this has reached a terminal point, where becoming-reactive expresses a becoming-nothingness as a quality of the will to power. However, insofar as the will to nothingness is expressed at all, it is *still the will to power*, and essentially affirmative, and creative. This affirmative character of the will to power can never be destroyed or removed from the will. What *can* be destroyed, however, are particular states of affairs, notably the human being as a reactive type. This is accomplished, on Deleuze's reading, by the negative and destructive face of the will to power *turning back on the reactive forces themselves*. The unity of the will to nothingness is broken at the extreme point: when nothing is left to deny, the will simply reappears as a pure, unbridled power of affirmation. This is how Deleuze puts it, in one of the key moments of his reading of Nietzsche:

> Destruction becomes *active* at the moment when, with the alliance between reactive forces and the will to nothingness broken, the will to nothingness is converted and crosses over to the side of *affirmation*, it is related to a *power of affirming* which destroys the reactive forces themselves. (NP 174)

We find here a third and final sense of the eternal return, or rather a reaffirmation of the first cosmological sense, but this time from the genealogical perspective rather than the structural sense we discussed earlier. We know that the eternal return names the absolute character of temporality—it is an affirmation of becoming. But becoming, the dynamism of reality itself, is absolutely opposed to everything that constitutes reactive forces and their avatar, nihilism: passivity, neutrality, the withdrawal of affirmation. Consequently, the eternal return really just names the impermanence of these reactive forces; it is the guarantee that nihilism will never have the last word.

This is what Deleuze describes as the *selective* characteristic of the eternal return—time 'selects out' everything passive because it is in itself only the affirmation of activity. This is true of the eternal return as an ethical thought, which selects out passivity in favour of a positive affirmation of each chosen act. But it is also true of the eternal return as a fact about reality. It grounds the dynamic flux of becoming which selects out the reactive and the passive elements in being and describes, by integrally affirming it, the errant arc, the tumultuous drama, of existence.

3

Kant's Critical Philosophy

La philosophie critique de Kant, Deleuze's third book, was published in 1963. It appeared in the series 'Les Philosophes', devoted to introducing key figures in the history of philosophy. The book is certainly introductory in some respects, running to a scant one hundred pages in the original French, and includes very little by way of the usual scholarly machinery of references and secondary sources. But Deleuze makes each page count, covering the entirety of Kant's philosophy, above all his three famous critiques: the *Critique of Pure Reason* (first edition 1781, second edition 1787), the *Critique of Practical Reason* (1788), and the *Critique of the Power of Judgment* (1790). As we will see, he also makes an important place for Kant's other works. Any invocation of *Kant's Critical Philosophy* must begin by noting this impressive act of concision itself.

Many years after its publication, Deleuze singles it out with the following remark: 'My book on Kant's different; I like it, I did it as a book about an enemy that tries to show how the system works'. (N 6) This critical spirit is all but impossible to discern in the text. Deleuze's goal instead appears exclusively positive and expository, even when famous and well-known problems with Kant's position appear quite clearly in the foreground.

THE DOCTRINE OF THE FACULTIES AND THE TRANSCENDENTAL METHOD

Deleuze's exposition of Kant's system turns around the concept of *faculty*. A faculty—the term itself can appear opaque or overly technical—is simply a capacity or power (*Kraft*) of thought. Perception, memory, imagination, desire, and so on, these are capacities that I can exercise, that is, faculties that I possess. What is decisive about Kant's doctrine of the faculties? Deleuze emphasizes four points, one of which we will postpone examining until later in our discussion.

First claim: we possess a plurality of different faculties

The first novel moment in Kant's account of faculties is his insistence on their plurality. This is why Deleuze writes that 'One of the most original points of Kantianism is the idea of a *difference in nature between our faculties*'. (KCP 19) This is not only of the greatest importance, but gives rise to serious problems for Kant's philosophy. The general name that Deleuze will use to describe this problem is *sensus communis*, that is, *common sense*: how can faculties that differ in kind nonetheless share a common purpose and a common frame of reference? We will return to this problem in detail.

Second claim: our faculties possess a higher form

As Deleuze reconstructs it, Kant's primary question of a given capacity in thought is: does it have a higher form? By 'higher form', Kant means *autonomous*, able to operate on its own terms and without the need or imposition of rules from elsewhere. As Deleuze puts it, 'a faculty has a higher form when it finds *in itself* the law of its own exercise'. (KCP 4) Consider the example of the faculty of knowledge—our capacity to know—whose higher form is what Kant calls the *understanding*. The contention here is that the understanding is a source of knowledge independent of any other source, and without it, knowledge in the everyday, empirical sense would be impossible. What the understanding provides, Kant argues, are the autonomous rules for knowing anything at all, what he calls the categories of the understanding. In turn, these rules define the notion of objecthood, or what Kant calls 'the object = x'. I know things about apples—how they grow, what they taste like, and even some things about their molecular composition. But my experience and knowledge of apples can never provide me with information about objects in general. Consequently, if I have any knowledge of this generality, it must be strictly *a priori*—that is, prior to any particular experience.

Third claim: faculties are hierarchically organized according to the ends of reason

This third claim brings together the previous two. How can the fact there are multiple faculties, and the fact that the faculties in their higher operation are autonomous in relation to the others be reconciled? The answer is that the faculties are organized differently depending on the given goal or end of thinking. In other words, different faculties can be brought together under the governance of one particular faculty—one will be in charge. The key point here is that the relative roles of the various faculties changes depending on the goal or *ends* to which thought has turned. To worry about a moral decision, to find a white lily beautiful, to critically examine Euclid's geometry, each of these activities of thought presupposes a different organization of the contributions of the various faculties. In each of these cases, a different organization of the faculties will be required. The three *Critiques* present three different accounts of what this 'being in charge' means in the various cases of epistemological, moral, aesthetic and teleological judgments (we will discuss the meaning of these terms in what follows).

But all of this can be put another way. In Deleuze's words: 'there are interests of reason which *differ in nature*'. (KCP 6) Reason, understood here as a name for thinking in general, has differing ends that require a different organization of the faculties. *Kant's Critical Philosophy* begins with the double assertion concerning these ends:

1. In Kant, these ends form a whole, an organic system
2. These ends cannot be explained either by empiricism (in which the relative position of the faculties is fixed and the ends are *natural*) nor by rationalism (in which the position of the faculties is fixed and there is only one end, that of reason in the narrow sense)

As Deleuze notes, the whole of Kant's philosophy is explicitly an investigation of a third alternative, what Kant himself famously calls a middle way between empiricism and rationalism (*Critique of Pure Reason* B167). This alternative will turn around the themes of *a dynamic community of faculties*, and Kant's conception of *autonomy*.

Before we continue, a note on terminology. Kant uses the term 'reason' in two distinct senses. In the current discussion, as I noted above, he takes it as a synonym for any kind of deliberative thinking, such as it is involved in judging art, doing mathematics, or resolving a moral issue. He also uses it to denote a very specific function in thinking. In keeping with the tradition of Kant scholarship, and with Deleuze's own usage, the lower-case 'reason' will be used when speaking in general terms, while the specific faculty of 'Reason' will always be capitalized.

The transcendental

We will see all of this unfold as we follow, with Deleuze, the respective arguments of the three *Critiques* in turn. But the main concern of Deleuze's reading can all be put another way yet again, this time in terms of the hallmark feature of Kant's philosophy, the *transcendental*. Kant's concern with the faculties in their higher sense is really a concern with the conditions of possible experience. In other words, the question 'what is the higher form of the faculty of knowledge?' can be reframed as 'what does our ordinary everyday capacity to know things necessarily presuppose?' This shift in focus is a shift from the empirical level of facts or habits of thought to the transcendental level of principles. There are always questions of fact involved when we claim to know something—a journalist must have his sources, the scientist her evidence. But beyond this remains the question about what accounts for the possibility of knowledge *in general and as such*. So this is what the term 'transcendental' names: the necessary, *a priori* conditions for the possibility of experience and of all of our capacities for thought.

THE DOCTRINE OF THE FACULTIES IN THE *CRITIQUE OF PURE REASON*

Let's now turn to the first case study of Kant's transcendental doctrine of the faculties, the *Critique of Pure Reason*, in which knowledge—epistemological judgment—is the main focus. And, as we should expect, Deleuze's argument proceeds through the various faculties that Kant treats with an eye to their organization when the goal of thinking is *knowing*.

The imagination

My knowledge of any object involves not one but a series of experiences in time and space: I *apprehend* the apple in this way and in this moment of time, and then the same thing happens in the next moment. But it is also the case that, if I know the apple, it is as a unified object and not just a series of profiles—I also *synthesise* these apprehensions into the apple as an object, reproducing the past profiles as I do. These two moments that are obviously in play in any objective knowledge are the acts of the faculty of the imagination for Kant. Why call it the imagination? Simply because, as a faculty, its power is the power to produce *images*—the image of the apple.

The subject, the object and the understanding

But this image is not really knowledge by itself. Knowledge also needs two other ingredients. On the one hand, there must be a subject of knowledge, a subject *for whom* the experience and knowledge of the apple is something experienced and known about. This subject is what Kant calls the *transcendental unity of apperception*, a long but apt name for what he's describing—as he famously writes, 'The **I think** must **be able** to accompany all my representations; for otherwise something would be represented in me that could not be thought at all, which is as much as to say that the representation would either be impossible or else at least would be nothing for me'. (*Critique of Pure Reason* B131-2) The point here is that my various experiences must be related to me as the one that experiences them, just like keys on my key ring, in order for me to be able to talk of *my* experience at all.

On the other hand, an image of the apple is not yet an object of knowledge in any robust sense. Knowledge also requires, as Deleuze says, an 'act by which the represented manifold is related to an object (recognition: this is a table, this is an apple, this is such and such an object)'. (KCP 15) Without this, there would be no difference between an image of a real thing and the image of, say, a unicorn that I can also easily produce. Now, as we noted earlier, the contours of objecthood are never given in experience directly, but are presupposed by it. For Kant, objecthood is determined in relation to the '*predicates of the concept of the object in general*'. (KCP 14) The faculty that provides these predicates is one I have already mentioned, the *understanding*, and these predicates are what Kant (ultimately following Aristotle), calls the categories of the understanding. Ultimately, these categories constitute the natural world as such, or, better, the laws of nature are found in the structure of human cognition and not in being itself.

Notice a key point here: the faculty of the understanding is 'in charge' when knowledge is the goal. I can always imagine crazed fictional scenarios, but the moment that I want to know something about a real object, the imagination is subordinated to the understanding. In other words, the understanding is the legislating faculty when the end of reason is knowledge. But it is even more important to keep in mind that Kant is presenting a transcendental philosophy, an account of the conditions for the possibility of experience and knowledge in general, and not an account of how particular knowledge claims come about. The consciousness in question isn't my empirical consciousness of this laptop, this desk, this city, but the form of consciousness as such. Conversely, the object that Kant is interested in isn't this laptop or this desk, but the formal object = x—the form of the object in general. The empty subject and the formal object are strict correlates and equally necessary presuppositions of knowledge.

Referring to Kant's outstripping of Descartes, Deleuze summarises these points in the following text: 'The real (synthetic) formula of the *cogito* is: I think myself and in thinking myself, I think the object in general to which I relate a represented diversity.' (KCP 14; see *Critique of Pure Reason* B138).

Sensibility

Both the understanding and the imagination are active and constitutive faculties in the constitution of experience and epistemological judgments, but something still remains missing, namely the origin of the materials on which these faculties go to work. There must be a further faculty through which I receive sensation, the faculty Kant calls *sensibility*. Unlike the understanding and the imagination, sensibility is necessarily passive—I do not constitute the sensations that I experience; they have to arise from a source beyond my control or direct apprehension.

But in addition to being passive, sensibility is characterized by a second important feature. All my encounters with the world immediately bear the stamp of time and space: they take place within a spatio-temporal framework. Sensibility is thus the faculty to which the forms of space and time belong. Now, it is not the case, Deleuze emphasises, that sensibility imposes these forms on the multiplicity of sensation. That my sensations are spatio-temporal in character is immediately given. And these spatio-temporally determined multiplicities are what Kant calls *intuitions*.

Reason

But now we arrive at a fourth and final faculty that plays a decisive part in the formation of knowledge in the first *Critique*, the faculty of *Reason*. This is the 'Reason' of Kant's title, and the first thing that the word 'critique' means in turn is that we need to reconstruct what we think of when we think of reason. It is true that I can think about the nature of the world without referring to experience—just as I can contemplate the nature of the soul, and debate the existence of a transcendent God with myself. But precisely because Reason does not refer itself directly to experience, it will be unable to resolve these questions either way. In fact, as Kant masterfully shows in the 'Antinomies of Pure Reason' section of the first *Critique*, questions like 'did the universe have a beginning?' or 'does God exist?' can be rigorously and consistently answered in both the affirmative and the negative.

Kant's interesting conclusion is that this problematic situation is a positive feature of Reason in the cause of knowledge, and not a weakness. The fact that Reason cannot represent the state of the world means that its concepts—what Kant calls the Ideas of reason—play a different role in the formation of knowledge. This role is a *regulative* one. Ideas contribute to knowledge by giving us a means to organize particular knowledge claims. Take the example of the Idea of the totality—the idea of 'everything' or the universe. This can never be an object of experience or knowledge, but what it can do is allow us to conceive of the systematic unity of knowledge itself. Without this, modern science would be completely impossible, reduced to a bric-a-brac collection of particular knowledge claims lacking any systematic interrelation—two chemistry labs working next to each other would not be able to correlate their research.

To be more specific, as Deleuze puts it, 'the Ideas of Reason refer to the concepts of the understanding in order to confer on them the maximum of both systematic unity and extension'. (KCP 17) Consequently the objects of the Ideas—Kant emphasises three: God, the soul, and totality—are not true objects, but a certain kind of ideal half-objects, or incomplete objects, completed each time they are called into play to give the representations produced by the understanding a breadth or depth that they do not possess on their own. Deleuze's summary passage is worth citing in full:

> Reason, at the very moment it abandons legislative power in the interest of knowledge to the understanding, nevertheless retains a role, or rather *receives in turn*, from the understanding itself, an original function: the constitution of ideal foci outside experience towards which the concepts of the understanding converge (maximum unity); the forming of higher horizons which reflect and contain the concepts of the understanding (maximum extension). (KCP 17)

Sensus communis logicus

We have now seen how the system of the faculties fits together in the first *Critique*. Together, 'The three active faculties (imagination, understanding, reason) [...] enter into a certain relation, which is a function of the speculative interest'. (KCP 18) This relation is dominated by the understanding, which has the role of the 'chairmanship' (KCP 10) when knowledge is the goal of thought. In particular, it gives to the other faculties the form of the object, to which their respective contributions are necessarily subordinated.

In other words, a certain kind of harmony or accord is established between the faculties—a certain *'common sense'*. (KCP 18) But now Deleuze asks an important critical question. Kant's reconstruction of the faculty of knowledge is founded on the claim that objectivity is only established *within* the subject, and that we must reject any belief that objects in themselves are somehow in harmony with our experience of them. However, hasn't Kant simply shifted the locus of this harmony, finding it now in the *sensus communis* of the faculties? Doesn't Kant 'once again come up with the idea of harmony, simply transposed to the level of faculties of the subject that differ in nature'? (KCP 19) Putting the point even more sharply, Deleuze notes that 'each time we assume the perspective of a relationship or an accord which is already determined, it is inevitable that common sense should seem to us a kind of *a priori* fact beyond which we cannot go'. (KCP 23)

Legitimate and illegitimate deployment of the faculties

As Deleuze will say, this seemingly illegitimate Kantian supposition arrived years before Kant develops an alternative approach in the third *Critique*. But for the moment, he sets aside this concern to discuss the unusual danger to thinking that Kant's reconstruction uncovers. It is this: because there is no natural harmony between thought and reality as it is in itself, and because the subject legislates autonomously, there is no guardrail against illegitimate uses of the powers of the mind. Nothing within the mind constrains it from crossing over into delirium.

Kant identifies two such illegitimate deployments, or rather two versions of a single complex error—the idea that we can grasp things as they are in themselves rather than as they are composed in our experience. As Deleuze puts it, 'understanding and reason are deeply tormented by the ambition to make things in themselves known to us'. (KCP 24) In the first instance, the understanding is at fault. If I get into an argument about, say, the colour of a dress, I can't ultimately have final recourse to what is physically in front of me to justify my knowledge claims, because the objects of experience are formed within thought and not produced by the things themselves. I can never to point to any further evidence than my representations, because there is no other evidence. But, nevertheless, this is what try I do (*Are you blind? It's clearly blue and black!* Etc.). This use of the understanding *neglects its limits*.

But secondly and more seriously, Reason can take itself to address the nature of reality directly. This is what Kant calls the *transcendent* use of Reason. It consists in the belief that Reason can constitute knowledge by itself. I come to think that because I can *reason* about God or my soul, I *know* about them. In this illegitimate use of Reason, I accede to an 'illusion of a positive domain to conquer outside experience'. (KCP 25) This issue is particularly serious, once again, because there is no way to stop it from happening. Reason on its own tends towards an illegitimate operation, engendering these fictions on its own terms. Kant famously calls this tendency *transcendental illusion*—the tendency to 'take a subjective necessity of a connection of our concept [...] for an objective necessity in the determination of things in themselves'. (*Critique of Pure Reason* A297/B354)

The need for a critique of *pure* Reason now appears; a critical vigilance will be required to keep this tendency in check. But, Deleuze asks, *why* does Reason tend to address itself to things in themselves? There is indeed something positive in this tendency, even if, in the service of knowledge, it can only be an aberration. In sum, if Reason exceeds the limits set by the understanding, it is because it is capable of more than being engaged in the search for knowledge. Its excesses speak to its deeper nature. As Deleuze puts it:

> There is then only one way out: it is that Reason, elsewhere, experiences an interest, itself legitimate and natural, for things in themselves, but an interest which is not speculative [not given over to the search for knowledge] [...] Speculative reason would never have been interested in things in themselves if these were not, primarily and genuinely, the object of another interest of reason. (KCP 23)

All of this, Deleuze writes, leaves us with two questions that we will need to find an answer for in Kant. The first concerns common sense: how can Kant justify his invocation of a harmony between the faculties? The second, and the one we will turn to now, concerns Reason: what is this other end that motivates reason to press beyond its legitimate operation in the service of knowledge?

THE DOCTRINE OF THE FACULTIES IN THE *CRITIQUE OF PRACTICAL REASON*

The question posed by the second *Critique*, the *Critique of Practical Reason* concerns desire: what is the higher form of this faculty? That is: what is the nature of desire when it is made autonomous from particular empirical needs and wants, pleasures and pains? The higher form of desire is, Kant concludes, the will itself, the will not constrained by any particular fact or feeling, or by any rule imposed upon it from elsewhere. It is the pure autonomy of subjectivity, 'such that practical reason and freedom are, perhaps, one and the same'. (KCP 29) However, this pure autonomy cannot be some kind of unbound randomness, unrelated to choice. This is after all what autonomy means—self-*rule*. Correlatively, though, this rule cannot be any particular stricture imposed on the basis of pleasure, or what other people think, since this would also cede its autonomy.

So now the question becomes what kind of rule is compatible with the will in this sense, and Kant's famous answer is that it is 'the pure form of universal legislation', (KCP 25) a completely general 'ought' that all rational beings can conform to without ceding their autonomy. This law is necessarily a moral law not just because it takes the form of a normative judgment ('One ought …'), but because it necessarily involves *universality*, a purchase on all rational beings. Here is Deleuze's excellent summary of Kant's point in his preface to the English translation of *Kant's Critical Philosophy*:

> It [the law] does not tell us *what* we must do, but to what (subjective) rule we must conform, whatever our action. Any action is moral if its maxim can be thought without contradiction as universal, and if its motive has no other object than this maxim. For example, the lie cannot be thought as formally universal without contradiction, since it at least implies people who believe in it, and who, in believing in it, are not lying. The moral law is thus defined as the pure form of universality. (KCP x)

The rule 'do not lie' has the normative character of the moral law, but to follow this rule for no other reason that that you have had it drilled into you since you were a kid is not to act autonomously. No, what confirms our freedom as moral agents is the fact that this secondary rule necessarily follows from the unity, in subjective freedom, of universality and normativity. Thus Kant expresses this moral law in the even more famous form of the *categorical imperative*. Here is one of his formulations: "So act that the maxim of your will could always hold at the same time as a principle of universal legislation." (*Critique of Practical Reason*, 45) As Deleuze indicates above, the rule 'do not lie' is a result that can always be deduced from this imperative, but it only has the purchase that it does because of it. This is why he connects Kant's moral philosophy to a sentiment from Kafka's *The Trial*: the good is what the law says. There are not particular goods for Kant, from which we might infer courses of action. There is only the formal rule of the law that allows us to determine what is good.

Before we continue, it is important to notice that the freedom Kant is speaking of cannot belong to the natural world. That world – the world of objects – is entirely bound by cause and effect and makes no place for subjective freedom, which is defined in turn by its power to 'begin a state *spontaneously*'. (*Critique of Pure Reason* A533/B561) The obvious question that this stance provokes is: what evidence Kant could possibly produce to justify the assertion that freedom exists? Deleuze emphasizes two elements of Kant's response to this line of questioning.

The first is uncovered by Kant in the first *Critique*. While objectivity is a product of the transcendental subject, in order for me to have any experience at all, I must have encountered something in the world that provides me with the sensible input that the understanding and the imagination can go to work on. Here we find Kant's empirical realism, which, as Deleuze emphasizes, 'is a constant feature of critical philosophy'. (KCP 14) This 'something' beyond the faculties of thought Kant calls the *noumenon*, as opposed to the *phenomenal* realm of subjective experience and knowledge about it. There must be something beyond my experiences in order for me to have them. The fact that there is such a beyond is a first justification for the belief in freedom—there is a realm beyond the world of cause and effect.

The second justification for the belief in freedom is found on the side of the subject. As thinking beings, we possess faculties that can act autonomously, just as the understanding does when knowledge is the end of thought. This autonomy is not vouched for by anything in the natural world precisely because it does not belong to that world at all. In fact, the autonomy of the faculty of the understanding is itself the source of our knowledge about the perennial role of cause and effect relations. At the root of the proof of the impossibility of freedom is the work of an autonomous faculty.

Reason

To flesh all of this out, we must turn to the interplay of the faculties in the case of morality, starting with the relative positions of Reason and the understanding. It would appear in the first instance that freedom is an Idea of reason akin to the Ideas of God, the soul and the world. But we have already seen that freedom is not a speculative element but a practical reality for the subject. It must, consequently, differ in kind from these other ideas when practical reason is in play. Kant will say instead that freedom constitutes the unique *fact* of Reason: it 'may be called a fact of reason because one cannot reason it out from antecedent data of reason'. (*Critique of Practical Reason*, 46) When morality is the end of thought, guided by the idea of freedom, it is reason rather than the understanding which legislates, and more than this, it is now *constitutive* rather than regulative. Reason constitutes freedom as an unquestionable fact, and whenever we choose against the categorical imperative, we at the same time choose, as if paradoxically, against both reason and freedom.

And though the fact of reason is decisive, the Ideas of the soul and God also play an important role, though one that differs from the first

Critique. In this context, Kant will call them the *postulates* of practical reason, and they function as presupposed conditions for the intelligibility or meaning of moral choice, 'the conditions under which the object of practical reason is itself posed as possible and realizable'. (KCP 42) As Deleuze puts it, 'The Ideas of the soul and of God are the necessary conditions under which the object of practical reason is itself posed as possible and realisable [...] an infinite progress (the immortal soul) and [...] the intermediary of an intelligible author of sensible nature or of a 'moral cause of the world' (God)' (KCP 42) are required.

The realization of practical reason: the understanding, sensibility and the imagination

With Reason adopting the legislative role, the understanding is displaced in moral thought. The self as a rational, free agent is not an object of sensible experience, and thus does not require the form of the object in general in order to proceed. Nevertheless, the understanding gives Reason a decisive resource by analogy. In essence, the understanding—in its legislative role—is nothing other than a complex rule that our intuitions must conform to. This is what Reason draws upon in morality. 'We retain only "the form of conformity to the law", as it is found in the legislative understanding. But we make use of this form, and of the understanding itself, following an interest and in a domain where the latter *is no longer* the legislator'. (KCP 42) Deleuze selects one aspect of knowledge as an example: causality. When morality is at issue, reason presents the causal agency of the free rational being as *analogous* to the causal agency possessed by nature.

On the same basis—because it does not belong to the world of cause and effect that characterizes nature—freedom it is not subject to the faculty of sensibility: 'Free beings and free causality are not the object of any intuition and [...] suprasensible Nature and sensible nature are separated by an abyss.' (KCP 33) Nonetheless, sensibility also plays a major role in morality: while freedom itself has no sensible reality, sensible reality is the necessary locus of its effects. It is even the case that free acts *only* have effects in the sensible realm. Practical reason must itself 'have causality in relation to phenomena'. (KCP 40) In short, sensibility provides us with the realm in which free will is *realized*.

The imagination is in the same situation. The exercise of freedom does not directly require its operations of apprehension and synthesis in the cause of knowledge. However, by function in this way, it gives to us the place where morality will have effects. As Deleuze puts it, 'the consciousness of morality, that is to say the moral common sense, not only includes beliefs, but the acts of an imagination through which sensible Nature appears as fit to receive the effect of the suprasensible. Imagination itself is thus really part of moral common sense'. (KCP 43)

It is in this context of this account of a moral *sensus communis*, a harmony of the faculties when subjective moral freedom is the guiding activity, that Deleuze addresses Kant's famous claim for the primacy of practical reason. From the perspective of free agency, the natural world now appears as a world constituted *in order that* moral action is possible. Deleuze is even more forceful: the world would never be of any speculative interest if it were *solely* an object of speculation. An obvious piece of evidence here is the transformation of the role of the Idea of God: 'as an object of knowledge, God is determinable only indirectly and analogically (as that from which phenomena draw a maximum of systematic unity); but, as object of belief, he acquires an exclusively practical determination and reality (moral author of the world)'. (KCP 44)

Illegitimate and legitimate deployment in morality

Just as in the first *Critique*, the *Critique of Practical Reason* addresses the troubling excesses that the operation of Reason courts. This time, though, the word 'critique' bears a different sense. The threat is posed not by a pure practical reason—since this is precisely the situation of the free agent operating in accordance with the categorical imperative—but by the *impurities* secreted by reason in its unguarded operation.

Kant recognizes the empiricist temptation to treat morality as motivated by sentiment, but this for him is not just false, but beside the point when we are talking about acting in accordance with a rule. However, when we act in accordance with the categorical imperative, we experience 'a satisfaction, a kind of negative enjoyment expressing our independence from sensible inclinations, a purely intellectual contentment immediately expressing the formal accord of our understanding with our reason'. (KCP 32) This is not in fact an emotion or sensation as such, Deleuze notes, but an intellectual '"analogue" of feeling'. (KCP 39) The threat to pure practical reason consists in taking this satisfaction to be evidence that motivations for moral action are in fact sensible and affective in character. Kant describes the situation well when he writes that we are confronted by 'an optical illusion [which] always lies in the self-consciousness of what one *does*'. This is 'an illusion that even the most experienced person cannot avoid."' (*Critique of Practical Reason*, 148) The difficult critical task is thus to bend our reflections back towards the exclusive mutual implication of freedom, reason and the law.

THE DOCTRINE OF THE FACULTIES IN THE *CRITIQUE OF THE POWER OF JUDGEMENT*

We have seen, in the first two cases, Kant's presumption that faculties that absolutely differ in kind can nevertheless enter into harmonious relations. One of the major orienting claims of *Kant's Critical Philosophy* is that the third *Critique* modifies and deepens the Kantian doctrine of the faculties in such a way that this troubling problem receives a definitive resolution. Earlier, I said that there are three major claims about the faculties that guide Deleuze's exposition:

1. There are a plurality of faculties that differ in kind
2. The higher sense of a faculty is that faculty operating autonomously
3. Depending on the goal of thinking in question, different faculties adopt the governing or legislating role, directing the contributions of the others

The Critique of the Power of Judgment will add a decisive further claim:

4. If the relationship between the faculties is able to change depending on the goals of thought, it must be because the faculties are capable of entering into a *spontaneous harmony in the first place*.

In other words, the fact that there can be different determinate relationships under the legislation of different faculty indicates that there must be the basic possibility for the faculties to enter a spontaneous accord:

> The indeterminate suprasensible unity of all the faculties, and the free accord which derives from it, are the deepest parts of the soul. Indeed, when the accord of faculties finds itself determined by one of them […] we assume that the faculties are *in the first place* capable of a free harmony […] without which none of these determinations would be possible. (KCP 55)

The two forms of common sense we have already seen (moral, and logical or speculative) therefore gesture to a third which would be the ground of their operation: an *aesthetic* common sense. Now the point here is not that all knowledge and morality are in some sense aesthetic—as if what is beautiful was immediately good or epistemologically significant. Instead, Kant will define this deeper spontaneity in the organization of the faculties as aesthetic. In a moment, we will see how he will do this, but first we must note, with Deleuze, that this shift in perspective is what will allow Kant to make progress on a problem he had long thought meaningless. The problem is simply this: '"Is there a higher form of pleasure and pain?"' (KCP 3)

Now, by shifting away from the emphasis on a single legislating faculty, several new situations open up. Specifically, three other kinds of judgments become able to be examined which we will examine in turn: aesthetic judgments of the beautiful, aesthetic judgments of the sublime, and teleological judgments, or judgments concerning the purposes or goals of Nature.

Aesthetic judgments of the beautiful

So let's consider a now-familiar form of question: what would a higher form of pleasure be? The hallmark of the higher form is always its autonomy, and here this means that pleasure must be autonomous not just from the demands of knowledge and morality, but also, Kant famously says, autonomous with respect to affect. Aesthetic judgments of the beautiful are always *disinterested* in character. In the same way that free moral choice must be an act that is not motivated by feeling, a judgment of the sort 'this is beautiful' cannot be an expression of a higher form of pleasure if it is really motivated by pleasure in the lower sense. Correlatively—and this is to be expected on the basis of what we've seen in the first two cases—the aesthetic interest in beauty is an interest in *form* and not content. At the same time, a judgment of this kind is completely particular—actually, not even particular, Deleuze notes, 'since it remains completely indifferent to its existence'. (KCP 47-8) I can, for instance, find the representation of a certain building beautiful even if it has never been built.

Now, when we pose the question 'what is the faculty of beauty in its higher form?', the answer is very striking: there is not one. The role played by the understanding and reason in speculative and moral judgments finds no analogue here. Something different is going on, and it concerns the aesthetic common sense we noted earlier. As Deleuze puts it, 'The faculty of feeling has no *domain* (neither phenomena nor things in themselves); it does not express the conditions to which a kind of object must be subject, but solely *the subjective conditions for the exercise of the faculties*'. (KCP 40)

The higher form of pleasure does not give rise to the autonomy of a particular faculty, but the autonomous organization of the whole system of the faculties. Consider Kant's example, repeated by Deleuze, of a white lily (*Critique of the Power of Judgment*, 181; KCP 54-5). What is at stake when I say 'this lily is beautiful'?

1. The image of the white lily is reflected in the *imagination*, but without any application of the categories (as in knowledge). Instead, the imagination 'plays' with the form of the thing, generating profiles and perspectives spontaneously and without guidance
2. The *understanding* nonetheless contributes the (negative) formal category of *indeterminacy*. It agrees with the imagination in general terms but without imposing any conceptual requirements. In other words, it engages the imagination but without any particular determined role
3. In turn, the image of the lily spontaneously gives rise in *Reason* to 'the Idea of pure innocence, whose object is merely a (reflexive) analogue of the white in the lily flower'. (KCP 54) . This *aesthetic Idea* gives us 'an intuition of a nature other than that which is given to us: another nature whose phenomena would be true spiritual events […] It "gives food for thought", it forces one to think'. (KCP 48) This other nature is, of course, the suprasensible nature of free, rational human agency.

The crucial point in all this is that no one faculty governs this interaction. So when I speak of pleasure here, it is not a pleasure inspired by the image of the flower, but a pleasure I feel thanks to *the free interplay of the faculties themselves*. The higher form of pleasure is thus nothing other than a kind of auto-affection of subjectivity in its free play.

Aesthetic judgments of the sublime

In addition to aesthetic judgments of beauty, there are also aesthetic judgments of the sublime, which are engendered in relation to an experience of the very powerful or the very large: 'The feeling of the sublime is experienced when faced with the formless or the deformed (immensity or power)'. (KCP 42) Confronted, for instance, with the immense power of a wild storm out at sea (think of the immortal Turner), what happens? What is going on when I say 'Oh my god!' or (if I've spent too much time reading philosophy) 'this is sublime!'?

1. The *imagination* strives to comprehend the experience and *fails*. To be more precise, it may have no trouble apprehending each particular moment of the storm, but it is incapable of bringing all of this together—it cannot *synthesise* these experiences into one storm.

2. This is *not* due to the storm itself—after all, all storms are in fact finite in character, and able as a result to be subject to the synthesis of the imagination under the chairmanship of the understanding ('Hurricane Lily started here, changed in this way, ended here, displayed the following characteristics, etc.'). The demand for the unity of phenomena is found in *Reason*: 'it is *Reason* which forces us to unite the immensity of the sensible world into a whole'. (KCP 51)

3. There is thus a spontaneous accord that emerges between the imagination and Reason, but it is a peculiar negative accord, one that forces the imagination 'to admit that all its power is nothing in comparison to an Idea'. (KCP 51) The pain of being unable to 'make sense' of the storm as I encounter it is therefore doubled by a peculiar pleasure that arises because I can nevertheless *think it*.

Two senses of 'judgment' in Kant

In both of these cases, we form a judgment—the lily is beautify, this storm is sublime—but clearly this is unlike the judgments that we produce in the spheres of knowledge and morality. Alongside this new—spontaneous and multilateral rather than *a priori* and unilateral—sense of facultative accord is a new sense of judgment itself. In the latter cases, judgment is *determinative*. Judgments are made *in accordance with* the categories of the understanding, or *in accordance* with the categorical imperative. But in aesthetic judgment, there is no legislating faculty and nothing with which judgment can accord. It is, instead, *reflective* in character. By this Kant means that to make an aesthetic judgment is to judge without rules.

Now, in keeping with the fact that the free play of the faculties are the ground of their determinative arrangement in knowledge and morality, determinative judgment must be conceived as a species of reflective judgment. As Deleuze puts it, 'Reflective judgment manifests and liberates a depth which remained hidden in the other'. (KCP 60) He adds that this is exactly what explains the title, the *Critique of the Power of Judgment*. It gives us an account of what judgment is capable of, over and beyond any particular interest of reason. It is not a faculty in the same sense as the imagination or sensibility, but it is nevertheless a capacity or *power of thought* that is in play every time the faculties are organized in any manner whatsoever.

Teleological judgments

We come now to the third kind of judgment treated in the third *Critique*. As I have said, teleological judgments are judgments about the point, goal or end of things (*telos* = end). They resemble aesthetic judgments in that they are reflective and do not involve a single faculty that plays the role of legislator. On the other hand, they uniquely involve something that aesthetic judgments do not—the positing of ends or goals. When I say 'the lily is beautiful', it is not and cannot be subject to a purpose, being disinterested even to the point that the lily's does not need to actually exist.

But there is a further, even more illuminating difference. We have seen that for Kant, aesthetic judgments prepare us for morality. This is not just because they present us with our own primary freedom in the form of the spontaneous accord of the faculties, but also because of the aesthetic Ideas these judgments give to Reason, such that 'the beautiful itself is a symbol of the good'. (KCP 55) Teleological judgments complement this by providing to speculative judgment something that it cannot provide on its own: the category of *end* itself. We saw in the case of speculative judgments that the Idea of totality has an important regulative role, giving to the ensemble of knowledge claims a horizon, an orientation, towards which they can be drawn together. But in the third *Critique*, Kant adds that something further is required in our inventory of the conditions of the possibility of knowledge. This is the sense that empirical reality and its own set of laws, whatever these are (we have no direct access to them), fit together into a meaningful whole on its own—that is, has a natural end, a *finality* or *purposiveness*—*Zweckmässigkeit* has been translated both ways—proper to it. Deleuze is particularly clear in his summary of this point:

> [It is] *on the basis of the concept of natural end we determine an object of the rational Idea*. The Idea doubtless does not have a determinate object in itself; but its object is determinable by analogy with the objects of experience. Now this indirect and analogical determination (which is perfectly reconcilable with the regulative function of the Idea) is possible only in so far as the objects of experience themselves display this final unity, in relation to which the object of the Idea must serve as principle, or substratum. (KCP 63-4)

Ultimately, then, the meaningfulness of any speculative judgment presupposes that the world is meaningfully organized. This is why Kant sometimes defines purposiveness as the lawfulness of the contingent (*Critique of the Power of Judgment* 20; 30; 76). Deleuze is more colloquial: 'in teleological judgment, we must consider that Nature is genuinely doing us a favour'. (KCP 65)

How does the spontaneity of the faculties manifest itself in this case, though? What is at stake in teleological judgments, when I assert, for example, that 'there is a purpose to the migratory activity of swallows'? This judgment is the product of a reflection on the natural world, and what it produces is, uniquely, a concept of reflection, which is nothing other than the concept of 'natural end' or purposiveness as such. It is as though the concept of natural end is a 'floating concept', belonging to reflection itself rather than to any one faculty. Whenever I reflect on the natural world, I spontaneously produce the concept of natural end as the object of the judgment that things must be governed by natural laws. This concept in turn then convokes the various faculties to organize around it in the cause of knowledge. Here is Deleuze's brief but illuminating summary of this spontaneous organization engendered by the concept of natural end:

> it intervenes to allow the imagination to 'reflect' on the object in an indeterminate way, so that the understanding 'acquires' concepts in accordance with the Ideas of reason itself. The concept of natural end is a concept of reflection which derives from the regulative Ideas: within it all our faculties are harmonized and enter a free accord which allows us to reflect on Nature from the standpoint of its empirical laws. (KCP 63)

HISTORY AND 'THE RUSE OF NATURE'

We ended our discussions of the first two *Critiques* with the same question: how can the presupposed harmony between the faculties be justified by Kant? We have just seen what Deleuze thinks is Kant's decisive rejoinder: the faculties are capable of a primary spontaneous accord. This approach certainly resolves the earlier form of the problem, but it seems to do so only by making it reappear in an even more profound sense: now the faculties are capable of *spontaneously generating harmony*. Deleuze notes this problem, but immediately responds that to look at Kant's system in this way is to miss something crucial: it is not that human thought is ultimately subordinated to the presupposition of these necessary accords, but that these accords are *produced in human thought*. We have already seen this genesis of subjective accord in the two forms of aesthetic judgment, but it is teleological judgment, and the production of the relationship between Nature and human freedom that Deleuze dwells on in the conclusion to *Kant's Critical Philosophy*.

We must begin by defining history. From the point of view of both speculative and teleological judgment, *homo sapiens* is just one species among many, governed by its own set of natural laws. Here, there is only nature. The only real option then appears to be to define history as a sphere proper to human beings as autonomous moral agents. So we can say that while speculative reason (qualified and extended by the teleological concept of natural end) finds its ultimate object in a law-bound Nature, practical reason finds its ultimate object in History.

It is here that Kant introduces his remarkable category of the ruse of Nature. This ruse is not, as the name might suggest, a trick played on us *by* Nature. It is a trick that thought plays on *itself*. The ruse of nature is the supposition *of* Nature, a natural order, governed by its own rules and completely beyond human agency. The notion of transcendental illusion examined with such power in the first two *Critiques* finds here its positive reinscription and indeed generalisation: Reason constitutes its self-conception in contradistinction to a Nature that it has itself produced, but only in order that its legitimate ends can be realized.

Now, this ruse is a necessary one for speculative reason, as we have seen, but we confuse its scope if we think it licenses us to say that history does not exist because of nature's anteriority and absolute exteriority. Because the ordered character of Nature is produced by the subject, 'whatever appears to be contingent in the accord of sensible nature with man's faculties is a supreme transcendental appearance, which hides a ruse of the suprasensible'. (KCP 74)

We could object that human history hardly looks like the forum for rational deliberation. It obviously looks a lot more like a make-shift arena of 'pure relations of forces, conflicts of tendencies, which weave a web of madness like childish vanity' (KCP 75) But as Deleuze points out, Kant does not think that history can be defined in terms of human reason's slow work of refashioning nature in a rational way, such that 'events would then manifest an "individual rational purpose"', (KCP 75) the kind of position advanced by Hegel for instance. Pointing out that a rational thinker cannot by herself produce a rational social order is no objection either.

So, on the one hand, our messy friend *homo sapiens* must remain at the centre of the picture—after all, this mad conflict of forces and drives *is* human nature from the point of view of knowledge. On the other hand and from the point of view of morality, nature provides the arena in which rational activity can be achieved, so long as we understand that this can only happen "*in conformity with its* [Nature's] *own laws*'. (KCP 75) History is *human* history, the novel which we collectively write as a species. Its protagonist human Reason is not an agent *beyond* or *better* than natural life, but one only capable of exceeding or bettering nature from within it.

4

Bergsonism

Though he was inordinately famous for most of his life, by the time the young Gilles Deleuze was preparing for his *agrégation* exams in 1948, Henri Bergson (1859-1941) and his philosophy were decidedly *déclassé*. Considered an obscurantist, an enemy of science and rational thought, and an ideologist for the bourgeoisie, his philosophy was steadily being buried by successive generations of existentialists, phenomenologists and structuralists. The widespread existential shock of the second world war had cast the philosopher of creative evolution in a very stark light.

Nevertheless, the young Gilles Deleuze was convinced of Bergson's enduring greatness. In his joint biography of Deleuze and Guattari, François Dosse reports a remarkable conversation between Deleuze and a group of his friends preparing for these exams, whose topics included

> Bergson's *Matter and Memory* and Emile Durkheim's *Rules for a Sociological Method*. [Olivier] Revault d'Allonnes recalls that he and [François] Châtelet, who had Marxist leanings, had no trouble whatsoever appropriating Durkheim's theses but considered Bergson to be a dusty and uninteresting spiritualist. 'At the Biarritz Café where we frequently meet, we told Gilles that Bergson sort of irritated us. He answered, "No, you're mistaken, you've read him badly. He's a very great philosopher."' Then Deleuze pulled *Matter and Memory* out of his briefcase and starts reading, commenting, and explaining a long passage to his pals. 'He had this expression on his face, "What! you don't like Bergson! I'm really disappointed."' (Dosse, *Intersecting Lives*, 97-8)

The young Deleuze's appreciation for Bergson's thought may have been a lonely one at the time, but it has borne remarkable fruit. Even more than his part in the rehabilitation of Nietzsche, Deleuze has played an absolutely central role in the reinstallation of Bergsonism in contemporary philosophy.

Le bergsonisme came out in 1966, though it is clearly of a piece with two long essays that appeared a decade earlier: 'Bergson 1859-1941', published in a collection edited by Maurice Merleau-Ponty, and 'Bergson's conception of difference'. Its goal is announced by Deleuze in its very first lines: 'Duration, Memory, Élan Vital mark the major stages of Bergson's philosophy. This book sets out to determine, first, the relationship between these three notions and, second, the progress they involve'. (B 13) Deleuze's presentation does proceed in this fashion, but it can also be read as a set of investigations into five of Bergson's major works in a not-entirely chronological order: *Time and Free Will* (the French title of this, Bergson's doctoral thesis, is *Essai sur la données immédiates de la conscience* [An Essay on the Immediate Data of Consciousness] 1889), *Matter and Memory* (1896), *Duration and Simultaneity* (1922), *Creative Evolution* (1907), and *The Two Sources of Religion and Morality* (1932).

TWO KINDS OF MULTIPLICITY AND THEIR CONFUSION

But we will begin here where Bergson does in his doctoral thesis, with the analysis of what is given immediately in first-person experience—for instance, the experience of walking across the room at a party, or miserably waiting for an aspirin to dissolve in a glass of water the morning after an evening of too much gin. Bergson's first observation about first-person experience is that it 'always gives us a composite of space and duration'. (B 37) Walking across the room at the party involves us in a movement in space, but it is also temporal in character. Now, while this is easy to recognize in an abstract sense, we nevertheless tend to collapse these two unequal halves together into spatiality. We have a tendency to treat what Bergson calls *duration* (*durée*) in terms of space—as homogenous, neutral and divisible: we 'introduce extrinsic distinctions into our duration; we decompose it into external parts and align it in a sort of homogenous time'. (B 38) This tendency itself is the source of our ideas of clock time and measurement, but also and more problematically the time of physics (which we'll return to below when we consider Bergson's critique of Einstein).

What this tendency obscures is the fact that space and duration *differ in kind*. On the one hand, space is 'an exteriority without succession', (B 37) homogenous, discrete and divisible. The space of the party is the same as the infamous space across which Achilles and the tortoise travel in Zeno's famous paradox, and it is the same space that I traverse from my bed to the medicine cabinet looking for merciful relief.

On the other hand, duration is *continuous*. My experience of the passage from boredom to anger in an overlong lecture cannot be divvied up into units or parts, because it forms an integral whole. If part of the experience was somehow extracted, it would not mean the same thing—in fact, it would be a different experience altogether. Duration is also *heterogenous* in character. One portion of space is the same as another, but the unfolding of experience shows us that duration is not like that. The continuity of my passage from boredom to anger in the lecture does not rule out various singular passages: moments of distraction and daydreaming, flashes of irritation. And the same is true of my experience as a whole, which is characterized by a profound range of experiential states or moments, but remains continuous nevertheless.

Two kinds of multiplicity

To put this point in Bergson's own terms, we can say that experience is a mixture of two kind of *multiplicity*. Deleuze emphasizes the mathematical heritage of this concept, and specifically GBR Riemann's distinction between discrete and continuous multiplicities (*Mannigfaltigkeit*) in geometry. As Deleuze points out, not only was Riemann's theory of multiplicities in geometry important for Husserl, but it plays a key role in Einstein's theory of general relativity, a theory that Bergson will come to directly challenge.

The fundamental importance of this category for Deleuze is the way that it displaces the ancient and orthodox opposition of the one and the multiple. 'Multiplicity' is not, therefore, 'a vague noun corresponding to the well-known philosophical notion of the Multiple in general. In fact, *for Bergson it is not a question of opposing the Multiple to the One but, on the contrary, of distinguishing two types of multiplicity*'. (B 39)

Later we will have to investigate the place of the categories of unity, simplicity and plurality in Bergson—in essence, Bergson is making a sideways move, displacing the opposition by shifting the philosophical terrain—but for the moment, it is enough to make explicit the connection between Riemann's continuous and discrete multiplicities and Bergson's duration and space. Both space and duration are multiple in character, but they are multiple in two different ways. Here is Deleuze's little summary text:

> The important thing here is that the decomposition of the composite [of lived experience] reveals to us two types of multiplicity. One is represented by space [...]: It is a multiplicity of exteriority, of simultaneity, of juxtaposition, of order, of quantitative differentiation, of *difference in degree*; it is numerical multiplicity, *discontinuous and actual*. The other type of multiplicity appears in pure duration: It is an internal multiplicity of succession, of fusion, of organisation, of heterogeneity, of qualitative discrimination, or of *difference in kind*; it is a *virtual and continuous* multiplicity that cannot be reduced to numbers. (B 38)

The wording of this passage is notable: one type of multiplicity is only *represented* by space, while the other *appears as such* in duration—Deleuze demonstrates a certain restraint here which indicates that more must be said about space than this initial characterization conveys. But the more notable term that appears here is 'virtual'—duration as a *virtual multiplicity*. This term sums up everything that we have seen about duration so far, and in fact *virtual* will be uniquely affiliated with temporality in Bergson's work, as we will see. In any case, *this concept of multiplicity, and the division into two kinds of multiplicity, is the heart of Bergson's philosophy*

THE METHOD OF INTUITION

It might already be clear why the question of philosophical method is important. In experience, we are given a mixture of space and duration. But in order to understand experience, space and duration themselves, we need a way to separate the two kinds of multiplicity out—we need a way to go *beyond* the given. Deleuze frequently insists on the high bar that Bergson sets for himself: we must constitute philosophy as a discipline every bit as rigorous and precise as science, 'as precise in *its* field, as capable of being prolonged and transmitted as science itself is'. (B 14) In this task, Plato is Bergson's inspiration: 'there is a Platonic tone in Bergson [...] Plato's metaphors of carving and the good cook (which Bergson likes so much) correspond to Bergson's invocation of the good tailor and the well-fitted outfit. This is what the precise concept must be like'. (B 44-5) Indeed, for Bergson, the aim of philosophy is to follow 'the articulations of the real'. ('Good Sense and Classical Studies', 350)

Now, the surprise: Bergson names his method *intuition*, a word that initially, as he himself says, might seem to be the opposite and even the enemy of precision. Deleuze points out that it shares with intuition in the ordinary sense an important feature: its 'simplicity as a lived act'. (B 14) But of course not all simple lived acts are equivalent, and we need to look at what constitutes this act in particular. Deleuze presents its constituents in the form of three main rules, along with two complements.

First rule of the method (true and false problems)

Deleuze states the first rule in this form: 'Apply the test of true and false to problems themselves. Condemn false problems and reconcile truth and creation at the level of problems'. (B 15) At issue here are two important points. The first, which Deleuze emphasizes with great force, is that it is a mistake to think that the essential in thought or life is the solution of pre-existing problems. Whenever we are confronted with this kind of schoolroom conception, we can be sure that social prejudice is in full effect, leaving us 'only a thin margin of freedom'. (B 15)

In fact, in both philosophy and life, what is essential is the *invention* of problems. Bergson marshals the examples of philosophy and mathematics to support his case: 'in mathematics, but still more in metaphysics, the effort of invention consists most often in raising the problem, in creating the terms in which it will be stated. The stating and solving of the problem are here very close to being equivalent'. (B 15-16, citing *Creative Evolution*) But Deleuze also invokes Marx's famous formula from *A Contribution to the Critique of Political Economy* here, according to which 'Humanity only sets itself problems that it is capable of solving'. (B 16) Human existence—and in fact existence in general—consists in the primary constitution of problems, whose solutions are only possible in their wake.

The second half of the rule involves the—at first glance—strange insistence that truth and falsity apply not to solutions but to problems as such. After all, 'how can this constitutive power which resides in the problem be reconciled with a norm of the true?' (B 16)

The two forms of false problems

Instead of answering the question directly, Deleuze introduces a first complementary rule, since, he says, Bergson's real genius concerns not exactly the opposition between true and false problems but the specification of the false. This complementary rule states that: 'False problems are of two sorts, "nonexistent problems," defined as problems whose very terms contain a confusion of the "more" and the "less"; and "badly stated questions", so defined because their terms represent badly analysed composites.' (B 17)

Let's take each of these kinds of false problems in turn. An example of a non-existent problem, key to Bergson's thought, concerns the notion of *possibility*. The false problems that this category give rise to are of the sort 'Why did this happen instead of that, when it too was possible?' (implicit in the great popular lament 'Why me?') The normal view of a possible state of the world is that it contains *less* reality than the real. These possible states pre-exist their realization as so many insubstantial present states, before one of them (somehow) comes into being. But, Bergson points out, the category of the possible actually contains *more* than the real. In fact, they are images of the present to which an act of thought has been *added*, in order to retroject them into the past: 'the possible is only the real with the addition of an act of mind that throws its image back into the past once it has been enacted'. ("The Possible and the Real,' 229; B 17).

The same critical line of argumentation can be made when we consider some other familiar chestnuts: 'why is there something rather than nothing?' and 'why is there order rather than chaos?' equally traffic in the same confusion; each time 'the more is mistaken for the less.' (B 19)

The second form of false problems are *badly-stated problems*, which trade in 'badly analyzed composites that arbitrarily group things that *differ in kind*'. (B 19) When we ask ourselves questions like 'given the laws of the physical universe, how can human beings be free?', we think we are addressing a unified reality that all falls under the rule of cause and effect, but which is in fact composed of the two irreducibly different multiplicities of space and duration.

Now, Deleuze notes, the first kind of false problems (involving a confusion of more or less) is really just a species of the second. A possible state of the world is no simple thing, but the confused composite of an image of the present and the retrojection of this image into an equally fabulated past. Indeed, this kind of confusion is, for Bergson, 'perhaps the most general error of thought, the error common to science and metaphysics'. (B 20)

In fact, we can and should be even more specific here. What this 'general error of thought' involves is not just any confusion, but the confusion of *differences in degree* and *differences in kind*. This is very clear in the supposed problem of freedom, which appears as a problem only when we create a confused composite of space (homogenous, and therefore characterized by differences in degree) and duration (virtual, characterized by an intrinsic heterogeneity, i.e., differences in kind).

Philosophy has never been innocent of this confusion. Earlier I invoked Zeno's paradox of Achilles and the tortoise (one that Bergson himself discusses in *Time and Free Will*), a paradox that Aristotle summarises in the following terms: 'the slowest runner will never be caught by the fastest runner, because the one behind has first to reach the point from which the one in front started, and so the slower one is bound always to be in front'. (Aristotle, *Physics*, VI: 9.239b15) In light of Bergson's work, Zeno's mistake becomes very clear: he has confused space and duration, thinking that the infinite divisibility of the former also characterised the latter. That is, Zeno confuses an order composed of differences in degree with one composed of differences in kind.

But for Deleuze, Bergson goes one step further again in his account of false problems, converging with Kant's famous theme of transcendental illusion. These errors are not, he insists, accidental or extrinsic, but are tied to the structure of rational thinking as such:

> The very notion of the false problem indeed implies that we have to struggle not against simple mistakes (false solutions), but against something more profound: an illusion that carries us along, or in which we are immersed, inseparable from our condition […] Bergson borrows an idea from Kant although he completely transforms it: It was Kant who showed that, deep within itself, reason engenders not mistakes but inevitable illusions […] The illusion is based in the deepest part of the intelligence: It is not, strictly speaking, dispelled or dispellable, rather it can only be repressed. (B 20-1)

Or, as Deleuze puts it later in the book, 'The retrograde movement of the true is not merely an illusion about the true, but belongs to the true itself'. (B 34)

Second rule of the method (the fundamental distinction)

Earlier I noted that the reason we need a method is to go beyond the mixture of space and duration that is given in experience, but now we see that the problem is more serious: experience doesn't merely give us this mixture, but tends to obscure the differences in kind that are mixed up within it.

This brings us to the second rule of the method. Given the tendency, intrinsic to experience, to confuse differences in degree with differences in kind, the method must above all affirm and pursue the latter. The rule is: 'rediscover the true differences in kind or articulations of the real'. (B 21) Intuition is thus the method concerned to establish with precision the *real differences in kind* in experience and in being itself.

Furthermore, as a method for going beyond experience, intuition necessarily involves us in a break with human experience itself, lending it an unavoidable alien character:

> Bergson is not one of those philosophers who ascribes a properly human wisdom and equilibrium to philosophy. To open us up to the inhuman and the superhuman (*durations* which are inferior or superior to our own), to go beyond the human condition: This is the meaning of philosophy, insofar as our condition condemns us to live among badly analysed composites, and to be badly analysed composites ourselves. (B 28)

Third rule of the method (duration as methodological foundation)

Here, finally, is the third rule of the method: 'State problems and solve them in terms of time rather than of space'. (B 31) Now, this might seem at first glance to be a strange feature to make a part of a general philosophical methodology—after all, time appears to be a problem for philosophy, not a methodological presupposition. But while it seems odd, we already know two things that will allow us to dispel the confusion. The first is what the second rule of the method tells us, that philosophy must orient itself around the search for differences in kind, and that these provide it with its *raison d'être*. The second is that time—that is, duration—is a virtual multiplicity, which is to say that it is composed of differences in kind as such. As Deleuze puts it, 'Duration is always the location and the environment of differences in kind; it is even their totality and multiplicity. There are no differences in kind except in duration—while space is nothing other than the location, the environment, the totality of degrees in difference'. (B 32)

Given this, to state that philosophy must be prosecuted in temporal terms clearly follows. Or, to put things the other way around, it is only by adopting the temporal point of view that the second rule of the method can hope to be upheld: 'Intuition is [...] the movement by which we emerge from our own duration, by which we make use of our own duration to affirm and immediately recognise the existence of other durations above or below us'. (B 33) Or again: it is only by adopting the temporal perspective that we are able to think beyond the perspective of the human being and grasp the nature of reality as such.

MEMORY AS VIRTUAL CO-EXISTENCE

Now we pass to a second Bergsonian problematic, what Deleuze calls 'one of the most profound, but perhaps also one of the least understood, aspects of Bergsonism: the theory of memory'. (B 55) It is also here that Deleuze turns from *Time and Free Will* to *Matter and Memory*. At issue once more is a certain composite notion that will need to be untangled by applying the method of intuition. Here, the composite is what Bergson calls *representation*, that is, the image I make for myself of the world as I encounter it. Representation has two sources though, which differ in kind: 'matter and memory, perception and recollection, objective and subjective'. (B 53) It is these that must be separated out, one from the other. What I perceive of the world is framed by a number of factors, including my physical needs as a living being. But recollection or memory also plays an irreducible role in the constitution of my representations of the world—in fact, without it, perception strictly speaking would be meaningless.

Paradox of Being

To put things this way is already to get ahead of ourselves a little, and it is better to turn first in more detail to Bergson's analysis of memory itself. Deleuze presents this analysis in the form of four propositions which, he adds, 'form as many paradoxes'. (B 61) Why paradoxes? These propositions are not paradoxes in the sense given to this term in logic, like, for instance, the famous Liar's Paradox ('All Cretans are liars. I am a Cretan'). Deleuze's use of this term derives from its literal meaning in the Greek: *para-doxa*, against opinion or expectation, against common sense, contrary to how things habitually appear. Now, given the way that experience constantly tends to present us with confused composites that we nevertheless take as obviously true, we must see paradox, in this sense, as the most important ally of critical thinking.

Deleuze calls the first paradox of memory the 'paradox of being'. We arrive at it by considering what, in the age of CT scans and MRIs, may seem a banal question: *where*, perhaps in the brain, are memories stored? This is, in fact, a classic false question for Bergson, because *memory is not matter*. The brain is certainly matter. Consequently, it does not differ in kind from any other material object, and cannot provide the explanation for a temporal phenomenon as a result. In fact, the very form of the question 'where?' is inappropriate for the same reason, since it presupposes a spatial context for what does not have one. No, if memory is to be grasped on its own terms, free of the confusion with matter, we have to understand that it does not have a location in space, but must be preserved *in itself*. The body, brain included, is actual and has an ongoing, active existence in space. But memory is *virtual*, unconscious and inactive—it does not act, it merely *is*. Here is Deleuze's summary text:

> The present *is not*; rather, it is pure becoming, always outside itself. It *is* not, but it acts. Its proper element is not being but the active or the useful. The past, on the other hand, has ceased to act or to be useful. But it has not ceased to be. Useless and inactive, impassive, it IS, in the full sense of the word: It is identical with being in itself. (B 55)

This obviously raises two difficult questions that will need to be addressed: how is memory constituted as memory, and how can this unconscious virtual memory be actualized once more?

Paradox of co-existence

For now, though, let's ask another question, more in keeping with the method of intuition: *when* are memories formed? Logically speaking, there appear to be three answers, but two fail to withstand much scrutiny. The first option would be for memories to be formed *before* the event (having a drink spilt on you at a party). This is clearly not a viable solution since the production of this image would be an act of imagination and not memory at all. The second is the view that we commonly hold, that memories are formed *after* the event (at the moment when we try to remember what exactly the spilt drink was). Bergson marshals a number of arguments against this view, but we need only consider that it presupposes that the past was in some sense *already* there—and not at all created when I try to remember—such that we could later access it. So this second option is not really an option at all, and points us in the direction of the third and correct explanation: memories are formed *at the same time* as our perceptions in the present: 'the past does not follow the present that it has been, but coexists with it'. (B 61) Incidentally, this is also what provides Bergson with the means to elegantly account for the phenomenon of *déjà-vu*: I encounter *in* this moment the memory *of* this moment itself, '*a memory of the present*'. ('Memory of the Present and False Recognition', 148)

Deleuze alludes here to Bergson's image of time splitting into two jets, one characterizing the ongoing movement of becoming in the present and towards the future, the other feeding into memory as such. So this is the second paradox of memory, the paradox of contemporaneity or co-existence: 'The past is "contemporaneous" with the present that it *has been*'. (B 58)

Paradox of psychic repetition

Now, if the past is conserved in itself, as a general ontological memory, then it is not, and cannot be, just *a* past. Instead, it is a *past as such*, *the* past as such, which exists on its own terms. This is the third paradox, what Deleuze calls the paradox of psychic repetition: 'Not only does the past coexist with the present that has been, but, as it preserves itself in itself (while the present passes), it is the whole, integral past; it is *all* of our past, coexisting with each present'. (B 59)
It is this paradox that is illustrated in illuminating fashion by Bergson's famous diagram of the cone:

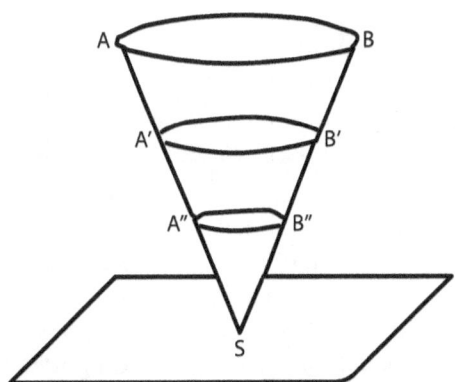

First let's note that, regardless of the level considered, each level of the cone (AB, A'B', A"B") includes the whole of the past. They are not past moments, arrayed in space like slices of pineapple one on top of the other, but the past in a particular state of contraction or relaxation; correlatively, each level is characterized by its 'ideal proximity or distance' (B 59-60) from the present and my body in it (S). Bergson is not saying that the past is itself characterized by slices of time, but that the various contractile states of the whole past are engendered from the point of view of the present. When I daydream about my first kiss, I engage the past in a relatively relaxed state, where this particular event is connected to many others in a looser, indirect fashion. But when I try to remember where I put my headphones when I came home from party last night, the circuit is much more contracted—that is, the past is in play in a condensed form.

Why does Deleuze invoke repetition here, when co-existence seems to be the hallmark of memory? It is true, he notes, that we are not dealing with repetition the way that it takes place in matter—that is, in terms of the successive repetition of a given state of affairs (stumbling over and over again on my way home from the party). He uses this term instead to indicate the fact that memory for Bergson is repetition as such: the entirety of the past is repeated in itself, and this repetition characterizes its very mode of being. Furthermore, as we have just seen, this repetition takes place at every level of the cone, which is to say at varying degrees of contraction and relaxation of the whole of the past. So it amounts to the same thing to say that memory is the integral repetition of the whole of the past, and to say that each degree of contraction of the whole of the past repeats every other.

The paradox of the leap

Given all this, what constitutes the act of remembering? We will see the second half of the answer in a moment, but given the ontological character of memory, it will necessarily involve something more than is implied in the (spatialized) image of a little *homunculus* flicking through a filing cabinet in the brain:

> According to Bergson, we first put ourselves back into the past in general: He describes in this way the *leap into ontology*. We really leap into being, into being-in-itself, into the being in itself of the past. It is a case of leaving psychology altogether [...] It is only then, once the leap has been made, that recollection will gradually take on a psychological existence. (B 57)

This is the final paradox of memory necessitated by the others: the paradox of the leap. To remember must involve an act that goes well beyond brain chemistry or psychological process. It must involve a 'true leap into Being', (B 57) even if this leap must have been motivated in the present for reasons that concern our psychological and physiological reality.

Before we continue, let's reflect for a moment on the fact that these paradoxes arise only when we take the distinction between virtual and actual multiplicity seriously, itself a distinction that only becomes viable from the point of view of the method of intuition. But now, from the other side of the paradoxes, our entire grasp on the world and our place in it has been ineluctably transformed.

THE ACTUALISATION OF VIRTUAL MEMORY IN EXPERIENCE

The force of Bergson's arguments about memory aside, we are still confronted with the nature of recollection, something that the invocation of a leap—however necessary it appears, given the ontological character of memory—does little to clarify. In fact, it is the very force of this account that puts us in such a difficult position. The truth is that the question 'How can pure recollection take on a psychological existence?' (B 62) remains in play.

As we have seen, the first moment, the moment of the leap, consists in situating oneself in the context of memory as a whole, at a certain level of contraction dictated by my current needs. Bergson calls this *translation*, which Deleuze will also dub *translation-contraction*. But things cannot stop here. To genuinely recall something—that is, constitute a recollection which feeds into action—requires a specificity lacking in the leap. Deleuze points out that to remain at the level of translation would be to treat our relationship with the past as if we were always asleep (B 66), lacking any *specific* motivated interests. The moment of the leap must therefore be met again—as if on the far side—by the needs of the present. Here's a key passage from *Matter and Memory*, cited by Deleuze as he unfolds Bergson's account of recollection (B 63-4), that spells out what is involved:

> Memory, laden with the whole of the past, responds to the appeal of the present state by two simultaneous movements, one of *translation*, by which it moves in its entirety to meet experience, thus *contracting* more or less, though without dividing, with a view to an action; the other of *rotation* upon itself, by which it *turns* toward the situation of the moment, presenting to it that side of itself which may prove the most useful. (*Matter and Memory*, 220)

The second moment, *rotation* (or *orientation-rotation*), therefore involves the taking up of memory for practical purposes. And in fact we find here a kind of positive analogue of Freud's 'censor': only those images that can be made use of are passed through to conscious thought: 'consciousness [lays] down the general rule that only what can serve action is allowed to pass'. (Bergson, *Creative Mind*, 155) Doubtless, this '*attention to life*' (*Matter and Memory*, xiv) fluctuates in intensity, depending on how important to us our practical situation happens to be, but these fluctuations always take place in the context of our engaged existence. Correlatively, the moment of rotation defines the psychological unconscious, 'the movement of recollection in the course of actualizing itself'. (B 71) Like Freud's drives, these unconscious recollections 'try to become embodied, they exert pressure to be admitted, such that a full-scale repression originating in the present and an "attention to life" are necessary to ward off useless and dangerous recollections'. (B 71-2)

The active body and the sensori-motor schema

But even at this point, Deleuze emphasizes, we have not yet fully described the actualization of a memory. This contractile rotation gives us a memory-image in the form 'which may prove the most useful', but it does not yet describe the actual use that the image is put to. In other words, what we require from the past is always an *image*, a recollection-image that would come to inform our perception-images and provide us with a way forward in our practical engagement. When I try to remember where I put my keys, what I am after is an image of their specific location. When I come to possess this image, it is not at all the past in general, but a very specific modulation of that past, framed by a very specific practical concern. However, what translation and rotation give us is not yet this image, but only what Deleuze calls the 'recollection-becoming-image', the virtual whole in the process of becoming the image that we require in our practical activity. We only arrive at a recollection-image properly speaking when memory has what Bergson refers to as a 'motor ally' (*Matter and Memory*, 152) and only then what is *useful* may be *put to use*.

We can equally look at things from the other side, one that Don Paterson brilliantly isolates when he writes that: 'Reality is the name that we give to everything that happens to face *up*'. (*The Book of Shadows*, 139) Our reality is a practical, habituated and dynamic reality, and one that makes use of the past only if it provides us with images that can inform it. But beneath, around, or within this reality is the realm of the mirror, of images insisting in the crystalline sterility of the past as such. Here is Bergson, using the example of recollecting a particular word for use in a conversation: 'motor habits ascending to seek similar images, in order to extract resemblances from them, and similar images coming down toward motor habits, to fuse themselves, for instance, in the automatic utterance of the word which makes them one'. (*Matter and Memory*, 153)

Bergson calls our 'motor ally' the *sensori-motor schema* (SMS), the set of habits that govern the interactions between the human body and the world that it encounters. To be more precise, what the SMS governs is the production of images—notably, perception-images and action-images—of the world for the body in question. We will discuss the nature of perception later when we examine Bergson's account of the brain, but for now it is enough to note that our encounter with the world is habitually organized, and that these habits regulate the passage from perception (sensory perception) to action (motricity). Like its illustrious precursors in the history of philosophy, notably Aristotle's *hexis*, the SMS is not a detached plan or structure that is imposed upon the body, but the habituality *of* the body, the body from the point of view of habit. In fact, we can even say that the SMS *is* the body itself, the active, perceiving body in its habitual being.

The passage from the virtual to the actual gives us a 'dynamic scheme', (B 66) the whole of the past at a certain level of contraction, which rotation then transforms into a 'recollection-becoming-image'. (B 67) This becoming is then completed when the habitual and habituated SMS transforms it into a genuine recollection-image, fitted to the needs of the present moment, the memorial supplement to embodied activity.

SPACE AND TIME IN SCIENCE AND METAPHYSICS

As I said earlier, *Bergsonism* effectively follows through on Deleuze's opening commitment to treat *duration, memory* and the *élan vital* one after the other. Nevertheless, he does devote a number of interesting pages to Bergson's famous argument with Einstein on the relative status of time in philosophy and physics. These pages are found in turn in a chapter devoted to the broadest and most difficult metaphysical questions Bergson confronts across his work: What is time? Is time unified or plural in character? Are the present and the past ontologically distinct? What are matter and space in relation to time?

One or many durations?

Deleuze begins this chapter discussing Bergson's various formulations of the nature of time, arguing that these formulations involve three distinct philosophical positions that are nevertheless able to be reconciled.

The first position, which we have already seen in some detail, is *dualist*. Not only is it oriented by the oppositions between space and duration, continuous and discrete, present and past as the two 'jets' of time, matter and memory, perception and recollection, it is also embedded into Bergson's method—intuition, let's recall, proceeds by opposing differences in kind to differences in degree.

This primary dualism, though, necessarily gives way to a certain *monism* of duration. In the final analysis, there is only one Time. Everything which exists participates in a single duration, one Time for every being in its concrete duration: 'there is only a single time, a single duration, in which everything would participate, including our consciousnesses, including living beings, including the whole material world'. (B 78)

Notice, Deleuze says, that even putting things this way means we must have passed from a generalized ontological monism to an equally generalized pluralism of duration. Or rather, we could say, Bergson's way of conceiving of this monism is at the same time the affirmation of its plural character. As I miserably wait for the aspirin to dissolve in the glass of water late one winter morning, various temporal rhythms are subordinated to my lived time, and the needs it involves. But beyond this subordination, the true plurality of durations appears—not only my shivering anticipation and the temporality of the aspirin's dissolution, but the hopefully revivifying eggs I've set to baking in sugo in the oven, the temporality proper to the slowly melting glass, the slow rain outside, the traffic shuddering through it, the gradual cycling of the seasons, and so on out into the cosmos and out to the whole of duration ...

Even the present moment, which seems like the exception to the whole virtual past is, for Bergson, '*only the most contracted level of the past*'. (B 74) And in fact, as Deleuze notes, it is the category of relaxation (*détente*) that allows for the marriage of monism and pluralism in Bergson's thought. The difference between the temporality of the aspirin, my unfortunately conscious experience of the hangover, and the hyper-glacial time of the solar system's dissolution, is in each case a difference in the degrees of contraction and relaxation of duration itself. It is true that, from the point of view of psychological consciousness, only human beings and other sufficiently complex natural systems seem to really participate in duration—a thesis considered in *Creative Evolution* (B 77)—but from the perspective of being itself, accessible through the aperture of intuition, this privilege of psychology seems to dissolve.

Classical, Relativist and Bergsonian view of time

In the context of these concerns, Bergson's engagement with Einstein's theory of general relativity is unsurprising. Here is a scientific theory of temporality that dispenses with the illegitimate treatment it is given in classical physics—doing away with the idea that time passes everywhere in the same unified way, along with the idea that space and time are parallel but completely independent.

And in the context of Einstein's theory of general relativity, the title of Bergson's book on this matter takes on a clear sense: *Duration and Simultaneity*. Though Bergson later distanced himself from this work, Deleuze will disagree with its author; he takes it to advance arguments that are central to Bergson's project. He will even go so far as to say that the obscurity of Bergson's various accounts of duration is only clarified, only made 'clear and convincing' (B 83) in the context of the disagreement with Einsteinian physics. In particular, he thinks that the encounter with Einstein convinced Bergson of the primacy of the monist account of time, over and above the other alternatives of dualism and pluralism.

How so? Classical science advances under the heading of a number of erroneous views, many of which turn around a very crude confusion of duration and space: time is thought about in strictly spatial terms. One feature of this confusion is the way in which the simultaneity proper to contiguous spaces passes over into a view about the homogeneity of time. At any given time, in this view, there is only one time—a universal 'now'. This is the feature of classical physics most dramatically overturned by general relativity; Einstein thus effects a profound 'dislocation of simultaneity'. (B 79) The present moment, and the passage of time more generally, is made *relative to the observer*. 'In this sense, there would be a multiplicity of times, a plurality of times, with different speeds of flow, all real, each one peculiar to a system of reference'. (B 79)

Such, in any case, is Einstein's claim, but it is one that Bergson would like to show—with a difficult and ingenious argument—contradicts itself. Let's break Deleuze's exposition down:

1. Einstein: time is relative to systems of reference (different observers), and therefore irreducibly plural.
2. Bergson responds: when you say that the time of another observer differs from yours, your apprehension of this other time is strictly in terms of extrinsic measurement, since the only way

to *compare* times is in terms of metric differences. But to talk like this is *to not talk about time at all but about space*.

3. Bergson adds (and this is the interesting argument): when you speak of a different system of reference, you are not talking about another real time at all, but a kind of abstract symbol of a time in which nobody actually lives. As Deleuze puts it, 'the *other* time is something that can neither be lived by Peter nor by Paul, nor by Paul as Peter imagines him. It is a pure symbol, excluding the lived and simply indicating that this system rather than another is taken as a reference point'. (B 84)

4. And then concludes: consequently, what you, Einstein, have shown despite yourself is that there is and can only be *one real Time*. Our capacity to abstract from this lived time does not mean that the resulting abstractions have a living reality.

The conclusion of all of this for Bergson is the necessity of affirming a *certain kind of simultaneity*, and of asserting that Einstein himself blindly endorses the same view. This is ultimately the consequence of his lack of the category of the virtual:

> From the first page of *Duration and Simultaneity* to the last, Bergson criticizes Einstein for having confused the virtual and the actual [...] By confusing the two types—actual spatial multiplicity and virtual temporal multiplicity—Einstein has merely invented a new way of spatialising time. And we cannot deny the originality of his space-time and the stupendous achievement it represents for science. (Spatialisation has never been pushed so far or in such a way). (B 85)

Correlatively, the form of simultaneity that Bergson endorses is nothing other than the *virtual* co-existence of all durations, that is, the state of co-existence proper to continuous and yet qualitatively distinct multiplicities. The whole question of whether time is one or multiple, Deleuze insists, misses the point on Bergson's view—time is *neither* an homogenous unity *nor* a set of extrinsic pluralities (as the letter of Einstein's text claims), but *a* virtual multiplicity: 'Being, or Time, is a *multiplicity*. But it is precisely not 'multiple'; it is One, in conformity with *its* type of multiplicity'. (B 85)

Bergson's mature account of matter and space

But this, in a way, returns us to the earlier oppositions we encountered: duration and space, memory and matter. If Being is Time, and if time is a virtual multiplicity, does this mean that space and matter are mere fictions? Certainly, the category of space, for the Bergson of *Time and Free Will*, presents a ripe opportunity for drastic misunderstanding, but we must be able to say more than this.

The question is thus: what is the relationship between matter and time? Again, the solution to the problem is found in the category of relaxation. Bergson will argue that matter is duration at its *most relaxed*. It is a 'duration that is infinitely slackened and relaxed [which] places its moments outside one another; one must have disappeared when another appears'. (B 86) Matter is time whose implicated folds unravel, lying next to one another discretely rather than in the form of a continuous multiplicity.

What is essential though, as Deleuze notes, is that matter and duration are always in fact co-implicated. Thanks to the method of intuition, the philosopher is always able to decompose the mixtures of matter and duration that exist into their two kinds. So we arrive at the definition of matter as the most relaxed form of duration, duration relaxed outside of itself. But *in fact* there is no matter in this pure state, and neither is there any duration lacking the portion of matter proper to it: 'duration is never contracted enough', (B 88) to be pure, and *'there is always extensity in our duration, and always duration in matter'*. (B 86-7)

Finally, we must ask: what is *space*? It is the artificial extrapolation of this passage from duration into matter beyond reality itself and into thought. Space is the abstract form of matter that we can create in thought, a symbol of materiality minus matter. Or, as Deleuze puts it, space 'is not matter or extension, but the "schema" of matter, that is, the representation of the limit where the movement of expansion would come to an end as the external envelope of all possible extensions'. (B 87)

THE *ÉLAN VITAL*

We arrive now at the third and final of the three key Bergsonian terms that Deleuze sets out to explain in *Bergsonism*: *élan vital*. Deleuze's translators wisely keep the term in the original French, preserving the complex of meanings that *élan* convokes: impetus, urge, surge, vigour and vivacity. But what it names for Bergson is the movement of being, of life itself, a forward-moving creative evolution.

The *élan vital* is thus the very nature of existence. And given Bergson's emphasis on multiplicity, it should come as no surprise that its movement is multiple and differential. As Deleuze says, '[t]o proceed 'by dissociation and division,' by 'dichotomy', is the essence of life'. (B 94) The following diagram, a minimal version of the one Deleuze provides in *Bergsonism* (B 102), maps out the major divisions Bergson concerns himself with in *Creative Evolution*. Key here is that these are dichotomies and not contradictions—we are not mapping out a vitalist version of Hegel. Each category here marks the divergent, creative solution of a problem posed to life by matter.

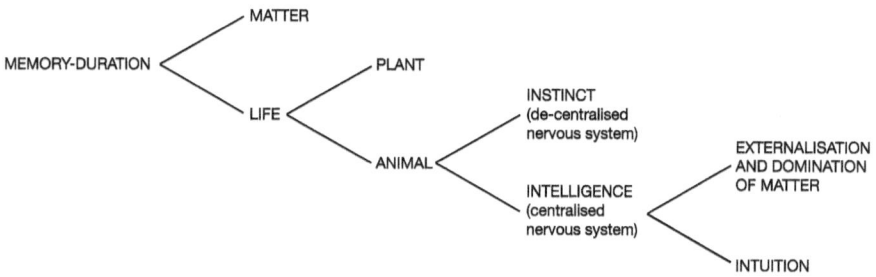

In what follows, we'll treat the key junctures indicated above, but it is worth noting that this movement of creative evolution through division is the inverse of the movement of intuition. Evolution carries us from a primary unity (memory) to a differentiated nature, while intuition takes us from mixture to identity. We will touch on this inverse complementarity again at the end of this chapter.

Realisation versus actualisation

Earlier, we saw Bergson's critique of the category of the possible as one object of the method of intuition: 'the possible is a false notion, the source of false problems'. (B 99) In Deleuze's view, though, it is in the context of the *élan vital* that this critique gains its true force. If we think that reality unfolds according to the realization of possible states of the world, we abandon not just the idea that the unfolding of life can be creative, but also any coherent notion of evolution. Why?

> The real is supposed to resemble it [the possible]. That is to say, we give ourselves a real that is ready-made, preformed, pre-existent to itself, and that will pass into existence [...] Everything is already *completely given:* all of the real in the image, in the pseudo-actuality of the possible. (B 99)

In sum, the notion of possibility *robs the present of a future.* Nothing new can ever be really new, because it is always already old, a literal foregone conclusion. This is indeed contradicted by all novelty and development, for instance, the advent of the eye in our ancient animal ancestors.

What takes its place? The answer is *actualization*. We know already that the past as such does not take the form of temporally displaced phantoms, but an ontologically real memory, a virtual multiplicity. We also know that the movement of the *élan vital*, which is creative evolution, proceeds by division or dichotomy. Together, these points lead to the following signal point—the movement of the *élan vital* actualizes the virtual through the creation of differences. Unlike the realization of the possible, the actualisation of the virtual is *creative* and *novel*. And in fact, this is what we have already seen in the restricted case of recollection: it only takes place because of a practical, material situation I find myself in, and it is entirely framed by and shot through with the body's sensori-motor engagement with the world.

Creative evolution

Now, Deleuze notes that in advancing his concept of creative evolution as the actualization of the virtual, Bergson parts ways with another misconception in addition to the 'possibilist' account we have just dispensed with. This other approach—one found in reductively materialist versions of evolution common in the sciences, or at least in their popular presentations—presents evolution as strictly actual in character. It claims that evolution involves the extrinsic encounter of elements '"indifferent" to each other', (B 99) that somehow accrue in quantity enough such that a qualitative transformation takes place.

For starters, once we adopt such a perspective, we leave ourselves with meagre means for understanding the relationship between the various moments in evolution (the various stages in the diagram above). The relationship between animal and human, for instance, can only be conceived as an abstract, external opposition, an oddly unevolutionary perspective which rules out any possibility of a line of development that links them together.

Bergson's critique of this approach is, for Deleuze, decisive. If we think that the movement of evolution takes us from actual state to actual state, as if through the random collision of material elements, we are not describing evolution at all. A collection of particles is not yet an animal, and these particles are 'incapable of functioning "*en bloc*," so as to control or utilize their causes'. (B 99) But the mutual indifference of the bodies that meet up is the real blunder here: 'since they are indifferent, they could not even have the means to really enter into such relations (for there would be no reason why the small successive variations should link up and add together in the same direction; nor any reason for sudden and simultaneous variations to be coordinated into a livable whole)'. (B 99)

On the contrary, there must be something over and above a particular accretion of material encounters that brings them into the active behavioural life of a living thing—and for Bergson, this is precisely virtual memory. We therefore arrive at the following Bergsonian alternative: 'evolution does not move from one actual term to another actual term in a homogeneous unilinear series, but from a virtual term to the heterogeneous terms that actualize it along a ramified series'. (B 100)

Deleuze alights at this point on one of Bergon's celebrated examples—and, of course, one of Darwin's—the evolution of the eye. At the most general level, and here we begin to return to the method of intuition, the relationship between life and matter is figured as a series of encounters with problems: 'Matter is presented as the obstacle that the *élan vital* must get around'. (B 101) In the case of the eye, the problem is light itself: 'the construction of an eye, for example, is primarily the solution to a problem posed in terms of light'. (B 103)

The means that the beings in question—the eukaryote *Euglena* and the mollusc as much as vertebrates like *homo sapiens*—have the whole of virtual memory at their disposal, which provides it with a general ontological resource to respond to the challenges it confronts in the course of its practical existence. It is this resource that allows us to attribute 'to organized matter a certain capacity *sui generis*, the mysterious power of building up very complicated machines to utilize the simple excitation that it undergoes'. (*Creative Evolution*, 54) To be more precise, the virtual is a virtual multiplicity—it is integrally differences in *kind*—that allow us to explain the qualitative changes in living beings, precisely what quantitative accumulation cannot.

This entire movement is just what Bergson means by *élan vital*—the creative movement into the future of life, passing through the virtual-actual (or memory-matter) circuit to transform itself into something new.

The brain

We now arrive at the case of human beings, or rather, arrive back there, at the place where we started. In *Time and Free Will*, the goal was to consider the nature of first-person experience. At the other end of the trajectory, we must discover how it is that this human perspective evolved in the first place—and, furthermore, what has constituted the human capacity to deploy intuition as a method.

For Bergson, the human being enjoys a genuine superiority over all other living things—'the *élan vital* successfully "gets through" only in human beings, and human beings are in this sense "the purpose of the entire process of evolution.' It could be said that in human beings, and only in human beings, the actual becomes adequate to the virtual'. (B 106) What this means is simply that human conscious experience is self-consciousness of experience *as duration*. All of life is duration unfolding, the *élan vital*, but in human experience the drama of this unfolding is present as an object of thought.

But now the question obviously becomes this: since human beings are a part of nature like everything else, what accounts for this fairly significant capacity? Bergson's famous answer is 'a certain state of cerebral matter' (B 107)—that is, *the brain*. Now, the brain is of course a part of nature, and 'nothing here goes beyond the physico-chemical properties of a particularly complicated type of matter'. (B 107) What is uniquely characteristic of the human brain though is that, in its complexity and malleability, it interrupts the immediate connection between stimulus and response: 'the brain [...] complicates the relationship between received movement (excitation) and an executed movement (response). Between the two, it establishes an interval (*écart*).' (B 24)

The importance of this *écart*, this gap, cannot be overemphasized. Rather than only being able to deploy memory in a strictly utilitarian fashion, we as humans have a direct access to the whole of the virtual past on its own terms—in other words, the actualizing movement of the *élan vital* is not merely constitutive of what we are, but is also a process which we can actively deploy ourselves.

If we return to the diagram of divisions, we can see the two divergent tendencies that characterize human being: instinct remains, but now it is doubled by something else. This would be the second point about the brain. The gap between stimulus and response makes possible a new kind of relationship to the world and to oneself: intelligence. Or rather, intelligence is the form that self-conscious thought takes thanks to the brain—the capacity to hesitate. We are no longer entirely identified with the SMS, but are able to modify the directions of our actions, which is also to say, we are able to recollect *differently*: freely and creatively.

Society, emotion and intuition

The final moment of Deleuze's analysis engages with what is perhaps, at first glance, a rather puzzling topic: emotion. Here, the main text he deals with is Bergson's last book, *The Two Sources of Religion and Morality*. Invoking this concept and this text, his goal is two-fold: to complete the analysis of what makes human beings different from all other animals, and to show how this completion also allows us to 'carry out a genesis of intuition, that is, determine the way in which intelligence itself was converted or is converted into intuition.' (B 110)

For Bergson, emotion is a correlate of the social character of human being. To merely point to the existence of society, premised on the intelligent organization of the satisfaction of needs, isn't to do much. The significant point is instead—perhaps unsurprisingly—a further divergence. As Deleuze notes, the interval constituted by the brain is met with a second interval, this time between the individual and society, or rather between the intelligence lodged in the individual and the quasi-instinctive role of social obligation. Emotion appears in this gap. And by emotion, Bergson means something quite specific: they are not simply *affects* that I *feel* (sadness, joy, pleasure), but general qualities or *essences* that I *produce*. One of Bergson's examples is of a song that expresses love—the song does not just evoke my love for a particular person or them for me, but love as something essential and in-itself, immediately available to every living person. This is equally so for sadness: 'When music weeps, all humanity, all nature, weeps with it.' (*Two Sources of Religion and Morality*, 28)

The essential feature of creative emotion is, of course, its creativity. Not only is it insubordinate to instinctual demands or the utilitarian requirements of intelligence, it plays out the very movement of the *élan vital* itself. In the freedom of emotion, the free and creative *élan* of being is expressed in its creativity and freedom.

The role of creative emotion in society could not be more important for Bergson. Beyond the story-telling function, which is a specific form of social instinct (a kind of intellectual instinct engendered within society to ease our subordination to shared values) there must be a means of encouraging sociability that does not involve such a subordination. What creative emotion gives to us is an inspired feeling of a shared humanity. For Bergson, it is truly emotion that is the avatar of an open society of equals: general essence leaps 'from soul to soul, it traces the design of an open society, a society of creators, where we pass from one genius to another, through the intermediary of disciples or spectators or hearers'. (B 111)

Now, Deleuze follows Bergson in singling out two kinds of human beings whose *raison d'être* is the production of emotion in this sense: the mystic and the artist, 'the great souls [...] who play with the whole of creation'. (B 112) What they reveal is that reality is not ultimately to be merely perceived or contemplated, but to be created and to be enjoyed.

Philosophy occupies an eccentric position here. Because of its unavoidable attachment to contemplation, it only grasps second-hand what the artist and the mystic produce directly. However, what is given to conceptual thought by creative emotion is an immediate aperture onto being itself—as *élan vital*, duration and creation. The method of intuition, therefore, is the conceptual transmutation of art and mysticism, the reinscription in philosophy of the open play of being that the artist and the mystic expose it to.

5

Coldness and Cruelty

In 1961, at the invitation of his friend Kostas Axelos, Deleuze contributed a short article to an issue of the journal *Arguments* on the topic of 'Problematic Love'. Entitled 'From Sacher-Masoch to Masochism', it was Deleuze's first published engagement, not only with literature, but also psychoanalysis. Six years later, the argument advanced in this piece reappeared in longer and more detailed form as 'Présentation de Sacher-Masoch. Le froid et le cruel'—'Coldness and Cruelty' in English—sharing the covers of a book with the full text of Leopold von Sacher-Masoch's *Venus in Furs*, and two letters also penned by Masoch. We will discuss the importance of these letters in what follows.

Deleuze's book not only draws heavily on psychoanalysis, in particular Freud, Reik, Klein and Lacan, it was held in particularly high regard by Jacques Lacan himself, who called it: 'undoubtedly the best book ever written' on masochism. He goes on to say that 'there is not a single one of the analytic texts which do not have to be [...] remade in this new perspective', and that it will be the basis for 'everything that I am, now, going to have effectively to say about it'. (*Seminar 14*, 109)

'ARE SADE AND MASOCH COMPLEMENTARY?'

But we can start by asking: why Masoch? Deleuze gives us two initial reasons for his interest. The first is that his work was no longer being read:

> Masoch has been treated unjustly, not because his name was unfairly given to the perversion of masochism, but quite the reverse, because his work fell into neglect whereas his name passed into current usage. Although we occasionally find books written on Sade that show no

knowledge of his work, this is increasingly rare [...] Even the best writings on Masoch, however, show a surprising ignorance of his work. (M 13)

The second reason is more specific, and more interesting: the clinical accounts of masochism, beginning with Richard von Krafft-Ebing's 1886 *Psychopathia Sexualis*, had entirely overlooked a key feature of the masochistic experience. This feature is the role of the *contracts*, composed by the masochist in order to prescribe the conduct of his or her would-be punisher. Deleuze's account of Masoch retrains our attention on this aspect of his work.

Now, as we will see, both of these claims are prominent in 'Coldness and Cruelty', though the first really operates as a pretext rather than a substantive part of the argumentation. But in truth a more profound goal is in play in Deleuze's book: to *disassociate sadism and masochism*, to treat them as different and unrelated phenomena rather than opposed and inverse. This goal is pursued in two registers, the artistic and the clinical. The first half of the book in particular dwells on the differences between the fictions of the Maquis de Sade and Masoch, differences which are found on the most granular, concrete level as much as in the highest goals of their respective work: 'Both in their art and in their language Masoch and Sade are totally different'. (M 34)

Emblematic here is the different position of the passive partner in the two cases. The idea that sadism and masochism are complementary would suggest that we would find Sade's fiction peopled by masochistic victims, and Masoch's with a full panoply of sadistic punishers. But, in the first instance, Sade's protagonists want *unwilling* victims and not masochists at all: as Sade writes in *Justine*, 'They [the sadists] wish to be certain their crimes cost tears; they would send away any girl who was to come here voluntarily'. (*Justine*, 124; M 40-1) In the case of Masoch, the last thing that his protagonists want is to be robbed of agency in the way that Sade's victims are. Being 'an integral part [...] of the masochistic fantasy', (M 41) the punishers are the real passive elements in this fantasy. That the masochist wants to be punished—and the meaning of this phenomenon will have to be discovered—in no way vitiates their essential agency in the masochistic arrangement.

The clinical facet of the argument, correlatively, is concerned with the trajectory that runs from Krafft-Ebing to Freud, and which is encapsulated in the single phrase that Deleuze wishes to challenge above all: *sadomasochism*. He does not pull his punches: 'Sadomasochism is one of these misbegotten names, a semiological abomination [*monstre*]. We found in every case that what appeared to be a common 'sign' linking the two perversions together [...] could be further broken down into irreducibly specific symptoms of one or other of the perversions'. (M 134)

The specifics of these two lines of argument will occupy us for the rest of the chapter, but we can begin by observing that in both cases (and particularly the clinical case), there are two general sources of the confusion. The first is that the concept of sadomasochism is *too abstract*, and trades in too many ungrounded and vague generalities: 'The belief in this unity is to a large extent the result of misunderstandings and careless reasoning.' (M 40) What is missing is the actual reality we are dealing with, what Deleuze calls the 'specific world of the perversion: we are not given a genuinely differential diagnosis because the symptoms themselves have been obscured by a preconceived etiology.' (M 58)

On the other hand, the sadomasochistic entity appears viable because the approaches adopted towards it are *not abstract enough*. Its proponents immediately settle for the immediate evidence given in sadism and masochism, Sade and Masoch: a certain combination of pleasure and pain. Of course, we do encounter such a combination everywhere in these texts and these living perversions, but—and on this point Deleuze is scathing not once but over and over again—this conjunction tells us literally nothing by itself. What we really need to know is 'whether the pleasure-pain link is being abstracted from the concrete formal conditions in which it arises'. (M 45) We need to move past the material givens of masochism and sadism and ask what role pleasure and pain actually play in their respective formations, and above all what the nature of the link itself is. What we need, therefore, is 'a genuinely formal, almost deductive psychoanalysis'. (M 74)

So, to summarise, we can say that the aim of 'Coldness and Cruelty' is fourfold:

1. To show the irreducibility of the two perversions at the respective level of Sade and Masoch's literature
2. To show the same irreducibility on the terrain of psychoanalytic thought
3. To enrich the concept of masochism by adding to it in particular i) an account of the role of the contract, and ii) a much more sophisticated understanding of the role of the mother.
4. Consequently, to theorize the relationship between literature and psychopathology more generally.

Let me add, in order to head off a familiar view that all of Deleuze's work is somehow always and everywhere opposed to psychoanalysis, that these aims positively require the materials furnished by psychoanalysis to be achieved. 'Coldness and Cruelty' certainly contests elements of the Freudian account in particular, but only in order to create a more rigorous account of masochism.

We might also add that the problematic way in which Freudian psychoanalysis formulates the sadomasochist complex is in part the result of the poor character of the readings of Masoch that it relies on. It is clear that, in Deleuze's view, we might have been able to avoid the whole mess if Krafft-Ebing, Freud and others had followed the path that was quite clear to Lacan some decades later: 'Read Mr. Sacher-Masoch!' (*Seminar VII*, 239)

Symptomatology

But we must pull the fourth thread of the argument before going any further, primarily because of a rather obvious critique of Deleuze's approach as I have just described it: why listen to novelists if we want to understand psychopathology? Don't we need a medical professional in here? It might be possible to respond that they are not just novelists but also, implicitly, great psychologists, but this is not exactly what Deleuze says. He wants to insist instead on their significance for thinking through the perversions of masochism and sadism *as artists*.

Now, Sade and Masoch are certainly *patients*, in the literal sense of this word—they were subject to their symptoms, and they continue to be subject to analyses both subtle and crude. Their work is symptomatic of their own time and place, of their own psychological states, and so on—they are passive in relation to the many factors of influence. But, Deleuze insists, this does not mean that they are *only* patients—they are also *clinicians*. In an interview that marked the publication of 'Coldness and Cruelty', he delineates the following three aspects of medicine:

> symptomology, or the study of signs; etiology, or the search for causes; and therapeutics, or the search for and application of a treatment. Whereas etiology and therapeutics are integral parts of medicine, symptomology appeals to a kind of neutral point, a limit that is pre-medical or sub-medical, belonging as much to art as to medicine: it's all about drawing a 'portrait.' The work of art exhibits symptoms, as do the body or the soul, albeit in a very different way. In this sense, the artist or writer can be a great symptomatologist, just like the best doctor: so it is with Sade or Masoch. (DI 132)

The genius of Masoch or Sade—but also Beckett, Duras, Kafka (DI 132-3), or any other great writer—consists in their having isolated distinct and interrelated groups of signs that express a certain way of existing, a way of living and feeling, of relating to the world. On this point, Deleuze thinks that Krafft-Ebing is quite right: 'In coining the term masochism, Krafft-Ebing was giving Masoch credit for having redefined a clinical entity not merely in terms of the link between pain and sexual pleasure, but in terms of something more fundamental connected with bondage and humiliation'. (M 16)

But to the degree that this creative symptomatology *is* creative, it means that Sade and Masoch do not merely discover something that already exists: they literally produce 'new ways of thinking and feeling and an entirely original language'. (M 16) Just as in medicine, a new symptomatology in art creates a new mode of human existence.

After a biographical foreword, 'Coldness and Cruelty' properly begins with the following question: 'What are the uses of literature?', (M 15) and now we know the answer. Fundamentally, literature is capable of not only diagnosing the state of the present, but also of creating new paths along which the future can unfold.

THE LANGUAGE OF MASOCH AND SADE

I said earlier that there are four main goals of 'Coldness and Cruelty'. We have just seen the fourth and broadest goal, but now we need to descend back into the details to make this dramatic vision concrete, to see if it can be something more than a striking gesture. So let's go back to the beginning, to the texts of Sade and Masoch themselves.

The position of the speaker

Deleuze highlights four points of difference between the two writers at the level of their respective texts. The first of these concerns the differing, and yet equally paradoxical, positions of the one who speaks. Despite the apparent authoritarianism and even fascism of sadist discourse, the paradoxical fact (and here Deleuze follows Georges Bataille's famous analysis) is that the one who speaks in Sade is necessarily a *victim*: 'Only the victim can describe torture; the torturer necessarily uses the language of established order and power'. (M 17) Deleuze means that the torturer themselves will never speak of torture, but instead of the law and of the necessity of upholding it. Only the victim of torture is in the position to describe it as such. And yet, at the same time, they are in a position that also forecloses the possibility of doing so. This is the true kernel of the paradox in Sade, which leads Bataille to note that, rather than buying into the fascistic discourse of the torturer, Sade's fiction actually identifies with its victim. In Masoch's fiction, we find an altogether different situation:

> We are no longer in the presence of a torturer seizing upon a victim and enjoying her all the more because she is unconsenting and unpersuaded. We are dealing instead with a victim in search of a torturer, who needs to educate, persuade and conclude and alliance with the torturer in order to realize the strangest of schemes. (M 20)

The masochistic protagonist speaks endlessly of wanting to be the victim, of their plans to bring their fantasy to life, both in a direct first-person voice and to their potential punisher, but the punisher never speaks on their own behalf. The passage of all of Masoch's fiction takes us from the anticipation of the masochistic scenario to the scenario itself—characterized by the education of their punisher—and yet at no point does the power to speak of the situation ever pass over to the punishing 'agent'.

The function of language

The second pair of discursive features follows from this, which concerns the role of language itself in Sade and Masoch. Deleuze notes that in both cases, we are well beyond the standard situation of pornographic writing, in which the use of language can be entirely reduced 'to elementary functions of ordering and describing'. (M 17)

In general terms, what role does language play in Sade? Deleuze here reflects on the most obvious and striking feature of Sade's fiction: its exhaustive (and exhausting) repetitiveness. It is in fact composed almost entirely of descriptions and orders, of 'endless repetitions', 'multiplying illustrations', 'adding victim upon victim'. (M 20) Nevertheless, it is not *only* composed of such elements. Among the most striking components of Sade's fiction are the moments of argument or *demonstration* that appear in the lacunae of the unending permutations of bodies. Perhaps the most well-known such demonstration is found in *Philosophy in the Bedroom*, when the Chevalier de Mirvel reads out a political pamphlet (whose title says it all) 'Yet Another Effort, Frenchmen, if You Would Become Republicans', which is then defended by Dolmancé. But throughout the whole of that book, and indeed all of Sade's work, the same intercalations of description and demonstration are to be found.

Now, as Deleuze points out, not only are these demonstrative elements an exception to the pornographic order, they provide it with a new *raison d'être*. The repetition of scenes and orders, descriptions and imperatives are properly to be understood as a working out—precisely in the spirit of a mathematician or even a Spinoza (M 20)—of the demonstrations across a series of cases, that is to say, bodies.

In Masoch's fiction, by contrast, the use of language is educational in function. The protagonist 'is essentially an educator' (M 20), and he conceives of his ideal punisher as someone he can 'educate and persuade'. (M 41) While the ordering function is displaced by its pedagogical double in Masoch, description still plays an important, but again transformed, role. As Deleuze notes, for a body of fiction so intimately engaged with the sexualized fate of the human body, Masoch's descriptions are remarkably chaste. Women's bodies do not appear naked, and even the body of the masochists themselves are only 'visible' at the precise points where and when the tools of pain are applied. Sade's descriptions sent him to prison, and his extant publications to the department of the Bibliothèque Nationale that was literally called 'Hell'; Masoch's descriptions brought him international fame during his lifetime, but their anodyne character may have cost his fame its afterlife.

But Masoch's descriptions are not just lacking the obscenity of Sade's. They are also characterized by a peculiar and marked frozenness or suspension—the coldness of Deleuze's title. Sade's language is kinetic, dynamic, but Masoch revels in the presentation of tableaus or still-lifes: 'any potential obscenity is disavowed or suspended', terms we will return to below, and in their place we find 'a strange and oppressive atmosphere, like a sickly perfume'. (M 34)

Two Ideals

Language is put to use as a means of logical investigation and as a refined pedagogical tool in Sade and Masoch respectively. But these characterisations open onto the broader question of the goals of the perverse use of language as such. Deleuze argues that both para-pornographic or 'pornological' (M 22) approaches are aimed at the attainment of a two very different Ideals.

Sade's fiction—and here Deleuze is following Pierre Klossowski—plays out a distinction between two natures. Secondary nature is what we normally identify with the word 'natural'. It concerns the organic processes of creation and destruction, it is both fecund and violent, a cycle of life and death. While this is the regime in which Sade's libertines operate, this is not the ultimate meaning or motivation of their actions. The negative is in play here, but as part of a nil-sum game with the positivity of living things. The true motivation is to be found in a primary nature, behind or beyond the world of living things. This nature consists in a pure negativity or negation, 'a primal delirium, an original and timeless chaos solely composed of wild and lacerating molecules'. (M 27) But, being beyond the organic rule of pleasure and pain, it is not something we have direct access to. Like Lacan before him, Deleuze emphasizes the Kantian quality of Sade's work: 'original nature is necessarily the object of an Idea, and pure negation is a delusion; but it is a delusion of reason itself'. (M 27)

Consequently, 'the libertine is confined to illustrating his total demonstration [of the fundamental character of evil] with partial inductive processes'. (M 29) The serial descriptions of bodies in the full range of their interlocking permutations are local results that imply the truth of a general theorem, but never succeed in any particular case in fully manifesting the general and unbound character of this Ideal evil. *120 Days of Sodom* is emblematic here—the number of days indicated in the title are divided up into an exhaustive sequence that runs through every imaginable perversion in a set sequence and is completed with the murder of the abductees.

Like Sade, Masoch aims his words at an Ideal, and in a sense the rest of our discussion here will aim to explain exactly what this is. But in general terms, it is a *supersensible* Ideal, extracted through the suspension of the natural order of a moment frozen in time: 'Everything is suggestive of coldness: marble body, women of stone, Venus of ice, are among Masoch's favourite expressions; his characters often serve their amorous apprenticeship with a cold statue, by the light of the moon'. (M 53) Masoch aims to show us this moment itself—the moment between crime and punishment, the past and the present, mastery and its forfeit, the blow and the pain—in order to convey its excessive character with respect to the quotidian experience of bodily pleasure.

So this moment of the ideal necessarily also implies a distinction between two orders of nature, as it does in Sade. For Masoch, 'Coarse nature is ruled by individual arbitrariness: cunning and violence, hatred and destruction, disorder and sensuality are everywhere at work. Beyond this lies the great primary nature, which is impersonal and self-conscious, sentimental and supersensual'. (M 54)

And, once again like Sade, Masoch's fiction is characterized by the repetition of a certain kind of scenario; their difference equally is striking here. Sade's repetitions are serial and (in principle) infinite, an impossible attempt to add together enough permutations of perversion to arrive at the Idea of negation. But Masoch's repetitions involve a qualitative intensification of the Ideal scene.

FROM THE DRIVES TO DISAVOWAL WITH FREUD

Now, in order to follow Deleuze's analysis further—and to understand both *how* Masoch's frozen moment can constitute a certain kind of Ideal, and the nature of the mechanisms involved—we'll need to introduce some concepts from Freudian psychoanalysis.

The plasticity of the drives

The first of these concepts is found in the Freudian account of the drives—the motivating forces that characterise behavior. In his 1915 piece 'Instincts and their Vicissitudes', Freud shows that these drives do not have a natural source or end, and are in fact subject to a variety of transformations which arise when the drives encounter various obstacles to their satisfaction. He identifies four transformations in particular. The most familiar of these are *repression* and *sublimation*. Freud defines repression (more properly what he calls secondary repression) as a 'fending off': '*the essence of repression lies simply in turning something away, and keeping it at a distance, from the conscious*'. ('Repression', 146) Correlatively, the drives that are subject to repression are those that in some way are unacceptable to the conscious mind, whose direct expression would increase the unpleasure or tension in the psychic system. Sublimation, on the other hand, involves a repurposing of such unacceptable drives. It is a process that 'consists in the instinct's directing itself towards an aim other than, and remote from, that of sexual satisfaction; in this process the accent falls upon deflection from sexuality'. ('On Narcissism', 94)

But it is the other two particularly interesting cases that are key for both Deleuze and Freud's account of masochism. The first involves the transformation of a drive into its opposite: the transformation of love into hate is Freud's example. The second involves a transformation in the aims of the drives in question. Instead of being directed towards an exterior object of investment, the drive turns inwards, taking the self (more properly, the ego) as its object. Two cases attract Freud's attention here: the transformation of voyeurism (a desire to watch) into exhibitionism (a desire to be watched), and—of course—the transformation of sadism into masochism.

Eros and Thanatos

This motif of transformation, not to mention the thematic of two orders of nature found in Sade and Masoch's fiction, is considerably complicated and enriched by Freud in 'the masterpiece which we know as *Beyond the Pleasure Principle*', (M 111) a text which also contains some important remarks on masochism and sadism for Deleuze's account.

Freud's earlier metapsychological writings present the drama of the drives as being entirely ruled by the pleasure principle. The definition of repression we've just seen bears this out: in the final analysis, repression is an economic function that only concerns the amount of unpleasure or discomfort the drive's coming to consciousness would give rise to. In *Beyond the Pleasure Principle* (1920), as the title suggests, Freud investigates whether or not there are psychic functions that exceed the apparently global reach of this principle.

One of Freud's key motivations for asking this question was the phenomenon of traumatic repetition. Why, he asked, are soldiers returning from the frontlines of the first world war subject to compulsively relive its horrors, especially given that this engenders unpleasure rather than resolving it? Furthermore and more generally, 'how is the compulsion to repeat [...] related to the pleasure principle?' (*Beyond the Pleasure Principle*, 20) This led him to speculate about the existence of the death drive (which Deleuze associates with the name *Thanatos*) in addition to the domination of the erotic drives (*Eros*). The death drive is characterized by a tendency to decomposition, disassembly, the return of life to inorganic materiality. This is how he puts it in a signal passage: 'If we are to take it as a truth that knows no exception that everything living dies for internal reasons—becomes inorganic once again—then we shall be compelled to say that "*the aim of all life is death*" and looking backwards, that "*inanimate things existed before living ones*".' (*Beyond the Pleasure Principle*, 38)

When he discusses this important Freudian hypothesis, Deleuze latches onto one of Freud's specifications: that the death drive never appears as such in psychic life. If we can detect aggressive or destructive features of the drives, we are always able to refer them back to the play of particular drives governed by *Eros*. *Thanatos*, Deleuze notes, 'remains essentially silent and all the more terrible' for it. (M 116) Later we will see Deleuze's surprising claim about what is beyond the pleasure principle (nothing!), but his aim in emphasizing this point is that we have no direct, experiential access to what is beyond the principle. Like Freud, we seem bound to accept the hypothesis of the death drive because of troubling features in human experience that point to a lacuna in the imperialism of pleasure: 'there is a residue irreducible to it'. (M 112) We will consequently need another mode of investigation, one not based in empirical observation, to grasp the nature and role of the death drive.

Disavowal

The final psychoanalytic category we need is *disavowal*, a mechanism crucial to the account of masochism that Deleuze provides. Deleuze's account here in truth draws more heavily on Lacan than Freud—the former considerably refined the relevant terminology—but this is a detail we can set to one side. Disavowal is the process whereby what is experienced is recognized and at the same time rejected by the self; it involves 'radically contesting the validity of that which is'. (M 31) Deleuze's account of disavowal leans heavily on the example of fetishism deployed by Freud:

> The fetishist's choice of a fetish is determined by the last object he saw as a child before becoming aware of [the mother's] missing penis (a shoe, for example, in the case of a glance directed from the feet upwards). The constant return to this object, this point of departure, enables him to validate the existence of the organ that is in dispute. (M 31)

The fetish itself is thus a special kind of quasi-ideal object, a kind of 'frozen, arrested two-dimensional image, a photograph to which one returns repeatedly to exorcise the dangerous consequences of movement'. Deleuze adds, in a fine phrase, that the fetish 'represents the last point at which it was still possible to believe'. (M 31)

Clearly, then, disavowal is no simple act, but involves two concomitant moments, *suspension* and *idealization*. The fetishist suspends the real world that they have encountered 'in order to secure an ideal which is itself suspended in fantasy [...] on the one hand the subject is aware of reality but suspends this awareness; on the other the subject clings to his ideal'. (M 33) Like repression, though, it functions in the first instance to grant the subject a reprieve from having to directly engage with traumatic material. But unlike repression, there is a conscious apprehension of the objects in question. Reality is neither negated nor repressed, but *displaced* and *replaced*. Notice, too, that the fetishist's 'returning to the moment *before* ...' is a *form of repetition*. This will become key later.

For Freud—the *Wolf Man* case study provides a good example of this—disavowal leads to a splitting of the ego, a split that embeds the contradiction between what is known and what is suspended. In Deleuze's view, however, something more complicated is in play as we will see shortly. The proximity to Masoch's fiction is hopefully already obvious—as Deleuze will say, 'the art of Masoch consists in multiplying disavowals in order to create the coldness of an aesthetic suspense' (M 133)—though we will require some more material to make this link explicit.

Freud's account of masochism

In light of these brief sketches, we can now present (equally briefly) Freud's account of sadism, masochism, and their alleged integral complementarity. In fact, Freud presents not one but two accounts of masochism, though for Deleuze their differences are relatively inconsequential, since both turn around the supposition of 'an original aggressive instinct followed by the turning around of aggression upon the subject'. (M 123) In both versions, too, the major agents are the *ego* and the *superego*. For Freud and in general terms, the ego is the active negotiator in charge of keeping order in the mind, managing the various demands made by the drives (the *id*) and by the real world (the reality principle). The superego, for Freud at least, is a refined portion of the ego fashioned like the biblical Eve from the biblical Adam's rib; it is a close analogue to the idea of conscience, a locus of critical moral judgment.

The first account of masochism has the following structure:

1. There exists a *primary sadism*, that is, an essential and basic aggressivity proper to all drives.
2. The prospect of the satisfaction of some of these drives—for instance, those that involve aggression towards the mother or father—is resisted by the ego; feelings of guilt arise.
3. These drives turn back on the self (*secondary masochism*).
4. At the same time, a particularly strong superego develops.
5. The superego is *projected* onto the punishing party, and my pain is experienced as deserved punishment.

The possibility of a second, improved account of masochism is mooted by Freud in *Beyond the Pleasure Principle* (55), in light of the hypothesis of the death drive. It is later presented in full detail in the 1924 text 'The Economic Problem of Masochism'. It has the following structure:

1. There exists a *primary masochism* (hypothesis of the death drive)
2. Under the influence of *Eros*, these drives are turned outwards (*secondary sadism*).
3. Resistance to, or guilt for, this aggressivity arises.
4. This aggressivity is turned back on the self again (*secondary* or *moral masochism*): 'I am guilty'.
5. This moral masochism is sexualized (*perverse masochism*).
6. The superego is *projected* onto the punishing party.

FIVE PROBLEMS WITH FREUD'S ACCOUNT OF MASOCHISM

Such is Freud's account. But before looking at Deleuze's own neo-Freudian version, let's take stock of its limitations. 'Coldness and Cruelty' presents five major immanent critiques of Freud on this point—and by 'immanent' I mean that these are problems that arise within Freud's system itself. Deleuze takes himself to be showing the confusions that arise if we follow through on Freud's presuppositions.

The first concerns the insufficiency of the hypothesis of inversion. Deleuze's point is this: if we take the sadistic position to be embodied in the assertion that 'I will punish you (for my own pleasure)', then its inversion is *not* the alleged masochist assertion 'I present myself, passive, ready for my well-deserved punishment', but rather the active, neurotic 'I punish myself'. This latter assertion involves nothing characteristically masochistic at all.

On the other hand—and this is the second point—we also lack any explanation for how the passage from moral to perverse masochism is effected; we lack any explanation for what Deleuze calls 'a particular masochistic erotogenicity'. (M 105) On their own terms, the fact of feeling guilt or suffering from repressed aggression explains nothing. As Deleuze says, the most it gives us is an explanation of an important condition for such a link, but it cannot constitute the link itself.

The third, somewhat more technical critique concerns the need to account for the projection of the ego onto the punishing agent (here Deleuze engages closely if implicitly with Freud's 1919 piece 'A Child is Being Beaten'). In Freud's view, masochism boils down to an attempt to deal with unacceptable drives, a complex deployment of disavowal that leads to pleasure being found in the punishment for having had such desires in the first place. These drives in turn are ultimately challenges to the patriarchal organization of the Oedipal family—that is, they all consist in challenging the rule of the father. It is easy to see therefore why Freud would say that in masochism, the super-ego is projected onto and identified with the Oedipal father. But for Deleuze (who engages in four pages of dense argument [M 106-9] that draws as heavily on the work of Melanie Klein as much as it does Freud) this dramatically simplifies things, overlooking, misrecognising and diminishing the status of the mother. She appears, in Freud's account, as both a stand-in for the father, and a stand-in for the ego (bearer of unacceptable aggression), without ever appearing on her own terms or as part of the masochistic fantasy as such.

In a moment we will turn to the role of mothers and fathers in perversion; but now, a fourth problem appears. Freud argues that whenever a drive is 'turned around', it necessarily involves a moment of *desexualisation*. That is, insofar as the drive is no longer bound to its former object of satisfaction, this former investment must have been withdrawn. Deleuze gives the example here of the formation of the ego and superego in Freud's own account of the resolution of the Oedipus complex, which requires exactly this kind of desexualisation in order to take place. 'A certain quantity of libido (Eros-energy) is neutralised, and becomes undifferentiated and freely mobile', (M 116) and only then, and with this neutral energy, can the ego and then the superego be formed. The problem Deleuze points out is this: when the sadistic drive is desexualized, why would we think it could *immediately* become a masochistic drive in the sexual-perverse sense? At the very least, a hiatus would exist, a moment of neutrality that would seem to rule out any necessity in the drive's subsequent investment.

But now, even assuming this kind of turning around could be effected and somehow would naturally follow, a fifth problem presents itself. Deleuze will ask: what characterizes the *specific* links between pleasure and pain, guilt and punishment in masochism? Because Freud's account remains abstract on this question, he overlooks the fact that 'any manner of transformation' (M 109) could account for the passages in question. In sum, *there must be a specific* concrete situation, "some material basis, some peculiar link," (105) that actually explains the masochistic arrangement, and Freud does not provide this.

FATHERS AND MOTHERS

These problems constitute, in Deleuze's view, fatal flaws in Freud's account of masochism, vitiating the plausibility of the clinical sadomasochistic entity. The path forward will nevertheless involve taking up Freud's account of the Oedipal situation—one that 'Coldness and Cruelty' fully deploys—and in particular the respective places of the father and the mother in the two different perversions. For Deleuze, properly situating these figures in sadism and masochism illuminates the true nature of the two perversions.

The role of the father and the mother in Sade and sadism

Sade equates the mother with secondary nature, nature understood in terms of 'creation, conservation and reproduction'. (M 59). Consequently, and here Deleuze is describing the arc of *Philosophy in the Bedroom* in particular, 'The sadistic fantasy ultimately rests on the theme of the father destroying his own family, by inciting the daughter to torture and murder the mother'. (M 59)

Correlatively, Sade identifies the father with primary nature, the embodiment of a pure Negation, Violence, Evil. We know too that this primary nature is beyond the reach of the world of the organic, the social and the conventional, and beyond its laws. This is why Deleuze will summarise the place of the father and the mother in Sade in the following terms: 'Sadism is in every sense an active negation of the mother and an exaltation of the father who is beyond all laws'. (M 60) Or again: 'Sadism stands for the active negation of the mother and the inflation of the father (who is placed above the law)' and 'an alliance of father and daughter'. (M 67)

The aggressivity of *Eros*, drawn in the final analysis from a hidden *Thanatos*, corresponds to Sade's secondary, 'feminine' nature, and constitutes the rule of libertine conduct. But primary nature corresponds to *Thanatos* itself. We saw before that Sade's protagonists are like logicians, endlessly trying to prove a universal truth through local inductive procedures. But now we see this truth as what it is: the death drive. 'The sadistic hero appears to have set himself the task of thinking out the Death Instinct (pure negation) in a demonstrative form'. (M 31) In another sense, they are like chemists who, having isolated a new physical element, restlessly seek to further and further purify it.

The role of the father and the mother in Masoch and masochism

We find here another differentiating factor, a tool to split open the alleged unity of sadomasochism, and a particularly important one for Deleuze. Freud assumes, he notes, 'that since the father-image is a determinant in sadism, this must also be true for masochism, since the same factors operate in both cases'. (M 57) The sadistic identification with the father, in this view, is merely projected onto the figure of the punisher. But is this really the case? Here is Deleuze:

> When we are told that the character who does the beating in masochism is the father, we are entitled to ask: who in reality is being beaten? Where is the father hidden? Could it not be in the person who is being beaten? The masochist feels guilty, he asks to be beaten, he expiates, but why and for what crime? Is it not precisely the father-image in him that is thus miniaturised, beaten, ridiculed and humiliated? *What the subject atones for is his resemblance to the father and the father's likeness in him*: the

formula of masochism is the humiliated father. Hence the father is not so much the beater as the beaten. (M 60-1, emphasis added)

This is the kernel of Deleuze's account of masochism: the father is identified not with the punisher but with the subject themselves—or rather, is identified with what is emblematic of the father in psychic organization, namely the *superego*.

All of this takes us back to the theme of disavowal, which assumes here its full significance. In Deleuze's view, the masochistic situation involves not one but two disavowals. On the one hand, there is the 'invalidating disavowal of the father (who is expelled from the symbolic order)'. (M 68) Freud is right to see masochism (and sadism) as dealing with desires that trouble the Oedipal order and the father's role as arbiter of the Law in it. But rather than masochism being a way of perversely adhering to the Law, it appears instead as a creative means for deposing the father and mocking the rule of his Law (in a way we will see in a moment). On the other hand, there is what Deleuze calls 'a positive, idealizing disavowal of the mother (who is identified with the law)'. (M 68)

But this analysis also allows us to explain, finally, the role of pain in masochism. Here, Deleuze is direct: 'in masochism, there is no direct relation to pain: pain should be regarded as an *effect* only'. (M 121)

Masoch's three women

Deleuze notes, though, that there are in fact *three* images of woman who are clustered around the ideal in Masoch's fiction, and only one of them is suitable for the position—despite the fact that in some of his works (like *Venus in Furs*), the main female protagonist passes through all three positions. Deleuze's discussion of these three types (M 47-55) makes use of a large number of examples drawn from Masoch, and is well worth consulting.

The first women is a sensualist—an hermaphrodite, an Aphrodite, a woman who 'lives for the moment', a pagan. 'She is sensual, she loves whoever attracts her and gives herself accordingly'. (M 47) The sensualist resembles the Sadean hero in rejecting the institutions of a corrupt society—morality, the church and its concomitants (marriage in particular), and the law of the State—but differs from them in every other regard. She is ruled by the ideal of unrestricted pleasure alone.

At the other end of the spectrum, in the third position, is the quasi-sadist, the woman who appropriates and transforms the position of punisher she has been educated into adopting, the woman who 'enjoys hurting and torturing others'. (M 48) This third type is also engaged entirely with the sensuous regime, if in the opposite modality—the hunger to inflict pain is only played out at the level of the body (in this sense, she is not and cannot be a sadist in the strong sense).

However, the ideal type in Masoch is the second woman. Deleuze cites a large number of examples, including that of the titular character of Masoch's story *Lola*: 'Lola likes to torture animals and dreams of witnessing or even taking part in executions, but "in spite of her peculiar tastes, the girl was neither brutal nor eccentric' on the contrary, she was reasonable and kind, and showed all the tenderness and delicacy of a sentimental nature."' (M 50-1) All of these examples bear out a general picture of the second type of 'cold, maternal and severe' woman: 'The trinity of the masochistic dream is summed up in the words: cold-maternal-severe, icy-sentimental-cruel'. (M 50) Deleuze emphasizes the significance of the term *supersensual* in Masoch. Indeed, it names the masochist Ideal, which is *beyond* the attachment to the sensuous (whether to pleasure or pain): 'their sensuality is replaced by her supersensuous sentimentality, their warmth and fire by her icy coldness, their confusion by her rigorous order'. (M 51)

The educational function of the masochist finds in this type its ideal, indeed only, object. Without the existence of the second type, there is no possibility of a masochistic situation: 'At one extreme masochism has yet to come into operation, and at the other it has already lost its *raison d'être*'. (M 50)

CONTRACTS AND INSTITUTIONS, HUMOUR AND IRONY

In light of this distribution of possible roles, the question now becomes this: how does the masochist avoid the mother turning into the third woman, or back into the first? In other words, how can the masochistic situation be maintained? This, Deleuze notes, is a constant issue both for Masoch himself and his characters. In the psychoanalytic register, the question takes this form: 'What are the masochistic defenses against both the reality and the hallucination of the father's aggressive return?' (M 65) We have already seen Deleuze's answer in passing, which is good for both registers: *the contract*. 'A contract is established between the hero and the woman, whereby at a precise point in time and for a determinate period she is given every right over him'. (M 66)

While Deleuze speaks of the contract as 'the masochist's pact with the devil', (M 20), it is important to note that we are speaking here of a quite literal material contract, a written list of rules to which both the masochist and his student-punisher are signatories. The contract plays a threefold role for the masochist:

1. *As a necessary pre-condition*: to establish access to the realm of fantasy and to give rise to the conditions under which the second type of woman can be engendered through education. In other words, the contract is the material condition of possibility for the advent of the masochist ritual.
2. *As a guarantee*: 'to ensure that [the masochist] will be beaten.' (M 66)
3. *As protection*: to rule out in advance the return of the father, i.e., the patriarchal order and the dominance of the superego in the form of the third woman.

The importance of the contract in masochism is the reason Deleuze elects to include two of Masoch's own contracts in the *Masochism* volume. They are well worth consulting.

Now, while there is no inverse or complement to the contract in the sadistic situation, there is a correlative socio-material context which is used to buttress the sadistic attempt to modify the relationship to the law: the institution. Sade not only denounces the conventional social and religious order of secondary nature, but argues for an extra-legal social structure oriented by a fidelity to the Ideal of negation and the practical transgression of all laws. In one sense, the ideal of the institution is best expressed in the image of the 'Society for the Friends of Crime' found in *Juliette*, which gives form to this radical impropriety. But more profoundly, it is another name for the extra-Oedipal position of the father. The institution-form, far from being an improved version of conventional patriarchy, is a way of transforming it into a weapon for to the destruction of convention *tout court*.

Classical conceptions of the Good, the Best, and the Law

The upshot of this contrast between the contract and the institution is that both sadism and masochism function by modifying the relationship with the law—and the concomitant position of the father in the Oedipal structure—and it is in this context that Deleuze presents a fascinating analysis of the history of the idea of the law and its relationship to perversion.

The first moment of the analysis considers the classical era. In ancient philosophy and then Christianity, Deleuze argues, the law is justified by recourse to either a *higher order* or the *most successful outcomes*. These two alternatives are figured as two principles, the *principle of the good* and the *principle of the best*.

The principle of the good is *ironic*—the law tells us to obey not it, but something higher than it, in full recognition that it is only through obeying the law that the good can be obeyed. This principle says: 'do not obey the law, pursue the good, which can only be pursued by obeying the law.' Irony is characterized therefore by a paradoxical ascent.

Conversely, the principle of the best is *humorous* in character. Here, the law tells us that everything turns around the good and bad in relative terms. There is nothing beyond the situations we find ourselves in, no Ideal, so we should weigh choices up and act with the goal of doing better than we might do otherwise. But this principle makes the law less than the law. This principle says: 'obey the law, an absolute, even though there is no absolute to be brought to bear in this world, where there is only the relative terrain of better and worse'. The paradoxical ascent of irony is thus doubled by a humorous descent, which leaves the rarefied air of the ideal in favour of the mixed means and ends of practical existence.

The Kantian and Lacanian paradoxes of the modern law

But this brings us to the second, specifically modern, moment. It is a mistake, Deleuze insists, to think that the ideal of the law gradually collapsed in light of the variety in kinds of legal systems typified in different societies (thanks to the discoveries of archeology and the social sciences). Instead, we can say that the thought of the law developed as the result of a new kind of investigation into the form of the law itself and as such, regardless of its affiliations with the Good or the Best—a development embodied by Kant's *Critique of Practical Reason* but which, Deleuze hypothesizes, 'probably reflected major changes in the world'. (M 83)

The Kantian revolution consists in treating the law strictly on its own terms. In the second *Critique*, Kant argues that only the form of free and rational action is action in accordance with the law, but that the law itself advocates no particular course of action. This is to say that Kant absolutely reverses the relationship between the law and the Good: the Law, as a pure empty form, is not justified by anything other than itself. There is only acting in accordance with the law—even though the law gives us no directions at all—or acting irrationally. And to 'act irrationally', for instance by 'being true to your feelings', is not really an action but a form of passivity, since it amounts to being determined by your emotions. But, Deleuze emphasizes, Kant equally deposes the principle of the Best. Confronted with only one genuine option (obey the law, or forfeit your freedom and rationality), I act in accordance with the law without any way of knowing whether or not a better outcome might be secured. The law in Kant's sense 'defines a realm in which one is already guilty, and where one oversteps the bounds without knowing what they are, as in the case of Oedipus [...] the man who obeys the law [...] feels guilty and is guilty in advance, and the more strict his obedience, the greater his guilt'. (M 84) This is what Deleuze refers to as the first modern paradox of the law: guilt comes before action.

The most profound developments of Kant's insight are found, according to Deleuze, in psychoanalysis. In the first instance it was 'Freud [who] made sense of this paradox: we are *a priori* guilty because "the renunciation of instinctual gratification is not the product of conscience, but on the contrary that conscience is born of such renunciation."' (M 84) I become a conscious individual as a *guilty* individual. Moreover, the degree to which I renounce the drives is also the degree to which the superego, the agent of conscience, gains in strength. The superego, as the internalization of the law itself, does not demand that we do or refrain from doing anything in particular—it merely manifests the force of repressed desire as such.

This point leads us to Lacan, and what Deleuze calls the second modern paradox of the law. The first paradox concerns the subject who is guilty before acting; the second paradox concerns the object of desire. What I desire defines my subjectivity, but this object itself is repressed, unconscious and unknown—it is my fundamental desire for this object that makes me *a priori* guilty. For this reason, and 'In Lacan's words, the law is the same as repressed desire [...] The object of the law and the object of desire are one and the same, and remain equally concealed'. (M 85)

This transformation of the law and its concomitant paradoxes bring about a change in the meaning of irony and humour. Because the law is not subordinated to any reference to the Good or the Best, any and all attempts to define the law in terms of any extrinsic factor necessarily constitute perversions. To be more precise, humour and irony constitute two ways of affirming the law in its modern form which are nevertheless at the same time ways of breaking with it. It's probably already obvious where we have now arrived—for Deleuze, sadism is the name for the ironic subversion of the law, and masochism the name for its humorous correlate.

Sadism, irony and the law

Sadism, and the Sadean doctrine of the institution turn around a single conviction: that the law itself must be transcended. In Sade's view, the law necessarily gives rise to tyranny: 'Sade's hatred of tyranny, his demonstration that the law enables the tyrant to exist, form the essence of his thinking. The tyrant speaks the language of the law, and acknowledges no other, for he lives "in the shadow of the laws." The heroes of Sade are inspired with an extraordinary passion against tyranny'. (M 87)

But more fundamentally, the sadist is motivated towards this transcendence by the Idea of Negation, or, to be more frank, Evil. According to the movement of irony, sadism constitutes 'a new attempt to transcend the law, this time no longer in the direction of the Good as superior principle and ground of the law, but in the direction of its opposite, the Idea of Evil, the supreme principle of wickedness'. (M 87) We already know, too, the figure who embodies this Evil beyond the law: the father. This is why Deleuze will write that 'In the case of sadism, the father is placed above the laws; he becomes a higher principle with the mother as his essential victim'. (M 90)

Masochism, humour and the law

Deleuze's first decisive point regarding masochism in this context is, unsurprisingly, that "While the Sadean hero subverts the law, the masochist should not by contrast be regarded as gladly submitting to it." (M 87-8). Such a conclusion would follow from any account that presupposes their complementarity, but once again runs into the concrete evidence of masochism itself. Instead, Deleuze argues, the masochist exploits the humorous approach in a different attempt at subversion.

This humorous attempt is a play on the law's consequences, and the masochist is for Deleuze nothing if not 'a logician of consequences'. (M 89) The masochist follows the law to the absolute letter, demanding to be punished for their crimes, aiming to demonstrate 'the law's absurdity' (M 88) by reducing it to its consequences alone. The masochist makes the law into a joke, showing that if you really go along with it to the very end, it reveals itself as mere convention.

Key to all this is the way the masochist *reverses the order of the law's prosecution:* 'The masochist regards the law as a punitive process and therefore begins by having the punishment inflicted upon himself; once he has undergone the punishment, he feels that he is allowed or indeed commanded to experience the pleasure that the law was supposed to forbid'. (M 88) In other words, 'he stands guilt on its head by making punishment into a condition that makes possible the forbidden pleasure'. (M 89) In more technical terms, Deleuze will say that, in masochism, 'the totality of the law is bestowed upon the mother, who expels the father from the symbolic realm'. (M 90)

So both sadism and masochism reveal the perverse character of the modern law, but in two entirely different ways. The two approaches lead, in turn, to the two very specific material, juridical and social formations that embody them that we have already seen. The (Sadean) institution 'establishes a power or an authority' (M 77), relatively permanent in character, and beyond the Law: when there is an absolute source of authority, there is only action in accordance with it or disobedience. The (masochist) contract, on the other hand, is extra-legal, instituting with the 'free consent of the contracting parties [...] a system of reciprocal rights and duties; it cannot affect a third party and is valid for a limited period'. (M 77) In sum, the institution and the contract are finely crafted tools that guarantee and support the two different perverse endeavours.

PERVERSION AND REPETITION

In the final two chapters of *Coldness and Cruelty*, Deleuze presents his own psychoanalytic theory of masochism, one that does not presuppose the hypothesis of their complementarity. His account leans most heavily on

> the masterpiece which we know as *Beyond the Pleasure Principle* [in which Freud] engaged most directly—and how penetratingly—in specifically philosophical reflection. Philosophical reflection should be understood as 'transcendental', that is to say, concerned with a particular kind of investigation of the question of principles. (M 111)

There is nothing ambiguous or merely rhetorical in this claim. Deleuze reads this remarkable work of Freud's as philosophical in character, and, what is more, as a transcendental investigation. As he says, this kind of investigation is a certain non-empirical consideration of principles, that is, *conditions*.

To see what this might mean, let's begin by describing the three major points that Deleuze advances in his reading of *Beyond the Pleasure Principle*. The first point is a restatement of Freud's elementary conviction about psychic organization. The psyche, as an organised set of drives seeking resolution, is governed by the pleasure principle. This principle brings it about that 'we systematically seek pleasure and avoid pain.' (M 113)

The title of the book, however, is misread if read literally. In fact, Deleuze claims, there is *nothing* beyond the pleasure principle. Everything *in* psychic life can be explained by this principle (however strange things can get). What *cannot* be explained by the principle is its own *applicability to the psyche*. The question 'what is beyond the pleasure principle?' thus means for Deleuze 'In virtue of what higher connection—what 'binding' power—is pleasure a principle, with the dominance that it has?' (M 113) That is:

what explains the fact that pleasure is the rule for the organization of psychic life?

What is beyond the principle is therefore what gives it its global scope as a rule for the resolution of drives. And this 'beyond' is a form of *repetition*, namely the habitual association of a drive with its means of resolution—*Eros*. It is no surprise that Deleuze alludes here to Hume, the first great modern thinker of habit. (M 112) The repetition that elevates pleasure to the status of a governing principle is the repetition that gives to mere coincidence (of desire and a source of its satisfaction) the relative necessity called habit.

Now, it is this 'second-order principle that we call transcendental' (M 114). We never encounter the ground of the pleasure principle directly in experience; our only access to it is through this investigation into what provides the principle with its force and scope. But there is a second virtue to the transcendental method. If we take experience on face value, it seems to show the very opposite of what we have just concluded. We would normally presume that repetition comes after pleasure—I have a pleasurable experience, and I then repeat it in order to gain the same pleasure again. It is only when we follow the transcendental method that we can see that this conclusion is a kind of optical effect that appears only once the psyche is constituted in the first place. A fundamental truth about psychic life is contained in this sentiment: 'I repeat in order to enjoy'.

Habitual repetition as the explanation of the pleasure principle's status is the second point Deleuze makes. But there is a third that is decisive for the whole account: *Eros*, the habitual repetition that systematizes the resolution of the drives itself presupposes another repetition, that is, *Thanatos*. Deleuze's explanation of this point is difficult, but we can reconstruct it in the following terms. *Eros* is a conservative modality of repetition. It normalizes and stabilizes the current organization of the resolution of the drives. We cannot overlook the fact though that drives press to be *resolved*. And when a drive is resolved, the psyche returns to a state of relative inactivity, of non-excitation. *Eros therefore presupposes Thanatos.*

Where Eros conserves, *Thanatos* dissipates. But this too is a form of repetition: *Thanatos* also repeats, but repeats the state *before* excitation, that is, the state of indifferent material existence, the degree zero of life and organization. Deleuze notes that while this repetition unbinds, it must not be seen as a strictly negative thing. In breaking down the current organization by repeating its prior, less organized state, it makes possible a different *afterwards* as well. The unbinding force of *Thanatos* thus binds together death and novelty.

Desexualisation, sadism and masochism

Thanatos makes possible changes to the organism, and Deleuze emphasizes one of these in particular: the advent of the ego and the superego. We have already seen that a desexualisation of certain drives is a necessary condition for this advent. The ego is not a natural development, and requires some drives to be neutralised and for their libidinal charge to be made fluid and freely displaceable. This is how thought itself is possible, too—if all drives remained bound to their source of resolution, it would be impossible for thinking to pass from one object to another.

Now, the desexualisation that gives rise to the ego and the superego can also have three additional consequences. It may, first, give rise to 'functional disturbances which affect the application of the [pleasure] principle'. (M 116) This is how neurosis begins, by maladapting the delicate balance between the drives, their conscious recognition, and their possible resolution. Sublimation, 'whereby pleasure is transcended in favour of gratifications of a different kind' (M 116) is another possible correlate. I may come to see that the well-being of the ones that I love, for example, is more important than my burgeoning second career on Tinder. When I do this, I deploy the desexualized drives that constitute the ego and superego to reorganize these drives.

The third consequence is the one that we are interested in: perversion. Here, as Deleuze puts it, it is the very split between the ego and the superego, produced through the process of desexualisation, that becomes an object of investment for the drives—that is, a perverse *resexualisation* takes place. How so? We know that both sadism and masochism function to the extent that ego and superego can be separated, and turned against each other: in masochism, the superego is the object of punishment and expulsion; in sadism, the superego takes the ego as the object to be destroyed. But what this really means is just that, in the two perversions, the two different agencies are the object of resexualisation: the superego for sadism, the ego for masochism

Masochism and repetition

Deleuze will repeat this analysis on a more fundamental level, that of repetition itself. As he memorably writes, 'Beneath the sound and fury of sadism and masochism the terrible force of repetition is at work'. (M 120) Again, how is this so?

As we have just noted, perversion in general is characterised by a dramatic modification of the regular form of ego-superego relations. In turn, though, these relations themselves are underwritten by the pleasure principle: the habitual production of a (relatively) stable libidinal framework. In the perverse formations of sadism and masochism, though, the link between repetition and pleasure is modified. Here is Deleuze:

> Instead of repetition being experienced as a form of behaviour related to a pleasure already obtained or anticipated, instead of repetition being governed by the idea of experiencing or reexperiencing pleasure, repetition runs wild and becomes independent of all previous pleasure [...] Pleasure and repetition have thus exchanged roles. (M 120)

As a pervert, I no longer repeat a habitual behavior in order to experience pleasure—pleasure is obtained through repetition *itself*. 'I enjoy repeating'. And, let's recall, we have already come to the same conclusion by reading Sade and Masoch. On the one hand, Sade's characters are engaged in an exhaustive but endless quantity of repetitions: cycling through all the possible permutations of meeting bodies, they aim to incarnate the idea of pure Negation—which is, of course, nothing other than *Thanatos* itself. So the sadist's most profound investment is not in pain and suffering, or even the anti-legal figure of the institution (which is only a tool, a means), but in repetition itself in its most profound and ungrounded sense.

But we can now return to the puzzle of masochistic repetition we dealt with hastily and partially earlier. If masochism is the art of suspension, if 'the masochist experiences waiting in its pure form', (M 71) in what way can repetition be involved? The key to understanding this point lies in grasping the kind of repetition that characterizes *Thanatos*. Unlike *Eros*, which constitutes an habitual bond between drive and means of satisfaction, *Thanatos* repeats the difference between the present order and the inorganic disorder of the past. This is why it is an unbinding agent in the psyche. The form of repetition it presents is not like the repetition of a word over and over again, or the repeated daily life of a university office drone. The same *thing* is not repeated over and over again. The death drive names the presence of the past in the psyche's present, an inorganic zero-degree state in which there is no life. So the masochistic situation, properly understood, consists in an attempt to break the hold of the law and the father on the ego by repeating and intensifying the state of disinvestment or death. The super-ego is thus not destroyed (as the ego is in sadism), but rather suspended at the very moment before it can come to bear, along with the entirety of the Oedipal arrangement.

And, of course, all of this brings us back to the beginning of our encounter with 'Coldness and Cruelty', and Deleuze's accusation that psychiatric and psychoanalytic accounts of sadism and masochism settle too quickly for their apparent complementarity. In contrast with these abstract theses, an adequate account of perversion must discover the 'concrete situation in which pleasure and pain are linked in an erotic fashion. This situation is the investment in repetition itself. This is the essential point: *pain only acquires significance in relation to the forms of repetition which condition its use*'. (M 119)

A tale of two perversions

We are in a position now to summarise Deleuze's conclusions, as he does himself at the end of 'Coldness and Cruelty', by speaking of the two respective stories of sadism and masochism. Sadism, he writes, 'tells a story. It relates how the ego [...] is beaten and expelled; how the unrestrained superego assumes an exclusive role—the mother and the ego becoming its choice victims'. (M 131) The sadist projects the ego into the world, and punishes it—'*The sadist has no other ego than that of his victims*'. (M 124)—identifying themselves entirely with the terrifying, superegoic father who is beyond the law.

The masochist's story is also striking but in a different and unrelated way. For the masochist, the ultimate goal is a certain kind of *rebirth*. Masoch's heroines, Deleuze points out, often say *I will make a man of you, Now I have made you into a man,* and often give new names to their subordinates. Given the abject position of the father in masochism, this rebirth cannot have the form described by 'normal' Oedipal genitality—in a word, it cannot be *sexual reproduction*. No, what the masochist seeks is a *parthenogenic rebirth*, that is, an asexual rebirth from a single progenitor: the mother.

Earlier we saw that Deleuze associates two disavowals with the practice of masochism, but now—in light of the ultimate goal of parthenogenesis—he adds a third:

> The masochist practices three forms of disavowal at once: the first magnifies the mother, by attributing to her the phallus instrumental to rebirth; the second excludes the father, since he has no part in this rebirth; and the third relates to sexual pleasure, which is interrupted, deprived of its genitality and transformed into the pleasure of being reborn. (M 100)

'Masochism is a story that relates how the superego was destroyed, by whom, and the consequences of this destruction', (M 130) Deleuze writes. Even better is the following summary: masochism 'is the story in which [the masochist] relates the triumph of the oral mother, the abolition of the father's likeness and the consequent birth of the new man'. (M 101) In this way, the ego aims to triumph over the father (that is, the Law, the superego), and experience a perpetual rebirth outside of the Oedipal compound—asexual and beyond the law.

The coldness and suspension that characterizes the masochistic situation therefore means something more than the simple suspension of the orgasm, the locus of 'normal' Oedipal sexuality. What the masochist aims to suspend is this Oedipal normality as a whole.

6

Proust and Signs

Proust and Signs is Deleuze's study of Marcel Proust's masterpiece *À la recherche du temps perdu*, published across seven volumes between 1913 and 1927. This title is now rendered in English as *In Search of Lost Time*—although an earlier version used the erroneous *Remembrance of Things Past*, a title inspired by Shakespeare's thirtieth sonnet but which even Proust thought butchered the original. Even putting aside its liberties with Proust's own words, the emphasis on memory that this latter demonstrates is, for Deleuze, highly problematic, for reasons that we will see shortly. Deleuze first published *Proust and Signs* in 1964, but he would come back to this book, supplementing and slightly reorganizing it twice in the early seventies, a revision that is unique in his body of work. The complete volume is now divided into two parts, contributions separated by a gap of almost ten years. It is consequently marked by a significant shift in focus.

Deleuze's aim in *Proust and Signs*, as the title indicates, is to analyse the nature and role of signs in Proust. Or rather, this is its principal aim. In fact, Deleuze will argue that Proust's novel is an investigation into the complex relationships that hold between *signs*, *time* and *thought*, and that it is only possible to grasp the Proustian sign by bringing these two other registers into play. More broadly, then, Deleuze's book examines the connections between: 1) different temporal regimes, or 'lines of time', (PS 25) including the titular 'lost time'; 2) different capacities in thought, such as memory and intelligence; and 3) different kinds of signs.

THE SPIDER, THE SIGN, THE APPRENTICESHIP

Clearly, the first question to be asked is: what is a sign? The final image in *Proust and Signs* is that of a spider, one that 'sees nothing, perceives nothing, remembers nothing. She receives only the slightest vibration at the edge of her web, which propagates itself in her body as an intensive wave and sends her leaping to the necessary place'. (PS 182) Just this relationship holds between the personages of Proust's novel and the sign, for Deleuze, it is also the elementary relationship we ourselves experience in relation to the world. The sign is the first thing we encounter in a given situation, before we know what it might signify, or who or what emitted it. This means two things immediately. The first is that, for us and in the first instance, the encounter with the sign takes the form of a shock. We are unprepared for it—so unprepared, in fact, that it is as though we are yet to develop the capacities required in order to recognize them for what they are. This is why Proust pairs discover and misery, for instance in the discovery of a hidden truth about a lover: 'It was a terrible *terra incognita* on which I had just landed, a new phase of unsuspected sufferings that was beginning'. (Proust, *Sodom and Gommorah*, 703)

The second thing is that the shock of encountering a sign is one that gives rise to thought: 'What forces us to think is the sign'. (PS 62) One of Deleuze's favourite examples here is love, and specifically the signs that the jealous lover encounters. *Why didn't she write back to my message straight away? Why did he take that phone call outside? What was she looking at over my shoulder at dinner last night?* These questions all arise because a sign is encountered, and in each case what makes them the index of genuine difficulty is the fact that the lover does not know what the beloved's signs mean—the lover feels the situation of love, the world that they share with the beloved, to be threatened. We can see the same logic at work in what is probably the single most famous moment in Proust's novel—and one we will return to—the account of the narrator's eating of the *petite madeleine* in *Swann's Way*. In this passage, the narrator eats a little bit of a sweet cake on a spoon with some tea, and, without any immediately obvious reason why, the memory of Combray, where he would go on holidays as a child, arises within him. Here, the sign is directly sensuous in nature, conveyed by the taste of the madeleine. This taste gives rise to a memory whose meaning seems, at least initially, to bear an entirely indeterminate relationship to this taste.

Now, it is because of the shock transmitted to us by signs that Deleuze will characterize Proust's novel as the recounting of the narrator's *apprenticeship*, in which he confronts a series of different signs and strives to make sense of them. For this reason, Deleuze argues, the Search constitutes a progressive act of the *interpretation* of signs. As such, Deleuze will say, it is concerned ultimately with the discovery of the truth to which signs refer us.

> Signs are the object of a temporal apprenticeship [...] To learn is first of all to consider a substance, an object, a being as if it emitted signs to be deciphered, interpreted. There is no apprentice who is not 'the Egyptologist' of something. One becomes a carpenter only by becoming sensitive to the signs of wood, a physician by becoming sensitive to the signs of disease. Vocation is always predestination with regard to signs. (PS 4)

The involuntary and plural character of the Search

Deleuze is a philosopher who is often considered to be hostile towards the notion of truth, but it is a central part of what he thinks is crucial in the Proustian search, so much so that he will write that 'The Search for lost time is in fact the Search for truth'. (PS 15) The truth of a sign is its meaning, but this is—as the two examples we have just seen indicate—impossible to grasp in the first instance. In fact, Deleuze will say that the truth of a sign is ultimately to be located in its relationship with an essence that is unavailable as such in all but the very particular context of art. We will see what this puzzling set of concepts means as we move through the taxonomy of sign-types that Deleuze investigates.

But before we do this, it is important to emphasise the *involuntary* character of the Search. The violence that the encounter with a sign necessarily involves is the only reason why thought begins. This is why *Proust and Signs* returns again and again to the example of the jealous lover: 'The truth seeker is the jealous man who catches a lying sign on the beloved's face'. (PS 97) Without the provocation of signs, there is no search, no true activity, and no thought.

For Proust, a certain idea of philosophy attends this belief in the voluntary nature of the search for truth. Philosophy is thought to originate in 'a mind seeking the truth,' (PS 91) and we believe this mind possesses, *a priori*, a 'benevolence of thought, a natural love of truth'. (PS 16) Now, it is true that thought conceived of as a voluntary activity does produce something—what is called 'philosophy' in public discourse today is proof of this. But the asymptotic proximity of these publications to the least volume of self-help proves something too. It may produce 'interesting ideas' that reflect 'conventional significations', (PS 16) but these will never equal the least thought born from the violence of an involuntary encounter.

The apprenticeship that constitutes the Search is however troubled in another way too. We have already seen that there is not one kind of sign, but a plurality, and the same holds for both time and truth. This complicated situation becomes even more of a thicket when we see that, in Proust, a range of combinations exists: 'Each kind of sign has a line of privileged time that corresponds to it. But there is also the pluralism that multiplies the combinations—each kind of sign participates in several lines of time; each line of time mingles several kinds of signs'. (PS 17) Correlatively, because there is no single, simple mastery of the sign, disappointment is a constant companion for the apprentice:

> The hero does not know certain things at the start, gradually learns them, and finally receives an ultimate revelation. Necessarily then, he suffers disappointments [...] The Search is given a rhythm [...] by series of discontinuous disappointments and also by the means employed to overcome them within each series. (PS 26)

On Deleuze's view, these two features of the Search place Proust's project under the heading of an *Antilogos* and even an anti-Platonism. The Search, being involuntary and irreducibly plural, breaks with the classical image of unified, eternal Truths, and if there is a meaning to the term 'eternal', it will have to involve a fundamental affirmation of difference. In sum, '*There is no* Logos; *there are only hieroglyphs*'. (PS 101)

We must take care, however, when we assign the Proustian Search the title of anti-Platonism, since no simple rejection of Plato's thought is in play. As Deleuze notes, Plato is the first to recognize the decisive role played by the constraint of the encounter. He will even insist that the '*Symposium*, the *Phaedrus*, and the *Phaedo* are the three great studies of signs'. (PS 101) Nevertheless, in Plato, 'the intelligence still comes before encounters'. (PS 101) Plato's capital error is to presuppose that the alleged autonomy of the intellect and the violence of the sign are compatible. For Deleuze, 'Proust is a Platonist' (PS 100) in that he fully endorses and elaborates Plato's insight into the nature of the sign; but he is an anti-Platonist in that he rejects the hypothesis of (subjective) autonomy, and—for reasons we will come to later—the supposed (objective) unity of the *Logos*.

FIRST REGIME: THE EMPTY WORLDLY SIGNS

Everything we've seen so far remains somewhat abstract, and only comes into full focus and attains its full force once it is added to the typology of signs that constitutes one of the major elements of Deleuze's analysis—indeed, in the final edition of *Proust and Signs*, the whole of the first version of the book falls under simple heading 'The Signs'.

There are, he argues, four kinds of signs that Proust's novel considers. The first of these are the *worldly signs*. The word Deleuze uses here is *mondanité*, a term that invokes something closer to what we mean by 'high society' or 'the in-crowd', and the particularly vapid kind of small talk that comes along with it.

> Nothing funny is said at the Verdurins', and Mme Verdurin does not laugh; but Cottard makes a sign that he is saying something funny, Mme Verdurin makes a sign that she is laughing, and her sign is so perfectly emitted that M. Verdurin, not to be outdone, seeks in his turn for an appropriate mimicry [...] She does not act for her friends, she does not think with them, she makes signs to them. (PS 6)

The primary characteristic of worldly signs is thus their emptiness; they function as place-holders for what is not there. This is not to say that they function as signifiers that point to a (differential) signified, as we might expect from a linguistic analysis. Emptiness characterizes worldly signs in their entirety, and they circulate without any reference to anything else at all. 'This is why worldliness, judged from the point of view of actions, appears to be disappointing and cruel, and why, from the point of view of thought, it appears stupid'. (PS 6) The function of these signs is therefore reduced to a kind of constant instantiation of the social and material context in which they take place. They demarcate a certain common realm, a group practice or 'way' (the Guermantes Way, the Méséglise Way …) that is irreducible to any other—that is, they express a certain kind of empty, formal 'ritual perfection'. (PS 7)

These facts, however, are not immediately apparent to the apprentice-narrator of the Search. Like all signs, they instigate an effort of interpretation. Despite, and even because of, their manifest emptiness, worldly signs make an interpretive demand. But upon discovering that they, as well as those that utter them, mean nothing at all, the narrator arrives at a first, crushing disappointment.

For Deleuze, to be more precise, the worldly signs engage us at the level of the *intelligence*, which 'dreams of objective content, of explicit objective significations that it is able, of its own accord, to discover or to receive or to communicate'. (PS 29) The intelligence is a capacity to think in terms of what is explicitly given to us in experience. But the problem, as we have just seen, is that what is explicitly given is a wholesale fake, a parade of simulacra that stand *in* for things (values, jokes, beliefs, loves) instead of standing *for* them. The address that the worldly signs make to the intelligence thus reveals its weakness for the merely apparent.

SECOND REGIME: THE SIGNS OF LOVE

Intelligence, Deleuze adds, also has an obvious affinity with friendship. Voluntary, mutual and placid, friendship also asks us to remain at the level of the explicit, and cannot withstand the whiplash that the encounter with signs inevitably brings—not least the violence of the signs of love.

These signs constitute the second type in Deleuze's analysis. In love, we pass beyond the groups constituted by worldly signs because the signs emitted by the beloved act to select us out from the group, and make us select them in turn. Thus, 'To fall in love is to individualise someone by the signs he bears or emits'. (PS 7) Equally, while the worldly signs ultimately refer us to nothing other than themselves, the signs of love express a hidden world. We begin, besotted, feeling we have been given the truth of the other person, invited into a secret communion. Here is Deleuze: 'The beloved appears as a sign, a 'soul'; the beloved expresses a possible world unknown to us, implying, enveloping, imprisoning a world that must be deciphered, that is, interpreted'. (PS 7)

But this invitation hides a double barb. The secret world of the beloved that beckons to us through her smiles, her lazy hand resting on the back of the chair at the restaurant and the way she eats off of your plate is a world that pre-exists your encounter with it. These signs seem to be emitted just for you, but there is no way to know this for certain. Her habit of eating off of your plate, for all you know, may have begun with another lover. More generally, the problem is that, being a secret world that you can only divine through the signs that the beloved emits, your lover will always remain hidden, secret: 'addressed to us, applied to us, the signs of love nonetheless express worlds that exclude us and that the beloved will not and cannot make us know'. (PS 9) Every sign of love addressed to us reminds us of the secret world from which it comes, and from which we are radically and necessarily excluded.

The signs of love are thus necessarily *deceptive*. They incite us to interpret the beloved's behavior with an eye to the secret world that they express, but what we can never do is gain access to this world itself. Note that this is not a subjective feature of the beloved, but a feature of amorous signs themselves, and the suffering that they give rise to cannot be ameliorated. Ultimately, then, love necessarily gives rise to jealousy:

The contradiction of love consists of this: the means we count on to preserve us from jealousy are the very means that develop that jealousy, giving it a kind of autonomy, of independence with regard to love. The first law of love is subjective: jealousy is deeper than love, it contains love's truth. (PS 6)

This is the first, subjective law of love, but it is doubled by a second, more profound 'objective' law. This objective law is most pithily expressed in an infamous line from *Sodom and Gomorrah* (whose title already carries its sense): 'The two sexes shall die, each in a place apart'. (Proust, *Sodom and Gomorrah*, 21). The hidden world of the beloved is (for the narrator) the world of women in general, just as the work of interpretation constitutes the world of men: 'We interpret all the signs of the loved woman, but, at the end of this painful decipherment, we come up against the sign of Gomorrah as though against the deepest expression of an original feminine reality'. (PS 7) The investigation undertaken by the narrator thus passes from the subjective sphere of a particular love to a correlative objective situation, deepening, generalizing and completing the realization of the identity of love and unavoidable deception.

Intelligence and memory in love

We saw before that the worldly signs address the faculty of intelligence, that is, our capacity to systematically think through what is explicitly given in experience, and the same is the case here. The signs of love also invoke the intelligence in the effort of interpretation. 'Why did she do that?' 'What did she mean when she …' 'What is his deal?', the whole ensemble of the lover's questions concern the attempt to pass—like detectives—from the signs that the beloved emits to the hidden world. As we know, this effort is in vain, because the signs are necessarily deceptive, hiding what they promise to reveal. But here, the intelligence has a further means at its disposal which is called upon to assist in the interpretation of the signs of love, namely *memory*. Like the intelligence, memory in this sense is a voluntary capacity, a means to grasp the past in the same way that the intelligence grasps the present. Unfortunately, it too is inadequate:

> memory always comes too late in relation to the signs to be deciphered. The jealous man's memory tries to retain everything because the slightest detail may turn out to be a sign or a symptom of deception [...] But it comes too late, for it cannot distinguish within the moment that phrase that should be retained [...] In short, memory intervenes in the interpretations of the signs of love only in a voluntary form that dooms it to a pathetic failure. (PS 34)

Simply put, I do not know which signs to make an effort to remember when I encounter them—it is impossible to know, as a love unfolds, which signs will become significant later on. The deceptiveness of the signs of love thus has both synchronic and diachronic characteristic which respectively defeat the efforts of the intelligence and memory to make sense of them.

THIRD REGIME: SENSUOUS SIGNS

We arrive now at the third regime of signs, *sensuous signs*. While the following passage is a long one, it is both an excellent example of Deleuze's sign-based reading of Proust, and a text whose fame is well-deserved. It appears relatively early in the first volume of the Search, and the pages that come right before it dwell on the narrator's memories (here, Marcel's) of living in Proust's confected town of Combray:

> Many years had elapsed during which nothing of Combray, except what lay in the theatre and the drama of going to bed there, had any existence for me, when one day in winter, on my return home, my mother, seeing that I was cold, offered me some tea, a thing I did not ordinarily take. I declined at first, and then, for no particular reason, changed my mind. She sent out for one of those squat, plump little cakes called 'petites madeleines,' which look as though they had been moulded in the fluted valve of a scallop shell. And soon, mechanically, dispirited after a dreary day with the prospect of a depressing morrow, I raised to my lips a spoonful of the tea in which I had soaked a morsel of the cake. No sooner had the warm liquid mixed with the crumbs touched my palate than a shiver ran through me and I stopped, intent upon the extraordinary thing that was happening to me. An exquisite pleasure had invaded my senses, something isolated, detached, with no suggestion of its origin. And at once the vicissitudes of life had become indifferent to me, its disasters innocuous, its brevity illusory—this new sensation having had the effect, which love has, of filling me with a precious essence; or rather this essence was not in me, it *was* me. I had ceased now to feel mediocre, contingent, mortal. Whence could it have come to me, this all-powerful joy? I sensed that it was connected with the taste of tea and cake, but that it infinitely transcended those savours, could not, indeed, be of the same nature. Where did it come from? What did it mean? How could I seize and apprehend it? (Proust, *Swann's Way*, 60)

These questions begin a long and detailed investigation of this phenomenon by Marcel. But first we should pay attention to the structure of the experience itself, which perfectly accords with Deleuze's analysis: there is a sensible encounter with a sign, and it forces the narrator to interpret, that is, to think. In the case of sensuous signs, this interpretive act consists in trying to identify—as the narrator says at the end of the passage—what '*altogether different* object' (PS 11) is hidden by the sensuous quality we have encountered. In this case, Marcel discovers that the taste of the cake and tea have invoked a memory of Combray—the town in which he spent some of his youth, and where he sometimes saw his aunt Léonie dipping her madeleines into her morning cup of tea—and it is this memory which is the true meaning of the sign. The taste of the cake involves a quality that it shares with Marcel's childhood, and it is this quality that hides or contains the memory itself.

This memory, though, is not a simple matter. Unlike the futile recollections of the jealous lover, Marcel's memory of Combray cannot be conceived in terms of a snapshot, a particular moment in the past that I can voluntarily recall. Instead, it 'rises up absolutely, in a form that was never experienced, in its "essence".' (PS 12) We will discuss what is meant by 'essence' in a moment, but the key point for now is that the involuntary memories that sensuous signs can invoke capture the past itself in a new form. When Marcel makes sense of the madeleine-sign, he finds himself in possession of a kind of mythical image of an eternal Combray, one that casts its light not just back onto his childhood but also onto his present moment, illuminating it in a new way. In short, this Combray-image has been *created* through the encounter with the sign.

Because of this, Deleuze will insist that we need to carefully distinguish between memory understood as a voluntary act (guided, as we have seen, by the intelligence), and involuntary memory, in which a sign is forced upon us for no reason we can initially understand. The second is the only kind of memory of real interest to Proust, in Deleuze's view. It is only because memory can operate without being subordinated to the voluntary pursuits of intelligence that it is capable of responding to sensuous signs.

The secondary role of memory in the Search

It is easy to see why the madeleine passage in particular might lead one to think that memory plays a foundational role in Proust, but Deleuze forcefully rejects this approach. In the first instance, this is because not only memory but also the faculties of imagination and desire may be invoked by the sensuous signs. Here is the case that Deleuze invokes:

> At a bend in the road I experienced, suddenly, that special pleasure which was unlike any other, on catching sight of the twin steeples of Martinville, bathed in the setting sun and constantly changing their position with the movement of the carriage and the windings of the road, and then of a third steeple, that of Vieuxvicq, which, although separated from them by a hill and a valley, and rising from rather higher ground in the distance, appeared none the less to be standing by their side.
>
> In noticing and registering the shape of their spires, their shifting lines, the sunny warmth of their surfaces, I felt that I was not penetrating to the core of my impression, that something more lay behind that mobility, that luminosity, something which they seemed at once to contain and to conceal (Proust, *Swann's Way*, 253-4)

In this case, it not a past memory but a certain kind of imaginative association that the narrator discovers, a certain resonance or parallel with the forms of three young girls from a story he had once read. The three trees invoke 'three maidens in a legend, abandoned in a solitary place over which night had begun to fall'. (*Swann's Way*, 256)

But there is a more important reason why memory cannot be taken to be essential for Proust: the sensuous signs remain inadequate in a certain key sense. Deleuze is very clear that, unlike in the cases of the worldly signs and the signs of love, the sensuous signs give us something that is profoundly true, and convey the powerful sense of joy—'that exquisite pleasure'—the madeleine gives rise to in Marcel. But like the other two signs, they find their meaning outside of themselves in a certain generality. The sensuous sign constituted by the madeleine only invokes Combray because it shares a quality with Marcel's life in Combray: 'the madeleine with its flavor and Combray with its qualities still have distinct substances that resist envelopment, resist mutual penetration'. (PS 64) This point by itself would be neither here nor there—maybe sensuous signs mark the end of the Search, and are as far as we can progress—if there was not a fourth and final regime of signs that would go beyond them and give us a reason to consider them inadequate. 'They represent only the effort of life to prepare us for art and for the final revelation of art'. (PS 65)

FOURTH REGIME: THE SIGNS OF ART

The signs of art both constitute the true goal of the Search and enable us to retrospectively make sense of the trajectory of the Search itself. Deleuze notes that the previous three regimes of signs are all subordinated to materiality, both in the sense that a material object is required to engender them (a party, a face, a madeleine) and insofar as the attempt to make sense of them is only possible by reference to these situations. This becomes particularly significant in light of the fact that, for Deleuze, the signs of art are *immaterial*.

What does this mean? After all—to invoke some well-known moments in Proust's novel—Berma's dance seems to require her body, just as Vinteuil's Sonata in F# must be played on a violin, or at least on some material instrument. What is key is that art is both *indifferent* to its context of materialization and cannot be explained by this context. To say that the signs of art are immaterial is to say, for Deleuze, that they are the expression of *essence*. Now, explaining one difficult term with another is not at first glance the best move that Deleuze could make, since now he has the formidable task of telling us what is meant by this most metaphysical of categories. And, to be clear, Deleuze does not shy away from insisting on Proust's Platonism at this point, or from explaining essence in terms of Leibniz's concept of the monad.

This latter connection conveys us to the key point: for Deleuze, essence as it is expressed in signs of art is nothing other than *point of view*. The signs of art express an irreducibly singular point of view. Here is Deleuze: 'Only by art can we emerge from ourselves […] Thanks to art, instead of seeing a single world, our own, we see it multiply, and as many original artists as there are, so many worlds will we have at our disposal'. (PS 28)

Now this passage initially seems to just point out that because there are many works of art, there are equally many ways of seeing the world 'through the artist's eyes'. Hardly profound. But for Deleuze this is not really Proust's claim. The signs of art express a point of view irreducible to *any* particular person's perspective. Or rather, the nature of art requires us to reverse the normal way we conceive of the category of point of view. It shows us that it is not we who each have a point of view; we instead *inhabit* points of view. In turn, artworks embody not just a *particular* point of view, a perspective on Mt. Saint-Victoire, for instance, but show the *irreducibility of viewpoint as such*. They give us not a mere extrinsic difference between points of view—of the kind we find in love, for instance—but this difference itself as the truth of experience.

In other words, a viewpoint *as a viewpoint* manifests difference of viewpoint. This is why Deleuze will offer the following definition: 'What is an essence as revealed in the work of art? It is a difference, an absolute and ultimate Difference. Difference is what constitutes being, what makes us conceive being'. (PS 41) When I come upon Turner's *Burial at Sea* or hear Debussey's *Pelléas et Mélisande*, what I am confronted with is not only one person's point of view on a boat or another on a pair of star-crossed, ill-fated lovers. As signs of art, they directly expose me to the multiplicity of points of view as such. 'Each subject [...] expresses an absolutely different world', (PS 28) but in art the plurality of worlds is expressed on its own terms.

So, this what Deleuze means by an essence in Proust. It is a point of view that makes subjective experience possible—indeed, 'it is essence that constitutes subjectivity' (PS 43)—but it remains implicit or implicated in subjective experience while we remain engaged with the worldly signs, the signs of love and the sensuous signs. Only in art does essence appear as such, precisely because it is no longer subordinated to this or that subject's way of being engaged with the world.

Art and thought

At this point, it becomes possible to reconstruct the Proustian doctrine of the faculties that we have discussed in passing a few times. Here's Deleuze's summary:

> Only the sensibility grasps the sign as such; only intelligence, memory, or imagination explicates this meaning, each according to a certain kind of sign; only pure thought discovers essence, is forced to conceive essence as the sufficient reason of the sign and its meaning. (PS 63)

So, sensibility comes first, in order that there can be any encounter with signs at all. Thought in its highest form, when it operates on its own terms and is not subordinated to any other exercise of thinking, is involuntary. The signs of art force me to think, just as involuntary memory does, but what they make me think is no longer any identity or generality: they make me think essence, which is difference itself.

Beyond these involuntary adventures we are drawn into because of the encounter with the sign, there are the faculties that appear in the first instance to be the natural and normal ones—intelligence, voluntary memory, imagination. They reveal their secondary and contingent relationship to signs to the extent that they are really quite unable to voluntarily attain what is only given to us in experience when we are forced to confront it.

And finally, what the signs of art reveal is the ultimate character of all signs—that they express a point of view or a differential essence. Even the emptiest form of the sign (in dinner party conversation at Professor Rorty's house, for instance) functions and can be made sense of because it expresses a point of view.

ESSENCE: SINGULARITY, COMMONALITY, SERIES, GROUPS

Having attained the point of view afforded by art into the nature of essence, Deleuze will now return to the three previous regimes of signs and explore the way in which essence is played out there. Once we have learnt the lesson of art, that is, the value and specificity of the other signs can be uncovered, as if despite themselves—as I have just said, art reveals that essence or point of view is always what is at stake in the encounter with signs, even when this is obscured by the regime of signs in question. Conversely, without art, 'we would not have understood this'. (PS 14)

A sign, any sign, expresses a point of view. But *whose*? The answer to this question differs for each regime of signs. As we return down the path that led to art furnished with its insight, we see that the subject that answers to this question becomes increasingly general, a generality that is reflected in the bond to materiality we noted earlier. In turn, this generality gives the first two regimes of signs the appearance that they fall under a governing law: the generalised law of the lie (in love) and the generic law of the void (in the salon).

Sensuous signs force us to recollect or imagine in order to establish their meaning. Because the sign and its meaning are extrinsically related, there is a necessary generality given to the (shared) quality in question. The quality borne by the madeleine, for instance, is an envelope for the present and the past moments. It may engender the memory of Combray, but this takes place indirectly. The essence that is directly expressed in works of art is here subordinated to the minimum of generality that this quality involves. It is true that a point of view is expressed through such a sign, but its singularity has been subordinated to this first—however minimal—*commonality*.

At best, as Deleuze notes on a few occasions, sensuous signs can act as *facsimiles* of signs of art that prepare us for them. We can see a kind of inversion of an argument Kant makes in the third *Critique* here: nature as it is encountered in the form of sensuous signs is and can only be a preparation for the higher form of the sign encountered in art.

This generality is greater again in the case of love. Essence or point of view is found, not in its singularity, or in a shared common world, but, first of all, *across a series of loves*. Each love repeats the same point of view, but in a way that obscures the fact that it is the same. While the narrator's love for Gilberte is repeated in his love for Albertine, this only becomes apparent after the regime of love has been reframed by the encounter with art.

To be more precise, the reason for the incapacity to grasp the serial character of love at the time is that the apparently objective details of the situation shift from one beloved to the next. But these accrued differences do not really tell us anything about love, because the essential truth of love is that what matters is necessarily hidden.

Love is serial in two further senses, Deleuze notes. There is, first of all, a serial character to every love on its own terms, and we pass with Proust's narrator 'from one Albertine to another'. (PS 45) Again, this is the case because there is no question of actually attaining the hidden world that the beloved expresses. All we can do is engage in a long series of investigations ('why did she make that gesture?' 'But last time you said you didn't want that!') that skate across the impenetrable surface of the beloved's world, with the truth of our lover sealed away forever beneath the ice. Conversely, the series of my loves—again, because it expresses precisely the same logic, regardless of how different the apparently objective details are—forms a part of the experience of love in general: 'Swann's love for Odette already constitutes part of the series that continues with the hero's love for Gilberte, for Mme de Guermantes, for Albertine'. (PS 45)

We return in the last step to the regime of worldly signs. Here, essence attains the greatest level of generality, the lowest degree of coherence and the greatest degree of obscurity with respect to the point of view that it expresses.

> Vacuity, stupidity, forgetfulness: such is the trinity of the worldly group. But worldliness thereby gains a speed, a mobility in the emission of signs, a perfection in formalism [vacuous circulation of signs], a generality in meaning [...] As essence is incarnated ever more loosely, the signs assume a comic power [...] Those who are like parrots, in a group, are also 'prophetic birds': their chatter indicates the presence of a law. (PS 53)

This law is the law of groups, the formal law of empty communication, which is overcome through the apprenticeship but revealed in retrospect at the end of the trajectory as what governs the diffuse act of polite society: fit in.

THE PLURALITY OF TIME

Earlier we saw some important reasons why Deleuze will reject the claim that Proust has any profound interest in memory. We now arrive at another such reason: the temporality that belongs to memory in the encounter with sensuous signs is only one temporal register in play in Proust's work. And in fact—as I said right at the start of the chapter—Deleuze will relate each regime of signs to a predominant mode of temporality.

The time of the worldly signs is *wasted* time. Nothing can be recuperated from time spent at vacuous dinner parties because nothing was ever there in the first place: there was nothing to be gained, and nothing to be uncovered. But this is not to say that the apprentice has learnt nothing—on the contrary, the value of the apprenticeship is to precisely realise this fact, the fact of this vacuity.

In turn, the time of love is *lost time*. This time is not lost through neglect, from spending too many hours at the office, or too much time gnawing your fingers in the grip of jealous thoughts. As Deleuze will insist, time is lost in love *in advance* and *necessarily so*. No amount of attention or care can recuperate anything from the time spent in love because, once again, the effort of interpretation will never carry us into the world of the beloved itself. Consequently, as Deleuze notes, 'Love unceasingly prepares its own disappearance, acts out its own dissolution'. (PS 13)

To the sensuous signs belongs time *rediscovered*. In what sense? We know that when the memory of Combray arises, unsummoned, it does so 'as it could not be experienced: not in reality, but in its truth; not in its external and contingent relations, but in its internalized difference, in its essence. Combray rises up in a pure past [...] out of reach of the present voluntary memory and of the past conscious perception.' (PS 61) What involuntary memory gives to us is, Deleuze suggests, nothing other than access to time in its pure state: eternity, the time proper to essences.

What about the other effects of sensuous signs? In the case where imagination is invoked, for instance (the case that Deleuze dwells on the most), the image I suddenly find myself contemplating appears to stand outside of time, as if it was eternal, unchanging. It is as though the sensuous signs have managed to invoke a little shard of eternity, made possible by the imaginative association of a material object, like the Martinville steeples or the three trees in the fading light. But whether we focus on what is discovered or rediscovered thanks to sensuous signs, a materiality and commonality remain the hallmark here.

Sensuous signs may lead to the rediscovery of time in its truth, but it is only in art that this time is present directly and on its own terms. Art exposes us to 'an absolute primordial time, a veritable eternity that unites sign and meaning'. (PS 56) Perhaps surprisingly, the key term in all of this is *eternal*. The nature of time in Proust is neither a kind of Bergsonian vital time, the time of the *élan vital* and the ongoing flourishing of being, nor the simple spatialized time of physics: it is a time in which the existence of essence and our capacity to apprehend them is united. We are finally able to complete the search for truth that marks the apprenticeship in general in art, because in art essence is no longer subject to the forms of temporal experience that obscured it in the previous regimes.

This in turn is the source of the joy that we feel before art—why we are dazed, why we weep: we are given immediately the feeling of what cannot be conquered by the other temporal modalities, the absolute superiority of essence over wasted and lost time in particular. Proust writes of the joyful indifference to death that involuntary memory can expose us to, but 'we are unable to say how' (PS 56) this joy arises. Only the signs of art, which show us essence directly, allow us to explain it. But now, there is no indifference left either, but instead an absolute affirmation of existence. This is a kind of intellectual joy, one that emerges from the troubled trials of the apprentice, and consists in being able finally to directly grasp not just the nature of these trials, but also the completely relative character of the suffering they involved: 'suddenly I did not care/if I had lived or died'. (Don Paterson, *Landing Light*, 81)

The difference between time rediscovered and time regained can now we explained more precisely. Involuntary memory exposes us to time in its truth, but it does so in a way that we cannot do anything with. We have an experience of immense joy, but cannot attain the perspective that gives rise to it: how can we 'save for ourselves the past as it is preserved in itself, as it survives in itself?' (PS 59) The only way that this eternal time can be preserved on its own terms is in art, there where no generality or commonality threatens to subordinate it.

With all of this said, Deleuze will make one final and general point:

> If each sign has its privileged temporal development, each also straddles the other lines and participates in the other dimensions of time. Time wasted extends into love and even into the sensuous signs. Time lost appears even in worldliness and also subsists in the signs of sensibility. Time regained reacts in its turn on time wasted and time lost. (PS 17)

The key point is that these lines of time are always in fact *mixed*. What remains 'the same' is essence qua point of view, which is played out according to mixtures of signs and their times. We can, nevertheless, schematically present the course of Deleuze's first version of *Proust and Signs* in the following table:

	Predominant temporal modality	**Faculty addressed by the sign**	**Degree of generality in expression of essence**
Worldly signs	Wasted time	Intelligence	The group
Signs of love	Lost time	Intelligence, voluntary memory	The series
Sensuous signs	Rediscovered time	Involuntary memory, imagination and desire	A common quality (minimal generality)
Signs of art	Regained time	Involuntary thought	Singularity

THE NATURE OF THE SEARCH

As I said at the start of the chapter, Deleuze returned to his study of Proust twice after its initial publication, in 1970 and 1973 respectively. These additions shift the terrain of our engagement with Proust away from the regimes of signs and times, introducing two new problematics. The first of these concerns the nature of Proust's novel itself, and how it works to produce its effects in its readers. The second concerns the nature—and more precisely the *unity*—of the Search.

We will take each of these points in turn, but first we should pause for a moment and note the peculiar move that Deleuze is making in these later sections. The first edition of *Proust and Signs* is about the content of Proust's novel. But when he returns to the project, Deleuze will take what he has discovered about this content and use it to explain the situation of this novel itself, and more broadly the meaning of literature. That is, he will use *In Search of Lost Time* to explain the state of the modern world and what this state demands of literature. Even the concept of art that he will use to explain the Search and the way it works is *drawn from the Search itself*. This fact is important to register: the passages Deleuze quotes from Proust in the parts of *Proust and Signs* added in the seventies are no longer being used to illustrate Proust's own procedure, but are instead the components of a new philosophy of literature.

Antilogos

The central point that Deleuze wants to make in the additional parts of the book is that any account of the unity of Proust's novel must not presuppose an identity, above all because a study of the Search demonstrates its irreducibly fragmentary character. This is why Deleuze uses the term *antilogos*, the title of the eighth chapter of *Proust and Signs*. In opposition to the Platonism we find in Plato himself, which leads from the shock of the sign to the self-identical and *objective* Idea, Proust's Platonism leads him to the subject, and to be more precise to the point of view that the subject inhabits: to the *proto-subjectivity* of essence. We already know that essence is difference, that it is nothing but viewpoint as differential perspective, but at an even more basic level the rejection of the Platonic organization of reality is already an affirmation of difference. If the Search is not organized around a return to an objectively unified vision of the world, we cannot but remain at the level of what cannot be unified: the *fragment*. Here is Deleuze:

> The essential point is that the parts of the Search remain partitioned, fragmented, *without anything lacking* [...] swept on by time without forming a whole or presupposing one, without lacking anything in this distribution, and denouncing in advance every organic unity we might seek to introduce into it. (PS 169)

So the key for Deleuze is that Proust's novel has no unity over and above its fragmentary parts—though it does, as we will see shortly, involve an affirmation of these fragments as fragments.

Now, these fragments themselves appear in two forms in Proust, according to Deleuze, and he will even go so far as to claim that 'each of the great categories of the Search marks [...] a commitment to one or the other figure'. (PS 118) The first is what he calls *boîtes*—literally, 'boxes'—which are translated in *Proust and Signs* as 'cells'. These kind of fragments involve closed or hidden elements in the novel. The second category, *vases*, which is translated here as 'vessels' appears at first glance to involve a basic feature of fluid physics. In French, the fact that two connected bodies of water (two small lakes, for instance) always come to an equilibrium (i.e., always end up with the same water level) is explained *par le principe des vases communicants*. We would expect this principle, as a result, to describe the communication of content between containers, but in fact Deleuze will assert the very opposite: vessels are the fragmentary elements in Proust's novel that *do not* communicate. A vessel 'involves the co-existence of asymmetric and noncommunicating parts'. (PS 117)

Ultimately then, these terms aren't much help in following what Deleuze is getting at here. Better are the terms from scholastic theology that he also deploys. In these terms, cells are containers that encompass a hidden, *implicated* content that is *explicated*, always in a new way, in the Search. Vessels, on the other hand, involve a *complication* of incommensurable parts—a common being for the disparate. Correlatively, the role of the narrator in Proust's novel is twofold: to explicate or unfold what is enclosed in the cells, and to select from between the incompatibles contained by vessels.

Deleuze gives a range of examples here, but let's consider some cases we're already familiar with. A good example of the way cells function is found in the sensuous sign of the madeleine. The cell in question is 'the sensuous quality, the flavour' of the madeleine itself, and the implicated content is nothing other than 'Combray as pure Viewpoint, superior to all that has been experienced'. (PS 119) We see too what explication will involve here—the attempt to make this viewpoint no longer a perplexing phantom but a way of seeing and feeling from Combray's point of view in the present, a 'reconquest', Deleuze insists, which is necessarily 'a creation'. (PS 119) This is just the conclusion of the work that Marcel does on his experience of the madeleine.

A first example of a vessel is the character of Albertine (although she goes both ways, embodying both cells and vessels). Far from being a simple container that includes something hidden that must be unfolded, she actually contains a multiplicity of irreducibly different 'Albertines'. What the narrator must do is, as if adjusting the focal distance on a camera, bring one of these Albertines into focus:

> To choose a certain girl in the group, a certain view or fixed notion of the girl, to choose a certain word in what she says, a certain suffering in what we feel for her, and, in order to experience this suffering, in order to decipher the word, in order to love this girl, to choose a certain self that we cause to live or relive among all the possible selves: such is the activity corresponding to complication. (PS 127)

The same thing is at issue in the case of common nouns (madeleine, tree, steeple). Common nouns in Proust, Deleuze writes, 'acquire their value by introducing into discourse certain noncommunicating fragments'. (PS 118)

These points might appear trivial, at least if we were to approach *In Search of Lost Time* looking for (or presupposing) a unity that belongs to it. But this is precisely Deleuze's point. That Proust does not invoke such a unity is what gives the Search its immense power—'the force with which the parts are projected into the world, violently stuck together despite their unmatching edges' (PS 123)—as a work of literature.

Three orders of truth

For Deleuze, then, Proust's novel has neither narrative *coherence* nor a single transcendent meaning, even a hidden one (as if it, too, was a vessel). But it is nevertheless capable of having *effects*, and this is the topic that Deleuze now turns to: given that the Search is a composite of fragments, what do these fragments *do*? His signal remark is thus the following: 'The modern work of art has no problem of meaning, but only a problem of use [...] the work of art, so understood, is essentially productive—productive of certain truths'. (PS 146)

There are three registers or orders of truth in Proust, according to Deleuze, to which correspond three machines for their production. In turn, these three machines give rise to three particular modalities of interpretation, the interpretation of our own existence in the world: "what is produced is not simply the interpretation Proust gives [...] it is the entire phenomenon itself that is interpretation." (PS 99) Here we need to be very specific. We are no longer dealing with the internal content and structure of the Search, but *the way that the Search as a work of art has effects on us, its readers.*

The first order of truth is oriented by sensuous signs and the involuntary memories that they invoke, and the essences that are expressed by the signs of art. It is true that involuntary memory and essence are distinct from the point of view of the regimes of signs, but here Deleuze draws them together since they both concern a certain *singularity* (of a particular essence, but also of Combray, the three young women of myth, etc.).

The second order of truth is defined by the failure to attain this singularity and are thus expressed by the worldly signs and the signs of love. Consequently, they characteristically concern *general laws*. The law of the series (love) and the law of the group (the salon) are truths about the world, but they are second-order truths that derive their force from their unrealized proximity to essence.

Finally, there are those truths that are concern 'death and the idea of death, the production of catastrophe (signs of aging, disease and death)'. (PS 149)

The three machines

In sum, then, the Search produces in us three types of truths: truths of essence, truths of law, and truths of catastrophe. Now, Deleuze notes that if we look at *In Search of Lost Time* as an ensemble of fragments rather than an apprenticeship oriented by time regained, it's clear that the second type of truth is by far the most prevalent. In turn, the most common kind of truth that the Search engenders in us concerns the complicated co-existence of specificity and orders of generality (group belonging and serial love), a co-existence in which specificity holds a very compromised position. In the middle region between art and death, we find the heterogeneous mixture of pleasures and pains, partial apprehensions of truth and the seemingly insurmountable feeling that we'll never really understand anything. As a result, the most common machine we find in Proust we can call the machine of 'partial objects'. (PS 151) This machine produces these fragments without producing at the same time the realization of their relationship to essence.

The second machine Deleuze calls the machine of *resonance*. It produces the truths of singularity found in sensuous existence and in art. Why resonance? The case of involuntary memory makes the point most clearly—the taste of the madeleine makes the present and the past resonate together. In doing this, the idea of Combray is made to appear, a new effect, a harmonious product.

Now, the machine of resonance produces what Deleuze calls 'a local or localizing essence' (PS 152) in the case of sensuous signs, but—as we know—it is only when we arrive at art that 'individuating essence' (PS 152) appears as such. Here, the production of truth appears directly and without mediation. Artistic production consists of a free act, a free production of a point of view that also conveys difference as such—recall the earlier discussion of essence in this context. It is again an act of resonance, but the choice of means (violin or piano?) and states or objects between which the resonance can be made to appear are not determined by an external factor.

Deleuze emphasizes that, in a sense, the second machine goes to work on the partial objects produced by the first, giving to them what they cannot attain in themselves, namely the realization of their point of view. The second machine does not *totalise* the fragments of the first, but sets up non-analogical connections between them—in other words, it makes their implicit point of view emerge: 'Combray as Point of View" (PS 98) *And from this point of view, the fragments can be brought into a new arrangement.*

Given this, we might expect the third machine to add something further to the production of the second, but—since the second machine already comprehends art as the highest act of life—what could this possibly be? The problem becomes even graver when we see that the third machine is a means of producing truths not of art or life but '*the idea of death*' (PS 157):

> Mme de Guermantes' salon, with the aging of its guests, makes us see the distortion of features, the fragmentation of gestures, the loss of coordination of muscles, the changes in colour, the formation of moss, lichen, patches of mold on bodies, sublime disguises, sublime senilities. Everywhere the approach of death, the sentiment of the presence of a 'terrible thing', the impression of an ending or even a final catastrophe. (PS 156)

The first observation Deleuze makes is that death is already ubiquitous at the first level, the level of the group and of love—not just in the degradation that we are made to see in Proust's account of the salons, but in the passage from one moment in the series of love to another (from lover to disappointment, 'first the joy then the debasement,' then from a new lover to a new disappointment …) on the way to the realization of love's futility as such. It appears that we find death 'imbuing all the fragments uniformly, carrying them towards a universal end'. (PS 157) But if this is the case at the first level, doesn't art ultimately end up confronting this situation and losing out? If death is the ultimate reality, then the bodily joy of sensuous signs and the intellectual joy that comes from encountering essence in art appear to be ultimately meaningless after all. So the question becomes this: 'Can we conceive of a machine capable of extracting something from this painful impression and producing certain truths?' (PS 158)

Here we find the analysis of *Proust and Signs* at its most subtle. True, death is a simple material fact that holds for everyone and everything. But the *idea* of death, produced in us by Proust's novel, is not some trite recognition of this fact. The idea of death is really the idea of *time*, of the reality of time and its presence in our existence. So being forced to realise the sensuous truth of time or death in our bodies supercharges the meaning of sensuous existence, rather than denigrating it. We are made to think the fleeting nature of existence, not in order to show how everything comes to nothing, but to show that we must make existence matter *now*.

What is crucial in this analysis is that this third machine comes to join forces with the second, and with the productive apparatus of art—the two machines 'mesh gears' (PS 160), as Deleuze puts it. We know that sensuous signs are precursors to the signs of art, and even function to prepare us for the encounter with essence. And now we see that the effect of the idea of death—an idea that *Proust's novel engenders in us*—does nothing but charge the sensuous realm of bodies with its true, profound meaning. The third machine *makes time sensuous* (PS 160), and by doing this *makes art matter*.

THE SUBJECT OF THE SEARCH

In his additions to *Proust and Signs* in the seventies, Deleuze presents the nature of the Search from two interrelated points of view. The first, which we have just seen, is internal to the organization of the novel and consists in the arrangement of fragments. The second is external to this structure and considers how the Search (and literature in general) functions. But the second will adopt a *subjective* point of view—Deleuze is interested, that is, in the kind of subjectivity that is put into play by the Search in particular and literature more generally.

He begins by noting that the modern novel participates in a general process of destitution, one we touched on above in passing: the destitution of objectivity. 'The world', Deleuze writes, 'has come apart, has become chaos'. (PS 134) Objectivity had appeared as given from two points of view: we either referred ourselves back to the stability of experience (presupposed, for instance, by scientific empiricism) or to the formal unity of ideality (as in philosophy, Platonism in particular). But these, Deleuze implies, have now failed us, and new means by which stability in the world can be guaranteed will have to be created: 'objectivity can no longer exist except in the work of art'. (PS 134) Proust's work is decisive in Deleuze's view, and for just this reason. It shows how what is given in experience (signs) lead to the production of thought and new capacities in thinking: 'to think is to create, and primarily to create the act of thinking within thought'. (PS 134) More importantly yet again, it shows us how the impetus of signs drives us in the direction of the only true objectivity that exists: the signs of art themselves, and the proto-subjective points of view that they express.

Now, the crisis of objectivity is not only addressed *by* the Search: it is also a feature *of* Proust's novel itself. The same two registers of objectivity that we took to ground the unity of experience are supposed to be able to account for the unity and meaning of novels: continuity of experience (narrative) on the one hand, and a 'meaning' or guiding idea of the book ('what is the book about?'). Here again, Deleuze will emphasise the importance of Proust's turn to *subjectivity* as a way of rejecting and overcoming these redundant approaches. The answer to the question 'what unifies the Search and gives it meaning?' will be the *subject* of the Search. But who is the subject of the Search itself?

In light of the nature of the Search, which is irreducibly fragmentary as we have just seen, there is no question of it being an omnipotent narrator-subject, who would lay out the narrative or employ recollections with an eye to a guiding theme or idea. No, the subject that unifies the search is not a person (or modelled on a person, as we are tempted to do by making reference to Proust's narrator [PS 170]) but a *selection machine*. Here is Deleuze: 'The "subject" of the Search is finally no self, it is that *we* without content that portions out Swann, the narrator, and Charlus, distributes or selects them without totalising them'. (PS 128) The subjectivity that unifies the Search, and indeed any work of literature, is the immanent organization of the novel in the novel itself. This is a strange notion of subjectivity, of course, but one that expresses what Deleuze thinks is key: the unity of creation and expression at the level of systems of signs, which is to say, *style*.

In a certain sense, this thesis expresses the most radical aspect of Deleuze's reading of Proust and, at least from the point of view of the concepts developed in *Proust and Signs*, his reading of literature more generally. What Deleuze contends is not just that we must dispense with any reference to the author when engaging with a literary work—an argument famously made by Roland Barthes, and more generally by thinkers like Foucault working in the wake of structuralism—but that any work of literature gains its unity from the particular mode of dispersion of a formally empty 'subject'.

There are ultimately no characters, no places and no events in a novel that are not expressions of a fundamentally irreducible multiplicity of points of view, brought together only in the unfolding of this multiplicity itself. And we must think of this unfolding as the spontaneous generativity proper, not to its author or reader, to the novel as an ensemble of signs. A work of literature is a web whose spider is the web itself in its spinning; 'the web and the spider, the web and the body are one and the same machine'. (PS 182)

All of this is to say, finally, that the unity of the Search is provided by *time itself*. This surely sound peculiar, but Deleuze's point is that time is the only thing that unifies what is different or disparate without reducing these differences to a fixed unity. This is why he writes that 'time [is] the dimension of the narrator, which has the power to be the whole *of* these parts without totalising them, the unity *of* these parts without unifying them' (PS 109):

it is in the meanders and rings of an anti-Logos style that it makes the requisite detours in order to gather up the ultimate fragments, to sweep along at different speeds all the pieces, each one of which refers to a different whole, to no whole at all, or to no other whole than that of style. (PS 115)

Consider the changes to your conscious experience as you've labored through this chapter, or mine as I've labored on it before you. These experiences are an ongoing process of shifting moods, affects and degrees of attention. It is easy enough to speak about them as unified things ('that hour I wasted reading a chapter on Deleuze's *Proust* book') but this unity is a product of the experience itself. And the only thing that gathers together a passage of experience in the process of its changes, its becomings, is time. It is what each accent, shift of attention, moment and mood share without, finally, sharing anything else.

7

Difference and Repetition

Difference and Repetition was the principal thesis submitted by Deleuze for his doctorate at the Sorbonne in 1968, alongside its complement, *Expressionism in Philosophy: Spinoza*.

Deleuze found its composition difficult. Writing to François Châtelet: 'Oh, my thesis, everything is swimming in this soup (the best must be at the bottom, but it's the least visible)'. (Dosse, *Intersecting Lives*, 135) The difficulty of the result has also been expressed in culinary terms: Clément Rosset reports hearing someone exclaim that reading *Difference and Repetition* 'is like eating a biscuit made without butter. It's excellent, but it's dry'. (Rosset, *Faits divers*, 217) There is no question that Deleuze's health made the process of composition particularly hard. After struggling with a fatigue even more intense than that which had dogged him throughout his life, a consultation with a doctor revealed the aggressive advance of tuberculosis, which had caused a large hole to form in one of his lungs. He consequently spent the latter part of 1968 hospitalised, before the defence of his thesis at the start of 1969. After the defence, the lung was removed.

The delay was not merely a matter of Deleuze's health, however. The events of May '68 had continued to roil the university system, making the prosecution of its official activities difficult. In a late interview with Claire Parnet, Deleuze recalls the circumstances of his examination with some amusement:

> [The jury] had only one fear: how to avoid the gangs who were at the Sorbonne. I recall that the president of the jury had told me that there were two options: "either we do your thesis on the ground floor, which has the advantage that there are two exits but the

disadvantage that the gangs are hanging around down there, or we do it on the first floor, which has the advantage that the gangs rarely go upstairs but the disadvantage that there is only one entrance and exit." So when I defended my thesis, the jury president stayed posted at the door to see whether the gangs were coming, and I never saw his eyes. (ABC, 'P as in Professor')

DIFFERENCE AND REPETITION RECONSIDERED

The overall project of *Difference and Repetition* can be put a number of ways. A first way is presented by Deleuze in its Preface:

> Two lines of research lie at the origin of this book: one concerns a concept of difference without negation, [not] subordinated to the identical [...] the other concerns a concept of repetition in which physical, mechanical or bare repetitions (repetitions of the Same) would find their *raison d'être* in the more profound structures of a hidden repetition [...] These two lines of research spontaneously came together, because on every occasion *these concepts of a pure difference and a complex repetition* seemed to connect and coalesce. (DR xix-xx)

That it would address the respective natures of difference and repetition and their interrelation is what we might expect from the book's title. But here, Deleuze also indicates his targets, namely specific existing accounts of the two categories. On the one hand, there is a conception of difference that makes it reliant on a prior identity—*the difference* between *those two loves*. On the other hand, there is a conception of repetition that makes it turn around the brute reiteration of a given identity—*we had the* same *argument over and over again.*

These existing accounts of difference and repetition are easily recognizable, as obvious—and, we will see, woven into the whole fabric of the history of western thought—as they are commonplace. What Deleuze calls 'pure difference' and 'complex repetition' are new concepts that he will have to create. He will do this by first advancing an absolute *critique* of the accepted accounts, and then *constructing* new concepts out of materials drawn from other thinkers, by gathering the finest of their arrows and firing them at this new target (DR xv).

But to characterize the book in these terms that Deleuze himself uses is to only present part of the picture. Indeed, his ambitions are considerably greater than two bits of precise conceptual work. Another—better, in my view—way of introducing the project of the book is to imagine that it bore a different, albeit famous and familiar, title: *Being and Time*. Now, it is certainly true that, like Heidegger, Deleuze will argue for a post-Kantian philosophy that emphasizes the primacy of temporality, and which will attack the way the nature of being is obscured by various spontaneous and reflective modes of thought. But in a broader sense, the constructive effort of *Difference and Repetition* involves conceiving of being as difference, as irreducibly differential, and of repetition in terms of time.

The outline I will present here will begin by discussing the critical facet of the book, and then turn to the constructive facet. This approach will force us to break with the order in which the book is published. This is less of a liability than it might seem. Not only does the book's Introduction, 'Repetition and Difference', present the new reader with a rather obtuse aperture on Deleuze's major lines of argumentation, it is certainly easier to appreciate the overall position he is trying to advance from the point of view of its third and fifth chapters, or even, as Deleuze himself suggests (DR xix), by reading the Conclusion first. Correlatively, as a reader's familiarity with the book grows, it will increasingly seems like each of the chapters address the same problems, and thus contains the whole argument of the book, each from their own point of view. *Difference and Repetition* is thus a book that repeats itself from a series of different perspectives.

CRITIQUE

OBJECTIVE AND SUBJECTIVE MISRECOGNITIONS OF DIFFERENCE

The first task is therefore to take stock of the critical facet of *Difference and Repetition*. But right from the beginning, we will need to distinguish between two registers in which the concept of difference in particular is mistaken.

First, there is the critique of what we can call objective misrecognitions of difference. These are explicit claims advanced by philosophers throughout the history of Western thought. In the first volume of the *Science of Logic*, for instance, Hegel asserts that 'Difference as such is already *implicitly* contradiction'. (II.279) This claim forms a decisive moment in Hegel's philosophy, but this definition and what it entails are themselves explicit moments in Hegel's argumentation. Like Hegel himself, however, Deleuze argues that there is also an implicit '*non-*

philosophical' (DR 132) misrecognition of difference. This second 'misrecognition is subjective in character'. Deleuze will call it the dogmatic image of thought, which, as we will see in more detail later, involves an habituated pre-reflective understanding of the nature of thinking.

Now, the dogmatic image does not explicitly involve any concept of difference, but what it does do is *imply* the primacy of identity with respect to difference in a number of ways. So, while Hegel explicitly argues that difference is contradiction, human thought in general implicitly construes reality in terms of identity rather than difference. The distinction Deleuze draws between these two kinds of misrecognitions also necessitates two different lines of critique. There will need to be an engagement at the level of philosophical argumentation with the objective presuppositions, and this is what *Difference and Repetition* predominantly offers in the first chapter. The three major case studies will be Aristotle, Leibniz and Hegel. There will also need to be an engagement of a different kind with the unreflective presuppositions of thought in its habitual operation, and this is what the third chapter 'The Image of Thought' pursues.

But while we must treat these two kinds of misrecognitions on their own terms, the broadest critical argument of *Difference and Repetition* is that the explicit philosophical errors concerning difference that permeate the history of Western thought are themselves a product of the implicit misrecognition built into our habituated human way of grasping the world.

This point allows us to emphasise a central feature of what Deleuze is up to in this book. His goal is not merely to denounce the misrecognitions of difference and repetition, but to account for the genesis of these misrecognitions themselves. When we arrive at the end of the chapter, we will see in fact that the kinds of mistaken positions advanced by Aristotle (for example) must be understood in relation to the very nature of reality itself.

THE OBJECTIVE MISRECOGNITION OF DIFFERENCE IN THE HISTORY OF PHILOSOPHY

The idea that *Difference and Repetition* is Deleuze's most important book is often debated, but there is no question that it constitutes his most significant work in the traditional format of the systematic philosophical treatise. It also displays the breadth of his mastery of the canon of Western philosophy—every significant and many more marginal figures are given consideration—that Deleuze would later declare he had been 'more or less bludgeoned to death with'. (N 5) Consequently, reading *Difference and Repetition* at times evokes the feeling of hurtling through this history at breakneck speed, and necessitates at least a general familiarity with it.

This will be reflected by the frequency of expository sequences in what follows, but nowhere is this more valuable than in relation to chapter one, 'Difference-in-itself'. We can appreciate the overarching goal of this chapter by thinking of it as an attempt to read the history of philosophy *from the point of view of the concept of difference.* Deleuze asks: where in this history can we find an adequate concept of difference, and, when it is not dealt with adequately, what do we find in its place?

Aristotle

According to Deleuze, difference appears in Aristotle's philosophy in two forms. The first of these is as contrariety. The concept 'bird' can be qualified in two contrary ways: flying and flightless.

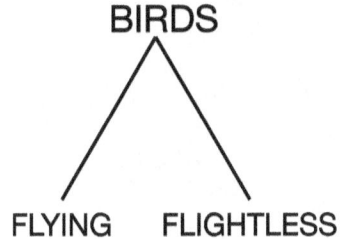

Of course, there are many other ways to qualify the concept 'bird' (red versus blue birds, for instance), but in Aristotle's view it is only when we attain contrariety, which is 'at once the greatest and most perfect' (DR 30) sense of difference, that we obtain real knowledge about birds. There is, as it were, 'not enough difference' between red birds and blue birds to allow us to think the concept of 'bird' adequately—the two qualifications don't go far enough to sketch out the whole range of birds. More generally, to possess knowledge about something is to be able to think about it in terms of its concept, and a concept is only properly qualified on the basis of contrary predicates.

We can immediately see the way that difference is subordinated to identity in Aristotle: the genus is always self-identical on its own terms, and difference only appears a contrariety between predicates or species. As he says in the *Categories*, a thing (a substance) is 'what is numerically one and the same,' and 'is able to receive contraries'. (4a9-10) The more general rule is therefore as follows: 'that which is different is different from some particular thing in some particular respect, so that there must be something identical whereby they differ'. (*Metaphysics* 1054b25)

This structure characterizes knowledge as such; for Aristotle, then, we should generalise it completely. If we consider 'substance' as the ultimate genus, and the position of 'human beings' as substances, for instance, we end up with the following diagram. Though Aristotle himself never presented things like this—the 'tree' structure is often traced back to the Plotinian philosophy Porphyry—it is nevertheless useful in the this context:

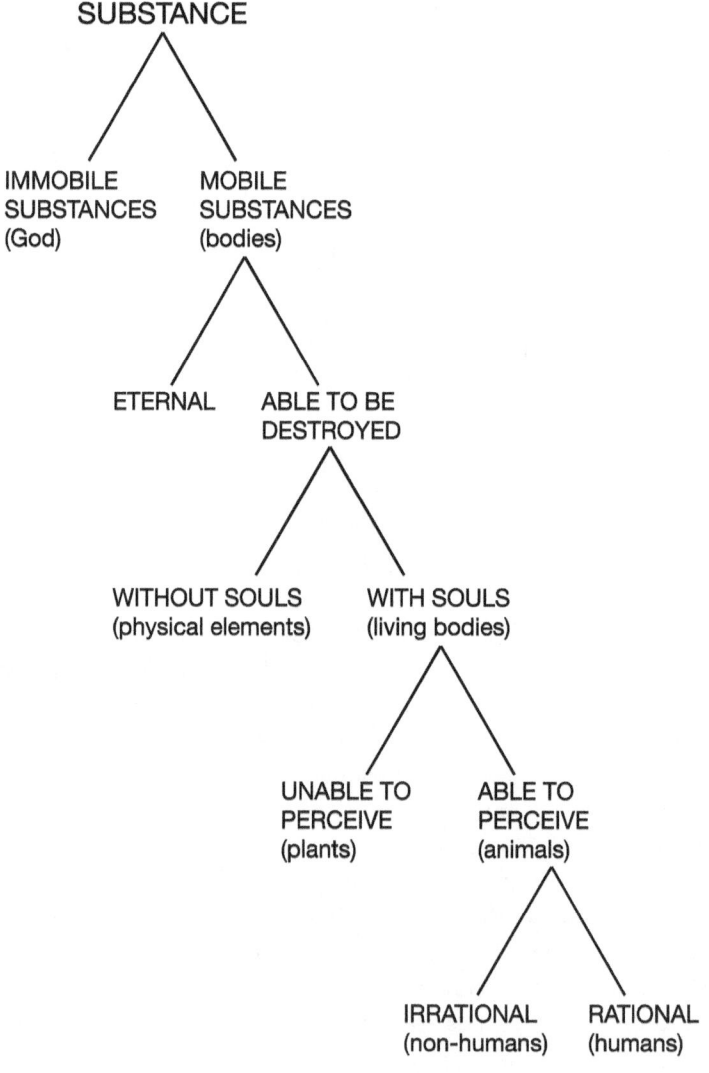

Such is the first sense of difference in Aristotle that Deleuze highlights. The second concerns the level on which 'substance' figures in this diagram. According to Aristotle, there are ten basic 'kinds' of being that are irreducible and cannot be attributed to anything further—what he famously calls the *categories*. Here are the first six:

SUBSTANCE ⟷ QUANTITY ⟷ QUALITY ⟷ RELATION ⟷ PLACE ⟷ TIME ....

Now, these categories name everything that has being for Aristotle, even if (like 'at six in the morning' or 'sitting at my desk') some of them are dependent on others ('I am writing this, sitting at my desk, at six in the morning'). They therefore share a single concept of being. But this concept of being is not and cannot be a genus like 'animal', and nor can it be some kind of meta-category. This is because, as Aristotle argues, in order for 'being' to be a genus, it would need to be differentiated from something else. But whatever could be counterposed to it would already have to have being, the very thing we were aiming to define. We would then be forced into a contradiction or an infinite regress. This problem clearly arises because Aristotle thinks that 'being' and 'oneness' are mutually implied: 'being and unity are the same and are one thing'. (*Metaphysics* 1003b22-3) In turn, differences can only be *between* unified beings or their properties.

What then is the nature of the relationship between the categories and being? We arrive now at his famous claim that 'There are many senses in which a thing may be said to "be"'. (*Metaphysics* 1003a33) In other words, being is said in many senses, or it is *equivocal*. These senses are the categories themselves, so that being is said *as* substance, *as* quantity, *as* quality, and so on.

It is here that Aristotle's second form of difference is in play. There are differences *between* the categories, but this difference clearly cannot be contrariety. Instead, Aristotle's position is that the categories express the unity of being *analogically*. Or, to use Heidegger's useful phrase, the categories express a '*unity of analogy*'. (*Being and Time* §3) This means that, as Deleuze tends to describe it, being's expression is a matter of distribution. Even though substance is the first or primary sense in which being is said (and the other categories are all said of substances: the cat is on the mat), the categories all express being. The nature of difference at the level of the categories therefore consists in a kind of harmony or shared (common) sense between these categories.

With these points in hand, we can now appreciate the three concerns that Deleuze has with Aristotle's account of difference. The first, which concerns what Deleuze calls 'the Large' (DR 29) is: what grounds the analogical relation between the categories? In his view, Aristotle's answer falls well short, turning as it does on the presupposition of a distribution of being that cannot be further detailed. That is, Aristotle's postulate of a generic difference inscribes 'difference in the quasi-identity of the most general determinable concepts', (DR 33) but lacks any resources to do anything more. Identity is *necessarily* gestured to, but it is an identity that cannot be thought or understood other than in terms of this gesture. Issues concerning the Large also plague the general effort to construct an ontology. So the concept of being Aristotle gives us only manages the status of quasi-concept.

The second problem concerns 'the Small'. If we ask what grounds the knowledge of various kinds of plants, for instance, Aristotle's answer is that we can establish the genuses and species according to contrariety as we directly experience it—that is, through 'a direct perception of *resemblances*'. (DR 34) He begins everywhere with the essential reliability of perception and our capacity to pass from *what appears* to be the case (this is the meaning of the Greek *phainomena*) to conceptual thought. The main problem with this reliance will appear later, but Deleuze's primary concern in this context is to note that for Aristotle, things in their individuality cannot be thought, and no knowledge in the strict sense can be attained of them. This is because in Aristotle's account there is 'too little difference' between individual ferns, or birds, or people. All we can think of these substances is contained at the level of their concept. The individual is strictly unthinkable. The rule of identity in the form of the concept is very clear here: outside of it, there is no rational thought, no science, no philosophy. The restrictions that Aristotle's conception of difference impose end up reducing his ontology to a taxonomic exercise that leaves out every real being in its being and becoming.

The third problem, finally, is nothing other than the absence of an adequate concept of difference. Or, to repeat what we have just said, Aristotle presents an explicit account of difference as both contrariety and analogical distribution, but in both cases it refers us back to a primary identity—the identity of the concept.

The definition of representation

If we have lingered for so long on the case of Aristotle, it is because Deleuze considers his thought to be both originary and paradigmatic. With respect to its originary character, Deleuze could not be more direct:

> Here we find the principle which lies behind a confusion disastrous for the entire philosophy of difference: assigning a distinctive concept of difference is confused with the inscription of difference within concepts in general—the determination of the concept of difference is confused with the inscription of difference in the identity of an undetermined concept. This is the sleight of hand involved in the propitious moment (and perhaps everything else follows: the subordination of difference to opposition, to analogy, and to resemblance, all the aspects of mediation). Difference can be no more than a predicate in the comprehension of a concept. (DR 32)

Aristotle is the intellectual source of western philosophy's destitution of difference.

But he is also paradigmatic for philosophy. Indeed, if we were to isolate the major target of *Difference and Repetition*, it would be what Deleuze calls *representation*, or the *world of representation*. This world is characterized by four interrelated ways in which difference is subordinated to identity or, better, by the subordination of difference to identity in four different registers of thought, all of which are easily recognizable in Aristotle's philosophy.

The first is the (already familiar) subordination of difference to identity in the form of the concept: various kinds of birds, defined on the basis of contrary predicates, fall under the concept 'bird'. We arrive not at a concept of difference, but *conceptual difference*, or difference subordinated to a self-identical concept.

The second concerns phenomenological experience or perception, and involves the subordination of difference to identity in the form of *perceived resemblance*. To say that two things look alike is to necessarily invoke a primary and shared identity.

The third register concerns analogy. As we have just seen very clearly with Aristotle, analogy always refers us back to the supposition of an identity that is distributed across the particular categories or kinds—there is always a 'something in common' that analogy invokes, even when this is not explicit. Analogical reasoning is, for Deleuze, nothing other than judgment, and to judge is always to distribute proportions according to an ideal. In the form of this presupposed ideal, 'the analogy of judgement allows the identity of a concept to subsist'. (DR 33)

The fourth register concerns *opposition*. The predicates that determine a concept ('flying' and 'flightless') are opposed. In Aristotle, this opposition takes the form of contrariety; in later thinkers, notably Hegel, it will appear as contradiction. But whatever its form, opposition is a negative presentation of difference. Like analogy, it implies the existence of an identity to which the opposed predicates will gain their significance. Opposition is difference as *implicit* invocation of identity.

There are many forceful passages in *Difference and Repetition*, but one of the more memorable addresses this fourfold world of representation:

> On precisely these branches, difference is crucified. They form quadripartite fetters under which only what is identical, similar, analogous or opposed can be considered different: *difference becomes an object of representation always in relation to a conceived identity, a judged analogy, an imagined opposition or a perceived similitude.* Under these four coincident figures, difference acquires a sufficient reason in the form of a *principium comparationis*. For this reason, the world of representation is characterised by its inability to conceive of difference in itself. (DR 138)

Three requirements for a philosophy of difference after Aristotle

Earlier I presented the three problems with Aristotle's account that Deleuze raises. But we can also present these in a positive way as the three requirements that Deleuze wishes to meet in order to advance an adequate philosophy of difference.

The **first** of these is the requirement we have already established as one of Deleuze's central goals: to create a concept of difference that is not subordinated to identity, and in particular one that does not confuse a concept of difference with conceptual difference in the way that Aristotle (and not just Aristotle) does.

Second, a fully worked out and explicit ontology will be needed. Aristotle's analogical ontology cannot but posit being as unity. If a genuine philosophy of difference is to be possible, it will need to be able to give difference its full due as fully real, and not as a subordinate conceptual attribution. To render the ideas of difference and being compatible is the second requirement.

Third, at the other end of the spectrum as it were, this concept of being and its concomitant ontology will have to be able to directly address individuality—not abstractly, generally or in the form of the concept, but on its own terms. Since the concept necessarily involves a generality, we can even say that Deleuze's account will have to show us how thought can 'penetrate the subrepresentational' (DI 115) level of reality.

Hegel

Deleuze's investigation of the history of western thought with respect to a concept of difference now turns to two modern philosophers, Leibniz and Hegel. Their specific interest for Deleuze concerns the way in which they overturn the Aristotelian legacy. Deleuze defines Aristotle's particular form of representational thinking as *finite* and *organic*. Aristotle considers both reality and conceptual thought to be constituted of established and discrete but mutually interrelated parts, forming an organic, natural whole. Both Leibniz and Hegel overturn these claims. On the one hand, they will argue for an *infinite* conception of representation; on the other, they break with the stable, naturalized organic world of Aristotle in favour of what Deleuze calls an *orgiastic* vision of reality.

We will begin with Hegel, even though he lived and wrote after Leibniz, for reasons that will become apparent. At the heart of Hegel's philosophy is the idea of a dynamic process. This process is the dialectic: every apparently finite and fixed thing is caught up in a movement that carries it beyond itself. In Platonic thought, 'dialectic' means dialogue in the familiar sense—Socrates and his interlocutors move from every day opinion (*doxa*) towards a higher understanding of something (piety, for instance, in the *Euthyphro*). In Hegel, the movement of what he calls mind or spirit (*Geist*) consists in a passage from what is implicit, abstract and particular towards the explicit, concrete and universal.

Now, Hegel's dynamic view of reality must not be conceived of in terms of some kind of blind vital flux. This processual unfolding not only can be understood rationally, it must be—it *is* rational, it possesses a logical structure.

The logical movement of the dialectic proceeds by way of negation. Consider the following schematized example of the formation of the State as discussed in the *Philosophy of Right*. Hegel begins with the family, which subsumes the individual family members into a single unit. The family unit therefore already involves a contradiction: it is necessarily composed of more than one person, but these individuals do not possess the freedom or the recognition of their freedom *as* family members. Individual freedom appears instead in the abstract individual presupposed by civil society, itself drawn from the model of the market and its individuated stake-holders. Civil society negates the family, takes the predicate 'belongs to the family of X' to be irrelevant to legal standing. But at the same time, the kind of legal individuality and freedom that it involves remains abstract—it is not strictly speaking *my* freedom, *my* individuality, but a kind of placeholder for anyone whatsoever. It appears to be real freedom, but it is, paradoxically, the freedom of nobody. In Hegel's view, it is only with the formation of the State that these implicit contradictions are overcome. State society—and in this sense it negates the abstract universal freedom of civil society—is the transformed unification of the family and the civil state, of togetherness and individuality, of freedom and constraint. The same claim about the constitution and transformation of nature and spirit is found everywhere in Hegel's work.

Now, difference takes the form of contradiction in Hegel's thought, and Deleuze quotes his *Science of Logic* to this effect: 'Difference as such is already *implicitly* contradiction'. (2.279) But that contradiction is the true sense of difference is clearly borne out by the movement of the dialectic itself. The more and the less, the relatively large and small do not get to the heart of the dialectical movement. More importantly, this conception completely exceeds the simple, static finite conception of difference at work in Aristotle. In Hegel, difference is the real productive movement of spirit, and one that he does not hesitate to speak of as *infinite* in character: in the movement of the dialectic, each particular finite moment comes to 'count for something infinite'. (*Encyclopedia Logic* §82)

Despite this, Deleuze finds Hegel's philosophy wanting, and in two ways that are of particular interest to us. First: while Hegel certainly outstrips Aristotle by situating difference outside of simple finite contrariety, he ultimately refers everything back to an identity, even if it is an identity that must each time be produced. 'The dialectic has a *positive* result [which] is not *simple, formal* unity, but a *unity of distinct determinations*'. (*Encyclopedia Logic* §82) He will even go so far as to describe his philosophy as 'a circle of circles' (*Encyclopedia Logic* §15)—a remark that explains the origin of Deleuze's denunciation of Hegel's 'insipid monocentricity'. (DR 263) Of course, Deleuze is quite aware that for Hegel this identity is an identity-in-difference, but in his view, this still gives identity an illegitimate pride of place.

The second point is a related one. What is it, after all (Deleuze asks), that is expressed in a continually more concrete and universal fashion through the dialectic? Hegel calls it the *Concept* [*Begriff*]: 'that which is truly *permanent* and *substantial* in the manifold and accidentality of appearance and fleeting externalization, is the *concept* of the thing, *the universal which is present in it*'. (*Science of Logic* 21.15) For all the reach and force of Hegel's thought, then, what Deleuze sees when he examines it from the point of view of the concept of difference is a gigantic replication of Aristotle's errors: difference is again subordinated to identity in the form of the concept.

> Thus, Hegelian contradiction appears to push difference to the limit, but this path is a dead end which brings it back to identity, making identity the sufficient condition for difference to exist and be thought. It is only in relation to the identical, as a function of the identical, that contradiction is the *greatest* difference. The intoxications and giddinesses are feigned, the obscure is already clarified from the outset. (DR 263)

Leibniz

But now we turn to a philosopher Deleuze presents, at least in this context, as Hegel's obverse: Leibniz. In Leibniz's philosophy as in Hegel's, we find an overturning of Aristotle's finite and static ontology, though in this case it is not the infinitely large movement of the Concept through history but the mutterings of the infinitely small that are drawn to our attention.

Leibniz's philosophy turns around his account of what exists: monads, 'the true atoms of nature and, in brief, the elements of things'. ('Monadology', §3) To speak of the monad as an atom is a little misleading however. Unlike the discrete bits of material stuff that the word 'atom' might invoke, monads are ideal or spiritual in character. 'We could call them *metaphysical points*', he says. ('A New System of Nature', 142) This means in the first instance that their relationship to each other and to the world in general is not like that of cogs in a watch.

On the one hand, the world is not made up of monads as if of elementary particles; neither does the world that Leibniz's God creates (the famous 'best of all possible worlds') exist apart from the monads. Instead, the world is a totality or whole expressed by each monad from its own point of view—two people standing beside each other at the sea's edge perceive the same sea, the same waves, but each from their own perspective. Or, to use an example favoured by Leibniz:

> Just as the same city viewed from different directions appears entirely different and, as it were, multiplied perspectivaly, in just the same way it happens that, because of the infinite multitude of simple substances, there are, as it were, just as many different universes, which are, nevertheless only perspectives on a single one, corresponding to the different points of view of each monad. (*Monadology* §57)

The great twentieth century Leibnizian Italo Calvino's *Invisible Cities* is, among other things, a meditation on this example:

> For those who pass it without entering, the city is one thing; it is another for those who are trapped by it and never leave. There is the city where you arrive for the first time; and there is another city which you leave never to return. Each deserves a different name; perhaps I have already spoken of Irene under other names; perhaps I have spoken only of Irene. (*Invisible Cities*, 124)

In short, every monad is a 'living mirror of the universe', ('Monadology', §56) which itself only exists as expressed in the monads. This concept of expression will play an essential part later in *Difference and Repetition* as we will see.

On the other hand, monads have no causal relations with each other. What monads perceive as these interactions—the respective experiences of two lovers kissing, for instance—unfolds in isolation within the enclosed reality of the respective monads. That they are coordinated arises from the nature of each monad. When God creates the world, then, he does not merely institute an initial state that then proceeds on the basis of its own laws. The world thus created is the whole world from beginning to end. From God's point of view, what appears to be a temporal sequence for us is really a perfectly organised logical structure, the analogue of the barrel in a roller organ or pianola, whose pre-established harmonies are played out perfectly because they are inscribed in advance. Or, to adopt the monadic point of view, we can say that 'the present is pregnant [*gros*] with the future and laden with the past', ('Preface to the New Essays', 296) a future and a past that all monads share because it is the past and future of the same world that they both express.

Now, if the world as the unity expressed by all the monads constitutes the 'higher' level of Leibniz's ontology, the 'lower' level—and the level of most interest to Deleuze here—is what explains the constitution of the unique experience of particular monads. The world that each monad experiences is the same world, but what is more, Leibniz will argue, every monad experiences the *whole* world: 'Monads all go confusedly to infinity, to the whole'. ('Monadology', §60) Each of us hear every least sound and feel the least motion. The smouldering of a cigarette in the bar downstairs, the sound of moth crawling along a wall in Prague, these are part of our experience of the world. Now, obviously we don't experience these immensely diminutive sensation in the same way that we experience what is in our nearer proximity, the sound of these keys as I type for instance. Leibniz will say that we only experience a portion of the world *clearly*, while this broader background is present in an *obscure* state.

Leibniz's signal example is the perception of the sea:

> I usually make use of the example of the roar or noise of the sea that strikes us when we are at the shore. In order to hear this noise as we do, we must hear the parts that make up this whole, that is, we must hear the noise of each wave, even though each of these small noises is known only in the confused assemblage of all the others, and would not be noticed if the wave making it were the only one. ('Preface to the New Essays', 295)

But in turn, the perception of each wave is made up of a multitude of small drops of water, which are also all perceived, but only obscurely. As both Leibniz and the poet Tomas Tranströmer indicate, the degree of our distinct perceptions is dynamic, shifting when we fall asleep, for instance, or get drunk,

> Or when a person goes so deep into a sickness
>
> that his days all become flickering sparks, a swarm,
>
> feeble and cold on the horizon (Tranströmer, 'Track', 35)

So each monad perceives a shifting part of the whole world clearly, and the rest obscurely—each monad is only in part conscious, a consciousness that flowers from an unconscious depth of what Leibniz calls *petites perceptions*, little perceptions. These little perceptions are not concepts, or things, but, Deleuze notes, infinitely small *subrepresentational* differences. Both the conscious experience of objects and conceptual thought—representational thought—arise through an integration or summing-up of these differences into identities; the essential, the real, is constructed from the inessential thoughtless muttering of being. In sum, then: 'Leibniz discovers in the clear, finite idea the restlessness of the infinitely small, a restlessness also made up of intoxication, giddiness, evanescence and even death'. (DR 45)

With this summary of Leibniz's thought in hand, one that will later serve us in good stead, we can now turn directly to his concept of difference, which is found in his differential conception of the unconscious. In Deleuze's view, 'No one has been better able to immerse thought in the element of difference and provide it with a differential unconscious, surround it with little glimmerings and singularities', than Leibniz. (DR 213)

And yet, he remains prey to representation in the form of his presupposition of the *unity of the world*. In a way that parallels the movement of the dialectic in Hegel, for Leibniz all monadic perception tends towards this identity, even if it never appears all at once or for itself. This is what Deleuze calls 'a principle of convergence'. (DR 51) The world appears as a limit, a form of the negative, that monadic perception is always oriented by—this was, he says, 'Leibniz's only error' (DR 51), but it is not a small one.

Difference beyond representation

Though Aristotle, Leibniz and Hegel hardly account for the whole of Western philosophy, Deleuze's survey of their respective positions shows how poorly difference has been treated along this trajectory. Neither finite nor infinite accounts of representation manage to ground an adequate concept of difference, since both, in the final analysis, insist on the primacy of the identity of the concept. Deleuze recognizes that neither Hegel nor Leibniz endorses identity in the way that Aristotle does. Nevertheless, they both have a way of 'taking the principle of identity particularly seriously, giving it an infinite value and rendering it coextensive with the whole, and in this manner allowing it to reign over existence itself'. (DR 49) He continues, writing that:

> The point is that in the last resort infinite representation does not free itself from the principle of identity as a presupposition of representation. This is why it remains subject to the condition of the convergence of series [harmony between the monads] in the case of Leibniz and to the condition of the monocentring of circles in the case of Hegel. (DR 49)

Of the three, it is Leibniz that will prove decisive for Deleuze's project in *Difference and Repetition*. Despite his remaining commitment to representation, Leibniz provides Deleuze with two partial resources. The first is the theory of *petites perceptions*, which constitutes an attempt to speak of difference in non- and sub-representational terms. This answers, of course, to the **first** requirement for a philosophy of difference identified in the wake of Aristotle; we will later see that Deleuze too will account for the constitution of reality beginning with a network of differential relations. The **second** is the Leibnizian theory of the monad. Recall Aristotle's failure with respect to individual beings, which he considered beneath the level of conceptual thought. Leibniz's monad is a positive theory of the individual as an expressive locus. Like the differential structure of the *petites perceptions*, this expressive individual will hold a key place in Deleuze's own positive account of reality.

UNIVOCITY

But if we now turn to the middle part of the first chapter of *Difference and Repetition*, we find Deleuze engaged with the **third** requirement, namely an ontology (an account of the nature of being) adequate to difference. He advances his argument by examining another trinity of figures from the history of philosophy, each of whom elaborate variously successful versions of a *univocal ontology*.

First exemplar: Duns Scotus

The term 'univocal' is drawn from the work of the first figure, the thirteenth century theologian John Duns Scotus. Like all scholastic thinkers, Duns Scotus worked within the ambient context of the thought of Aristotle, who was so influential at the time he was just known as 'the Philosopher'. Duns Scotus' major contribution, in Deleuze's view, was to break with the Aristotelian foreclosure of an explicit highest genus ('being'). In fact, Scotus writes, being 'has a primacy of commonness in regard to [...] the quidditative concepts of the genera, species, individuals, and all their essential parts, and to the Uncreated Being'. (Duns Scotus, 'Concerning Metaphysics', 4) The assertions 'there are scarfs', 'this cat is grey', 'you were still sleeping', affirm being of you, the cat and scarfs in the same way, regardless of their particularities. Being is not a genus to which you, the scarf and the cat belong, but the commonness *of* being that they share. Philosophy can therefore affirm the being *of* each being *as* a being.

Deleuze's endorsement of this position is very strong: 'There has only ever been one ontology, that of Duns Scotus, which gave being a single voice'. (DR 35) In light of this, it is perhaps already clear why he will advance his famous claim that 'A single voice raises the clamor of being'. (DR 35)

Nevertheless, he identifies a major limitation with the way in which Scotus deploys this insight. As a theologian, he was concerned to avoid falling into pantheism—and also, no doubt, being thrown into a fire nailed to a log. The doctrine of the univocity of being could be no more than a speculative claim without any follow-on effects. This is why he understood 'univocal being as neutral or indifferent' (DR 40)—so that his discovery would have no further consequences for his thought.

Second exemplar: Spinoza

The great rationalist philosopher Benedict de Spinoza constitutes Deleuze's second exemplary thinker of univocity. Indeed, Deleuze posits him as something like Scotus' direct successor, and one who makes good on the promise of the notion of univocity. He does this by making univocal being 'an object of pure affirmation'. (DR 40)

Spinoza's philosophy revolves around the assertion that there exists a single *substance*, which we can call God or Nature (the famous *Deus sive Natura*). Particular things do not have reality independent of this substance, but are modifications or *modes* of this substance. These modes—you and I, that book, this cigarette ash—exist as expressions of substance's power to exist, a power which is the essence of substance, what defines it.

This means, for Deleuze, that Spinoza's affirmation of the univocal being of substance is immediately and necessarily an affirmation of every individual being. It is not a claim that can be made in a neutral, abstract fashion like Scotus did: 'With Spinoza, univocal being ceases to be neutralised and becomes expressive; it becomes a truly expressive and affirmative proposition'. (DR 40) Even this cigarette, this flame, this smattering of ash are affirmed as a real and full expressions of being.

Nonetheless, Deleuze detects a problem in Spinoza's account. It lies in the fact that 'there still remains a difference between substance and the modes: Spinoza's substance appears independent of the modes, while the modes are dependent on substance, but as though on something other than themselves'. (DR 40) That is to say: the level of individual being is made to turn around a substance that is *self-identical*. However sophisticated Spinoza's thought might be in affirming difference at the level of the modes—and it certainly is—everything redounds upon substance, the incomparable One. The problem here is therefore different from the one he detects in Duns Scotus. In that case, the ontological proposition of univocity had no consequences; in Spinoza, the problem is that univocity seems to have been confused with monism, the view that a single thing exists. So, even given his unquestionable superiority with respect to Scotus, Deleuze thinks that Spinoza has still taken a step backwards from the point of view of a philosophy of difference.

Third exemplar: Nietzsche

Scotus gives us a shallow, stage-prop formulation of univocity; Spinoza's affirmation is full-throated, but it still leaves us in the thrall of identity. What is required is to extend this affirmation of univocity beyond the confines of identity thinking and to difference itself. Or, as Deleuze puts it in a fine passage,

> Substance must itself be said of the modes and only of the modes. Such a condition can be satisfied only at the price of a more general categorical reversal according to which being is said of becoming, identity, of that which is different, of the multiple, etc. That identity not be first, that it exist as a principle but as a second principle, as a principle *become*; that it revolve around the Different: such would be the nature of a Copernican revolution which opens up the possibility of difference having its own concept, rather than being maintained under the domination of a concept in general already understood as identical. (DR 40-1)

How can this be accomplished? Deleuze finds the answer in a perhaps surprising third exemplar: Friedrich Nietzsche. More than this, he indicates that a particular, and particularly difficult, concept is the key. To make identity turn around difference? 'Nietzsche meant nothing more than this by the eternal return'. (DR 41)

For our purposes here, we can gloss Deleuze's reading of the doctrine of the eternal return by saying that it is, for him, Nietzsche's conception of time. It presents time not as a neutral container analogous to space that does not affect its contents, but as the reality of becoming itself. To say that becoming is prior to being amounts to saying that *there is time*, and therefore that nothing is timeless, changeless.

But this means in turn that, for Nietzsche, the time of the eternal return is absolute, absolutely fundamental. Nothing stands outside of it. It is in this sense that the eternal return is a thought of univocal being— it names the commonness of all beings without affirming any kind of identity. All that beings share is their merciless subjection to time. This is why Deleuze will say that the eternal return 'is the being-equal of all that is unequal'. (DR 41) All that beings share—the only 'thing'—is a subordination to time as the motor of the different.

But because we are now speaking in terms of time, which really exists and conditions reality, and no longer speculative thought, we must stop thinking about univocity as a doctrine, and start thinking of it— Deleuze insists—as something that is genuinely accomplished: 'eternal return is the univocity of being, the effective realisation of that univocity.

In the eternal return, univocal being is not only thought and even affirmed, but effectively realised'. (DR 41-2)

The essential point here is this: that the univocity of being is not secured by a thought of *substance* but by the reality of *time*. Consequently, the full sense of this proposal will have to wait until we give Deleuze's analysis of time in *Difference and Repetition* its proper due at the end of this chapter. But before we move on, we cannot avoid reading or re-reading the capstone text of the first chapter of the book, in which the stakes of univocity are clearly stated:

> In effect, the essential in univocity is not that Being is said in a single and same sense, but that it is said, in a single and same sense, *of* all its individuating differences or intrinsic modalities. Being is the same for all these modalities, but these modalities are not the same. It is 'equal' for all, but they themselves are not equal. It is said of all in a single sense, but they themselves do not have the same sense [...] Being is said in a single and same sense of everything of which it is said, but that of which it is said differs: it is said of difference itself. (DR 36)

THE SUBJECTIVE MISRECOGNITION OF DIFFERENCE

A series of objective misrecognitions of difference are found in the history of Western thought. They consist in paralogisms—arguments that appear sound but involve false or confused premises. But for Deleuze, the head-on critique of these errors is accompanied by the realization that the major obstacles for a philosophy of difference are to be located at a more profound level and are consequently difficult to overturn in this direct fashion.

We can directly challenge *what* philosophers have said about difference, but, Deleuze will insist, the greater difficulty lies in *how* we think about everything, including the nature of thought itself. There is, he says, an habituated set of presuppositions that skew thinking in advance. They constitute what Deleuze will call the *dogmatic image of thought*, and constitutes the basis for the subjective misrecognition of difference.

This image of thought is made manifest whenever a phrase like 'Everybody knows, no one can deny' (DR 130) is appended, explicitly or implicitly, to any assertion. At a first level, this pertains to philosophy's perennial enemy, *opinion* or *doxa*. Deleuze refers us to a famous opening line penned by Descartes: 'Good sense is the best distributed thing in the world'. (*Discourse on the Method*, 1) The idea that everyone actually possesses good sense cannot bear even a single moment of scrutiny, Deleuze notes, but that does not get in the way of its broad and uncritical acceptance as an opinion about human beings.

But it is not the case that Descartes is simply and unreflectively advancing a ludicrous opinion in the *Discourse on the Method*. 'What makes Descartes a philosopher is that he makes use of that saying in order to erect an image of thought as it is *in principle:* good nature and an affinity with the true belong in principle to thought, whatever the difficulty of translating this principle into fact or rediscovering it behind the facts'. (DR 132) So there is a second level to the dogmatic image: the first Deleuze calls its 'natural' form, while the second is characterised as 'philosophical'. It is important to see that the philosophical form of the dogmatic image *derives from* the natural form. It extrapolates or *traces* (a term Deleuze is fond of for this operation) from the level of opinion or doxa in order to establish an unexamined but quasi-formalised basis from which to proceed in relation to theoretical questions. At the very end of this chapter, we will see that it is this second-order image of thought which is the implicit foundation for the objective conceptual errors we have diagnosed above.

For now, though, there are four things that should be kept in mind before we go into the details of the third chapter of *Difference and Repetition*. The first, to repeat, is that the dogmatic image does not explicitly assert any particular claim, but rather involves implicit beliefs about the nature of thinking itself: 'It is *in terms of* this image that everybody knows and is presumed to know what it means to think'. (DR 131) Second, and as we will see in more detail, the image functions by spontaneously but implicitly subordinating difference to identity. Third, Deleuze's description of the image identifies its eight main traits, what he calls the *postulates* of the dogmatic image. Postulates, for Deleuze, 'are not propositions the acceptance of which the philosopher demands; but, on the contrary, propositional themes which remain implicit and are understood in a pre-philosophical manner'. (DR 131) Finally, his goal will *not* be to propose an alternative image of thought, but to show how thought has no natural state such that we could extract its universal features. In a magnificent passage—one of several in this chapter—he writes that

> the conditions of a philosophy which would be without any kind of presuppositions appear all the more clearly: instead of being supported by the moral Image of thought, it would take as its point of departure a radical critique of this Image [...] It would find its difference or its true beginning, not in an agreement with the *pre-*

> *philosophical* Image but in a rigorous struggle against this Image, which it would denounce as *non-philosophical*. As a result, it would discover its authentic repetition in a thought without an Image, even at the cost of the greatest destructions and the greatest demoralisations, and a philosophical obstinacy with no ally but paradox [...] As though thought could begin to think, and continually begin again, only when liberated from the Image and its postulates. (DR 132)

In what follows, and rather than detailing each postulate in its two forms (natural and philosophical), we will follow the central narrative thread of Deleuze's account.

Good will, common sense, recognition

The first three postulates of the dogmatic image of thought constitute its kernel. Invoking Descartes, Deleuze calls the first the postulate of *the principle*. This is the supposition that thought naturally—as a matter of principle—seeks the truth and is oriented by it. It claims that 'there is a natural capacity for thought endowed with a talent for truth or an affinity with the true, under the double aspect of a *good will on the part of the thinker* and an *upright nature on the part of thought*'. (DR 131)

Consider the term 'natural' in this quote. The postulate tells us that thought has a nature, eternal and unchanging. Regardless of what kind of person I in fact am, my thought possesses this character by its very nature. It is, moreover, quite transparently a moral supposition—and this is the real meaning of the 'good' in 'good sense' (not to mention the 'upright' in 'upright nature'). Deleuze insists on this point:

> Morality alone is capable of persuading us that thought has a good nature and the thinker a good will, and only the good can ground the supposed affinity between thought and the True—what else if not this Morality, this Good which gives thought to the true and the true to thought? (DR 132)

The second postulate of *common sense* is both more complex and more interesting. If thought is naturally oriented towards the truth, how does it function? We know, first, that there is not one sense of the word 'thought': you remember, you sense, you reason, you imagine, and so on. Thought is a common noun that describes a whole set of capacities, or *faculties*, of thinking. The postulate of common sense presents us with two correlative claims, the natural and philosophical versions. On the one hand (natural form), it assures us of the *commonness* of the object of thought. The cigarette whose scent you first imagine from the other room when you hear the match strike, the cigarette whose heat you feel when you take a drag, the cigarette you reason about as you justify smoking it to yourself, and that you later ruefully and guiltily remember—these are the same cigarette. On the other hand (philosophical form), these various faculties of thinking are supposed to involve a naturally harmonious interrelationship: thought as a placid council.

The third postulate in this foundational triad is the postulate of *the model*. How, in general terms, do we grasp the world? What is the fundamental act of thinking—whether I sense, remember, reason, or whatever—relative to an object? The dogmatic answer is that thought *recognizes* its objects. What is that I'm smelling? Ah yes, an apricot. I see it now, the Hagia Sophia. Yes, I remember: her name was Bella. Key here is the fact that, on the dogmatic view, *nothing can fundamentally surprise us*. The very form of thought, on the dogmatic model, already anticipates every possible content. Deleuze is more direct: 'The form of recognition has never sanctioned anything but the recognisable and the recognised; form will never inspire anything but conformities'. (DR 134)

Together, as I said, these first three postulates—'a naturally upright thought, an in principle natural common sense, and a transcendental model of recognition' (DR 134)—give us the kernel of the dogmatic image. They describe not what we think at any given moment, but *how* we think about thought.

Kant's transcendental idealism

Deleuze's discussion of the image of thought begins with an invocation of Descartes, but with these opening postulates we find ourselves on Kantian rather than Cartesian grounds. And indeed, the 'Image of Thought' chapter is from start to finish framed by Kantian terminology and aims at a radical critique of Kant's project, so much so that these initial postulates already give us a clear sense of what Kant is up to and where its shortcomings lie.

Here, we will just sketch the account of the first of his three great Critiques, the *Critique of Pure Reason*. Given our concerns, we can say that Kant's approach in the first *Critique* involves two essential commitments (later we will come back to considerably complicate this summary). The first is that human thought has formal or logical characteristics that are not derived from empirical experience. *What* we encounter in the world belongs to the world, but *how* we experience belongs only to the sphere of thought. This leads him to distinguish between reality as it is *in itself*, and reality as it is *for us*. Kant's second essential commitment is to the idea that human cognition is not simple, but involves a plurality of different functions, capacities or *faculties* in thought. In the first *Critique*, he is interested in four of these faculties, all of which are required in order that human knowledge and experience can be possible.

First is the faculty of *sensibility* (though because all four of these faculties are integral to and function together in experience for Kant, this 'first' is relative). Sensibility names our passive capacity to receive sensations, our receptiveness to encounters with the world as it is in itself. Through it, we acquire sensory manifolds or multiplicities (think of the sensory elements of the experience of the cigarette), which Kant terms *intuitions*. Now, while sensibility is passive, receptive, intuitions are not undifferentiated; they possess spatio-temporal characteristics, which is to say that intuitions are reciprocally *located*. That is, sensibility is the locus of the empty forms of space and time; when I encounter something in sensation, its *apprehension* (as Kant calls it) is subject to these two forms.

Sensibility is a passive faculty, in the sense that it has no control over what is experienced and cannot fabricate sensations by itself, but it is also *constitutive* of experience. Without intuitions, there can be no knowledge, and no experience. It is not, however, the sole source of experience. The other major contributor is a second faculty which Kant calls the *understanding*. The understanding is the locus of the rules of cognition, the concepts of the understanding or the *categories*. Like a conceptual grid that is actively applied to the intuitions produced by sensibility, the categories provide us with the elementary rules for meaningfulness in experience. Or, as Kant puts it, the categories provide us with the laws of nature themselves:

> we ourselves bring into the appearances that order and regularity that we call nature, and moreover we would not be able to find it there if we, or the nature of our mind, had not originally put it there [...] The understanding is thus not merely a faculty for making rules through the comparison of the appearances: it is itself the legislation for nature, i.e., without understanding there would not be any nature at all. (*Critique of Pure Reason* A125–126).

Between these two, there is the *imagination*, the faculty that has the task of bringing together the two sources of experience, the concepts of the understanding and the intuitions of sensibility. Kant calls this task *reproduction*, the synthesis of a 'manifold of intuitions into the form of an image'. (*Critique of Pure Reason* A120) His account of the imagination as this productive middle ground between intuition and concept—'a blind but indispensable function of the soul' (A78B103)—is infamous, and we will return to it a little later. For now, we need only to note its role as the third faculty required for the constitution of experience in Kant's system.

Sensibility, the understanding and the imagination together constitute experience and knowledge. Kant now adds that a fourth faculty, *Reason*, plays a *regulative* rather than a constitutive role in the formation of knowledge and experience. What does this mean? Consider the fact that the ongoing production of experience is not itself systematic. It responds to contingent encounters in sensation as they are encountered. But knowledge and experience do possess an order. This order is provided through the operation of the Ideas of Reason. Unlike the categories, these ideas do not apply directly to intuitions; neither are they representations of real objects. The idea of *totality* is a useful illustration here. Clearly, we can never experience 'everything'. The idea of this totality, however, guides the organization of scientific knowledge: contributions from physics, botany, cell biology are on their own terms discrete, but they each build together in a systematic way towards a knowledge of everything. Without this idea, science would be strictly speaking impossible. So the genuine function of Reason is to provide human thought with a set of internal horizons that—like the perceptual horizon—systematize and organize without imposing any particular form on what is organized.

We will return to the nature of these Ideas in the next section of this chapter, which provide Deleuze an important component of his own construction in *Difference and Repetition*. But for now, there is a final important pair of concepts that round out Kant's account, and these concern the nature of human subjectivity. On the one hand, there is a subject who is subject *to* experience. This self is passive, the locus of *what I undergo*, as Kant puts it in his *Anthropology from a Pragmatic Point of View* (1.1.§24). If I smoke a lit cigar like the Spanish women of Lima, I can describe its taste, and the way the plumes hang in the air, but I can also describe how the cigar *makes me feel*.

This empirical self is doubled by a formal subject. In a famous passage, Kant writes that 'The **I think** must **be able** to accompany all my representations; for otherwise something would be represented in me that could not be thought at all, which is as much as to say that the representation would either be impossible or else at least would be nothing for me'. (*Critique of Pure Reason* B131-2) His point is that in order for my experiences to be *mine*—to be unified *for* me—they must be formally attributed to the same subject. Kant calls this aspect of subjectivity the *transcendental unity of apperception* (i.e., reflective consciousness). I never experience this formal subjectivity—indeed, it cannot be experienced, since it is only the formal guarantee of the coherence of my experience as mine. As Kant puts it: 'In attaching "I" to our thoughts, we designate the subject only transcendentally ... without noting in it any quality whatsoever—in fact, without knowing anything of it either directly or by inference'. (*Critique of Pure Reason* A355)

Notice, finally, that these two forms of subjectivity are separated from each other by the form of time in sensibility. I experience myself *in* time (the time in which I smoke the cigar, the time of writing this book, etc.), but the formal unity that the coherence of my experience presupposes—the pure and empty form of subjectivity—is indifferent to time. This is a point of the highest significance for Deleuze, as we will see; he thinks that it is this that makes Kant the first truly modern philosopher.

Sensation: (from) the shock to thought

The fact that the whole of the 'Image of Thought' chapter is framed in exactly these Kantian terms can be difficult to appreciate. This is because of the dramatic way in which Deleuze overturns, scrambles and reassembles them. This critical reassembly begins with the category of sensation.

As I said above, the postulate of the model fundamentally means that nothing we encounter can surprise us. But we *are* surprised. I am not always able to immediately cope with and make sense of what I encounter in the world. It is at the point of contact with the world that this shock originates, which is, for both Kant and Deleuze, the point at which I encounter *sensation*, prior to any formal or conceptual element coming into play. So, to return to Kant's transcendental idealism again for a moment, Deleuze's claim is 1) that Kant has illegitimately presupposed that sensation is amenable to the categories, that it is, as it were, *pre-digested*. But worse than this, 2) he assumes that we engage with the placid recognizable world on our own account—that thought naturally *thinks*.

For Deleuze, though, both are entirely unjustified assumptions. Contrary to the first postulate, thought only *begins as a result of a shock*: 'Something in the world forces us to think. This something is an object not of recognition but of a fundamental encounter'. (DR 139) And, to quote an amazing passage that extends this point:

> Certainties force us to think no more than doubts. [Truths, like] concepts [...] lack the claws of absolute necessity—in other words, of an original violence inflicted upon thought; the claws of a strangeness or an enmity which alone would awaken thought from its natural stupor or eternal possibility: there is only involuntary thought, aroused but constrained within thought, and all the more absolutely necessary for being born, illegitimately, of fortuitousness in the world. Thought is primarily trespass and violence, the enemy, and nothing presupposes philosophy: everything begins with misophy. Do not count upon thought to ensure the relative necessity of what it thinks. Rather, count upon the contingency of an encounter with that which forces thought to raise up and educate the absolute necessity of an act of thought or a passion to think. (DR 139)

Telling here is the description of trauma provided by that tragicomic almanac of received opinion, the American Psychological Association's *Diagnostic and Statistical Manual*: 'The person has experienced an event that is outside the range of human experience.' (120) This sentiment is, from the point of view of *Difference and Repetition*, more true than it knows and certainly less tautological. Not only is it not natural to think, the fact that we think about anything at all is only the result of having encountered something in sensation—something that is entirely alien to us, and certainly to our everyday recognition-based knowledge of the world—that forces us to think. In sum: Deleuze opposes the first three postulates of the dogmatic image by insisting on the *non-natural, contingent* nature of thought, and its origin in an *encounter in sensation*.

Four components for a new doctrine of the faculties

Deleuze's account of sensation as a shock that gives rise to thought is not an isolated moment in this chapter. Aside from its centrality in the account, and the primacy that he will give sensation throughout, it provides him with the cornerstone of his attempt to explain what he calls 'thought without an image'. In the more technical Kantian terms we have just introduced, Deleuze wants to develop his own doctrine of the faculties. He says in fact that this is not precisely his aim. Despite the fact that 'the doctrine of the faculties is an entirely necessary component of the system of philosophy,' (DR 143) the immediate goal is instead just to 'determine the nature of its requirements.' (DR 144) This means that Deleuze is not going to provide us with a comprehensive list of the faculties. Instead, he will dwell on four components any such account would have to include.

We have just seen the first component: the new account of the faculties must begin with the assertion that thought is *not natural*, but is the object of a *genesis* in relation to *sensation*. But what is meant by 'thought' here? The main point of any doctrine of the faculties is surely that there is more than one kind of thinking. In Kant, we have seen four: sensibility, imagination, understanding and reason. Or again, in the *Meditations*, Descartes also proposes four—the intellect, the senses, the will and the imagination—which differ in nature and their interrelations to Kant's. The previous question can thus be refined: what accounts for the genesis, not of thought in general, but of *particular* faculties in thought? In these passages, following Kant, Deleuze sometimes uses the word 'thought' to denote a particular faculty of thought, but for the moment we'll use the word in a general sense; we'll come back to this at the very end of this chapter in order to clarify the two senses in which he uses the word.

Deleuze thinks that the identification of thought as plural is decisive. A primary reason for this is that, if thought is engendered through a shock—the encounter with something we cannot recognize, are not prepared for—then the resulting 'ways of thinking', or faculties, will differ depending on the kind of shock we experience: each faculty has its *own* 'involuntary adventures'. (DR 145) An example that is familiar to everyone who reads this is that of reading Deleuze, or any great philosopher, for the first time. This constitutes a confrontation that immediately presses your capacity to think in concepts right up against its limit. You encounter something that demands you think it, and yet you cannot. It's not a matter of another kind of thought—you're not trying to *imagine* what Deleuze means, you're trying to *think* it. This is the initial and primary act of thinking for Deleuze: the impulsion, the involuntary grasp of thought that involves a particular and peculiar kind of problematic object. The object addresses itself to one faculty, engendering its activity.

Reading the work of a new philosopher imposes itself on your capacity to think with concepts, but at the limit of this capacity, where your capacity to think and your incapacity to do so meet; an involuntary memory imposes itself on your capacity to remember but at the limit of this capacity, the point where remembering and forgetting meet. Deleuze calls this primary activity of thought the *transcendent* operation of a faculty. He means by this that the problematic object encountered forces thought *beyond* what it is currently capable of, and that in doing so it breaks any connection that thought, or memory, or imagination have with the simple empirical act of 'thinking about', or 'remembering where', or 'imagining that'.

So, the second component of this proto-theory of the faculties is that they first and fundamentally operate in a transcendent, *monomaniacal* fashion in response to their unique problematic object.

Deleuze's third component is a response to the postulate of common sense; it answers the question 'how do different faculties of thought interact?' For the dogmatic image of thought, the answer is that faculties function together harmoniously—they exhibit a spontaneous harmony, such that the object of sensation is the same as the object of memory, of understanding, and so on. But this cannot be the case for Deleuze, given the second point we've just seen. As he quips, 'there is no *amicability*' (DR 145). The portrait of the faculties working in placid harmony in the service of knowledge that Kant draws in the *Critique of Pure Reason* only gives us thought in its least significant aspect. Or, as Deleuze will also put it, 'the harmony between the faculties can appear only in the form of a *discordant harmony*, since each communicates to the other only the violence which confronts it with its own difference and its divergence from the others'. (DR 146) Simply put, if the faculties communicate with each other, it is not calmly, with reference to a supposedly identical object, but *violently*, by troubling each other, transmitting shocks and imposing the need for new leaps and transformations on each other. The first encounter with Szechuan food demands a transformation not just for sensibility, but also for memory (it troubles your recollection of the pantheon of past great meals), for your imagination (what you imagine good food—and even food itself—to be like), and so on. Through the haze, it becomes clear that nothing will be the same again. Or, overcome by a memory that arises in me involuntarily of the taste of a kiss, the sentence I was in the middle of writing is interrupted, forcing me to begin the work of argument again, my concentration shattered. Or to return to the example of first reading Deleuze, the effort to think what is unthinkable ends up at moments provoking memory too—some echoes of things Deleuze says seem to sound in the corners of your memory, but you can't place where they're from.

Instead of the first *Critique*'s water-colour painting of a hand-cranked machine in a bucolic setting, we should picture thought in its discordant operation as what a roiling lightning storm would look like from the inside. Sharp differences in pressure and temperature give rise to a lightning bolt and clap of thunder, shifting the entire storm around, setting up new loci of pressure and heat, and transmitting the potential for another explosion at a different level.

Fourth and final is Deleuze's emphasis on the particular role of sensation in thought. It is true that all faculties arise in the encounter with a problematic object that addresses only it, but we nevertheless need to appreciate the fact that problems are *first* encountered in sensation. In other words, in a passage that presages some important later developments in *Difference and Repetition*, 'it is always by means of an intensity that thought comes to us'. (DR 144) So the advent of faculties in thinking happens, as Deleuze puts it, along a fuse that is lit in sensation. I encounter a problem *in* sensation, which conveys this shock to, for instance, memory—I suddenly smell her perfume, and this freezes me in place on the Metro, grasping for the memory that I can't recall, overwhelmed and transfixed.

From error to stupidity and madness

Now, if we take a look again at the postulates of common sense and recognition, we can identify a further problem. Taken together, these postulates tell us that there are no radical gaps in thought. Common sense says that there are no gaps between the different faculties, that they converge around a supposedly self-identical object. 'Recognition' tells us that there is no gap between us and the world, and that what we encounter we are already prepared to make sense of. But then, how can we explain failures in thought? We often misrecognize things, for starters—maybe a small ruby red grapefruit is mistaken for an orange in the supermarket, but maybe I also mistakenly embrace someone else from behind who is not him. Worse than this, sometimes we forget things: where we put the lighter, but also the names of close friends. Worse again, our capacity to think can completely collapse: we can, indeed, in fact, go mad, and we do, some of us, every day. How can any of this be explained?

The dogmatic image includes an answer to this question, in the form of another postulate, the *postulate of error*. It states that if thought fails, it does so for merely empirical contingent reasons *unrelated to thinking itself*. This is why 'error' is paradigmatic: thought itself naturally seeks the truth. Human beings can stray from the path by virtue of being fallible finite creatures—but not by virtue of being thinkers. The 'terrible Trinity of madness, stupidity and malevolence' (DR 149) appears, from this point of view, to be a catalogue of merely empirical circumstances that befall particular people, but which tells us nothing about the nature of thinking itself. Descartes again gives us perhaps the most famous example. Near the very beginning of the *Meditations*, he considers a series of ways in which he had perhaps been led to believe things that weren't true. One such way is through the fallibility of the senses: I see a tower in the distance that appears round, but when I'm closer it becomes clear that it's really a rectangular in shape. Another is the possibility that I am in fact dreaming instead of awake. But he also considers a further possibility: that he is himself like one of those

> madmen, whose brains are so damaged by the persistent vapours of melancholia that they firmly maintain they are kings when they are paupers, or say they are dressed in purple when they are naked, or that their heads are made of earthenware, or that they are pumpkins, or made of glass. But such people are insane, and I would be thought equally mad if I took anything from them as a model for myself. (Descartes, *Meditations*, 13)

The first thing to note is how trite Descartes' images of madness are in this passage. The close horror of real suffering—for instance that of the schizophrenic, whose whole life and being is at stake in this suffering—is absented here, obscured behind a clownish façade. We should pay attention to trite examples of this kind, Deleuze insists, because they reveal the character of the image of thought that animates or attracts them: 'how can we accept that such puerile and artificial textbook examples justify an image of thought?' (DR 154). But Deleuze also wants to make another point. Descartes takes the hypothesis that he might be mad to be one that falls outside of thought itself. To the degree that he is a rational thinking being, he would be (figuratively) mad to take the (literally) mad person as a model for what might go wrong in thought. In other words, madness is a simple fact that is true of some people as living beings, but cannot be true of people as thinkers. *Thought itself cannot go mad*: 'Stupidity, malevolence and madness are regarded as facts occasioned by external causes, which bring into play external forces capable of subverting the honest character of thought from without—all this to the extent that we are not only thinkers'. (DR 149)

Deleuze's attack on this postulate begins by briefly discussing moments in the history of philosophy where the postulate of error was at least put in question, already in Plato, Lucretius, Spinoza and the eighteenth-century French *philosophes*. But it is Kant, in his view, who makes the essential discovery: that thought possesses its *own* dangers, dangers *immanent to thought*. Kant's identifies one species of these under the heading of *transcendental illusion*, a '**natural** and unavoidable **illusion**' which 'cannot be avoided at all' (*Critique of Pure Reason* A298/B354). To return to an earlier example: though we can demonstrate that the Idea of the whole or the totality is not an object of experience, but a regulative horizon for the systematization of knowledge, we nevertheless cannot help but to drift towards treating it as a real thing, to speak of 'the universe' as if it were something we know directly.

Kant's novelty is striking here—*thought misleads itself*—and Deleuze is genuinely struck by his intervention. But he thinks nevertheless that the significance of Kant's insight only really appears once it has been completely radicalized, and it is the French writer Antonin Artaud that he thinks achieves this radicalization, at the cost of his own self and thought:

> Artaud said that the problem (for him) was not to orientate his thought, or to perfect the expression of what he thought, or to acquire application and method or to perfect his poems, but simply to manage to think something. [...] Henceforth, thought is also forced to think its central collapse, its fracture, its own natural 'powerlessness' [...] He knows that thinking is not innate, but must be engendered in thought. He knows that the problem is not to direct or methodically apply a thought which pre-exists in principle and in nature, but to bring into being that which does not yet exist (there is no other work, all the rest is arbitrary, mere decoration). To think is to create - there is no other creation - but to create is first of all to engender 'thinking' in thought. (DR 147)

There is an essential, foundational *stupidity* that belongs to thought, and there is nothing that guarantees that we will manage to think. And the same point holds for *madness*: 'schizophrenia is not only a human fact but also a possibility for thought'. (DR 148 At the most general level, then, Deleuze will insist that thought's essential dangers are immanent to thought itself.

Culture

> The limits of the faculties are encased one in the other in the broken shape of that which bears and transmits difference. There is no more a method for learning than there is a method for finding treasures, but a violent training, a culture or *paideïa* which affects the entire individual. (DR 165)

This passage effectively identifies a further problem that arises on the basis of Deleuze's account of thinking, one that he discusses in the final pages of the 'Image of Thought' chapter. Given the involuntary origins of thinking and the primary, discordant operation of the faculties, what explains the fact that a placid mode of thinking whose model is recognition is so very general—and not just general, but standard and *standardized*?

The passage also gives us the answer: *culture*. For Deleuze we must understand the work of culture to be an additional involuntary element involved in thought. We do not become 'able to think', even in the placid everyday sense by following a natural method of learning, which would take us from childhood of thought to the maturity of the thinker—we already know that such a path does not naturally exist. Instead, culture functions to at once engender and organize thinking by determining in advance *which* encounters in sensation we are likely to confront, and then what will constitute the legitimate activity of the faculties.

The child is fed certain foods, allowed to see certain images, taught to know and say certain words. This nexus already constitutes an implicit network for the training of sensibility (what is the right way to feel?), for the training of the imagination (what images are capable of being produced are drawn from those already seen) for the training of memory (what is significant to recall?). More than this, culture as training establishes certain sanctioned connections *between* the faculties themselves. Here Deleuze glosses this point before citing, somewhat out of context, a passage from Nietzsche's *On the Genealogy of Morality*:

> Culture [...] is an involuntary adventure, the movement of learning which links a sensibility, a memory and then a thought, with all the cruelties and violence necessary, as Nietzsche said, precisely in order to "train a 'nation of thinkers'" or to "provide a training for the mind." (DR 165-6)

Nietzsche is discussing the formation of a group of individuals; Deleuze, on the other hand, is talking about the training of a community of faculties'. The organization of thought, the training of its habitual forms and acceptable permutations, is the ambit of culture. Thus, in a way, the great irony of Kant's thought from Deleuze's point of view is that it has discovered the activity of culture in reverse, and determined it to be universal and necessary nature—he has confused the attentive schoolchild for human thought as such.

CONSTRUCTION

WHAT IS DELEUZE'S POSITIVE PROJECT IN DIFFERENCE AND REPETITION?

At this point it is worth taking stock of what we have discussed so far, and casting an eye at the general positive project that Deleuze will advance in its wake. We have essentially seen a two-step argument. The first step consists in presenting the objective misrecognition of difference in the history of Western philosophy—hence our tour through Aristotle, Hegel and Leibniz. It turns out, though, that the misrecognition of difference Deleuze identifies in the history of Western philosophy is grounded in a much more problematic substrate: the dogmatic image of thought. This was the second step, and consisted in showing that a certain set of implicit presuppositions organize our thought about the world. But now we can describe this step in more salient terms: *it is because thought is presupposed to be oriented around the recognition of the Same and the placidity of the world that the figure of identity arises and comes to possess such a sense of obviousness.* And later we will see that a third, even broader consideration is in play here, one that subtends both the objective and subjective misrecognitions of difference: it is the conditions under which reality itself, including human thinking, is produced that explains its own occultation.

But this is only to list the critical facet of Deleuze's argument. Earlier we saw what I termed the **three requirements** for a philosophy of difference after Aristotle.

1. to create a concept of difference that is not subordinated to identity;
2. a general ontological framework that affirms this concept of difference;
3. an account of the composition of reality at the level of the individual.

As we saw earlier, Deleuze thinks that the **first** of these requirements is at least obscurely grasped by Leibniz in his theory of sub-representational differences in perception. The **second** requirement, in turn, is met (at least in part) by the theory of the univocity of being. This affirms difference by making, in general terms, time the foundational ontological category rather than substance—time conceived of in keeping with Nietzsche's eternal return, and we'll see more on this point later in the chapter.

A differential, genetic ontology

With this in mind, we can say that Deleuze's aim in the rest of *Difference and Repetition* is going to be to address the **third** requirement, and he will do this by constructing a genetic, differential account of reality. That it should be *differential* is to say that it will have to make difference come first, it should take difference as the fundamental category in thinking about being. But it will also be *genetic*, and this will be the major focus moving forward. A genetic ontology is one that accounts for the ongoing production of reality.

In other words, having cleared the way with the critical parts of the book, Deleuze wants to give direct, positive answers to two questions:

1. What are the conditions of novelty? What must be in play such that things change? The answer to this question will lead Deleuze to an account of conditions, which is to say, a transcendental investigation broadly in the Kantian tradition. And it also requires a theory of time, since if things really change, then they will be different over time.
2. How are these conditions realised? This question—which turns out to be the same question as 'what is difference-in-itself?'—will require a thought of material reality.

Conditions, time, materiality: these are the topics of chapters four, two and five of *Difference and Repetition* respectively, which we will discuss in turn. But they go under more well-known technical names in Deleuze's work too: the virtual, repetition, and intensity. Once we work through these chapters, we will be able to grasp Deleuze's answer to these two signal questions: in what sense is difference-in-itself the fundamental name for being, and precisely how does novelty arise in being?

THE VIRTUAL I: KANT AND MAIMON

The first major positive contribution we need to consider here concerns the idea of conditions, and the question 'what are the conditions of the new?' Once again, Deleuze will turn to Kant to begin his construction, and this is because it is in the *Critique of Pure Reason* that a new question in the history of philosophy was first asked: 'what are the *conditions of possibility* for experience?' Deleuze will draw some key materials from Kant's argument, but then subject them to a number of critical transformations, themselves presaged in the work of one of Kant's great contemporaries and critics, Solomon Maimon. We will follow in his footsteps.

The problematic Idea in Kant

Let's begin by recalling our earlier outline of Kant's doctrine of the faculties. Three faculties are constitutive of knowledge and experience. *Sensibility* is the receptive faculty, the point of contact with sensation and objects-in-themselves. It produces spatio-temporalised multiplicities, or what Kant calls *intuitions*. The *understanding* is the faculty of rules for thought, or *categories*, which are actively applied to intuitions through the medium of the *imagination*. It is in the imagination that the generality of thought's logical structure and the particularity of encounters in sensation are brought together.

In addition to these three constitutive faculties is the faculty of *Reason*, which is regulative rather than constitutive. When it functions legitimately, it provides thought with the means to systematize the individual instances of knowledge into a systematic structure. To be more precise, this systematizing function is due to the Ideas of Reason—of which the three most general examples are God, the Soul and the Totality—'objects' of thought which have no correlate in experience. Once again, I never experience the totality (the universe), but as an Idea(l) it allows for the organization of particular pieces of knowledge in a systematic fashion, just like the horizon over the sea allows me to locate objects relative to each other in space.

Deleuze begins the fourth chapter of *Difference and Repetition* by focusing on a key detail of Kant's account of the Idea. He notes that Kant will call them 'problematic'—an Idea is a 'problematic concept', that is 'a **problem** without any solution' (*Critique of Pure Reason* A339/B397; A328B384). In turn, Reason for Kant is 'the faculty of posing problems in general.' (DR 168) What does all this mean? Consider again the analogy between the Ideas of Reason and the horizon. Each time I look out this window and across to the burnt-out house, then the riven oak tree, and then the line where sky and land meet up, a meaningful whole is produced. But if I was to get up and look out the kitchen window instead, then the same thing has to happen again. Every time I look at the world, the horizon allows me to unify my perceptual field—to 'resolve' all of the distinct things I can see into a whole. But the horizon itself is never exhausted. Here's another way to put it: each time I look out the window, the 'problem' of the horizon is solved by the particular organization of visible things, but it is only 'solved' momentarily, until I look once more.

Now consider Kant's Idea of totality again. Each time I 'totalise' or systematize all my knowledge about, for instance, *Difference and Repetition*, the Idea is momentarily determined by all of the particular things I know about the book. But then I begin to read again, and this prior determination is set aside as I learn more. It is in this sense, then, that the Ideas are problems *without permanent solutions*; 'Ideas are themselves problematic or problematising'. (DR 168)

So, for Kant, Ideas have a rather unusual status. They are, on their own terms, *undetermined*. The concept of totality does not correspond to anything in experience. However, they are nevertheless *determinable*, which is to say, temporarily solvable with respect to particular cases of experience and knowledge. But then a final twist: Deleuze notes that Ideas are also, in a very specific sense, completely determined. We just need to remember that, for Kant, experience and knowledge presuppose the categories of the understanding—the rules for all thought. This means that every time an Idea is *determined*, it enters into a relationship with these categories. But this relationship between the understanding and Reason *is always present* in experience, such that we can say that the outline of all experience and knowledge always already completely determines the Ideas of Reason. In sum, Ideas 'present three moments: undetermined with regard to their object, determinable with regard to objects of experience, and bearing the ideal of an infinite determination with regard to concepts of the understanding'. (DR 169)

Maimon's critical reconstruction of Kant's critical philosophy

If I have dwelt on this account at such length, this is because it substantially underpins what comes next—which is to say that Deleuze's infamous idea of the virtual is fundamentally based in and derived from Kant. He will, however, subject it to some rather dramatic modifications. The first of these is best appreciated by turning to one of Kant's contemporaries and critics, Solomon Maimon, a philosopher Deleuze admired a great deal. So, in fact, did Kant, writing to his friend Marcus Herz that 'not only [have] none of my opponents understood me so well, but [...] very few could claim so much penetration and subtlety of mind in profound inquiries of this sort.' Fichte was even more effusive: 'My respect for Maimon's talent is limitless'. (Beiser, *The Fate of Reason*, 285; 370n2)

In constructing his concept of the virtual, Deleuze isolates and develops two of Maimon's criticisms of Kant in particular. The first of these concerns the way that Kant explains the constitution of knowledge through the work of sensibility and the understanding. Maimon asks: given that we never have any experience that isn't already conceptualized—that doesn't bear the marks of the categories of the understanding—then why should we think that there is a non-conceptual element to experience and knowledge? Kant wants to think of the categories as what condition sensible intuitions, but on his own terms he doesn't have any way of showing that these sensible intuitions actually exist.

Now to the second line of criticism. Bertrand Russell famously described his first impression of Leibniz's philosophy as 'a kind of fantastic fairy tale, coherent perhaps, but wholly arbitrary'. (*The Philosophy of Leibniz*, xxi) It is this same charge that Maimon levels at Kant. Kant says that he wants to identify the conditions for all *possible* experience, but how can we know that they *really apply* in experience? Perhaps Kant's system is internally coherent, but it may be wholly unrelated to *real* experience. In other words, Kant doesn't have the means to answer the question: how do you know that the conditions of possible experience apply *in fact*?

In Deleuze's view, both of Maimon's criticisms target a central supposition of Kant's: that the relationship between thought and experience is one of *conditioning*. A non-conceptual matter presents itself to thought, which it subjects to certain conditions (the categories in particular) in order to produce a regulated and meaningful Nature. But Maimon has just shown that Kant cannot justify his own position. What is required instead is a new theory of experience that takes *genesis* rather than *conditioning* as its central category: how is experience actually *produced*?

So, to summarise,

1. Kant's claim that the categories are the conditions for sensible experience can't be demonstrated on the basis of his own account.
2. The applicability of Kant's conditions for possible experience to real experience can't be demonstrated on the basis of the first *Critique*.
3. The root of these problems is that, at least in the first *Critique*, 'Kant neglected the demands of a genetic method', (DI 61)

effectively producing a hypothetical description of experience's conditions rather than an explanation of the production of real experience.

The path forward is as follows. Maimon and Deleuze (but also Fichte, Schelling, Hegel, etc.), will adopt the point of view of genesis, asking: how is experience produced within thought? How is thinking engendered within thought? Let's consider Maimon's solution first—at least in the form that Deleuze seems to interpret it—before seeing how Deleuze will modify it again in turn.

For Maimon, how are the objects of experience *produced*? Instead of taking a sensory experience as the starting point, he begins with 'the rule for the production of object[s]' (*Essay*, 40) within thinking. Like Leibniz, Maimon thinks that what is primary in relation to all objects is a field of differential relations, lacking any extension or homogeneity. What we think of as objects are *integrations* of these differentials, the production of discrete, unified and homogenous things out of this field of relations. Or, as Deleuze writes, it is the 'reciprocal synthesis of differential relations [that is] the source of the production of real objects.' (DR 173)

Maimon will also call these differentials the 'ideas of the Understanding' (*Essay*, 9). This rather curious-seeming mash-up of Kantian terminology means to convey two things. On the one hand, the way in which the differentials of thought function as the rules for the production of objects is *problematically*, in just the way that the Ideas of Reason function in Kant. They are never themselves the object of either sensible experience or rational knowledge, but are presupposed by both. On the other hand, these Ideas are not merely regulative but *constitutive*, in the way that Kant's categories of the understanding are. Consider: walking past a jewelry store in downtown L.A., I happen to see through the window a golden sphere. Both my knowledge of it as a sphere and my experience of it as an object involve a resolution of the problem posed by the conditions that produce the sphere as an object within thought—the particular differentials of thought in play in this particular instance. In turn, the origin of experience is not a thing-in-itself outside of thought. Maimon takes Kant's notion of the *noumena* and identifies it with the differentials of thought themselves.

As I have just implied, Kant's dualism between sensibility and the understanding is resolved by Maimon on the basis of an insistence that the two syntheses engage with the same 'raw materials' (the differentials of thought) in two different ways. Sensibility (along with the imagination) integrates the differentials into objects of experience. And, contrary to Kant, the understanding does not apply itself to the objects of sensibility but also to the differentials of thought, working to produce an adequate concept of the differentials in question.

> the understanding [...] produces the real relations of qualities themselves from the real relations of their differentials. So, if we judge that fire melts wax, then this judgement does not relate to fire and wax as objects of intuition, but to their elements. (Maimon, *Essay*, 183)

So, if I ask myself about 'the area of a circle, or its relation to a square', (*Essay*, 46) my answer will not have to go by way of a sensory intuition, but will instead involve the production of the object of the circle and the square from the differentials of thought directly. Keeping all this in mind, we can see why Maimon will summarise matters like this:

> Sensibility thus provides the differentials to a determined consciousness [...] Out of the relations of these different differentials, which are its objects, the understanding produces the relation of the sensible objects arising from them.
>
> These differentials of objects are the so-called *noumena;* but the objects themselves arising from them are the *phenomena* [...] These *noumena* are ideas of reason serving as principles to explain how objects arise according to certain rules of the understanding. (Maimon, *Essay*, 21)

Deleuze and Maimon

As I said earlier, Deleuze greatly admires Maimon, and draws quite profoundly from his modification of transcendental philosophy in *Difference and Repetition*. Even if this admiration is not unequivocal, we can still identify four points at which the two thinkers intersect.

First, Deleuze is in absolute agreement with the shift to the thematic of genesis: 'Maimon's genius lies in showing how inadequate the point of view of conditioning is for a transcendental philosophy'. (DR 173) In other words, he thinks that the only effective approach to understanding thought and reality is in terms of how it is produced. Transcendental philosophy no longer turns around conditions of possibility, but of real genesis.

Second, like Maimon, he thinks that the Kantian notion of the problematic Idea will be a decisive part of any genetic transcendental philosophy. The production of reality will not make reference, in the final analysis, to a fixed structure of reality (the great chain of being) or a fixed order of self-identical idealities (a certain Plato), but to *problems*. Genesis will be defined as the ongoing solution of problems.

But third—and this is a topic I will return to right near the end of the chapter—Deleuze's goal will not just be to explain the genesis of objects of experience, but also of objects in their full material reality.

Fourth and finally, Deleuze is in full agreement with Maimon that an invocation of mathematics—and specifically the differential and integral calculus as inaugurated by Leibniz—provides the project of a genetic philosophy with an essential component. It's to this we will now turn, before giving a synthetic summary of what Deleuze means by his signal concept of the virtual.

THE VIRTUAL II: DIFFERENTIAL CALCULUS

The presentation of the calculus I'll give here, a very simple one, will only invoke first-order differentials, and we'll take a very simple function as our example: $y = -x^2 + 5$. Rendered as a graph, the most interesting part of the function looks like this:

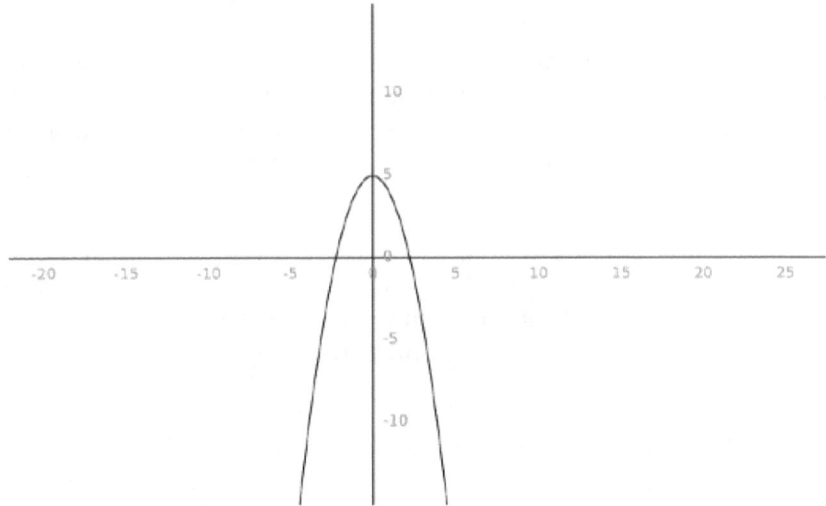

And we're going to compare it to an even simpler function $y = x + 5$, which looks just as boring at every point:

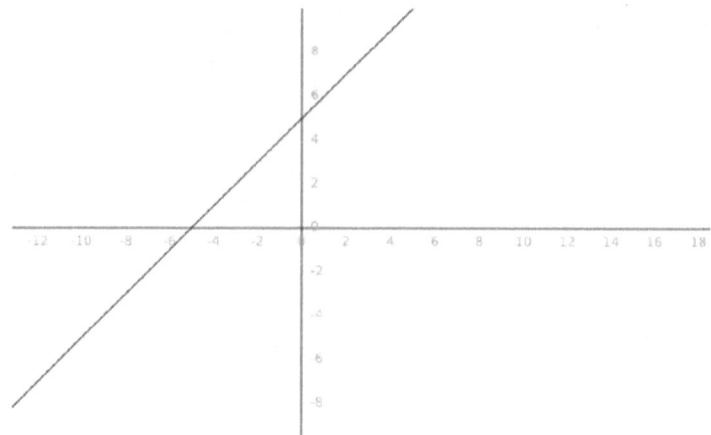

If this were a school text book introducing the calculus, it would probably work through the following points:

1. Let's begin with the second function and its graph, and consider two questions: *what is the gradient of the function at a given point*, and *what is the area under the line between the x- and y-axes?* Now, because the function is linear, it doesn't matter which part of it we select to figure out the gradient, since it will be the same wherever. So let's take the section which runs from (0, -5) to (5, 0), forming a triangle with the two axes. To determine the slope of this line, we divide the distance travelled along the y-axis (we'll call it Δy, which reads 'the change in y') by the distance travelled along the x-axis (Δx). So we get: $\frac{\Delta y}{\Delta x} = \frac{5}{5} = 1$. Again, notice that if we took a section twice as long—or half as long—we'd get the same result. Now, how can we determine the area between the function over the same values, and the axes? Well, this area is a regular shape, a triangle, whose area (A) is length by height divided by 2. Here, this is
$$A = \frac{(5 \times 5)}{2} = 12.5$$

2. Now, suppose we ask the same questions of the first function and its graph. In both cases, there's an obvious problem that prevents us from using the simple approach adopted above. In the case of the slope of the function, the problem is that it is not linear. This means that its slope changes *at every point*. No matter which portion of the curve we choose to apply our previous formula $\frac{\Delta y}{\Delta x}$ to, it will only be an approximation. The paradoxical-seeming requirement is this: to discover the gradient of the curve *at a point*. But how can we do this when figuring out what the gradient of

a curve is requires that we consider the way the function changes over a certain distance? In the case of the area under the curve above the x-axis, the problem is even more obvious: it is not a regular shape. The resolution of these two related problems only became possible with the invention of the two branches of the calculus, *differential calculus* and *integral calculus*.

3. Let's begin with the *integral calculus*, and the problem of the area under the curve. The first attempt to resolve this problem, invented by ancient Greek mathematicians, consisted in trying to find the measurable shape that most closely approximated the unmeasurable one. For instance, Archimedes' attempt to find out the area of a circle followed a process similar to this:

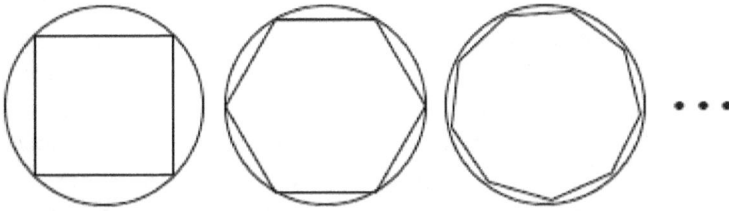

This approach is known as the method of exhaustion, since the aim is to exhaust the space left over by considering polygons with more and more sides, and which therefore tend towards the circumference of the circle itself (without ever getting there). A related approach could be used to grapple with our problem:

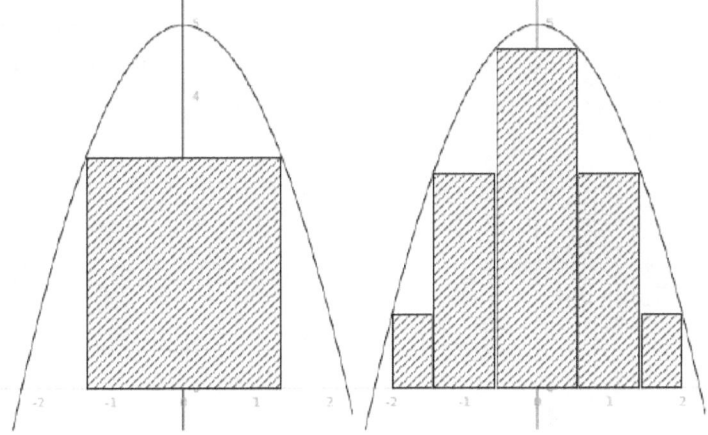

The second iteration here indicates the limits of the approach. What we would need to do to exhaust the entire area under the curve would be to include an infinite number of infinitely thin rectangles. Only then would we actually have determined the complete area. And there it is in a nutshell: the infinitesimal calculus, as it was invented by Leibniz, is a means of summing up an infinite number of infinitely small quantities. In our case, the integral equation and its result will be (leaving aside the working-out, which isn't relevant for our purposes):

$A = \int_{-5}^{5}(-x^2 + 5)dx = 33.3$. The long S indicates a summation, so this can be read as 'the area A is the sum of the infinite number of infinitely small quantities (dx) that constitute the space of the function between -5 and 5 on the x-axis'.

4. But now, let's consider the branch of the calculus that will be so key for Deleuze in *Difference and Repetition*, the *differential calculus*. The remaining question to answer is this: how can we calculate the gradient of the curve for the function $y = -x^2 + 5$? The problem is closely related to the issue of integration. In the latter case, the issue was about obtaining a sum of an infinite number of infinitely small quantities. In the case of the gradient, the problem will be managing to determine the slope of the curve over an infinitely small portion of the curve – in effect, we want to find out what $\frac{\Delta y}{\Delta x}$ is in the cases where these quantities are infinitely small. In this case, we will use slightly different terminology to indicate what is at issue here: $\frac{dy}{dx}$. Again, without going through the details, the differential equation for $y = -x^2 + 5$ is $\frac{dy}{dx} = -2x$. This is to say that the gradient of the slope to the curve is $-2x$. Here's an example: when $x = 0$, the function of the tangent to the curve is $\frac{dy}{dx} = 0$. That is, the tangent to the curve at the very point that it changes direction is an uninclined line:

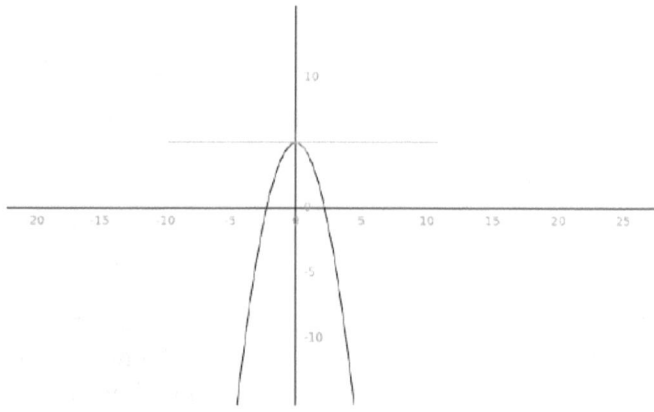

Deleuze's modern metaphysics of the calculus

The calculus is a key element of Deleuze's account of the virtual, but his uptake of it will be heavily inflected and modified by a range of factors and developments. Above all, we need to recognize that this way of presenting the calculus is mired not just in seventh grade but in the seventeenth century. There are three main points to make here.

One of the primary elements of the early formulations of the calculus in Leibniz and Newton that subsequent philosophers and mathematicians were troubled by was the very idea of an infinitely small or 'vanishing' quantity. How could this idea be justified, above all in mathematics? Bishop Berkeley's scornful remark is rightly famous: 'And what are these [infinitesimals]? They are neither finite Quantities nor Quantities infinitely small, nor yet nothing. May we not call them the Ghosts of departed Quantities?' (*The Analyst* §35) The solution, advanced first by Bernard Bolzano and Augustin-Louis Cauchy, but then rigorously pursued in the work of Karl Weierstrass, involved dispensing with this idea altogether. From their work onwards, the idea of the limit would replace any reference to infinitely small quantities. That is, instead of asking what the tangent of the function is when $\frac{dy}{dx}$, where these two are taken to indicate a vanishingly small portion of the curve relative to the two axes, differentiation now works by describing the behavior of the function with respect to a limit: $\lim_{x \to 0}(-x^2 + 5)$. That is: what characterizes the function as x approaches 0?

Deleuze takes all of this as an unquestionable given. Nevertheless, he wants to resist completely breaking with the heritage of certain metaphysical conceptions of the calculus. In an important passage, he writes that:

> it is a mistake to tie the value of the symbol dx to the existence of infinitesimals; but it is also a mistake to refuse it any ontological or gnoseological value in the name of a refusal of the latter. In fact, there is a treasure buried within the old so-called barbaric or prescientific interpretations of the differential calculus, which must be separated from its infinitesimal matrix. A great deal of heart and a great deal of truly philosophical naivety is needed in order to take the symbol dx seriously. (DR 170)

Why does this terminology require such a striking warning label? The answer becomes clear when we ask what dx means if it no longer designates an infinitely small quantity. The answer would seem to be that it means nothing at all. As Deleuze puts it, 'it is therefore completely undetermined: dx is strictly nothing in relation to x, as dy is in relation to y.' But, as he immediately adds, 'The whole problem, however, lies in the signification of these zeros.' (DR 171) We know that differentials are no longer to be considered to be quantities, so they can't be determined to be zero in the sense of null quantity. Instead, they are elements that are undetermined in themselves and as such. But now, a further step:

> In relation to x, dx is completely undetermined, as dy is to y, but they are perfectly determinable in relation to one another. For this reason, a principle of determinability corresponds to the undetermined as such. [...] The relation $\frac{dy}{dx}$ is not like a fraction which is established between particular quanta in intuition, but neither is it a general relation between variable algebraic magnitudes or quantities. Each term exists absolutely only in its relation to the other: it is no longer necessary, or even possible, to indicate an independent variable. For this reason, a principle of reciprocal determinability as such here corresponds to the determinability of the relation. (DR 172)

This is the second point: to the undetermined dx and dy corresponds the reciprocal determination of $\frac{dy}{dx}$. The terms themselves only gain any consistency insofar as they are related to each other. Put another way, the differential relation is primary in relation to the terms themselves.

We've just seen again the terms of undetermined and reciprocally determined – precisely the same terms we saw earlier in our discussion of Kant's Ideas of Reason. This is of course no coincidence. What Deleuze is looking for in the calculus is a way of correcting and extending Kant's transcendental philosophy. Given this, it will come as no surprise that the third moment concerns what Deleuze will call complete determination, and it corresponds to the ideal of determination in Kant. The mathematical category that Deleuze puts into play here is singularity. As before, we'll set aside here the more complicated elements of this analysis and settle for the main point.

Take a look at the graph for our main function $y = -x^2 + 5$ again. Where $x = 0$, the curve changes direction. This point is a singularity, a singular point that determines the distribution of all of the correlative ordinary points composing the curve in its neighbourhood. This distribution of singularities is what distinguishes one function from another. Here is Deleuze: 'the distinctness of Ideas [...] consists precisely in the distribution of the ordinary and the distinctive, the singular and the regular, and in the extension of the singular across regular points into the vicinity of another singularity.' (DR 176)

The singular points of any function constitute the potentiality of the function. This is to say that on the basis of these points, it is possible to generate the function itself. Deleuze is again drawing on a post-Kantian reconstruction of the calculus in making this point, this time one proposed by Höene Wronski—the differential relation is presupposed as the basis from which the function can be generated. Or again: the distribution of singular and ordinary points which the differential relation describes constitutes a problem which is solved by the function itself. Or, one more time: the singularities of a function provide the means to completely determine the function itself.

THE VIRTUAL III: DEFINING THE VIRTUAL

We're now at the point where, drawing on the resources we've just rehearsed, it is possible to define Deleuze's concept of the virtual quite precisely. Before we do so, let's summarise what has been discussed so far:

1. With Kant, Deleuze will insist on the problematic character of Ideas.
2. But with Maimon, he takes these Ideas to be constitutive rather than regulative—they are genetic conditions.
3. Against Maimon, Deleuze takes problematic Ideas to be constitutive of reality as such, and not just the experience of reality.
4. Again with Maimon, Deleuze will redefine the problematic Idea in terms of the differential calculus
5. Drawing on the modern mathematical reformulation of the calculus, he will reject Leibniz and Maimon's reference to the infinitely small, and take the differential to be an undetermined ideality
6. These undetermined idealities nevertheless determine each other reciprocally. In this sense, it is the relation between them that is decisive.
7. To reciprocal determination is added complete determination: any function is primarily to be described in terms of the distribution of singular and ordinary points.

Now, as it happens, this list already effectively provides the definition of the virtual in *Difference and Repetition*. The virtual is the ideal, problematic, differential field, which constitutes the genetic conditions for the production of reality: 'The reality of the virtual consists of the differential elements and relations along with the singular points which correspond to them.' (DR 209)

A word, finally, on the word itself: why 'virtual'? Deleuze draws it from Bergson. He means it to convey the fact that for him problematic Ideas are at once *ideal* and *genetic*, but that they are not *possibilities*. As genetic conditions, they do not resemble what they will provoke into being (this was already Maimon's point, you may recall). It's thus no surprise that he admires a phrase from Proust: 'The virtual is opposed not to the real but to the actual. *The virtual is fully real in so far as it is virtual.* Exactly what Proust said of states of resonance must be said of the virtual: "Real without being actual, ideal without being abstract"'. (DR 208) At the same time, it is irreducible to anything negative or lacking in being. True, the virtual is not actual—it is not another determined material thing in the world. And to convey this strange modal status, Deleuze choses some interesting phrases: 'The being of the problem is not *negative*, it is not a lack. A positive mode of problematicity: not non-being but "(non)-being or ?-being"'. (DR 205)

But now a new question appears on the horizon: if the virtual is the set of structural conditions for the production of reality, how does this production come about? 'How does actualisation occur in things themselves?' (DR 214). Later he puts the question, and then its answer, like this: 'how is the Idea determined to incarnate itself [...] The answer lies precisely in intensive quantities'. (DR 245)

INTENSITY

With an eye to impressing her, you put a pan of water on the stove to poach some eggs and hit the gas. If this was an example from a school science book, it might involve the quantity of an homogenous substance we call 'water' in the half-filled pan, or a lesson about the transfer of heat, or the boiling temperature of that same water. But what's strange about every pot of water is the fact that it is nowhere homogenous. Even ultrapurified water has traces of other elements—and you're about to put in a lash of vinegar yourself—but more notable is the fact that, even before the gas flame strikes, the water is not a single temperature. We have become accustomed to thinking of the ocean as a heterogenous assemblage of currents and rivers of different temperatures engaged in a complicated ecosystem, but the same is true of every body of water, including the pot on the stove. As you wait for it to heat up, you notice here and there small eddies emerge, temporary local structures in the water. These are explained by the very fact that the water is neither pure nor homogenous in temperature. There is a complex series of differences in temperature that give this pot of water its particular structure.

Meanwhile, about two kilometres above the kitchen, a menagerie of cumulonimbus clouds are forming, their increasingly angry virga tendrils intermingling. None of these clouds are homogenous either, composed instead of a dynamic interplay of heterogenous temperatures and centres of turbulence that mirror their much smaller confrères below in the now-simmering pot of water. The clouds are internally dynamic, changing in relation to internal tendencies but also to other clouds, the cold surrounding air, and the hotter air roiling up from the ground. Ongoing, then, is polarisation. Within the clouds, positively charged ions are pulling away from negatively charged electrons, molecules straining at the limits of their habitual shapes, before breaking. The loosed ions form plasma tracks in the atmosphere along which energy can easily flow. And then, lightning: a dissipation of the difference in intensity that hammers electrons down along these ionized paths, while, running up from the upper branches of an unfortunate oak tree, comes the flash of lightning itself.

And then, the following morning. Instead of enjoying your carriage across the crewcut grass and the treetops and out into the city—seeing, off in the distance, cranes still slowly gnawing on the Sagrada Família and the storm dissipating over the sea—you spend most of your ride in the Montjuïc cable car desperately crouching among shoes and shopping bags on the dirty floor. Unannounced, you've been gripped by vertigo, suddenly every point of stable reference slipped away, and the world is now being sickeningly slung around you like a giant off-kilter hula hoop.

The first trait of intensity: the unequal

Each in different ways, these three cases illustrate the concept of *intensity*, the next major concept in Deleuze's construction of a philosophy of difference in *Difference and Repetition*. But before we get into his sometimes opaque way of talking about this concept, we need to recognize that it is not some mysterious unknowable, hyper-metaphysical concept, but a basic cornerstone of the physical sciences.

Consider the difference between length, which is an extensive quantity, and temperature, which is an intensive quantity. Length is homogenous in nature and readily divisible. You can cut a one-meter piece of string into four pieces, but by joining them back together again they once again measure the *same* meter. Temperature, on the other hand, is not composed of homogenous parts in this way. To speak of 50° celsius as *half* of 100° is to speak metaphorically. If we add two pots of 50° water together, the temperature will not become 100°. More to the point, temperature is not additive in the same way that length is. In order to bring a pot of water to the boil at (around) 100° celsius, we do not add 1° at a time. There is instead a dynamic process of genuine transformation. At each moment, the water differs from its previous state, a difference in kind and not merely degree.

But what then is the relationship between 50° and 100° celsius? Here, Deleuze deploys a basic mathematical contrast between two ways of thinking about number. The first way takes numbers in terms of their size or *cardinality*. The number 5, taken as a cardinal, is exactly half of the cardinal 10, and this 10 can be broken down into homogenous component numbers (5 x 2, or 10 x 1). Cardinal numbers are therefore an ideal framework for thinking about homogenous quantities like length. But numbers can also be conceived as *ordinals*, that is to say, as an *ordered* ranking: 1st, 2nd, 3rd ... The key difference is that, unlike the standard 'distance' that falls between each of the cardinals, there is no fixed, homogenous measure between any two ordinals. Three lobsters (Gérard, Thibault and Salvador) are set to racing along a strip of AstroTurf. The order in which they arrive at the far side is perfectly captured in the ordinal series (first, second, third), but this tells us nothing about the relative distance between first and second, or second and third. No metric is implied in the ordinal series, only this ordering itself. These are simply differences or distances without a common measure.

Intensive quantities like temperature—but we can equally think of depth, distance, altitude, speed, resistance, and so on—are ordinal in just this way. We can say that 50° is hotter than 40°, and not as hot as 100°, but it would be wrong to think that we can do so because we are referring to an underlying metric of the kind that the cardinal number series provides. Ordinal numbers are in this sense close to proper names, each marking something irreducible.

With these points in mind, and the three examples from before in the background, we can now discuss what Deleuze calls the 'three characteristics' of intensity. 'According to the first, intensive quantity includes the unequal in itself'. (DR 232) Though this appears odd at first blush, think about the ordinal series again. The reason why the distance between first and second is incomparable to that between second and third is because there is no homogenous standard of measure. Indeed, in intensive quantity, there is no homogeneity at any level. Here is Deleuze:

> when it is pointed out that a temperature is not composed of other temperatures, or a speed of other speeds, what is meant is that each temperature is already a difference, and that differences are not composed of differences of the same order but imply series of heterogeneous terms. (DR 237)

So the point is not just that temperature, for instance, can never be subtracted from physical states of affairs (everything 'has' a temperature); it is not even just that there is no such thing as an homogenous temperature, as the pot of water example displays (everything is caught up in an heterogenous play of temperatures). What is crucial is that temperature is different *in itself*, unequal *in itself*.

Second trait of intensity: difference-in-itself and the being of the sensible

That last sentence hopefully rang a bell—after all, one of the key aims of *Difference and Repetition* is to develop a concept of difference-in-itself. Have we found it in intensive quantity? *Yes.* 'A second characteristic flows from the first: since it is already difference in itself and comprises inequality as such, intensity affirms difference. It makes difference an object of affirmation'. (DR 234) So, as if all of a sudden—Deleuze himself doesn't announce it with any particular fanfare—we've found what we were looking for.

He presents this claim from two complementary points of view. The first is ontological: intensity is a name for being itself—it constitutes, he says, 'the being of the sensible'. (DR 236) So it is not just lightning that is the product of intensive differences, but the cloud within which this difference forms, the atmosphere in general, and then, finally, everything. Everything that exists arises from an interplay of intensive quantities or differences-in-themselves. Putting things this way gives a sense of the enormity of the task Deleuze has set for himself. He will have to explain how it is that extended and qualified things (two litres of water, a chicken egg, a lobster, AstroTurf) come into being on the basis of the regime of intensity. We'll get to this genetic perspective in a moment.

The second point of view is that of the human being who encounters intensity as something in excess of the world of stable objects that she is capable of recognizing. From the point of view of placid, established thought, identifying the dynamism in being is a work of 'tracing hardly recognisable intensive paths through the ulterior world of qualified extensity', (DR 236) something akin to the detective work of a scientist. But the direct encounter with intensity does take place, and when it does, we find ourselves forced outside of our habits of recognition and into a confrontation with our very limits as thinking being:

> It is intensity or difference in intensity which constitutes the peculiar limit of sensibility. As such, it has the paradoxical character of that limit: it is the imperceptible, that which cannot be sensed [...] But in another sense, it is that which can only be sensed or that which defines the transcendent exercise of sensibility, because it allows us to sense, and thereby awakens memory and forces thought. (DR 237)

It is from this point of view that we can appreciate the earlier example of vertigo:

> Pharmacodynamic experiences or physical experiences such as vertigo approach the same result: they reveal to us that difference in itself, that depth in itself or that intensity in itself at the original moment at which it is neither qualified nor extended. At this point, the harrowing character of intensity, however weak, restores its true meaning. (DR 237)

The experience of vertigo is not at all, as we normally think, an *aberration*. Instead, it reveals to us the primary nature of our perceptual relationship with being, which is not neatly parceled up into stable, recognizable objects, but consists of encounters in intensity. Some of these are simply *too much*—for our habits, our expectations, our bodily intertwining with the world. But what is too much is being itself in its primary aspect.

We will return to this point, but before going any further, it's worth noting that the concept of intensity or intensive quantity thus answers, to a certain degree, the first two of what I called the requirements of a philosophy of difference after Aristotle. The **first** requirement was to develop an adequate concept of difference. We have just seen that intensity fits the bill here. The **second** requirement is to elaborate an ontology adequate to this concept of difference. Part of this requirement is answered by the notion of the univocity of being in the form of the eternal return. But another, equally important part, is provided by the notion of intensity as difference-in-itself. For Deleuze, univocity affirms difference, but now we have a proper idea of what the being of difference is. This complementarity between intensity and time is at the very centre of the positive project of *Difference and Repetition*; we'll touch on it once again when we arrive at our discussion of repetition in what follows. But there's still the **third** requirement: to be able to think individuality directly, to think the reality of each thing on its own terms rather than asserting that it falls below the level of thought. Indeed, Deleuze will say, Aristotle is right to think that individuality is below the level of conceptual, representational thinking. But there remains a way to think it nevertheless. We will need to wait until the next section on 'The Intensive Individual' to see how this works, but the point for now is to recognise how just significant this notion of intensity is for Deleuze's project, and just how much it allows him to do.

Third trait of intensity: the implication of quantity

The third trait of intensity takes us back to the notion of ordinality and our example of the racing lobsters.

> In terms of a third characteristic which includes the other two, intensity is an implicated, enveloped or 'embryonised' quantity. Not implicated in quality, for it is only secondarily so. Intensity is primarily implicated in itself: implicating and implicated. We must conceive of implication as a perfectly determined form of being. Within intensity, we call that which is really implicating and enveloping *difference*; and we call that which is really implicated or enveloped *distance*. (DR 237)

In terms of our lobsters, third envelops second and first, but without otherwise providing a rule for the measurement of the distances between them. In terms of the two ways of conceiving number, Deleuze will insist that 'natural numbers are first ordinal—in other words, originally intensive. Cardinal numbers result from these and are presented as the explication of the ordinal. [...] Ordinal construction does not imply a supposed same unit but only [...] an irreducible notion of distance'. (DR 232) And the same is true yet again of temperature (and then for all intensive quantities): 100° envelops or implicates 50°, which in turn envelops 48°, which in turn envelops .... There is a very clear idea of structure here, but it is one that in no way determines anything—distances including other distances, differences including other differences.

While this trait seems to be relatively insignificant in comparison to the previous two, it reveals something important about how intensity is related to the world of apparently stable, given things. Intensity will somehow have to pass from its implicated state, and 'unfurl' into things.

In other words, the genesis of material reality will go by way of an *explication* of intensity. We now have: perplication (reciprocal determination) in the virtual, implication in intensity, explication and qualification in the realm of actual things.

Fourth trait of intensity: genetic priority

Deleuze's explicit list of the traits of intensity only involves these three. But a good way of unpacking the rest of chapter five of *Difference and Repetition* is to add another two to the list, items which draw out and extend some of the sense of the first three. The fourth trait of intensity is this: it is genetically prior to the extended and qualified material world (a smouldering cigar from Lima, this school of fish, a printing press). This means both that implicated intensity is logically and causally prior to extended reality, and that the reality of stable objects is 'made up of' intensity.

In one sense, this is the most difficult claim of *Difference and Repetition* to grasp. We may have no trouble agreeing that intensive quantities like temperature cannot be grasped in extensive terms, or even that they are the vectors of change (as the example of lightning was meant to convey). But what Deleuze wants to convince us of is that every relatively stable given object and state of affairs in the world is *composed of intensity*, that the 'fields of fluid intensive factors' (DR 152) do not just perturb the stable world of things but *are* these things in their primary state.

To unravel all of this requires a bit more than we have to hand at the moment—though we will get there—but it will be useful to consider one of Deleuze's examples to make a bit of progress. In fact, this is really *the* key example in *Difference and Repetition*, the one that he repeats numerous times and which he takes to be emblematic of his entire construction: the *egg* or *embryo*. In the background here is the work of Raymond Ruyer, a remarkable and still little-known French philosopher whose work is oriented by precisely the same example. Both philosophers in turn draw on the astonishing discoveries of modern embryology, which essentially turn around one point: at least up to a certain moment in their development, embryos possess neither fixed structure nor any homogeneity. The tissues that would 'normally' develop into a nervous system can, if transplanted, instead become the epidermis—and if the tissue that would presumptively become the skin of one embryo is grafted into another at the right place, it will become that animal's nervous system. As the embryologist Hans Driesch famously discovered to his shock, if you cut the first two cells of a sea urchin embryo into two halves, each of them will develop into a whole new animal.

All of these experimental results show us that embryonic tissue is not yet one thing. Indeed it is not *a thing* in the strict sense at all: it possesses neither fixed extension, nor established qualities; neither a determining structure, nor a pre-determined destiny. Capable of becoming every part of the organism, this tissue is instead a site for heterogenic processes of an enormous range. It is, simply put, an example of difference-in-itself. Embryonic development, as a result, is completely unlike the assembly of a fixed object out of indifferent parts. Instead, we should think in terms of 'An intensity forming a wave of variation throughout the protoplasm [that] distributes its difference along the axes and from one pole to another [...] In order to plumb the intensive depths or the *spatium* of an egg, the directions and distances, the dynamisms and dramas, the potentials and potentialities must be multiplied'. (DR 250)

Keeping the example of the egg in mind is a useful way to keep hold of what Deleuze is getting at in this important fifth chapter of *Difference and Repetition*.

Fifth trait of intensity: transcendental illusion

Fortunately, Deleuze has an explanation for our sense of bewilderment when confronting the genetic primacy of intensity. The first trait of intensity, noted above, is that intensity is what is uncancellable in quantity. But Deleuze is clear that it is also and at the same time *cancelled*. How does this work? Let's go back to a key passage:

> Intensity is the uncancellable in difference of quantity, but this difference of quantity is cancelled by extension, extension being precisely the process by which intensive difference is turned inside out and distributed in such a way as to be dispelled, compensated, equalised and suppressed in the extensity which it creates. (DR 233)

We have just seen that the genesis of material reality will go by way of an explication of intensity. But now we can add that this genesis does not take place without at the same time obscuring its intensive conditions. This *is why the world appears in the first instance as fixed and stable, reliable and recognisable*. We are not wrong to think that it is, only that this is its most profound state, and the state that can explain everything else. In this way, all common sense experience of the world labours under the shadow of a transcendental illusion.

The notion of transcendental illusion is, as we saw earlier when talking about the dogmatic image of thought, from Kant, but (at least in the first *Critique*), it's an illusion that only pertains to knowledge. Reason tends towards an illegitimate exercise of its power, making claims as if it had direct access to reality. For Deleuze, the stakes are considerably higher. In fact, the transcendental illusion he is interested in is inseparable from the genesis of the material world itself, which is why he refers to it as an 'objective or transcendental illusion'. (DR 208) As intensity is explicated, it is in fact, really and materially covered over, obscured and consumed: 'It is a transcendental illusion because it is entirely true that difference is cancelled qualitatively and in extension. It is nevertheless an illusion, since the nature of difference lies neither in the quality by which it is covered nor in the extensity by which it is explicated'. (DR 266)

This point is crucial for Deleuze, and explains why it is that we take the stable, recognizable world *as what the world really is*, so let me repeat it for emphasis: the very process of ontogenesis, since it obscures its intensive grounds, *is the reason for its own misunderstanding*. Let's invoke Ruyer once again, who illustrates this point in the following amusing passage:

> When an embryologist publishes her observations concerning a developmental phenomenon, following her name with a list of her achievements, academic and otherwise, she forgets the most important of her circumstances, which is that she is an 'ex-embryo' [...] The embryologist—*in other words, the embryo all grown-up*—certainly observes the young embryo under study in a way that the embryo does not observe the biologist, on account of the fact that it does not yet have eyes and its brain is little more than a gutter. But this superiority of the biologist is, first of all, short-lived. Nothing prevents the observed embryo from becoming, in its turn, an eminent biologist or great neurosurgeon, who will observe, with a profound sense of superiority, the now-deficient brain of its earlier observer. And above all, this very observation clearly takes place on the basis of the subjacent condition that a development has occurred in the organism of the observer, who has passed from the state of a fertilised egg or 'neurula', occupied some thirty years earlier, to that of the adult organism, endowed with eyes and a functional nervous system. (Ruyer, *La genèse*, 217-8)

Indeed, as far as Deleuze is concerned, the history of Western philosophy has been predominantly and massively written from an analogous point of view, that of 'an adult observer who contemplates [ontogenesis] from without'. (DR 214)

THE INTENSIVE INDIVIDUAL

Why does water boil at 100°C? In fact, here's a better question: why does any given volume of water *not* boil at 100°C exactly, but at some other point? Which point, and why at this point? Why does one egg give rise to a tortoise and another a platypus? *That* water boils, *that* an embryo develops can be explained by what we have said so far about intensity and its dynamisms, but this kind of specificity is at present out of our reach. In other words, what we have described so far is the heterogeneity of intensity, but this heterogeneity is not for all this *random*. What provides it with its structure and its specificity? The answer to this question will take us back to Leibniz.

Memories of a monad

Let's recall the lineaments of Leibniz's account once again. At the most general level, we have the world. From God's point of view, the world is the totality of logical relations between subjects and predicates, which all fit together perfectly (principle of pre-established harmony). That *this can* of Red Bull Zero is on *this table* requires the two subjects to also be predicates of each other at this particular moment in the unfolding of the universe. It happens that I moved this table over into the middle of the room earlier today, so I too am a part of the set of pre-conditions for the can being on the table such as it currently exists, and so on up to the totality of the world (principle of sufficient reason).

From the point of view of the finite beings or monads that compose the universe, the world is perceived more or less clearly, more or less obscurely, from its own particular point of view: 'each simple substance is a perpetual, living mirror of the universe', (Leibniz, *Monadology* §56) My point of view, centred around my body, takes in my shirt and shoes, this laptop and table, and the empty can of Red Bull. Out the window, a building is being demolished, which I can still vaguely hear over the sounds of the Geotic track playing through my headphones. And if I pay attention, I can hear the rumble of traffic outside. This zone is in perpetual change, however. If I turn off the music, it would grow to incorporate more sounds from outside, and if I had just drunk a gin and tonic rather than a Red Bull, it would be shrinking.

More important again is the fact that what I perceive clearly is in fact an integration of what Leibniz calls *petites perceptions*—small perceptions, the murmuring of the world beneath the threshold of my consciousness apprehension of it. You might recall Leibniz's example of the sea discussed much earlier in the chapter: I clearly perceive the roar of the sea, but this clear perception is also a confused one. What is confused are the infinite number of infinitely small sounds made by the waves crashing together, and then the droplets of water that compose the wave, and so on down into infinity: 'Each portion of matter can be conceived as a garden full of plants, and as pond full of fish. But each branch of a plant, each limb of an animal, each drop of its humours, is still another such garden or pond'. (*Monadology* §57) The noise of traffic is another good example of the same kind—so that each portion of matter is a muttering gridlock, down to infinity. Everywhere, the imperceptible murmuring of cars. The imperceptible muttering of stars.

I perceive the whole of the world, but only a small part is expressed clearly. This relationship of expression is crucial. The world or universe is not outside the monad, as if it were a separate thing. It only exists in each monad. But again, it is not 'in' each monad the way that a fortune is inside a cookie. So it would be better to say that the world subsists or insists, rather than exists, in each monad. Each monad expresses the whole of the world; the world only exists in its expressions. Hence Deleuze's definition of expression itself: 'By "expression" we mean, as always, that relation which involves a torsion between an expressor and an expressed such that the expressed does not exist apart from the expressor, even though the expressor relates to it as though to something completely different'. (DR 260)

One more detail. What differentiates one monad from another is its ever-shifting zone of clear perceptions. But this zone is in turn characterized by certain singularities that dominate in it.

> The idea of the sea, for example, as Leibniz showed, is a system of liaisons or differential relations between particulars and singularities corresponding to the degrees of variation among these relations—the totality of the system being incarnated in the real movement of the waves. (DR 165)

A wave peaks. This peak is a singularity in the dynamic system of movement in the water, as is the trough that forms next to it, and the locus of the turbulence that forms when this wave strikes another. In Leibniz, Deleuze notes, these singularities that characterize monadic perception are *events*. The cresting of a wave is an event that has consequences for the surrounding movement of water, just as the event 'to eat the apple' is definitive of the existence of Adam and Eve, and as the event 'to cross the Rubicon' is for Caesar's existence.

As a little coda to this account of Leibniz, let's also briefly recall Maimon's system. Taking up the Leibnizian model of perception, Maimon recast the *petites perceptions* as the differentials of thought. He shares with Leibniz the idea that objects of experience are the result of a resolution or integration of these differentials. And, drawing on Kant, he will insist on a difference in kind between the objects of perception and their conditions, which do not resemble the objects for which they are the rules of construction. The key passage, once again, is this: 'These differentials of objects are the so-called *noumena;* but the objects themselves arising from them are the *phenomena* […] These *noumena* are ideas of reason serving as principles to explain how objects arise'. (Maimon, *Essay*, 21)

The individual

Hopefully all of this talk about differential relations and singularities sounds familiar. For indeed, not only does Deleuze take up (via Maimon) Leibniz's account of the differential constitution of object, he takes up the 'differentials and singularities—expression—object' series as a whole in order to explain the very questions about specificity and individuality that we raised at the beginning of this section.

The best way to grasp what is going on in this second half of the final chapter of *Difference and Repetition* is to ask two questions. The first is: if Deleuze is going to deploy a modified version of Leibniz, what takes the place of the monad? The answer is the *intensive individual*. The individual is the expressive locus in Deleuze, though unlike Leibniz we are here in the realm of materiality. If there was anything that (very broadly) corresponded to the idea of a material building block, this would be it. And in fact we've already seen one example of the intensive individual—the egg, 'the individual-embryo in its field of individuation'. (DR 214)

Now, the second question: what allows us to define a particular individual, and thus differentiate between intensive individuals? For Leibniz, monads are 1) distinguished by their specific zone of clarity and 2) the singularities that organize it, even though 3) they express the whole world. For Deleuze, the answer is very similar: individuals are distinguished by 1) which virtual differential relations they clearly express and the 2) singularities that correspond to them, even though 3) every individual expresses the virtual as such.

So, we begin with the point that virtual Ideas 'are expressed in individuating factors, in the implicated world of intensive quantities' (DR

259). This is to say that we are here dealing with two ontological registers: 'individuation is essentially intensive, and [...] the pre-individual field is a virtual-ideal field, made up of differential relations'. (DR 246) Between the two, as in Leibniz, there is the relationship of expression. The virtual is not transcendent, but exists or rather insists in its expressions at the level of intensive individuality.

Like Leibniz once again, Deleuze thinks that the difference between individuals is to be thought in terms of the *clear-confused* pair: each individual expresses

> the changing totality of Ideas, the variable ensemble of differential relations. However, each intensity *clearly* expresses only certain relations or certain degrees of variation. Those that it expresses clearly are precisely those on which it is focused when it has the *enveloping* role. In its role as the *enveloped*, it still expresses all relations and all degrees, but *confusedly*. (DR 252)

To see what this enveloping-enveloped distinction means, let's return to the embryo once again. One of the earliest processes that introduce structure in embryogenesis for most animals is gastrulation, the formation of an inside and an outside. Here is Ruyer's description of this process for the amphioxus, a small marine invertebrate:

> Without growing, the egg is segmented into two, then four, then eight cells of roughly equal size. Those cells that continue to divide constitute a small sphere the size of a blackberry (*morula*), before becoming a hollow sac (*blastula*). The lower section flattens, collapses and subsides (*gastrulation*) into the higher hemisphere as if an invisible thumb were pressing on a rubber ball. The cavity of the blastula is then reduced, and a new cavity, which constitutes the primitive intestine, is formed. This primitive intestine communicates with the outside through the residual orifice: the blastopore. (Ruyer, *La genèse*, 14)

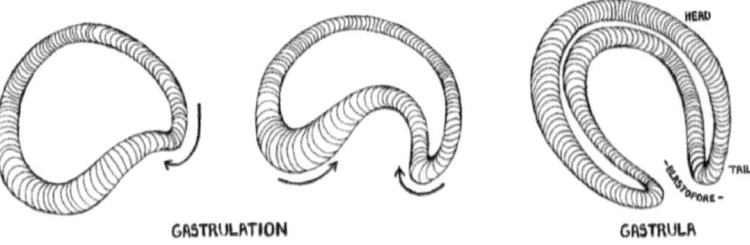

The subordinate or enveloped character of the processes local to each cell is also demonstrated by the kinds of transplanting experiments we touched on earlier. If any of the cells in the embryo are transplanted to elsewhere at this stage of development, they will take up the role that belong to their new location, the overall dynamic uninterrupted. But the same point is also conveyed by the way in which the processes taking place on the 'head' side (the dorsal arch) of the gastrula, where a much higher rate of activity is found, envelop and direct those on the 'tail' or ventral side. As Deleuze puts it, 'The region of maximal activity exercises a dominant influence on the development of the corresponding parts at a lower rate: the individual in the egg is a genuine descent, going from the highest to the lowest and affirming the differences which comprise it and in which it falls'. (DR 250) In other words, embryogenesis cannot be understood in terms of a set of discrete parts coming together *en masse* to achieve a certain extrinsic outcome, but is instead a set of nested or enveloped dynamisms that implicate those of a lower degree of intensity. And at no level is there any fixed structure, nor any stable extended mass that remains what it is throughout.

Now, there are a couple of points on which Deleuze will entirely reject Leibniz's position. They concern the principle of pre-established harmony, and the principle of closure. The world is not given once and for all in Deleuze, and the individual is always caught up in relations with others and with the intensive field more generally—the way that the embryogenesis of a yellow walleye is a part of dynamic intensive system in the bend of Flint River, which is itself a part of ever-broader dynamisms that include the upriver farmlands larded with fertilizers, and the Flint General Motors factory that dumps arsenic, mercury, lead and elements of petroleum into the water. 'Indeterminate, floating, fluid, communicative', (DR 258) such is the nature of the intensive individual. So, at the limit, the notion of the intensive individual is nothing other than a particular process of intensive individuation: 'The essential process of intensive quantities is individuation. Intensity is individuating, and intensive quantities are individuating factors'. (DR 246)

Now we can see how Deleuze would answer questions like 'why did this pot of water boil at that temperature?' or 'why did that egg hatch to reveal a chicken and not a platypus?' His answer would always turn around the fact that any given intensive individual or process of individuation expresses a *particular* set of differential relations and singularities clearly.

Hopefully at this point a very rough outline of Deleuze's picture of reality is beginning to emerge. At this point, it would have the following components:

Virtual Ideas

are *expressed* by

Dynamic intensive individuals

which are the genetic kernels of

Actual objects and subjects

But a fairly pressing issue still remains. It concerns the fact that the account so far is completely static. It's all well and good to say that Deleuze has sought out the genetic conditions for the ongoing production of reality, but if this is the goal, then an explanation for why things *in fact change* will be required.

TEMPORAL SYNTHESIS: IDENTITY AND CHANGE OVER TIME

The last major piece of the puzzle, then, will be *time*. A few opening remarks. In the discussion of the doctrine of univocity, we saw already that time plays an important role in *Difference and Repetition*. There, Deleuze advances the claim that the Nietzschean eternal return (essentially, the emphasis on the irreducibility of temporality on Deleuze's reading) should be understood as both the true affirmation of univocity and the only fundamental ontological position that affirms difference itself. This is so because time, insofar as it affects everything, rules out anything being necessary, absolute, essential, or self-identical over time. If being *is* becoming, then nothing has a permanence in being.

This idea is the centerpiece and logical terminus of the second chapter of *Difference and Repetition*, 'Repetition-for-itself'. But there is also another equally significant if more modest idea that runs through the whole of this chapter, one that initially seems to contradict the thought of the eternal return: the idea that temporality is synthetic. In fact, Deleuze's claim is that temporality is first of all a matter of *passive* synthesis. In the immediate background here are Kant and Husserl. It was Husserl who first developed a thorough-going account of passive synthesis. His idea was that the constitution of objects of experience—for instance, this bottle of Chinkiang vinegar slowly moving around the table on the *cānzhuō zhuànpán*—takes place at a level prior to any conscious act. That it belongs on the table, that it has a sticker on the back that gives its ingredients in English, all of this is constituted in my experience of the world, but it is constituted without any activity on my part as a conscious being. That I can ask my friend to pass me the vinegar, or I think back to remember the first time I tasted it—which are conscious *acts*—presuppose this synthetic substratum. But lying just behind this for both Husserl and Deleuze is the notion of synthesis advanced in Kant's first *Critique*, where it is defined as 'a blind though indispensable function of the soul, without which we would have no cognition at all, but of which we are seldom even conscious'. (*Critique of Pure Reason* A78/B103) So, passive synthesis is not an act of a conscious thinker, even if it constitutes the object that they think about. It is nevertheless more than an inert passivity. It consists in a gathering together without any reference to a governing concept.

A passive synthesis of what? This question will have to be delayed, since it has a different answer for each of the temporal registers. But there is another question that often remains unasked when encountering this chapter of Deleuze, and its omission leads to serious confusions. The question is this: what is produced by the passive syntheses, what is the result or outcome? The answer, which seems really very strange at first, is that they produce *time itself*. To be more precise, the present and the past are produced through two corresponding passive syntheses, though the future is something of a different matter. But instead of trying to unravel all of this at a general level, it will be more useful to get down to cases.

First synthesis: habit and the present

The first synthesis of time is the synthesis of habit, or *Habitus*. This synthesis produces the present. But how, and on the basis of what material? Deleuze's discussion of time and repetition begins with the instant. One of his examples is a ticking clock. Both the 'tick' and the 'tock' are independent instants. Not only do they have no necessary relationship, neither of them by themselves possesses or conveys a real temporality: 'A succession of instants does not constitute time'. (DR 70) Of course when I'm listening to the clock in my shrink's waiting room, the 'tick tock' takes place in time, but this is not Deleuze's point. A collection of instants is not enough by itself to compose the present. Precisely, a certain synthesis is required. 'Time is constituted [...] in the originary synthesis which operates on the repetition of instants'. (DR 70) What is required is for the sequence of instants to be gathered together, for the 'tick' and the 'tock' to begin to imply one another.

As I said above, Deleuze designates this synthesis the synthesis of habit. It consists in *contracting* these instants, which is to say that 'habit is contraction'. (DR 73) When I hear the 'tick', I expect to then hear the 'tock'. This contracted, habitual expectation is not the result of a conscious act on my part. I can certainly work to pay attention to a series of instants in order to habituate my grasp of them, like a card counter hustling a dealer on Lake Tahoe. But *that* I contract a habit is the result of a passive synthesis taking place beneath the level of conscious agency: 'Passive synthesis [...] constitutes our habit of living, our expectation that 'it' will continue'. (DR 74) Prior to our self-conscious activity in the world, we grasp it as part of it, our presents are filled out with retained past moments, and our habits reach out into the future, anticipating what is to come—as Leibniz said, we are laden with the past and pregnant with the future (*Monadology* §22).

Such is the first step of the analysis. But this way of describing things doesn't quite get to the heart of the issue. It is not just that I contract the habit of expecting the 'tock' to follow the 'tick', which would presuppose that I exist before hand, as a stable subject capable of taking on new habits, an already old dog learning new tricks. Deleuze's more radical point is that the passive synthesis of habit first of all *composes me*: 'habit here manifests its full generality: it concerns not only the sensory-motor habits that we have (psychologically), but also, before these, the primary habits that we are; the thousands of passive syntheses of which we are organically composed'. (DR 74) Or, as he memorably puts it a little later on:

> Underneath the self which acts are little selves which contemplate and which render possible both the action and the active subject. We speak of our 'self only in virtue of these thousands of little witnesses which contemplate within us: it is always a third party who says 'me'. These contemplative souls must be assigned even to the rat in the labyrinth and to each muscle of the rat. (DR 75)

As this passage already indicates, the radicalization of habit that Deleuze advances here concerns not just human experience and subjectivity, but 'the whole of organic and psychic life'. (DR 78) To exist *in general* is to be engaged in a multitude of passive habitual syntheses that account for our ongoing composition. Deleuze composes a rhapsody to this effect:

> What we call wheat is a contraction of the earth and humidity, and this contraction is both a contemplation and an auto-satisfaction of that contemplation. By its existence alone, the lily of the field sings

the glory of the heavens [...] What organism is not made of elements and cases of repetition, of contemplated and contracted water, nitrogen, carbon, chlorides and sulphates, thereby intertwining all the habits of which it is composed? (DR 75)

Setting aside this ecstatic language for a moment and adopting a more general perspective, we can say that: the object or material that the first passive synthesis works on is intensity itself. *Habitus* is the contraction of intensities and the composition of objects from these intensities.

Now: this description of the first synthesis might give the impression that it really produces two things: objects, via contraction, and the present in which they exist. But it is key to see that, for Deleuze, these are the same thing. The present is not an empty container in which things happen; neither are contractile beings within time. The living present of the wheat is the wheat's existence itself. The tissue of habits that I am *is* the ongoing genesis of a living present.

Correlatively, there is no such thing as *the* present on this account. My present, sitting at the bar with a beer and a docket indicating that I bet on Gérard in the lobster race, Gérard's present, and the present of my beer itself, as it slowly grows warm and flat, possess different rhythms. In each case, there is an elastic capacity to 'hold onto the present' that has its limits. Despite the fantastic image of nineteenth century dilettantes touring them around town on ribbons, lobsters quickly become exhausted by unfamiliar terrestrial activity. My own capacity to remain engaged with Gérard's (entirely predictable) serial racing failures is likewise limited. As Deleuze puts it, 'Fatigue marks the point at which the soul can no longer contract what it contemplates, the moment at which contemplation and contraction come apart. We are made up of fatigues as much as of contemplations'. (DR 77)

Active synthesis

Deleuze's next move will be to insist that this first passive synthesis of habit is the foundation for agency or activity in general terms. When a honey bee smells food less than fifty feet away, it dances in a circle, signaling to other bees that food is nearby. But this active response to the environment presupposes the habituated and finely nuanced contraction of scent from the air. Deleuze even suggests that 'cellular heredity' (DR 73) constitutes a set of passive contractions, which hold not just for one bee, but for the bee's entire lineage. Likewise, the card shark will bet at just the right time to maximise winnings without attracting undue attention from the mobsters that run the casino, but this already presupposes the contraction of information during the previous hour playing poker, the 'taking in' of facts about which cards have already been played, and so on.

Deleuze never presents a definitive list of active syntheses (though Kant's syntheses of apprehension, reproduction and recognition are in the background). What he does say, though, is that the passive synthesis of habit is the foundation for 'the active faculties of reflective representation, memory and intelligence'. (DR 77) These three faculties effectively correspond to the present ('this is a pipe'), the past ('the ace of spades has already been played') and the future ('I predict that it will rain tomorrow morning'). All of these capacities are underwritten by the habituated living present, but they are genuine capacities nevertheless. I can recall what I had for dinner last night; I can scan the lemons at the supermarket and pick out the lime that has snuck in; I can sourly anticipate what would have happened if I used that lime instead of a lemon in the vinaigrette.

The inadequacy of the first synthesis

The account of habit already gives us a very rich theory of time. Deleuze will even say that 'The synthesis of time constitutes the present in time. It is not that the present is a dimension of time: the present alone exists. Rather, synthesis constitutes time as a living present, and the past and the future as dimensions of this present'. (DR 76) However, the present is not for all this a sufficient account of time. Why not? Deleuze's answer to this question occupies a dense few of pages (DR 80-2), which can be summarised in terms of two related lines of argument.

The first is as follows. The present passes. This is to say that there is a *next* present moment, and the current present will then become a past present. But when we say that time passes, into what time does it pass? 'We cannot avoid the necessary conclusion—*that there must be another time in which the first synthesis of time can occur*'. (DR 79)

The second line of argument, broadly drawn from Kant, turns around the active faculty of memory. In order for the card shark to remember how many aces have been played since the dealer last changed the deck, she needs to have access to the past present *in* the present. But this act of recollection doesn't simply return a past moment into the stream of passing presents, because what matters is that the recollection of when the aces were played is recalled in the present *along with the present itself*. This is why Deleuze writes that 'The present and the former present are not, therefore, like two successive instants on the "line of time". Rather, the present one necessarily contains an extra dimension in which it represents the former and also represents itself'. (DR 80) And if you think about it (Deleuze says), this is true not just for the act of remembering, but for any act of thought whatsoever. For instance, in order to recognize the lime amidst the lemons at the supermarket, I need to be able to invoke a past understanding of the two fruits, and to concurrently be able to deploy this knowledge in the present, in order to discriminate between them. 'The past,' then, 'is presupposed by every representation'. (DR 81)

Both arguments lead to the same conclusion: there must be a second passive synthesis, a past in relation to which the present passes and on which present acts of thought can draw.

Second synthesis: memory and the past

The second synthesis of memory, or *Mnemosyne*, constitutes the past in time. As we have just seen, a second synthesis is required by the very nature of the passing present. These arguments show, in effect, that there is no way we could ever strictly identify the past with the totality of past presents, which is close to the common-sense view of what constitutes the past. But then what is it?

Deleuze's answer draws primarily from Henri Bergson, and in particular his masterpiece *Matter and Memory*. He follows Bergson in presenting the nature of the past in terms of what he calls the three paradoxes of the past. These theses are paradoxical in a specific, if unfamiliar sense, a sense indicated by the Greek *paradoxa*—against opinion, contrary to what is accepted. The three paradoxes are only contradictory or nonsensical from the point of view of the common-sense view of the past I just mentioned. But they nevertheless constitute a true description of the nature of the past.

The first paradox asserts 'the contemporaneity of the past with the present that it was'. (DR 81) If we ask ourselves when it is that memory is formed, Bergson suggests, we quickly come to realise that there is only one viable answer. A memory cannot be formed *before* the perception it is the memory of. But neither can it be formed *after* the perception—what could account for the sudden genesis of a memory, which bears a necessary relationship with a perception, spontaneously after the passing of any amount of time whatever? If we extrapolate from examples like remembering where I put my keys to remembering a whole relationship, now ended, the ludicrousness of this idea becomes particularly obvious: how could I somehow produce *ex nihilo* recollections that correspond to that whole tragic course? So the truth remains: memories must be produced at the precise moment of the encounter itself. In *Mind-Energy*, Bergson describes this situation with an image much admired by Deleuze. The movement of the present splits into 'two perfectly symmetrical jets, one of which falls back towards the past while the other springs forward towards the future' (160). In other words, the past is the repetition of the present.

The second paradox concerns, not one present moment and its memory, but the whole of the past. Here is Deleuze: 'If each past is contemporaneous with the present that it was, then *all* of the past coexists with the new present in relation to which it is now past'. (DR 81-2) We must therefore think of the past as one massive memory, one that grows and changes at every moment as new memories are added to it. In other words, the past is an integral repetition of *every* past present, and forms an implicit but open whole of them all.

The third paradox, finally, asserts the pre-existence of the past itself as a temporal register. Because the present must pass into a time, this time must already exist—it is presupposed by the first passive synthesis. This third paradox is really what illuminates the scope of the claim Deleuze wants to make. The past is not a graveyard for former presents, but the ground of the passing of time and the being of memory as such: 'We cannot say that it was. It no longer exists, it does not exist, but it insists, it consists, it *is*. It insists with the former present, it consists with the new or present present. It is the in-itself of time as the final ground of the passage of time. In this sense it forms a pure, general, *a priori* element of all time'. (DR 82)

This is an ontological vision of the past: a total, if always open, memory, in which an image of each past present is progressively included. But it is the result of what Deleuze calls the *transcendental* passive synthesis of memory. The habitual synthesis of the present is *empirical* and *material*, and comes to bear on the matter of intensity. But this synthesis presupposes the transcendental synthesis of memory at each point: the past is the transcendental ground for the present, memory the transcendental ground for habit and its concomitant active syntheses. Correlatively, memory is unable to be conceived of as a set of material traces in the brain. It is, as Deleuze often likes to say, a past that was never present.

Involuntary memory and the virtual past

At this point in his argument, Deleuze poses the following, seemingly odd question: 'The entire past is conserved in itself, but how can we save it for ourselves, how can we penetrate that in-itself without reducing it to the former present that it was, or to the present present in relation to which it is past? How can we save it *for ourselves*?' (DR 84) Think again of the image of time splitting into two jets. The ongoing passing of the present is one jet, and it is in this time of the living present produced by the synthesis of habit. As Deleuze says, this is a time that 'we live'. (DR 84) But the other jet streams into the impassive and inactive past-in-itself of memory. So Deleuze is asking: is there any way in which we can live the past itself? Two answers to this question are ruled out in advance—he is not interested in either the active synthesis of memory, which is certainly lived but is lived on the basis of habit, and neither are we interested here in the way in which the past is always presupposed in the present. It's true of course that I cannot listen to a piece of music without the memory of the past notes and passages being passively recalled as I do so, and in this sense to live is always to live in the ambient context of a memory that enriches everything. The question is more precise: is there any way that the past *in-itself* can come to bear once more, come to matter *as past*?

Deleuze finds his answer in the work of the great Marcel Proust, in relation to one of his famous themes: involuntary memory. In a famous passage in first volume of *In Search of Lost Time*, the narrator eats a bit of a madeleine, a small cake, on a spoon with a little tea. This taste sends him into a near-rapturous state, one somehow tied up with a memory of childhood holidays in the seaside town of Combray. But, as Deleuze points out, the memory of Combray that rises up in the narrator is not any reproduction of a moment from the past—it is not the image of a past present, but, precisely, a past that was never present. 'Combray reappears, not as it was or as it could be, but in a splendour which was never lived'. (DR 85) Recall that memory on Deleuze's account is actually never lived, even in the first instance: on the one hand, it is the transcendental ground for the passing present, and on the other, it is composed of images of the passing present, and not the past presents themselves (the image of the two jets again). Consequently, the experience of involuntary memory involves the rising up of the past in-itself, unmediated by and foreign to the living present of habit.

Granted, not all experiences of involuntary memory are as filled with joy. The smell of your ex-lover's perfume in a supermarket is enough to paralyse you in your tracks; the sight of the half-untouched bed threatens to break you, in an instant, with grief. And spare a thought for the rare Luna moth whose embryogenesis expresses the recessive gene for albinism—and which hatches onto a vibrant red sumac plant. Involuntary memory is how the past is lived in-itself—it is lived as *an encounter with a problem in sensation*.

I've italicized this phrase—and discussed this passing reference to Proust—because it provides us with a very important insight into the argument of *Difference and Repetition* as a whole. For what is a problem in Deleuze? It is a virtual Idea. But if this is true, then involuntary memory would involve an encounter with the differential structure of the virtual we discussed above via Kant, Maimon and the calculus. Indeed. So here is the key point: this virtual differential structure is nothing but the past in-itself, and the past is, for Deleuze as for Bergson, virtual.

Deleuze himself only signals this identity between the past in-itself of memory and the virtual as differential structure briefly and for the most part indirectly, to the chagrin of anyone who has tried to read *Difference and Repetition* as a single coherent argument. Nevertheless, the two are indeed the same thing. Here then are the three theses that summarise the whole account of the virtual:

1. The past in-itself is a virtual memory which is constantly changing as new memories are added;
2. The structure of the past in-itself is best thought through the lens of a mathematised version of Kant's problematic ideas; and
3. The past in-itself, construed in this way, constitutes the set of structural, genetic conditions for the production and organization of reality in the future.

Identity over time: the conservative character of habit and memory

Let's continue our consideration of involuntary memory by posing a further question: why is this experience so rare? We already know the answer: *habit*. The first passive synthesis gathers together intensities in producing the lived present, which is to say that it gathers together the vectors of change into stable and self-stabilising contractile formations. In the example from Proust, a certain encounter in sensation—the taste of the madeleine—triggers the involuntary memory of Combray, but rare is the person who takes tea with their cake and finds themselves in the presence of an 'all-powerful joy'. (Proust, *Swann's Way*, 60)

The real crux of the issue here is the role of memory in habit. Involuntary memories arise only in the context where the synthesis of habit is overcome, incapable of contracting what it encounters. Otherwise, memory functions simply to ground and supplement the synthesis of the present and never appears as such: memory tends to 'represent itself as a former present and to enter into the circle which it organized in principle'. (DR 274) Or, to use one of Deleuze's most enigmatic but also weirdly beautiful turns of phrase, '*The ground is strangely bent*'. (DR 275) The past as the ground of the present bends towards the present, favours the present and gives itself over to the present in the name of the success of the first passive synthesis.

We began this discussion of time in order to explain how the static triad 'virtual—intensity—actuality' functions dynamically, but in a way the problem has only been made more serious, because (involuntary memory aside) habit and memory, the present and the past, collude in the name of stability and self-identity. Time by its very nature resists change ... 'Unless we have not yet found the last word, unless there is a third synthesis of time ...' (DR 85)

The future I: Kant, Nietzsche and the empty form of time

The first synthesis constitutes the present in time. The second synthesis constitutes the past in time, a past into which the present passes. But *why* exactly is it that the present passes? The answer to this question is revealed by considering another: what does the word 'future' mean? An obvious answer is that it is the future present. It would be the next moment like the current one, and in the endless sequence of presents. But we already know that this can't be Deleuze's answer. The future understood in this way belongs entirely to the present, to the first passive synthesis of habit and the active faculty of intelligence that is founded on it. In other words, it is not really the future at all.

If the word means anything, it must describe a temporal modality that is not subordinated to the present or the past and their respective contents. After all, if the future—as the time that is not yet—already had some content, then this content would be *necessary*. If in every future there is a God, then God is necessary and nothing in the present could act to evict it. This is another way of making the word future mean nothing, but this time in the name of the eternal rather than the present. Consequently, if there is a future, it must be radically empty.

Two philosophical precursors are in the background here. The first is, once more, Kant. Here's a useful passage from the first *Critique*:

> the empirical unity of consciousness, through association of the representations, itself concerns an appearance, and is entirely contingent. The pure form of intuition in time, on the contrary, merely as intuition in general, which contains a given manifold, stands under the original unity of consciousness, solely by means of the necessary relation of the manifold of Intuition to the one **I think**, thus through the pure synthesis of the understanding, which grounds *a priori* the empirical synthesis. (Kant, *Critique of Pure Reason* B140)

Let's consider the three main elements that Kant identifies here. First, that the content of everyday empirical experience is completely contingent—though it presupposes the operation of the faculties, it depends on what we *happen to encounter*. Second, that the only thing necessary in subjectivity is the 'original unity of consciousness', which is to say, the completely formal and empty 'I think' in relation to which all experience can be considered to be *my experience*. But third, and this is key, between the empirical content of my experience and the formal guarantee of its unity lies the pure form of time.

Now Deleuze wants no part of the Kantian commitment to the transcendental unity of apperception—the subject conceived of as a static, formal unity of the 'I think'. In fact, one point that he wants to make is that we don't need to invoke such an idea to explain the unity of subjective experience, because this is already given by the passive synthesis of habit. But he thinks Kant's account of time as the pure form of inner sense—that is, of all experience, including the experience of thought itself—constitutes a radical moment in the history of Western thought. *Every contingent occurrence is subordinated to time*, without exception. Time itself is the absolute.

But Deleuze modifies Kant on this point in the same way that he does with respect to the problematic Ideas. Exploding Kant's subjectivism, he will take this claim to be about the whole of reality. Consequently, the pure form of time will not just insist as a split between the active and passive moments of subjectivity, but will constitute a rift or ungrounding proper to the structure of being. The empty form of time will become what rules out the possibility of any unity whatsoever.

The second precursor is Nietzsche, who we have already encountered on this very topic. If Kant gives us a picture of what the empty form of time means for the apparent unity of subjectivity, Nietzsche gives us a picture of the empty form of time on its own terms. Recall that, for Deleuze, the doctrine of the eternal return is not and cannot be described as the return of the same thing over and over again. It must instead be understood as a thesis about the nature of time, namely that there is nothing more fundamental than time, and that nothing stands outside of it. But this is to identify the eternal return with the empty form of time itself—if the reality of time is the fundamental reality, this means that nothing more fundamental exists outside of its scope and function.

Like Nietzsche, Deleuze also figures the eternal return as a *test* and a *selection*: only that which is not 'selected out' by the eternal return is affirmed, but because the eternal return is the empty form of time, all that it 'selects' or affirms is what differs. Why? Because the self-identical does not subsist over time. One somewhat metaphorical way to put it is that the future, being empty, has no 'room' for identity. All that it could possibly affirm is what can undergo transformation.

The future constitutes the third synthesis of time. Unlike the other two, however, this is a *static* rather than a passive synthesis. Instead of gathering, the future is simply imposed as empty form, as 'rigorous formal and static order' and 'crushing unity'. (DR 111) Or rather, it is a mode of gathering at the very limit of itself, since what it gathers or affirms is the asymmetry of or rupture between the present and the future. As Deleuze likes to say, situating himself in a long philosophical trajectory that begins with Plato, 'time is the most radical form of change, but the form of change does not change'. (DR 89) The difference is that Deleuze is unwilling to take the point in anything but its most serious sense and with its full set of consequences for being and thought.

Two points by way of summary here. Deleuze answers the question of *how* novelty comes about by invoking the encounter that takes place in the present with an intensity that cannot be habituated, an intensity that expresses a virtual problem. But *that* novelty takes place at all is explained by the future as the third synthesis. It is only because of the empty form of time that anything *can* change, and it is the empty form that guarantees that everything *will* change. In this sense, the fundamental agent in *Difference and Repetition* is time itself, as the implacable law of the 'once and for all' that imposes itself on the present. As Deleuze puts it, 'The expulsive and selective force of the eternal return, its centrifugal force, consists in [...] ensuring that the first two repetitions do not return, that they occur only once and for all, and that only the third repetition which turns upon itself returns for all times'. (DR 297)

The future II: three figures

Deleuze makes use of a number of topological figures to flesh out his account of the future, of which we will make use of three to illustrate and summarise what's just been said about the future. The first figure is that of the *caesura*, a term Deleuze takes from Friedrich Hölderlin's enigmatic discussions of Greek tragedy. What the future introduces into time is an absolute rupture or break, a gap that nothing can bring together: it introduces 'a kind of disequilibrium, a fissure or crack [...] an alienation in principle, insurmountable in principle'. (DR 58) In this sense, the future is essentially to be thought of as a trauma or disaster that befalls the stable organization presented by the present and past. In some memorable words, this is how Deleuze describes this figure:

> the caesura, of whatever kind, must be determined in the image of a unique and tremendous event, an act which is adequate to time as a whole. This image [...] adequate to the totality of time may be expressed in many ways: to throw time out of joint, to make the sun explode, to throw oneself into the volcano, to kill God or the father. This symbolic image constitutes the totality of time to the extent that it draws together the caesura, the before and the after. (DR 89)

As Hölderlin says of Sophocles' tragedies, 'beginning and end can simply no longer rhyme with each other' ('Remarks on Oedipus', 108)

This leads into the second, initially unpromising, figure, given that the goal is to convey the radical ungrounding effected by the future: it is the figure of the *line*. Deleuze presents this image to contrast it with that of the circle. In their collusion, the present and the past make time in the image of habit: that is, as circular, as a repetition of the same (the daily routine of the stock broker, the life-cycle of the cicada). This conservative, habitual movement is broken open by the future as empty form: 'Time itself unfolds [...] instead of things unfolding within it' (DR 88). The caesura, as the 'too much', is the agent of this new linear distribution. It is with respect to this figure that Deleuze often invokes the famous line from *Hamlet*: 'time is out of joint'.

The third figure, the *series*, is implicit in the two previous figures and completes them. In breaking open the circle of habit in its complicity with memory, the future as caesura distributes the temporal registers into their respective places, no longer on the basis of the habitual present but from the point of view of the time of the future. From this point of view, the past appears as a state of affairs which is inadequate to deal with the encounter. Think, Deleuze says, of the first act of Hamlet. He knows that his father has been murdered by his uncle, but is frozen, unwilling and unable to act in the way that this calls for. The present, then, describes the moment of 'becoming equal to the act'—Hamlet's sea voyage. But then there is

> the third time in which the future appears, this signifies that the event and the act possess a secret coherence which excludes that of the self; that they turn back against the self which has become their equal and smash it to pieces, as though the bearer of the new world were carried away and dispersed by the shock of the multiplicity to which it gives birth: what the self has become equal to is the unequal in itself. (DR 89-90)

The fate of Hamlet is the most extreme exemplar here, but in more mundane terms, Deleuze's point is that what the encounter with a problem demands is the transformation of the one who encounters it. When the scientist increases the salinity of a rat's drinking water, the rat must change, or die, just as a divorcee only survives by becoming someone unrecognizable to their former partner. In sum: it is *this serial order*, and not the half-awake, half-dreaming life of habit and memory, that is the truth of time.

HUMAN BEING

We're now in a position to register two very important facts about the argument of *Difference and Repetition*. The first is that while Deleuze draws from philosophical positions that are uniquely concerned with human thought and experience, he does so in order to reflect *both* on human thought and being in general. The obvious case here is Kant. Kant's critical philosophy as a whole concerns grounding all universal and necessary claims in the structure of human thought. Certainly the parts of Kant that Deleuze draws on seem to be applicable only to human thought. But Deleuze wants to take parts of his philosophy and apply them in absolutely general, ontological terms.

The second point is that, in *Difference and Repetition*, Deleuze distinguishes human reality from being in general, and thinks that there are things that must be said to explain human being *in excess* of what is required to explain wheat growing in a field, or the embryogenesis of a tortoise. The best way to make this point is to say that the word 'thought' has *two* main meanings in the book. At times, it refers to a human capacity—this, for instance, is the primary sense of thought and thinking in the third 'Image of Thought' chapter. At other times, it refers to the production of reality itself. The fifth chapter baldly asserts this: 'The thinker is the individual'. (DR 253) The individual in turn thinks virtual Ideas—Deleuze takes 'the intensity that expresses the Idea' to be synonymous with 'the individual which thinks it'. (DR 253) A particularly taxing part of reading the book is keeping straight which of these two registers are in play at a given moment, especially because there are certainly times when the one follows the other remarkably quickly and without any warning.

As you might have noticed, these two points are closely related. They are so close, in fact, that their proximity has been the source of significant misunderstandings. It is common, for instance, to think that Deleuze has no specific account of human being, but sophisticated readers of Deleuze have also made arguments to the opposite end. Both such accounts have to work hard to ignore the explicit statements that support their counterparts' positions. So, to conclude our discussion in this chapter, we will now isolate what Deleuze says in particular about human being from the broader project of *Difference and Repetition*, repeating the trajectory from intensity through the temporal syntheses in this specific register.

Human beings as psychic systems

Let's begin by insisting that Deleuze has no trouble at all conceiving of human beings as biological systems in just the way that a stalk of wheat or a tortoise are. Like them, we are, as living beings, solutions to virtual problems expressed by intensity. The human embryo, like the embryo of the tortoise, is an intensive field characterized by tendencies that express the differential relations and singular points of the virtual, but which are not yet qualified and extended. The human embryo is capable of undergoing many things that the adult (actualized) human being, as a biological being, simply cannot.

But we are more than mammals, and human being is on the far side of a difference in kind from the animal kingdom. To use Deleuze's terminology, we are also *psychic systems*. The biological life of wheat includes within it subordinate chemical processes ('contracted water, nitrogen, carbon, chlorides and sulphates' [DR 75]). Conversely, the biological life of the human body is the subordinate material element which makes possible consciousness and representational thought.

So the project of this last section now comes into more focus. What we need to understand is how the major categories of *Difference and Repetition* will play out for psychic systems, above and beyond what we have already seen with respect to the other registers of being. He does this, as we are about to see, in close quarters combat with Freudian and Lacanian psychoanalysis.

The id and the pleasure principle

The constitution of psychic systems begins with the biological human being; it begins in the same way as the constitution of wheat or tortoises, with the habitual contraction of intensive differences:

> Biopsychical life implies a field of individuation in which differences in intensity are distributed here and there in the form of excitations. The quantitative and qualitative process of the resolution of such differences is what we call pleasure. A totality of this kind—a mobile distribution of differences and local resolutions within an intensive field—corresponds to what Freud called the Id, or at least the primary layer of the Id. (DR 96)

The psyche begins, then, as a disparate field—an intensive field. But, Deleuze asks, what is it exactly that constitutes the systematization of these resolutions—what is it that makes pleasure a general principle and initiates the passage from intensity to actuality? The answer is the first passive synthesis, which, following Freud, he gives the name binding: 'Binding represents a pure passive synthesis, a Habitus which confers on pleasure the value of being a principle of satisfaction in general. Habit underlies the organisation of the Id'. (DR 97) So, for Deleuze, the first level of subjectivity is radically passive with respect to any idea of human agency. This will come much later in the order of things. So far, this is perfectly in keeping with Freud.

The ego and the reality principle

The effects of the first passive synthesis in the psyche correspond to the active synthesis founded on it. In Freudian terms, this concerns the formation of the ego and the reality principle. But Deleuze breaks with Freud on both points. He first disagrees with Freud that the primary function of the ego is to mediate the respective demands of the id and the external world. Here is one canonical formulation of that view, with which Deleuze would disagrees almost entirely:

> the ego seeks to bring the influence of the external world to bear on the id and its tendencies, and endeavours to substitute the reality principle for the pleasure principle which reigns unrestrictedly in the id. For the ego, perception plays the part which in the id falls to

> instinct. The ego represents what may be called reason and common sense, in contrast to the id, which contains the passions. (Freud, *The Ego and the Id*, 25)

In Deleuze's view it is rather that the ego functions primarily, not to *recognize* objects (supposed as pre-given) that can satisfy the drives in the id as they are encountered in the world, but to *construct* psychic objects that can function as templates or guides for conscious activity:

> an active synthesis is established upon the foundation of the passive syntheses: this consists in relating the bound excitation to an object supposed to be both real and the end of our actions [...] Active synthesis is defined by the test of reality in an 'objectal' relation, and it is precisely according to the reality principle that the Ego tends to 'be activated', to be actively unified. (DR 98)

Consider: there is no one natural kind of object in the world that satisfies thirst. Eating an orange does this just as does drinking a glass of water. The idea of a 'drink' in general is one produced by the ego on the basis of prior habitual contractions—it is neither exhaustive nor definitive, and yet it functions as a means of organizing conscious activity with respect to this need. More generally, the ego functions to construct general objects that would satisfy the drives, by drawing from the flux of encounters.

Consequently, Deleuze bridles at the idea that the reality principle functions in a strictly negative fashion, the expression of a constraint on the psyche or as a principle opposed to the pleasure principle. It is instead primarily an *extension* of the pleasure principle in the direction of reality; it provides the pleasure principle with a set of ready-made directions in which to unfold: 'The two principles are on the same track, even though one goes further than the other'. (DR 98)

It is also worth noting at this point that Deleuze's deployment of the reality principle is not a simple copy of Freud's—it is not meant to simply account for the role of 'the real world' in psychic organization—but has a very significant range. Consider the fact that this active synthesis functions to *create self-identical and stable objects* (production of identity) interior to thought that constitute the human relationship to the world. In turn, the reality principle explains the stability of human thought. Since the objects of thought are constituted by the subject in the image of the *resolved drives*, their placidity is to be expected. To cut to the chase: the advent of the reality principle and the active synthesis of the ego are what give rise to the dogmatic image of thought. Here is Deleuze with respect to the first postulate of good sense: 'Good sense is based upon a synthesis of time, in particular the one which we have determined as the first synthesis, that of habit'. (DR 225) And if we were to return to the critical sequence of the 'Image of Thought' chapter, we would be able to see this play out with respect to the other postulates too.

The past and the object of desire

So far, Deleuze's account of the three syntheses in the case of psychic systems completely tracks with the more general account. This continues with his account of the second passive synthesis. Consequently we should expect to read that the first synthesis of habit is insufficient on its own terms to account for psychic life, and that an additional virtual register is required.

First, what constitutes the insufficiency of the first passive synthesis in this specific instance? Deleuze frames this question in some memorable passages on early childhood:

> A child who begins to walk does not only bind excitations in a passive synthesis, even supposing that these were endogenous excitations born of its own movements. No one has ever walked endogenously. On the one hand, the child goes beyond the bound excitations towards the supposition or the intentionality of an object, such as the mother, as the goal of an effort, the end to be actively reached 'in reality' and in relation to which success and failure may be measured. But *on the other hand and at the same time,* the child constructs for itself another object, a quite different kind of object which is a *virtual* object or centre and which then governs and compensates for the progresses and failures of its real activity: it puts several fingers in its mouth, wraps the other arm around this virtual centre, and appraises the whole situation from the point of view of this virtual mother. (DR 99)

In general terms, and without yet talking about what this object is exactly, what Deleuze is pointing at here is the constitution of an *orientation* or *meaning* of an action in the psychic life of the child. No child would learn to walk should it stay at the level of the first passive synthesis—this is Deleuze's claim. The mother, as the motive for this action, appears first of all as a global object of satisfaction produced by the active synthesis of the ego. But when the mother doesn't satisfy the child, even in her presence, who does the child cry to? What allows the child to remain attached to the real mother even when she disappoints? Here's another version of the question, this time from the other end of the spectrum of reproduction: what explains the fact that we sometimes cry out someone else's name in bed?

In both cases, and in psychic life more generally, what makes the psychic system function is the presence of two orienting objects, one of which gives depth (the virtual object) and significance to the other (the real object). Deleuze suggests as a result that we should think of the structure of subjectivity as a figure eight, where each of the two loops are occupied by one of the two objects: the real object and its virtual counterpart. At the point of intersection, we find the ego itself: no longer conceived as a thing or stable person, it is instead the ongoing synthetic product that takes place in the space between the two objects.

The virtual object is the product of a second passive synthesis of memory or the past. At first blush, this seems peculiar. What does the virtual mother, who orientates and compensates for the real mother, have to do with the past? More generally, why would we conceive of the object of desire in this way? Recall the second synthesis in general terms: it consists in the production of a virtual past that has never been present. The virtual mother is not a real person, not even a memory of the real mother in a previous present moment—it is the mother-as-supplement, the mother-as-meaning, the mother-as-inexhaustible depths. Likewise, when I call out someone *else's* name, I am not invoking them in person, not really calling for them to be there. I am instead invoking a virtual lover who has never existed, but who supplements sex, makes it a matter of desire rather than a process of animal impulse. Of course, it is a shame that the name in question was uttered, and that it didn't correspond to the real person in the bed—hence the value of the virtual lover's many pseudonyms (*baby, daddy*, etc.). But nevertheless, the second, virtual object— 'a shred of pure past' (DR 101)—is a necessary element in the formation and functioning of desire.

With respect to psychoanalysis, Deleuze identifies this object with Lacan's object-cause of desire, *l'objet petit a*. For Lacan, this object does not exist, it has no proper place, and is constitutively incomplete—all the features that Deleuze identifies with the virtual object. The *a* is that 'special something' that makes one person in the room stand out, seem novel, exceptional, entirely unknown and mysterious, unknowable. It supplements the material reality of the person as I experience them by giving to them a hidden depth (a profundity) and a difference from everything else. The object of desire, that is, has an effect akin to an optical effect or mirage, intimating a depth or difference from a specific point of view (that of the object itself). It is for this reason that Deleuze insists on the disguising and displacing character of the virtual object. Rather than being an object *in* the field of experience, it is an object that modifies the field of experience itself, charging it with depth, giving it a rich but anobjective meaningfulness. This is why, conversely, Deleuze will make the apparently enigmatic claim that every reminiscence is erotic (DR 85). In the psyche, memory plays in habit, the past plays in the present, in the form of the object of desire.

Deleuze takes this account to explain a wide variety of things, from left-handedness to the effectiveness of psychoanalysis as a therapy. But perhaps the most impressive application he makes of it—and the most useful for us here as an illustration—concerns the very famous psychoanalytic account of childhood trauma. A familiar critique of psychoanalysis' emphasis on childhood experience would be to claim that the resurfacing of events claimed to be the cause of trauma could easily be fictions (since they are old memories and the memories of a child). There is also the fact that what triggers the past sequence and awakens effects in the present often doesn't resemble in any direct way the past sequence itself. But this whole way of framing the question is entirely secondary and misleading.

> When Freud shows that a *phantasy* is constituted on the basis of at least two series, one infantile and pre-genital, the other genital and post-pubescent, it is clear that the series succeed one another in time from the point of view of the solipsistic unconscious of the subject in question. The question then arises how to explain the phenomenon of 'delay' which is involved in the time it takes for the supposedly original infantile scene to produce its effect at a distance, in an adult scene which resembles it and which we call 'derived' [...] In fact the two series—one infantile, the other adult—are not distributed within the same subject. The childhood event is not one of the two real series but, rather, the dark precursor which establishes communication between the basic series, that of the adults we knew as a child and that of the adult we are among other adults and other children. (DR 124)

In truth, then, there is no 'original' or 'originary' sequence of present moments which then explains the later traumatic affects that appear in a 'derivative' or 'resulting' sequence. There are two sequences or series of present moments, but what brings them together is not a factual sequence of occurrences, but this 'dark precursor'—virtual problem, object of desire, problematic Idea—that brings the two into communication without making the one follow on from the other in accordance with a strict material identity between them.

In other words, the real cause of the trauma in the present, and what makes the two series of present moments resonate, has never existed and has no proper place: 'We do not know *when* or *where* we have seen it, in accordance with the objective nature of the problematic; and ultimately, it is only the strange which is familiar and only difference which is repeated'. (DR 109) Precisely this same sentiment holds for the work of desire more generally: 'I feel like I have been waiting for you my whole life', 'You gave me something I didn't even know I wanted', et cetera, et cetera. The whole parade of romantic clichés is perhaps the result of the always displaced, never present object of desire.

This discussion also reveals the site at which the conservatism of the first two syntheses operates. Recall that, at the general level, habit and memory form a circle around the figure of identity. This results from the fact that the habitual present takes the past to be a past present. In the psyche, the problem arises in the same way. The past appears in the form of a former present, one charged with all of the force of desire— the mythical present of *firsts* (first love, first love lost, first affair, first 'transgression', etc.) As a result, the decentering, derailing effect of the object of desire as shred of the pure past is subordinated to the subject's ongoing identity in the present. This is how desire and the ego tend to cover over the intensive dynamisms and passive syntheses on which they are founded—'Always the same ambiguity on the part of the ground: to represent itself in the circle that it imposes on what it grounds, to return as an element in the circuit of representation that it determines in principle'. (DR 110)

The future III: the narcissistic ego

Finally, what is the place of the static synthesis of the future in psychic life? The key thing to grasp here is that the third synthesis will appear not in person—as the pact between difference and repetition in the pure empty form of time—but in terms of its effects on psychic systems. At the limit, this will take the form of death in the psyche, since death is the name for the dissolution of identity—but death in what sense? And what other, more 'moderate' transformations will it also ensure? Here is the key passage:

> The narcissistic ego indeed appears in time, but does not constitute a temporal content: the narcissistic libido, the reflux of the libido into the ego, abstracts from all content. The narcissistic ego is, rather, the

phenomenon which corresponds to the empty form of time without filling it. (DR 110)

Narcissism describes the situation in which the ego is libidinally invested in itself. For the narcissist, other people appear as elements in their own psychic processes, as means to ends or representatives of their own desires. The narcissistic ego is therefore no longer invested in either the real object of the active synthesis or the virtual object of the passive synthesis. But how is this at all possible? Strictly speaking, such a state is unlivable, because it means the breaking down of all binding in the id and all identification and investment in and through the ego. In this state, the psyche would literally be an empty form, an ego in the form of an ouroboros. And indeed, Deleuze is not presenting the narcissist as some kind of ideal form of subjectivity, or even as a viable form of subjectivity. The point he's making is more subtle and profound: when the psyche confronts a problem, a trauma, it is forced to change. In other words, the existing bindings in the id and investments and identifications in the ego are—necessarily—broken in order to forge new connections suitable to the new situation. It is to this moment of rupture that the narcissistic ego corresponds, as the quote above indicates. Without the impact of ruptures of this kind—the impact of trauma, to be blunt—the collusion between the bound id and the invested ego would close out any novelty and change.

It is also on the basis of these traumatic ruptures that Deleuze will explain thought itself. When existing investments are broken, the energy that they had bound up is released, furnishing to the psyche a certain quantity of 'neutral and displaceable' (DR 114) energy, that is, *desexualised* libido—or, to be more precise, *intensity unbound from any synthesis*. And this unbinding, like the escape of difference from identity affirmed by the static synthesis of the future more generally, is only possible because every particular binding is rendered contingent by the static synthesis of the future, or what Deleuze will not hesitate to call *Thanatos*.

Now, thinking involves being able to pass from one idea to another, to invert them, to entertain concepts in order to assess their validity, to hypothesise and project, to wonder and to predict. All of this is impossible at the level of habit and memory, where all intensity is bound and its resolution oriented. When I think about what might have been with a lover long past, I make use of a mobile, displaceable energy in the psyche that is not invested in any given image (active synthesis), nor any habitual reception or virtual identification (first two passive syntheses). Instead, I am able to think this alternative hypothesis without investment. Here and in general, thinking requires this dis-invested psychic energy, and without it, only habit and desire are possible. Thought is therefore, strictly speaking, *dead desire*.

The first synthesis brings about the systematisation of the drives in the service of *need*. The second synthesis transforms the resolution of needs into an existence oriented by *desire*, thanks to the stereoscope of the double object. But only the third synthesis guarantees that *thought is possible*, that it is possible for psychic energy to be neutralised, freed from all commitments in advance and open to an empty future in which the demand for thinking falls upon the thinker as an implacable event.

Individuality and trauma in psychic systems

So far, we've examined psychic systems from the point of view of the three syntheses, but it is also worth asking how the human being looks from the two extreme points of the process of ontogenesis: intensity on the one hand, and the final products of active synthesis on the other.

What composes the level of intensive individuation in the psyche? Here is Deleuze's initially surprising response: 'Dreams are our eggs, our larvae and our properly psychic individuals'. (DR 250) At first, this seems to conflict with the account given above. After all, how can dreams pre-exist the formation of the psyche itself as that psyche's own component elements? The notion of dreaming that Deleuze is using here is psychoanalytic, if in a very broad sense. It comes closest to Freud's notion of the 'dream-work':

> This dream-work proper diverges further from our picture of waking thought than has been supposed even by the most determined depredator of psychical functioning during the formation of dreams. The dream-work is not simply more careless, more irrational, more forgetful and more incomplete than waking thought; it is completely different from it qualitatively and for that reason not immediately comparable with it. It does not think, calculate or judge in any way at all; it restricts itself to giving things a new form [...] the dream-work makes use of a *displacement of psychical intensities* to the point of a transvaluation of all psychical values. (Freud, *Interpretation of Dream*, 510-11)

Now, Deleuze—following in the wake of Leibniz and Maimon—rejects the idea of a conflictual relationship between the unconscious and conscious thought, siding instead with the model of integration and production. But otherwise, this passage from Freud provides a good basis upon which to understand his own theory of the dream. The psychic processes in play is qualitatively different—pre-judicative, heterological and asignifying—from the habituated and structured processes of waking thought, above all the reflexive machinations of active synthesis. More to the point, it is these dynamisms themselves that form the primary layer of the id for Deleuze. In this sense, he uses the term 'dream' to describe something much more profound than Freud does—not just an effort to work through repressed desire, but as a return to the ontogenetic matter of subjectivity itself.

So this accounts for the reference to dreams. But what of the return to the thematic of the egg? We have already seen that the embryo provides Deleuze with the principal example of the intensive individual; here is how he brings the topics together explicitly:

> Embryology already displays the truth that there are systematic vital movements, torsions and drifts, that only the embryo can sustain: an adult would be torn apart by them. There are movements for which one can only be a patient, but the patient in turn can only be a larva. Evolution does not take place in the open air, and only the involuted evolves. A nightmare is perhaps a psychic dynamism that could be sustained neither awake *nor even in dreams,* but only in profound sleep, in a dreamless sleep. In this sense, it is not even clear that thought, in so far as it constitutes the dynamism peculiar to philosophical systems, may be related to a substantial, completed and well-constituted subject, such as the Cartesian Cogito: thought is, rather, one of those terrible movements which can be sustained only under the conditions of a larval subject. (DR 118)

Trauma. To be thrown back on the intensive individuals that are our larval selves at the level of human thought is, then, to be thrown back on a disorganized layer of psychic life in which our upright concepts no longer find purchase, and the proper names for things slide off like wet stamps. As psychic systems, and even more as thinkers, we remain part embryo, and the stable formations of 'waking' thought—rational, systematic thinking, the fruits of active syntheses—are all in the final analysis drawn from the reservoir of the unconscious dynamisms of intensity.

The genesis of the dogmatic image of thought

One final step. If human thought arises through this process of synthetic ontogenesis, we should also be able to explain why it congenitally misunderstands this process itself. As I've noted a couple of times in passing, this is Deleuze's most general ambition for his genetic philosophy: to explain not just the advent of reality, but the advent of its own misrecognition. We saw earlier that the root of this misrecognition is found in intensity itself, or rather in the way in which intensity is covered over in the process of its explication.

Recall the role of the active synthesis of the ego, which produces the real objects of recognition and in turn provides a stable basis for prediction, representation and recognition—this is a piece of wax, the sun will rise tomorrow, good morning Theaetetus. As Deleuze notes, these kinds of acts of thought 'occupy a large part of our daily life,' even though we would be mortally mistaken to think that 'the destiny of thought is at stake in these acts'. (DR 135) It is the collusion of habit and memory that make these acts possible, but what is more, grounds the dogmatic image of thought. The stable identity of each of the two objects of experience, and their collusion in the name of that experience, explain the tendency to think starting with the category of identity.

But this provides us with a way to return, at last, to the first chapter of *Difference and Repetition*, to its serial examination of Aristotle, Hegel and Leibniz, and a way to close the circle of our investigation. We are now in the position to understand why it is that the history of Western philosophy tended to explicitly and systematically subjugate difference to identity. It was not because Aristotle was an idiot. Human thought is always undergirded by the dogmatic image. This is not something we can simply do away with once and for all, because, as we have just seen, it arises on the basis of the ontogenetic processes that engender thought. Or, to use the terminology we began with, objective misrecognitions of difference (explicit arguments that subordinate difference to identity) are grounded in the subjective misrecognition of difference (the dogmatic image), which is given rise to in turn by the very processes that generate reality itself, including the reality of conscious human experience. Certainly, 'Difference is inverted, first, by the requirements of representation which subordinate it to identity', but this is itself finally explained by the fact that 'extensity and quality [...] cover or explicate intensity'. (DR 235)

INDI-DRAMA-DIFFERENT/CIATION

To summarise his position in *Difference and Repetition*, Deleuze introduces what is surely his most unkempt neologism: indi-drama-different/ciation. It nevertheless remains a useful touchpoint and will provide us with a good way to take in the sweep of his project. The virtual is *differentiated*, which is to say that it is a reciprocally determined differential structure populated by singularities. This structure is expressed in and through intensive individuals in a process Deleuze calls *individuation*. These intensive individuals are the immediate material taken up by the three syntheses in a process called *dramatization*. The first two syntheses are responsible for producing and maintaining the existence of objects in general: the actual, that is to say, is *differenciated*. This includes the particular subset of objects that we call subjects (*psychic systems*). The third synthesis, finally, functions to rule out this processual ontology ever grinding to a halt. No differenciated object is ever guaranteed to continue existing because time itself, the empty form of time or the third static synthesis, guarantees that it will continue to undergo new encounters, at least until it runs up against something that is terminally too much for it. This is death, 'the last form of the problematic'. (DR 112)

8

Logic of Sense

Though Deleuze's *Logic of Sense* was published early in 1969, he indicates that its composition had taken place alongside that of *Difference and Repetition* earlier in the decade (N 7). That year was a busy one for Deleuze—or rather, not at all busy. It began in hospital; the balance was spent convalescing in his wife Fanny's Limousin country house after the springtime removal of his tubercular lung. Near the end of December, Deleuze writes to Pierre Klossowski to say that he was feeling much better, and that the 'filthy surgery' had dealt with the 'craven organic regression' of his diseased lung. (LAT 58)

While it forms a careful and systematic argument on its own terms, the *Logic of Sense* is nevertheless related to two series of articles that Deleuze published in the years before the book appeared. On the one hand, Deleuze had published work on Artaud and Lewis Carroll, schizophrenia and language throughout the sixties. As we will see, these are key elements in the book, even if his final position is sometimes a modification of what the earlier pieces advance. On the other hand, he also published a number of pieces which 'develop certain points which are only briefly touched on' (LS xiv) in the book proper, but are included as appendices in *The Logic of Sense*. They address Plato, Lucretius, Klossowski and language, the concept of the Other in Michel Tournier's fiction, and on Zola and naturalism, a range of topics that conveys a good sense of the scope of *Logic of Sense* itself.

But perhaps the most notable aspect of the book overall is the degree to which it explicitly endorses and deploys psychoanalysis. Deleuze will even go so far as to describe his book as 'an attempt to develop a logical, psychoanalytic novel'. (LS xiv—not a 'psychological' novel as the translators unfortunately have it) We are not just talking about Freud either: the work of both Melanie Klein and Jacques Lacan play an irreducible role in the construction of Deleuze's argument in *Logic of Sense*. When he later reflects on the prominence of psychoanalysis, he plays its significance down (e.g. N 144), but this is a revisionist take. His affirmation of its value as a modality of thinking and a clinical practice is unalloyed here. And it happens that the respect was mutual. In his seminar of March 12, 1969, Lacan remarks the pleasant surprise of finding a new book of Deleuze's on his desk. In inimitable fashion, he couches his admiration of Deleuze's work in the recognition that it is, after all, an elaboration of his own: 'he has, to his credit, been able to take the time to articulate, to assemble in a single text not simply what is involved at the heart of what my discourse has stated [...] but all of these things that have nourished my discourse'. (*Le Séminaire Livre XVI*, 208-9)

There is one other general feature of the *Logic of Sense* that should be discussed at the outset. This is the first time that Deleuze will begin to explicitly play with the organization of his books. Rather than chapters, *Logic of Sense* is composed of *series*. The overall significance of this choice can be difficult to make sense of at the outset, because *Logic of Sense* develops its own account of the nature of series. The key idea, though, is this: no one series has any meaning without a relationship with another series. The classic case would is the series of signifiers (the noises and graphic marks that are involved in language) and its necessary relationship to a series of signifieds (ideas, concepts or meanings). Without the latter, the former really are just noises, however well differentiated they may be. Structuralist linguistics takes the reciprocal determination of these two series as its starting point.

So, in the case of the *Logic of Sense*, this would appear to mean that no one chapter has meaning other than in its relationship to the others. But so what? Isn't this true for the composition of any book? The difference lies in the fact that the normal organization of chapters (first, second, third ...) presumes that we will read them in their given order. What Deleuze wants to convey in writing a book composed of series is that there is no fixed order in which it should be read.

Putting aside the trivial fact that we can, of course, read any book out of order if we want to, there's the unfortunate problem that this is simply not true in any profound way for the *Logic of Sense*. With the exception of a few somewhat isolated series—the best example is the magnificent 'Eighteenth Series of the Three Images of the Philosophers', which could have been published as a little pocket book—*Logic of Sense* has a quite linear structure. There are also series that begin by explicitly continuing the work of the previous one. The chapter with the best title, 'Twenty-Ninth Series—Good Intentions are Inevitably Punished' begins with the words 'It is necessary therefore …' (LS 202) So we would be better off seeing the book in terms of *three* overall parts that form a *clearly ordered progression*, plus a few interludes on specific topics.

THE THREE GUIDING QUESTIONS OF THE *LOGIC OF SENSE*

These three main parts correspond to three questions:
1. What are events, and how do they relate to the physical world on the one hand, and language on the other?
2. What makes language-use possible, not to mention critical thought? That is: how can we explain the passage from the screaming newborn to the poet and the philosopher?
3. What meaning can be given to ethics if the physical world is causally determined? Or: what is the relationship between freedom and events?

Each of these questions in turn occupies a segment of *Logic of Sense*'s argument, and Deleuze draws upon a particular set of philosophical and literary resources to answer them.

The answer to the first question leads Deleuze to present an account of the structure of reality (we will refer to this moment as the *structural account*)—*being and event*. This structure will include places for the causal network of bodies, language-use, and events. To elaborate this account, Deleuze will draw on a wide range of thinkers: Stoic and Epicurean philosophers, Leibniz and Nietzsche, Lacan and Bertrand Russell, but also Lewis Carroll and Antonin Artaud. Roughly speaking, this account takes up the first eighteen series of the book, and then from the twenty-third to the twenty-sixth.

The second question is dealt with on the basis of a *genetic account* of the speaking subject—it concerns *sex and surfaces*. It is this aspect of *Logic of Sense* which draws on psychoanalysis, but also on a pair of radical French writers, Artaud once again, but also Pierre Klossowski. This account is more or less the object of the book's last chapters, from the twenty-seventh to the thirty-fourth series.

The third question concerns an ethics, one based on the ontology of the event elaborated in the structural account. The explicit references here are the Stoics and Artaud once more, but also F. Scott Fitzgerald and Jöe Bosquet, two other literary figures; implicitly, Nietzsche is key. Each of them cast some light, for Deleuze, on the pair of *freedom and death*. In order to better see the continuity of the structural and genetic accounts, we will consider this ethical question last, but its elaboration is in fact found near the middle of the book, across the twentieth, twenty-first and twenty-second series.

TWO EVENTS

Early in the morning on May 27, 1918, the German army launched a surprise attack on the French position at a strategically decisive ridge known as the Chemin des Dames, about eighty miles north-east of Paris. A massive bombardment from 4000 artillery pieces—some have estimated that around two million shells were fired—was followed by an enormous gas attack, the aim of which was to neutralize defensive gunnery positions. In their wake came seventeen German stormtrooper divisions—almost 300,000 soldiers—on foot. At the end of the day, taking into account soldiers on both sides, over a quarter of a million people had been killed.

This event is known as the Third Battle of the Aisne, and it will serve as the first of two guiding examples as we consider Deleuze's definition of the event. Why start with such a grim example? It is because, for Deleuze, 'the battle is not an example of an event among others, but rather the Event in its essence'. (LS 100) What gives the battle such a significance? When we start thinking about what the Third Battle of the Aisne involved as an event, we begin to see that nothing at all about it is simple.

Let's start with an apparently straightforward question: *when* was the battle? In standard military histories of the first world war, the Third Battle of the Aisne occupies a discrete period of time. The German army began the assault at 1am in the morning, and was concluded that evening when, 'after a forty-mile advance, [this] tactical masterpiece faded to strategic inconsequence'. (Cowley, 'The Ludendorff Offensive', 274) But the battle was also already an event for the German troops weeks before it was one for the French troops. The plan for the battle was concocted by General Erich Ludendorff; for Ludendorff, as a result, the third Battle of the Aisne had been happening for years before 1918. But it is also true that he never ceased to live the battle after it was 'over'. Convinced that if he had been given a more substantial number of soldiers he would have succeeded, the remainder of his life was tormented by the spectre of his failure. This torment led, for instance, to the composition of *Der Totale Krieg*, a book that proposed a theory of total war. Consequently, the answer to the question 'when was the battle?' cannot be given in the simple and discrete terms of historical time. The most that can be said is that the battle is never exhausted by any one present moment: 'Never present but always yet to come and already passed' (LS 100).

Deleuze for his part poses another question which has an equally complicated answer: *where* is the battle? Well, the Third Battle of Aisne was focused around the Chemin des Dames, but it was also in Sweden, where Ludendorff fled, a failure, at the end of the war. It was in the offices of the German National Army in Berlin; it's there with you now, as you read this.

Let's linger over one final question for now: who was the Third Battle of Aisne an event *for*? I said above that the soldiers who were the initial target of the assault were predominantly French. But four divisions of British soldiers, from Middlesex, Devon and West Yorkshire and elsewhere were also killed on May 27, many of them in the initial onslaught. And of course the battle wasn't just an event for the Allied forces, but for the German soldiers too. Then there were all of the thousands of people not a part of the military that were caught up in the battle as it hammered towards Paris—those literally in the way of the army, but also all of those at home, fearful for both news and its absence. It's an event for scholars of military history, but also for those tourists looking for the French countryside of Camille Claudel but who come upon marked earth. So, who was the battle an event for? This enormous, ever-expanding host—the subject of the Third Battle of Aisne—is a kind of anonymous, impersonal 'someone', a name that has to be vague enough to be able to designate both those that survived and those that died; those that won and those that lost; those that lived the battle in the months before April 1918 and those, like you and me, who are living it now; and so on.

So we begin to see that the event of the Third Battle of Aisne is not at all simple. We can of course locate quite precise material circumstances in which the battle was actualized (to use a technical term that we'll have to make sense of)—for instance the bodily existence of General Ludendorff. But locating the event itself proves to be something altogether different. It begins to appear as something like 'an immense black and neutral cloud, or a noisy crow [that] hovers over the combatants and separates or disperses them only in order to render them even more indistinct'. (LS 101)

Alice's adventures

Now let's take a different case, one that may be more whimsical but is no less serious, the one with which Deleuze begins the *Logic of Sense*. Throughout Lewis Carroll's *Alice's Adventures in Wonderland*, Alice finds herself engaged in various processes of growing and shrinking. Quite early on, she drinks a small bottle whose flavor is a mixture of a large variety of foods: 'cherry-tart, custard, pine-apple, roast turkey, toffy, and hot buttered toast.' (*Wonderland*, 19) Upon finishing it, she finds herself shrinking down, as if 'shutting up like a telescope,' (*Wonderland*, 19) becoming in the end ten inches high.

The value of this particular example lies in the unbounded mixture it presents to us, but Deleuze's various discussions of Alice growing and shrinking are likely invocations of a more famous case from later in the tale:

> By this time she had found her way into a tidy little room with a table in the window, and on it (as she had hoped) a fan and two or three pairs of tiny white kid-gloves: she took up the fan and a pair of the gloves, and was just going to leave the room, when her eye fell upon a little bottle that stood near the looking-glass. There was no label this time with the words "DRINK ME," but nevertheless she uncorked it and put it to her lips. "I know *something* interesting is sure to happen," she said to herself, "whenever I eat or drink anything: so I'll just see what this bottle does. I do hope it'll make me grow large again, for really I'm quite tired of being such a tiny little thing!"
>
> It did so indeed, and much sooner than she had expected: before she had drunk half the bottle, she found her head pressing against the ceiling, and had to stoop to save her neck from being broken. She hastily put down the bottle, saying to herself "That's quite enough—I hope I shan't grow any more—As it is, I can't get out at the door—I do wish I hadn't drunk quite so much!"
>
> Alas! It was too late to wish that! She went on growing, and growing, and very soon had to kneel down on the floor: in another minute there was not even room for this, and she tried the effect of lying down with one elbow against the door, and the other arm curled around her head. Still she went on growing, and, as a last resource, she put one arm out the window, and one foot up the

chimney, and said to herself "Now I can do no more, whatever happens. What *will* become of me?" (45-6)

Here is Deleuze:

> *Alice* and *Through the Looking-Glass* involve a category of very special things: events, pure events. When I say 'Alice becomes larger,' I mean that she becomes larger than she was. By the same token, however, she becomes smaller than she is now. Certainly, she is not bigger and smaller at the same time. She is larger now; she was smaller before. But it is at the same moment that one becomes larger than one was and smaller than one becomes. (LS 1)

This passage is deceptively simple, something that becomes obvious when you start to think about how Alice is becoming larger and smaller at the same time. We first need to distinguish between two registers or levels of this remark. On the one hand, we have the level associated with fixed states of affairs and a linear, unidirectional movement of time. At this level, Deleuze points out, Alice is a certain, fixed, measurable height at every moment. We are capable of comparing the various states of Alice as a result. But there is also a second level that no longer pertains to a fixed state of being for Alice, but to the event 'to grow'. If we look from this point of view, things appear very differently. Certainly Alice^2 is larger than Alice^1, but Alice^2 is also *becoming smaller* than she will be if we consider things from the point of view of Alice^3. From this point of view, the entire process moves in reverse: Alice^3 grows smaller, becoming Alice^2 and then Alice^1, and (as she does earlier in the story), worries about becoming Alice^0.

But, you might object, time only moves in one direction—forward, from the past to the future—so there is no meaning at all to be attached to this reverse perspective. This objection is based on the idea that the first level of stable, discrete identities is the only correct basis for understanding what things are and how they change. Deleuze wants instead to insist that we can adopt the point of view of the event itself. Considered independently, the event 'to grow' has no natural orientation with respect to the present, past or future. It only involves a movement of becoming that affects size. 'To grow smaller' and 'to grow larger' are like 'to win the battle' and 'to lose the battle'—both are true, depending on which point of view you adopt. But in both cases, if we shift our attention to the events themselves, we discover a full suite of paradoxical features: one can grow in reverse, and the battle can be won and lost at the same time. The pure event is a pure process that needs to be understood on its own terms.

There is another illuminating connection between the events of the battle and 'to grow': when we examine Alice's adventures from the point of view of the event or her unlimited becoming, the name 'Alice' becomes somewhat precarious. It now denotes not a stable person (Alice^1 or Alice^2) with determined features, but a process without any stability at all (all of the Alice's together, an Alice^x). This other Alice from the other side of the mirror is anonymous, anomalous, unfixed, fluid—she is the kin of 'the young soldier,' the indistinct protagonist of Stephen Crane's *The Red Badge of Courage*, who Deleuze identifies as the subject of the battle.

I used the word paradoxical just before—and indeed, all of this is clearly paradoxical. But we need to pay attention to the etymological sense of this adjective: *paradoxa* is a break with *doxa*, or opinion. Certainly, common sense rules out any meaningful talk of growing backwards, and it would be easy enough to say that what is written in children's books should stay there. This is an objection anticipated by Deleuze: 'We cannot get rid of paradoxes by saying that they are more worthy of Carroll's work than they are of [Russell and Whitehead's] *Principia Mathematica*. What is good for Carroll is good for logic'. (LS 74) In other words, instead of dismissing this strange Carrollian thesis about the event as paradoxical, we should take the paradoxical character of the event itself seriously. More than this, Deleuze insists, the fight against *doxa* or common sense has always been the task of philosophy. Common sense holds faith with a world that is easily recognizable, easily digestible, and never fundamentally changes. But if we need to think change seriously, we will need to tackle the event in all of its paradoxical character.

For now, though, let me simply note that these two examples provide useful points of reference to understand the difficult claims that Deleuze will make about the nature of the event in *Logic of Sense*. The next task will be to understand the nature of the event as such, given that it has these peculiar features, and to understand the nature of the relationship between events and the particular material states of affairs or bodies in which they are actualized.

THE STOIC DISTINCTION BETWEEN BODIES AND EVENTS

Deleuze points out that the duality of being (stable states of affairs) and becoming (events) we discovered in the case of Alice is already discussed in penetrating detail in Plato's *Philebus* and *Parmenides*. But the first resource from the history of philosophy that he will draw on extensively is Stoicism, a school of Hellenistic philosophy that arose in Greece after Aristotle. We will see that Deleuze returns to the Stoics a number of times throughout the *Logic of Sense*, but his first and most significant debt to them concerns their theory of the event, and its relationship to the regime of bodies. As we will see, everything that he goes on to say about this dualism is grounded in this account. But let's begin with a brief sketch, essentially following what Deleuze writes in the 'Second Series of Paradoxes of Surface Effects'.

The Stoic body

Stoic physics presents us with a complete vision of Nature as composed of *an infinite mixture of bodies*. By 'complete', I mean that as far as the Stoics are concerned, *only bodies exist*. There is not a second level of reality populated by souls, for example, or a realm of self-identical Platonic Ideas, but only the one corporeal realm. In fact the Stoics did believe in the existence of the soul, but the soul too is corporeal, a kind of body.

In turn, by 'mixture' I mean that there is no exteriority in Nature. To be a body is to be intermixed: 'Mixtures are in bodies, and in the depths of bodies: a body penetrates another and coexists with it in all of its parts, like a drop of wine the ocean, or fire in iron. One body withdraws from another, like liquid from a vase'. (LS 5-6) Consequently, as the twentieth-century Stoic Billy Idol puts it in a text we will return to again below, 'There is nothing pure in this world' ('White Wedding'). A series of *prima facie* shocking consequences follow from this, Deleuze insists (though this perhaps pushes at the limits of a robust reading of the Stoics). If Nature is just mixture, then no one mixture is any more or less natural than any other: gluttony is equal to starvation, and there could be no legitimate prohibition against either incest or cannibalism. (LS 130)

Now, for the Stoics the whole of Nature unfolds in a total network of causal relations. A body is active in relation to another body that it causes to change, and it is passive when it is caused to change in turn. It is crucial to note—for a reason we're about to see—that the full network of bodily causation *does not include any effects*. When one body causes another to change in some way, the changed body is not itself an effect, but just a different body. Nature is thus defined as an infinite sequence of causal relations that modify the interpenetration of bodies. The other name the Stoics gave to this set-up will likely come as no surprise: *fate*, 'a sequence of causes, that is, an inescapable ordering and interconnexion'. (Aetius, 'Causation and Fate', 55J)

The other initial thing to recognize about corporeal Nature is that this unlimited series of causal relations takes place in the present. This is the companion thesis to the Stoic claim that Nature is exclusively composed by bodies. As Deleuze puts it, 'only bodies exist in space, and only the present exists in time.' (LS 4)

The Stoic event

How exactly can effects, let alone events, be brought back into the picture then? The following fragment from Sextus Empiricus provides the most direct answer:

> The Stoics say that every cause is a body which becomes the cause *to* a body *of* something incorporeal. For instance the scalpel, a body, becomes the cause *to* the flesh, a body, *of* the incorporeal predicate 'being cut'. And again, the fire, a body, becomes the cause *to* the wood, a body, *of* the incorporeal predicate 'being burnt'. (Sextus, 'Causation and Fate,' 55B; my emphasis)

I have italicized the two key prepositions, 'to' and 'of'. For the Stoics, bodies are causes *to* each other—this is what we've already seen—but there are also effects *of* these causes. These effects are, in turn, *events*. On the one hand, fire is a cause *to* the wood because the fire is the active party, and the wood the passive party. On the other, both the fire and the wood are the causal antecedents *of* an event or effect, 'being burnt' or 'to burn'.

Now, Deleuze says, notice that an event is not a *quality* of a body: the heaviness of a billiard ball is not an event or attribute. Its heaviness, however, might be key in certain events: the billiard ball knocked the Tsing Tao over onto her copy of the *Phenomenology*. It is for this reason (though not only for this reason, as we will come to see) that Deleuze will insist that events are best expressed with the infinitive form of the verb. To say a tree is green is to identify a quality of a body; to say '*The tree greens*' (LS 21) is to grasp an event expressed by the tree; and, finally, the event itself is 'to green'. Each of these perspectives has its merits. The first speaks to the nature of a body in the present; the second, to the processes or events that characterize a body in way that points beyond the present; and the third recognizes that, while the event is the effect of bodily causes, it possesses an independence or neutrality with respect to Nature as a whole. It is this neutrality, an important facet of the event that we will return to in detail, that allows events to 'take place' in such different, even apparently contradictory, ways: the battle is both won and lost, finished and yet to come, and so on. This multiplicity of expressions corresponds exactly to the multiplicity of ways in which an infinitive verb, like 'to cut' can be conjugated: I cut you; you cut me; you will cut me; I had cut you; she cut you; if you cut me; when she cut me, and so on … All the modalities of the verb are in play; all the modalities of the event are in play.

We can now fix some terminology. An event is an *effect* of a cause, one that *inheres* in bodies. The immediate upshot of this point is that—contrary to both the everyday sense of the word and more sophisticated modern scientific and philosophical accounts—events *are not causes*. Deleuze will say that they are therefore impassive or neutral. But if this is the case, then aren't we just saying that events are less effects than *side-effects*, pure epiphenomena that, in doing, mean less than nothing? This disappointing conclusion is avoided by Deleuze through the introduction of two further terms, *expression* and *quasi-causality* (though we will hold off on quasi-causality for the moment).

Rather than 'taking place', Deleuze will say that an event is *expressed by* a body or state of affairs. A relationship of expression is very particular in nature: in it, what is expressed does not exist independently of its expressor; its expressor is nevertheless characterized by the expressed. A good example is emotion: despite what excessively optimistic neurobiologists might hypothesise, being infatuated cannot be explained in terms of chemical interactions. The complex set of emotions involved do not exist independently of the lovers in question, but is instead entirely found through its expression in behaviour—inability to conjugate verbs, embarrassing blushing, tendency to lose track of

Another useful example is systemic discrimination, such as racism. Contrary to a lamentable liberal perspective, racism cannot be explained solely (if at all) as a set of consciously held beliefs about certain groups of people. As Eduardo Bonilla-Silva's sociological classic *Racism without Racists* demonstrates, racism is in fact a set of socio-political and experiential norms *expressed through and in* individual behavior—'expressions at the symbolic level of dominance'. (54) The expressive character of racism is indeed such that the subjects who are its expressors can quite often be in no way aware that they are reproducing the very system that they may even think no longer exists.

So, as the tree gets greener and greener during the early weeks of spring, the tree expresses the event in an ongoing and variable fashion depending on a huge range of other causal interactions: sunlight, temperature, nutrients in the soil, and so on. The event itself neither exists independently, nor is a causal agent in the change of the tree, nor changes itself. It is that which is capable of being expressed in each of these ways without changing, or existing, or changing.

Nature, as the ensemble of bodies, is all that *exists*. Contrary to Platonism, a transcendent realm of Ideas does not exist. However, events as effects *insist* or *subsist*. This is not just a matter of splitting hares. One of the main problems that Plato confronts is how to explain the interactions between Ideas and the material states of affairs that participate in them: to take the topic of the *Crito*, what is the relationship between the Ideal of Justice and the just person? This problem is so difficult because of the *kind* of dualism Plato pursues—for him, there are two levels of Being, distributed in terms of purity and identity (Ideas), and then degraded material copies. Precisely how does this participation function? By distinguishing between what exists (bodies) and the attributes of these bodies that inhere in them without existing (events). As a result, the general ontological category cannot be 'Being', somehow divided between the ideal and the material, the eternal and the fleeting: 'The highest term therefore is not Being, but *Something* (*aliquid*), insofar as it subsumes being and non-being, existence and inherence'. (LS 7) At the same time, by making ideal events the neutral effects of bodily interactions, the Stoics have avoided having to explain how the Ideal (in the quasi-moral sense) can be transmitted from the perfect and eternal to the 'compromised' regime of materiality.

A philosophy of the surface

As these latter remarks may have hinted, Deleuze considers the Stoic dualism to be an original move in the history of philosophy, though not one often followed by subsequent philosophers. This history has been dominated by various forms of Platonism, which is not content to speak of the immanence of events, but necessarily invokes (as we've just seen) the transcendence of the Idea. Platonism is thus a philosophy of the *heights*, and it is this orientation that we invoke when we think of the cliché, 'the popular image of the philosopher with his head in the clouds'. (LS 127) The following famous lines, spoken by Socrates shortly before imbibing the hemlock, are rightly considered emblematic:

> when the soul makes use of the body to investigate something, be it through hearing or seeing or some other sense—for to investigate something through the body is to do it through the senses—it is dragged by the body to the things that are never the same, and the soul itself strays and is confused and dizzy, as if it were drunk, in so far as it is in contact with that kind of thing [...] But when the soul investigates by itself it passes into the realm of what is pure, ever existing, immortal and unchanging. (Plato, *Phaedo* 79c-d)

The countering tendency in the history of philosophy evokes no longer the heights but the *depths*. For Deleuze, the great pre-Socratic philosophers, possessed with the composition of Nature, constitute some of the main examples. Philosopher-physicists, Deleuze will say of them that they 'philosophised with [...] the hammer of the geologist'. (LS 128) But the great modern thinker of the depths is Nietzsche, and Deleuze partially quotes the following (equally famous) lines from *Beyond Good and Evil*:

> The hermit does not believe that a philosopher—given that a philosopher was always a hermit first—has ever expressed his actual and final opinions in books: don't people write books precisely to keep what they hide to themselves? In fact, he will doubt whether a philosopher could even *have* "final and actual" opinions, whether for a philosopher every cave does not have, *must* not have, an even deeper cave behind it—a more extensive, stranger, richer world above the surface, an abyss behind every ground, under every "groundwork." Every philosophy is a foreground philosophy—that is a hermit's judgment: "There is something arbitrary in *his* stopping here, looking back, looking around, in his not digging any deeper *here*, and putting his spade away—there is also something suspicious about it." Every philosophy *conceals* a philosophy too: every opinion is also a hiding place, every word is also a mask. ('What is Noble?', §289)

This second orientation therefore has a critical edge: it takes the ideal to be derivative of what is happening in the depths, a stopping-point whose validity can always be called into question. Thinkers of the depths agree with Socrates that the realm of bodies is a realm of absolute impurity and mixture, but reject the allegation of anything like the ideal *purity* he espouses. The Nietzschean notion of the drives is emblematic in this case: any idea, representation or philosophical concept is animated by a complex and antagonistic bodily dynamism.

The Stoic account institutes a radical break with both perspectives. It agrees without reserve with the identification of being and the unlimited mixture of Nature—there is no *higher* Being from which this derives. However, it agrees too with Platonism by affirming, not the being of ideal and unchanging Forms, but the subsistence or inherence of ideal events. These events are the result of bodily interactions, but they do not exist in the way bodies do—in fact, they do not *exist at* all, but instead *subsist* as pure, ideal attributes of the bodies that express them. And they subsist, Deleuze will say, *at the surface* of bodies.

FIVE PROPOSITIONS ON THE EVENT

We now have a good sense of the basic ontological framework of the *Logic of Sense*, one that underpins both its structural and genetic moments: bodies mixed together in the depths, accompanied by an ideal or metaphysical surface populated with events. With this is in place, we are now in a position to elaborate our understanding of the event in Deleuze, before considering what this has to do with language and the notion of sense. We will undertake the former by elaborating five propositions on the event in Deleuze.

First proposition: the event is neither an accident nor an essence

The first proposition constitutes, for Deleuze, a necessary warning. In trying to work through the difficult metaphysical status of the event, we confront at this point two opposite temptations which correlate with the orientations towards the depths and the heights.

The first temptation is to define the event as a mere occurrence, a happening with no lasting status or significance. Deleuze calls this the 'empiricist confusion', (LS 54) a confusion of the event with the play of bodies in the depths. Contrary to such a view, the *Logic of Sense* asserts that 'Events are ideal'. (LS 53) The empiricist temptation also involves a tendency to collapse the gap between the event and expression, (LS 22) to the detriment of the former. Such a view, for instance, would explain a beer being knocked over in a bar, or a divorce, or the composition of a poem, solely in terms of the material circumstances involved. Once again, though, the ideal status of the event for Deleuze rules this out. The empiricist temptation can also take the form of identifying events with accidental features of things. Here, Deleuze is perhaps thinking of Aristotle, for whom an accident is a secondary and inessential feature of a substance. For him, the greenness of the tree is accidental—when the leaves turn yellow in advance of winter, the tree remains the thing that it is. This characteristic empiricist position—the distinction between primary and secondary qualities is a notable feature of early scientific and empiricist thought prior to Hume—robs the event of something crucial once more, namely its capacity for expression. Events are not epiphenomenal but expressive: they, and they alone, give to bodies their significance, even if we don't yet know how this will work.

The second temptation is a manifestation of the orientation towards the heights and constitutes a form of Platonism of the event. By thinking of events as ideal, Deleuze is challenging the Platonic view that what is ideal must be eternal, universal, and unchanging, which is to say, *self-identical*. The Idea of Justice, for example, constitutes once and for all the standard against which actions can be tested, and the model in relation to which just conduct can be formed—in general and without exception. Now, we already know that for Deleuze events are the effects of specific causal relationships between bodies. They therefore possess a specificity in origin. But he is more interested in the fact that events never have just one meaning, and that they can be expressed in an unlimited number of different ways, just as we have seen with the event of the Third Battle of Aisne. Unlike the Platonic Idea, Deleuze wants to affirm the ideal event in its irreducibly multiple expressions.

We might also frame Deleuze's anti-Platonism of the event in more critical terms: we must avoid reifying particular events as if they should constitute the universal and necessary conditions for all other interactions between bodies. From this point of view, the temptation takes the form of a belief that an event—for instance, the founding of democracy in Athens—can be *once and for all*.

Second proposition: the event escapes the time of the present

Now, Deleuze does not hesitate to speak of the 'eternal truth' (LS 53) of an event, but here the word 'eternal' does not mean what it does for Plato, for instance in the *Philebus*, where he has Socrates speak of 'what is really and forever in every way eternally self-same'. (58a) He is instead referring to the temporality proper to the event, which is the point of the second proposition.

The peculiar temporality of the event already appeared in our two opening examples. The Third Battle of Aisne is not exhausted by any particular present moment—it is both always already finished and yet to come. The same holds for Alice: she is a certain fixed height at each moment, but the 'to grow' which she expresses exceeds this moment into the future (shorter than she will be) and into the past (taller than she was). Hence our second proposition: the event is irreducible to any present moment.

But we can be more precise. In the 'Tenth Series of the Ideal Game', and then the 'Twenty-Third Series of the Aion', Deleuze shows that our puzzlement in the face of the event's temporality arises because we are implicitly relying on another sense of time. This is the time of bodies or states of affairs, to which he gives the name *Chronos*.

Chronos is the time of the present. In it, we find only bodies engaged in their ongoing mixtures. Because nature is fundamentally a heterogenous mixture, this time is not at all simple. Consider the respective presents involved in an encounter between a hummingbird, whose heart beats at more than 1,200 beats a minute, and the flowers of the delphinium. When feeding, the hummingbird dips its tongue in and out of a flower up to fifteen times a second, and is capable of fully digesting what it eats within twenty minutes; the present that encompasses its actions in Nature is extremely contracted. The delphinium, despite being a perennial, blooms at most two times a year. Its present is thus comparatively distended, stretching out to meet the edges of seasons. Consequently, when we speak of the past and the future in Nature, we are really invoking a present of greater magnitude within which the lesser presents are nested: 'Chronos is an encasement, a coiling up of relative presents', and 'There is always a vaster present which absorbs the past and the future'. (LS 162) For the Stoics, the outer limit is Zeus himself, who lives an eternal present incorporating everything.

But the time of the event escapes this natural, corporeal realm of encased presents. Deploying a term invented by the pre-Socratic philosopher Anaximander that is also used by Plato, Deleuze calls this time *Aion*. Aion possesses a key feature we have already noted—in it, there is no present. The event has *had* meanings, and *has* been expressed, but these past attributions have no hold on the future of the same event. Now, as Deleuze says, we can formally speak of an 'instant', the smallest possible time of the event. But this is a purely logical figure—no matter how small the time of the instant is, it would nevertheless be divided into present and past, and the point of their meeting would once again be evacuated. This unlimited divisibility of Aion is thus the formal counterpart of the infinite nesting of various presents in Chronos.

Summarily then, we can say that while

> Chronos was inseparable from the bodies which filled it out entirely as causes and matter, Aion is populated by effects which haunt it without ever filling it up [...] Aion stretched out in a straight line, limitless in either direction. Always already passed and eternally yet to come, Aion is the eternal truth of time: *pure empty form of time*, which has freed itself of its present corporeal content. (LS 165)

Despite the fact that I have presented these two times as incongruent counterparts—two meanings of 'time', one for each register of being—it is important to grasp that, for Deleuze, Aion imposes itself on, and troubles, Chronos. The expression of events by bodies or states of affairs necessarily 'opens up' the present to the future. Nature is not a closed system of causes for this exact reason: what happens is always caught up in events, whose expression evades the present moment. The event 'perverts the present into the inhering future and past'. (LS 165) Alice may be a certain height in any given present, but because she is caught up in the event 'to grow', that state of affairs is unable, as it were, to "stop" the event from being actualized. If we return to the point of view of Nature as a whole (the Stoic's Zeus), we see then that the exhaustive causal network is really not some kind of ultimately constricting iron cage because it opens onto events that are not subject to causal determination.

Let's again briefly reflect on what this means for subjectivity or agency in the *Logic of Sense*. I 'do things' in the present, engage with other bodies, but the events that result from these causal acts can never be mastered, definitively grasped or exhausted by interpretation, or by the things that I do in response later on. To invoke a famous line from John Ashberry's 'The Other Tradition', the individual agent is always already 'the ex-president of the event'. (*Three Books*, 4) Conversely, this means that every event has the structure of a trauma: though it belongs in some way to the past, it will always come to us, unpredictable, from the future. 'When will I suffer the trauma again?' The question cannot be answered—and neither can the questions 'What will an event come to mean? When will that event once again come into play in my life?', for precisely the same reason. So Deleuze will write: 'The agonizing aspect of the pure event is that it is always and at the same time something which has just happened and something about to happen; never something which is happening'. (LS 63)

There is also a positive sense to this declaration. Recall once again Billy Idol's *White Wedding*: it is the song of the event. A white wedding is one that involves bodies in a particular state of mixture. But, as an event, the white wedding is never exhausted by any particular occurrence. It belongs to the future as much as the past, and it can always be taken up again, actualized once more. The capacity to begin again, to renew a relationship or a promise, is never exhausted; any wedding can express the event 'to whiten'; and if it is always a 'nice day for a white wedding,' this is because it is always 'a nice day to start again'—by virtue of the temporality proper to the event.

Third proposition: all events co-exist in their differences

This third proposition provides a response to two closely related questions. The first is: if all bodies exist in the present in the form of mixtures, what is the corresponding nature of the relationship between events on the surface? The second follows from the previous proposition: if events are not subject to causal determination (since they don't belong to Nature), then what rule or rules govern their interrelation?

The answer to these questions are given in the 'Twenty-Fourth Series of the Communication of Events', and the 'Twenty-Fifth Series of Univocity', which constitute a kind of brief, critical survey of the history of philosophy on the topic of the event. This survey passes through two moments (Stoic and Leibnizian), before arriving at a conclusion that Deleuze will endorse. We'll consider each in turn, but let's begin by providing an example—drawn from the work of Georges Canguilhem—that can function as a touchpoint:

> It is held, for example, that a species of butterfly cannot be at once gray and vigorous. Either the specimens are gray and weak, or they are vigorous and black. We can always assign a causal physical mechanism to explain this incompatibility, a hormone, for example, on which the predicate gray would depend, and which would soften or weaken the corresponding class. And we can conclude from this causal condition that there is a logical contradiction between gray and vigorous. But if we isolate the pure events, we see that *to turn gray* is no less positive than *to turn black*: it expresses an increase in security (to be hidden, to be taken for the bark of a tree), as much as the becoming black is an increase in vigour (to invigorate). (LS 171)

Now, we have seen that Stoicism was the first philosophical tradition to develop an adequate thought of the relationship between bodies, or states of affairs, and events for Deleuze. This is primarily because they grasped the difference in kind between the two, and abjured the 'empiricist confusion' that would treat events as if they could be thought about in the same way that we think about bodies. In other words, it is the first philosophy to think 'to turn black' and 'to turn gray' as resulting from, but independent of, the moths that express them.

But this initial success is shadowed by at least the threat of a subsequent failure. When the Stoics come to consider the relationships between events on their own level, Deleuze argues, they tend to import criteria that belong to the interactions between physical bodies (causes), extrapolated into a conceptual contradiction that would apply to events, perhaps succumbing to the thought a gray vigorous moth is a contradiction in terms or a physical impossibility, thereby scrambling the body-event structure. While recognising that we only have fragments of the texts to work with, he writes that 'The Stoics may not have been able to resist the double temptation of returning to simple physical causality or to logical compatibilities'. (LS 200) Note that Deleuze is not saying that it is wrong to assert that gray butterflies are weak and black butterflies strong—there may indeed be good, causal reasons for thinking this—but that this difference at the level of the bodies should not be projected onto the relationship between 'to turn gray' and 'to turn black' according to the logic of contradiction.

The philosopher who makes an enormous step forward on this question for Deleuze is Leibniz, 'the first theoretician of alogical incompatibilities, and for this reason the first important theoretician of the event'. (LS 171) The phrase 'alogical incompatibility' appears forbidding, but it simply means that *contradiction* will no longer be taken as the rule for thinking about the relationship between events. In other words, Leibniz will have invented a new, *positive* way to think about the relationship between incompatible events, like 'to turn gray' and 'to turn black', or 'to invigorate' and 'to weaken'. What is this?

Leibniz reasons in the following way: in our world (the one that exists), black butterflies are vigorous, while gray butterflies are weak. But there is nothing logically contradictory in the concept of a vigorous gray moth. It is just that such moths are incompatible with *this* world— or, as Leibniz famously argues, they are *incompossible* with this world. Deleuze emphasizes the need to be more precise: in this world, the event 'to invigorate' is incompatible with the events that compose the trajectory of the existence of gray butterfly species. In another possible world, one of the infinite number which God conceived but did not create, the event 'to invigorate' would instead be incompatible with black butterflies.

Leibniz's genius was therefore to displace incompatibilities between events, which now hold not between bodies and events, or concepts and predicates, but between possible worlds. Deleuze is greatly impressed with this innovation, which he declares to be 'an essential component of the theory of sense'. (LS 172) Despite this, he also thinks that Leibniz has also fallen into the same temptation that troubled the Stoics. After all, the rule of compossibility is still a 'principle of exclusion'. (LS 174) Leibniz still has no way of saying that events that are incompatible with each other can co-exist *in this world*, our world. His theological commitments are what constrain him here: God could not create a world that affirmed both incompatibility and rationality or order at the same time. The former had to be banished into other possible worlds so that the latter could be taken to be the rule.

Now, strictly speaking Deleuze does not take a further step in this sequence. Instead, his move is to interrupt the desire to think about the compatibility of events in terms derived from anywhere else. We must instead appreciate the affirmation of difference that is characteristic of events in their co-existence. Here is the key passage:

> As a general rule, two things are simultaneously affirmed only to the extent that their difference is denied, suppressed from within [...] it is generally *through* identity that opposites are affirmed at the same time [...] We speak, on the contrary, of an operation according to which two things or two determinations are affirmed *through* their difference, that is to say, that they are the objects of simultaneous affirmation only insofar as their difference is itself affirmed and is itself affirmative. (LS 172)

The name Deleuze gives to this affirmation is *disjunctive synthesis*, a phrase whose paradoxical character he is fully aware of. Normally, synthesis involves the subordination of a plurality to an identity (black moths are vigorous); and disjunction is normally thought of as a rule of discrimination (either/or) rather than a synthesis in any positive sense. But events *do* differ, do subsist in their plurality, without dissolving or ruling each other out. Events do co-exist *in their difference* from other events. As an ensemble, Deleuze will call all of the co-existent events 'the Event'.

Freud's theory of the drives provides us with a useful analogy. In the unconscious, there is no contradiction—I can, and do, at once love and hate every important person in my life. In themselves, the drives are at once plural and different, even if, at the level of my conscious experience of the world, this plurality is organized in a variety of ways with the general aim of satisfaction. The desire to masturbate and the desire to sleep are organized in a sequence, so that one is put off until later; my hatred of my friend is repressed or sublimated. In sum, my conscious existence is an organized sequence of activities in which managing contradiction is essential. But the drives themselves are not subject to the logic of conscious thought, instead subsisting in their plurality without subordination or negation. The unconscious drives here are the analogues of events in Deleuze's sense—subject to none of the rules that pertain to bodies, they subsist in their plurality, and are affirmed as such. The question of compatibility only arises insofar as events are actualized in bodies.

Fourth proposition: events are inter-expressive
Fifth proposition: events are quasi-causal factors in the organization of bodies

These final propositions follow on from the previous one. Disjunctive synthesis affirms the plurality of events in their co-existence and distance from each other. But Deleuze will extend the point: 'The communication of events replaces the exclusion of predicates'. (LS 174) How can events, as sterile idealities, communicate with each other? And what would this mean for bodies? We'll take each of these questions in turn, but both answers will turn around one of the most enigmatic concepts in the *Logic of Sense*, that of the *quasi-cause*. Whereas bodily causality gives rise to incorporeal effects, the event itself, 'is nevertheless the locus of a quasi-cause'. (LS 150) The relationships between events, and those between events and bodies, will involve this category.

Events are neutral in relation to the bodies that are their causes, and—as incorporeal attributes—they indeed cannot engage in causal relationships with each other. They are, however, interrelated. When the scalpel cuts into the body, the event 'to cut' engages a whole series of other events, for instance, 'to heal', 'to scar'—and indeed, both 'to die' and 'to live'. Consequently, events must be understood to be '"inter-expressive"', (LS 177) none radically independent of any other.

At this general level, it is difficult to see what such a claim adds—and it is a puzzling one. After all, a cut might heal, with or without a scar, but it might lead to someone dying from an infection. Nothing about the nature of events allows us to explain why one of these alternatives will take place, especially since, as we know, events are not causes. What makes the difference between living and dying from a wound? The answer concerns the way in which the implicated field of events is expressed or actualized in *particular* bodies. The crucial passage is this one:

> Incorporeal effects are never themselves causes in relation to each other; they are instead only 'quasi-causes' following laws which perhaps express in each case the relative unity or mixture of bodies on which they depend for their real causes. (LS 6)

In other words: at any given present moment, each body expresses the entire field of events, each of them relative to the nature of this body and the causal relations it is engaged in. For instance, the wounded body might heal in the right setting, but if it is the body of someone without access to the appropriate medicine or care, or who has preexisting conditions that hamper recovery, they may sicken and perish—that is, the fate of this body will be to express the events that run through the sequence 'to infect', 'to weaken', and 'to die', to the increasing exclusion of 'to heal', 'to thrive', and 'to live'.

Given Deleuze's interest in thinking about events as singularities, we can borrow an image from catastrophe theory to further illustrate what is going on.

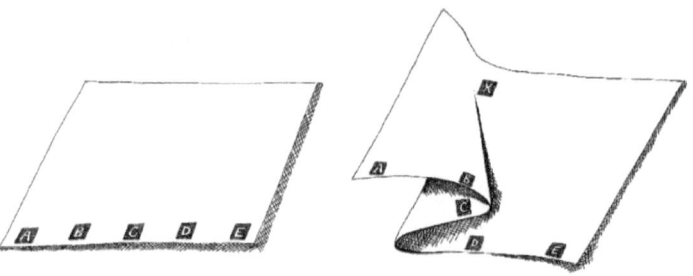

The left hand side presents the field of events in a kind of hypothetical neutral state. But in fact, any particular body will express the field of events as if it were 'buckled' or 'folded' around certain dominant singular points. Take x to be the locus of the body, just now expressive of the event 'to cut' by a scalpel. By virtue of the other events that are quasi-causally related (or 'inter-expressive') to this event, relative to this body, the whole structure of events is transformed, foregrounding some in particular. In this example, we can take b as 'to sleep' and d as 'to become infected', events that as they are actualized to a certain degree will then come to affect the prominence of e, 'to heal'.

There are two complementary points to draw from all of this. On the one hand, we can say that the field of events as such—the Event or *eventum tantum*—is the *quasi-cause* of changes in bodies or states of affairs. This is to say that bodies *express* events, or that the causal activity of a body is characterized by the ongoing incarnation of events. It is true of course that causal changes in a tree and its environment are the cause of its 'greening', but it is also the case that the field of events constitutes an orientation or locus for the future causes that the tree will engage in—a range of predominant tendencies will present themselves. Because 'the tree greens'—because the body of the tree expresses the event 'to green'—it will also develop a proximity to other events, like 'to bloom' and 'to fruit'. Each of these events in turn transform the relationship between the body of the tree and the whole field of events—'to fruit' will develop a proximity with 'to wither', and 'to go to seed'.

On the other hand, these particular events will be expressed by the tree not because of any kind of necessity, but because of the kind of body the tree is, such that its expression of the event 'to green' will transform its relationship with other events, some becoming more proximate on the surface of events, and others less so. A bruise or a moldy cheese may also express the event 'to green', but in relation to a whole set of other events that are pertinent to the ankle or the cheese in question. In other words, the *specificity* of the quasi-causal or interexpressive relations that develop between events themselves is explained by the specific nature of the body in question.

In the *Twilight of the Idols*, Nietzsche famously declares that 'Whatever does not kill me makes me stronger'. ('Maxims and Barbs', §8) This determination is much too simple, and, as he himself declares only a few lines earlier, the very idea of a simple truth is 'a compound lie'. (§4) The kernel of truth in the sentiment lies in the fact that it refers to Nietzsche himself—it is *his* truth. It is the body of each individual that determines the proximity of a trauma to the other events it is liable to express; there can be no general ethical maxim. But what is false is the simple opposition—there is an unrestricted affinity between events, a quasi-causality, that assures the proximity of many events whenever anything happens. An event that does not kill can nevertheless also engage a becoming-weak. Mere weeks after receiving the typescript for *Twilight of the Idols*, Nietzsche collapsed in Turin, never to recover, the patient for causes that he could not, or no longer, master.

But there is a mystery that still remains: how can we be more than just the sum of the causes and effects that compose our routine existence? Why is it that the name 'Nietzsche' must not be reduced to a name for 'his general paralysis, the ocular migraines and the vomiting from which he suffered', but instead describe his work, describe the 'style in an *oeuvre* instead of a mixture in the body'? (LS 108) In the final section of this chapter, we will address this question, which is a question not of ontology but of ethics.

Summary

We are now in a position to describe the entire novel system of causes and effects that lies at the heart of the *Logic of Sense*

1. Bodies, or states of affairs, causally interact. The modification of bodies is doubled by the production of effects: *events*, which are incorporeal attributes *of* the bodies that caused them (the attribute 'having been cut' is the effect of the scalpel's causal relation to the body);
2. Events co-exists in their differences: they are inter-expressive, or constitute a quasi-causal structure;
3. This structure is perpetually shifting in accordance with the changes in the bodies that express it ('to cut' is related to 'to heal', 'to scar', 'to become infected', and so on;
4. This specified structure constitutes a set of tendencies that orient the future causal actions and passions of the body (consider the relative dominance of 'to heal' and 'to become infected' as outlining the future of the body and what it is capable of).

As we have just seen in the case of Nietzsche, Deleuze will give a rather striking name to the way in which the totality of events is expressed, in its particularity, in a given body: *style*. (LS 108) Each body has a style of living that consists in the proportional expression of some events more than others, some only because of others.

LANGUAGE AND SENSE

Deleuze's book is entitled *Logique du sens* and not *Logique des événement*, or *Logique de l'Evénement*. As a result, we now confront two problems. First, what does Deleuze mean by sense? And second, given the course we have been following, what does it have to do with the dualism between events, and bodies or states of affairs? An answer to both can be stated quite directly: language is meaningful because it expresses events. An event is an incorporeal attribute of a body, but it is also the expressible of an utterance: 'it is the same thing which occurs and is said: the attributable to all bodies or states of affairs and the expressible of every proposition'. (LS 180) Consequently, and this is the banner headline: 'Events make language possible'. (LS 181) But what does this mean? And, really, what exactly is *sense* when it comes to language?

Beyond denotation, manifestation and signification

In the Third Series 'Of The Proposition', Deleuze invites us to consider this question in terms of the nature of the proposition. There are, he notes, three prominent functions of the proposition (or relations between the proposition and something else). The first is *denotation*. When I say 'That's a South American lizard!', the proposition functions to point to some external state of affairs—the tegu in question. As Deleuze indicates, it is denotation that provides us with our everyday sense of truth and falsity in language-use: if the lizard is in fact a native Australian goanna, then the proposition will be false. The same point holds no matter how oblique a denotation is at issue. The proposition 'Smoking makes me taste like metal' equally invokes a state of affairs that can be subject to examination for its truth-value in the routine sense of the word.

The second function is *manifestation*, which concerns a relationship between the proposition and the person speaking. Here, instead of pointing to an external state of affairs, the proposition functions to express desires or beliefs: 'I'm so sick of how petty you always are'. Now, Deleuze says, notice that denotation presupposes manifestation—there must be a motivation on the part of the speaker to speak. In more technical terms, this is to say that beliefs about the world already anticipate what is meaningful in what we might encounter. For the arachnophobe, the presence of certain psychological tendencies are what explain the fact that they can—in a room full of all kinds of other potentially notable things—pick out the small beast lurking on the sill of the window. At the limit, as Deleuze points out, the use of the word 'I' immediately signals the primacy of manifestation. Whatever I go on to say in the proposition, it is only explicable because it arises in relation to *my* thoughts, *my* beliefs and desires.

The third function is *signification*. In this case, a proposition no longer relates to a real state of affairs or a framework of beliefs and desires, but to possibilities—'to *universal or general* concepts'. (LS 14) When a scientist speaks about lizards or spiders, they are addressing no particular animal, but a general type of thing; the amateur admirer of reptiles approaches the scaly body it sees in the bushes and begins to try to fit it into a general category—snake or lizard? Venomous? Nocturnal?

This kind of attempt to define an animal is taken to a certain extreme in Lewis Carrol's 'The Hunting of the Snark', where the various features that might be taken to mark out the borders of the concept 'Snark' push at the edges of credulity. In the 'Fit the Second, The Bellman's Speech' section of the poem we read the following 'definition':

> 'Come, listen, my men, while I tell you again
> The five unmistakable marks
> By which you may know, wheresoever you go,
> The warranted genuine Snarks.
>
> 'Let us take them in order. The first is the taste,
> Which is meagre and hollow, but crisp:
> Like a coat that is rather too tight in the waist,
> With a flavour of Will-o'-the-wisp.
>
> 'Its habit of getting up late you'll agree
> That it carries too far, when I say
> That it frequently breakfasts at five-o'clock tea,
> And dines on the following day.
>
> 'The third is its slowness in taking a jest.
> Should you happen to venture on one,
> It will sigh like a thing that is deeply distressed:
> And it always looks grave at a pun.
>
> 'The fourth is its fondness for bathing-machines,
> Which it constantly carries about,
> And believes that they add to the beauty of scenes—
> A sentiment open to doubt.
>
> 'The fifth is ambition. It next will be right
> To describe each particular batch:
> Distinguishing those that have feathers, and bite,

From those that have whiskers, and scratch.
(Carroll, *The Hunting of the Snark*, 13-14)

This definition also recalls another very famous fictional account by Jorge Luis Borges concerned with what the word 'animal' signifies, one framed by another fiction, that is,

> a certain Chinese encyclopedia called the *Heavenly Emporium of Benevolent Knowledge*. In its distant pages it is written that animals are divided into (a) those that belong to the emperor; (b) embalmed ones; (c) those that are trained; (d) suckling pigs; (e) mermaids; (f) fabulous ones; (g) stray dogs; (h) those that are included in this classification; (i) those that tremble as if they were mad; (j) in numerable ones; (k) those drawn with a very fine camel's-hair brush; (l) etcetera; (m) those that have just broken the flower vase; (n) those that at a distance resemble flies. (Borges, 'John Wilkins' Analytical Language', 231)

The nonsensical character of these definitions is obvious, and, as we will see, very important for Deleuze. But for now let's just note that they provide a very clear sense of how signification functions: it outlines a general type by providing features that allow us to collect things under its heading. As he puts it, 'The logical value of signification or demonstration thus understood is no longer the truth, as is shown by the hypothetical mode of implications, but rather the *condition of truth*, the aggregate of conditions under which the proposition "would be" true'. (LS 14)

Now, from one point of view, it seems clear that signification also presupposes manifestation. No matter how abstract the proposition might be—for instance, 'everything which exists is strictly physical in character'—it still presupposes the motivations of the speaker. However, as Deleuze points out, there is another sense in which signification is clearly primary. This is because, no matter how specific or personal a statement is—for instance, 'this is best romescu sauce I have ever tasted'—it presupposes a framework of general concepts that would allow me to denote the object I've just eaten as one sauce among others, as one romescu sauce, and so on. And at the same time—a 'paradox which lies at the heart of logic' (LS 16)—there can be no signification, no ascent to general concepts, without denotation first. The general is obtained through a *generalization*: the concept 'tree' can only be arrived at starting with particular trees, real or represented.

So we arrive at a rather unusual situation: 'From denotation to manifestation, then to signification, but also from signification to manifestation and denotation, we are carried around in a circle, which is the circle of the proposition'. (LS 16-17)

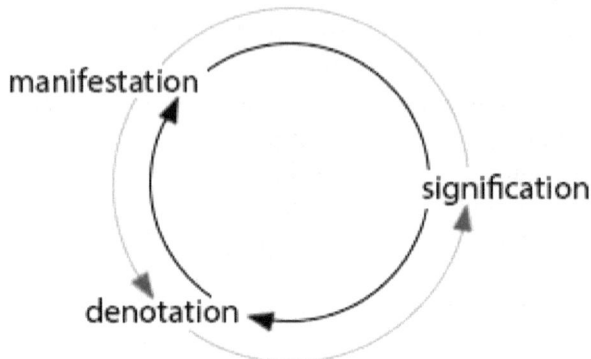

In other words, *concepts* presuppose the *objects* about which they are generalisations, which in turn presuppose the *subjects* (what Deleuze calls *persons*) who speak about them; at the same time, subjects presuppose particular objects, which are in turn nothing other than instantiations of general concepts. We confront a serious problem of foundation: none of these functions are ultimately primary in relation to any of the others. Manifestation presupposes signification in order for speech to be *about* anything, while signification is reduced to an empty formalism if what it allows to be designated is not selected by a manifester. And this is not merely an abstract problem, because if we remained caught in the circle, there would be no way to explain how speech ever actually *starts*.

Let me put the point as directly as possible: if we ask 'what does this proposition mean?', we mostly have no trouble at all answering. 'This is definitely not a persimmon' is hardly a troubling claim, even when this definitely is a persimmon. But if we ask what function of the proposition explains its meaningfulness, neither subject, nor object, nor concept fit the bill. This is because the meaning of each of these instances themselves can be fixed without a regression to the others. In sum, the meaning that language use involves appears 'irreducible to individual states of affairs, particular images, personal beliefs, and universal or general concepts'. (LS 19)

We seem led as a result to conclude that a fourth element is required, one that would be capable of explaining both how language is concerned with meaning, *and* how it begins:

> Sense is the fourth dimension of the proposition. The Stoics discovered it along with the event: sense, *the expressed of the proposition*, is an incorporeal, complex and irreducible entity, at the surface of things, a pure event which inheres or subsists in the proposition. (LS 19)

Lekta: *Deleuze and the Stoic philosophy of language*

Deleuze attributes the discovery of sense or meaning to the Stoics. This discovery also involved a work of distinction, akin to the one we have just seen Deleuze himself prosecute. On the one hand, what is spoken of are bodies. On the other, there is the act of speaking itself. These two are close to Deleuze's categories of denotation and manifestation. But in addition to these two are *what is said of* bodies. These the Stoics called *lekta*: incorporeal attributes expressed *by* statements in the act of speaking *about* bodies. In identifying *lekta* as incorporeal, the Stoics for Deleuze give sense a very particular ontological status. It does not exist on its own terms, but instead can be said to 'subsist or inhere', (LS 5) in the proposition or utterance (the Stoics term is *phōnē*).

Even if the quote at the end of the last section didn't telegraph my point here, this characterization of sense should sound eerily familiar. Deleuze appears, and does not just appear, to be describing the Stoic account of sense in the way that he also described the event. For Deleuze, it is not just that 'The Stoics discovered it [sense] along with the event' (LS 19)—*it is the same discovery*.

It is therefore unsurprising that, throughout the *Logic of Sense*, Deleuze oscillates between speaking of events and sense—depending on whether he is considering their relationship to language (or the proposition) or bodies (or states of affairs)—but that what he says about them both is so similar. The two are strictly identical. The sense or meaning of propositions are events, the same events that are a) the result of bodily interactions, b) the incorporeal attributes of, and c) quasi-causes, or orienting tendencies of, bodies. For this reason, though I will also oscillate between referring to the 'event' or to 'sense', the best general term is Deleuze's compound 'sense-event'. (LS 22)

Summarising Deleuze's philosophy of language

With these points in hand, we can now give a summary account of Deleuze's philosophy of language in the *Logic of Sense*. We need to start by recognizing that, as speaking beings—that is, putting aside the question of how and why anyone begins to speak—we are always already in the middle of a meaningful world. To recall a famous remark of Claude Lévi-Strauss', 'The universe signified long before people began to know what it signified'. (*Introduction to the work of Marcel Mauss*, 61). Or, as Deleuze puts it, quoting Bergson, 'one is established "from the outset" within sense. Sense is like the sphere in which I am already established [...] Sense is always presupposed as soon as *I* begin to speak'. (LS 28)

Sense is always already in play. However, in everyday speech, we can in fact 'only infer it indirectly, on the basis of the circle where the ordinary dimensions of the proposition lead us'. (LS 20) The sense of a proposition can never be isolated out as something discreet in the act of language-use. When we try to do so, we end up back with subjects, objects and concepts. And for the same reason, Deleuze stresses, no proposition can ever say its own sense. We are always capable of speaking about the sense of another proposition ('what he meant to say was ...'), but the proposition itself can only indirectly invoke—designate, manifest or signify—its sense. This is what animates the following amusing sequence cited by Deleuze early in the *Logic of Sense* (LS 29). The White Knight declares to Alice that he will sing her a song, introducing it by saying:

> 'The name of the song is called *"Haddock's Eyes"*'—'Oh, that's the name of the song, is it?' Alice said, trying to feel interested.—'No, you don't understand,' the Knight said, looking a little vexed. 'That's what the name of the song is *called*. The name really is *"The Aged Aged Man."*'—'Then I ought to have said "That's what the *song* is called"?' Alice corrected herself.—'No, you oughtn't: that's quite another thing! The song is called *"Ways and Means"*; but that's only what it's *called,* you know!'—'Well, what is the song then?' said Alice, who was by this time completely bewildered.—'I was coming to that,' the Knight said. 'The song really is *"A-sitting on a Gate"*!' (Carroll, *Through the Looking-Glass*, 81)

So how does sense appear in the proposition? Perhaps the most concise answer Deleuze gives is the following: 'Sense is thus expressed as the problem to which propositions correspond insofar as they indicate particular responses, signify instances of a general solution, and manifest subjective acts of resolution'. (LS 121) A proposition, no matter how abstract or vacuous in character, is always a complex response to the event as a *problem*. Or again: language-use is never the spontaneous act of a radically free, sovereign subject, but the situated resolution of a problem posed to a finite person (who is always in the middle of their embodied agency) caught up in the actualization of an event. *I am provoked to speak by the events that are actualized in my body and the world around me; the changes that these involve are what I speak about; and the general categories that we develop to talk about and understand the world are attempts to grasp the underlying structure of what is happening.*

A final point before we move on. Deleuze does not want to give us the impression that each proposition corresponds to one event, which would be played out in three correlative ways. And indeed, we already know—by virtue of the inter-expressive nature of the event—that no one event is ever expressed in isolation from the others. Consequently, we need to see that what any given proposition expresses is the whole field of events as an ever-shifting field of sub-representational *meaningfulness*, as a 'complex *theme* which does not allow itself to be reduced to any propositional *thesis*'. (LS 122) This field is shifting, of course, because events are ceaselessly taking place, ensuring the kinds of topological modifications I invoked earlier.

SENSE AND NONSENSE

Deleuze doubles his analysis of sense in the *Logic of Sense* with a theory of *nonsense*. He emphasizes two main claims in this respect. The first is that nonsense cannot be thought in terms of a failure of sense, or some kind of derivative, impoverished state of discourse—a diagnosis that only arises, let's note, if we take denotation to be the primary function of the proposition, and think of 'true' and 'false' as its two fundamental states. Properly understood, sense and nonsense enjoy a unique relationship of co-implication, 'an original type of intrinsic relation, a mode of co-presence'. (LS 82) Nonsense is not to sense what the true is to the false (LS 68), but the always present field from which sense is derived. The second claim is that the capacity to express sense in language is *fragile*—indeed, 'Nothing is more fragile'. (LS 82) It is constantly under threat. Deleuze relates these two claims to Lewis Carroll and Antonin Artaud respectively.

Nonsense in Carroll

We now know that for Deleuze the event is sense. It is sense that is expressed in language, and what makes language an activity that involves meaning. In light of this we might revisit some of the characteristics of the event already discussed, but this time from the point of view of sense, and what this means for language. For our purposes here, there is one key characteristic: the affirmation of all events in their disparity from each other, or what Deleuze called the inter-expressivity of all events. All events are affirmed in their disparity—this means that sense is also integrally affirmed in the same fashion.

Consider (very briefly) the conspiratorial claim that Finland does not exist. At the level of the proposition, and in its denotative function, we can say that the statements 'Finland exists' and 'Finland does not exist, but is a conspiracy of cartographers and Japanese fisheries' are *contradictory*. Now, neither contradiction nor the criterion of true and false are applicable to sense, which is one reason why these kinds of arguments can become infernally interminable. In other words, while this conspiracy is ridiculous, it is not nonsensical; both people having this argument are legitimately operating the levers of the proposition (it is, after all, a debate about the denotation of the word 'Finland').

But now compare this situation to Carroll's famous use of portmanteau words, which Deleuze returns to on a number of occasions in the *Logic of Sense*. A first set of examples consists in collapsing a whole proposition into a single word, what Carroll refers to as the 'Unpronounceable Monosyllable'. Deleuze gives an example from *Sylvie and Bruno*, where '*y'reince*' takes the place of '*Your royal Highness*', and 'aims at the extraction of the global sense of the entire proposition in order to name it with a single syllable'. (LS 43) Some related examples are helpfully provided by Humpty Dumpty: *slithy* (lithe-slimy-active) and *mimsy* ('flimsy-miserable'). The meaning of *slithy* can never be finally determined, because there is no way of legitimating the order and therefore significance of its three 'components', *lithe, slimy* and *active*. There is a kind of indeterminacy here—or, better, the portmanteau presents us with a problem that has no pre-given solution. The only way forward is, each time, to create a new meaning *on the basis of this nonsense word*, or what Deleuze will call, following Leibniz, an 'ambiguous sign'. (LS 114)

So: the sense of the nonsense word or proposition is *created* through the convergence of a plurality of senses—'slithy' forces its readers to produce a sense for themselves through such a convergence. Correlatively, though, the field of sense itself is not governed by any requirement for convergence. As a result, it affirms all meanings at once *in* its cacophony: nonsense. What we before called the quasi-causal inter-expressivity of events is nothing other than the field of sense-nonsense: it is the field of sense from the point of view of its expression in language use; it is the field of nonsense when taken on its own terms: 'This quasi-cause, this surface nonsense'. (LS 176)

Artaud and the fragility of sense

The nonsense of Carroll is the nonsense of sense itself, the nonsense of the surface from which sense is continuously generated *for* bodies and expressed *by* and *through* bodies. But there is another nonsense, one that Deleuze will call the nonsense *of* the bodily depths, whose discovery and traumatic investigation he attributes to Antonin Artaud in some memorable words:

> We would not give a page of Artaud for all of Carroll. Artaud is alone in having been an absolute depth in literature, and in having discovered a vital body and the prodigious language of this body. As he says, he discovered them through suffering. He explored the infra-sense, which is still unknown today. (LS 93)

Unlike the nonsense Carroll's work champions—the positive, constitutive aspect of nonsense—this primary nonsense is only arrived at with the collapse of the very capacity to make the divergence of sense converge.

Deleuze does a remarkable job in the *Logic of Sense* of capturing a troubling experience—the moment that you realise that what you are hearing is no longer someone trying to express themselves in language, but the immediate sonorous presence of madness. It is the experience few of us have failed to have: waiting at a bus stop, or lingering in the foyer of the public library, you suddenly realise that this person's body and face, words and gestures, have broken away from the tacit expectations we all hold for each other, and that a *thing* which is not them is now moving and talking instead. The passage in question concerns Artaud's attempt to translate Carroll's "Jabberwocky". Here is the opening stanza of the poem, and Artaud's rendering:

> 'Twas brillig, and the slithy toves
> Did gyre and gimble in the wabe:
> All mimsy were the borogoves,
> And the mome raths outgrabe.
> (Carroll, *Through the Looking Glass*, 10)

> Il était roparant, et les vliqueux tarands
> Allaient en gibroyant et en brimbulkdriquant

> Jusque là lò la rourghe est à rouarghe a rangmbde
> Et rangmd a rouarghambde:
> Tous les falomitards étaint les chat-huants
> Et le Ghoré Uk'hatis dans le Grabugeument. (LS 342)

As Deleuze says, everything seems in order at the start:

> As we read the first stanza of 'Jabberwocky,' as Artaud renders it, we have the impression that the two opening lines still correspond to Carroll's criteria and conform to the rules of translation generally held by Carroll's other French translators [...] But beginning with the last word of the second line, from the third line onward, a sliding is produced, and even a creative, central collapse, causing us to be in another world and in an entirely different language. With horror, we easily recognize it: it is the language of schizophrenia. (LS 82)

This text recalls the evening of Artaud's last public performance in 1947, a little over a year before his death. He had spent much of the previous decade in an asylum, subject to the innumerable bouts of electroshock treatment which had left his body broken. The performance, billed as 'Tête-à-tête avec Antonin Artaud', was attended by over nine hundred people, well over capacity for the Vieux-Colombier. Beginning at 9pm, it ran until midnight.

> Artaud comes on stage alone. Dressed like a *clochard* [a beggar], he looks emaciated and a little startled. When he starts reading from the pile of papers, his voice sounds emasculated, yet undeniably powerful. There is some heckling, then a tight silence. Artaud declaims, whispers, roars, and comes to an awkward pause. He seems to have lost his place or his nerve, shuffles his papers, takes his head in his hands as if he were giving up. Yet he starts again. Now he is not reading but haranguing the audience [...] The denunciation of language, of sex, of himself goes on and on. Artaud appears a man possessed, lunatic beyond recall. Yet he remains an actor, a painful ham, clowning, mocking himself, spouting his outrage and conscious of his excess, forcing it. With the audience at bay in front of him, he is watching the combustion of his own mind. He wants to drop not words but bombs. There is no end to it, no stopping him, until [André] Gide climbs on stage and throws his arms around the exhausted performer. (Roger Shattuck, *The Innocent Eye*, 169-70)

The distinction between bodily noise and speech collapses, and with it so does Artaud himself. Silences no longer function as necessary breaks between sounds in order that they can be distinguished, but as another assault.

What Carroll's method shows is that nonsense and sense are co-present and co-originary in language. But the case of Artaud is entirely different. Words like 'rouarghambde' in his version of the 'Jabberwocky' do not show the immanent proximity of nonsense and sense in language, but instead *collapse meaningful language into noise*. As Deleuze points out, even 'the portmanteau words seem to function differently, being caught up in syncopes and being overloaded with gutturals'. (LS 84) The emphasis on syncopes (the 'dropping-out' or loss of vowels from a word) is particularly illuminating. Instead of the nonsense apparent in an unrestricted ramification of sense (lithe *and* slimy *and* active), it emerges through a recrudescence of words to the strictly sonorous, physical level. And this is the key point: the nonsense that Artaud shows to us in his suffering is an 'infra-sense', and reveals the difficult proximity of language use and bodily noises. In his work, 'There is no longer anything to prevent propositions from falling back onto bodies and from mingling their sonorous elements with the body's olfactory, gustatory, or digestive affects': 'Ratara ratara ratara Atara tatara rana Otara otara katara'. (LS 91; 83) Artaud himself is unremitting on this point: 'All true language / is incomprehensible. / Like the chatter / Of beggar's teeth'. (*Selected Writings*, 549)

ELEMENTS OF PSYCHOANALYSIS

The opening lines of the 'Twenty-Sixth Series of Language' rather abruptly mark the major shift in Deleuze's argument in *Logic of Sense*: 'Events make language possible. But making possible does not mean causing to begin'. (LS 180) In fact, these two sentences neatly describe two main goals of the book. We have already seen the *structural* account, which describes how it is that events make language possible—events being the sense that language expresses. But, Deleuze indicates, an entirely different question remains to be answered. This question is a *genetic* one: what is the process whereby a newly born baby, unable to do anything more with its mouth than make noises, eat (or suckle on objects) and vomit, comes to be able to use language to invoke the world (denotation), express themselves (manifestation) and operate within the sphere of generalities (signification)? In other words, how can the element of sense possibly be attained by the human animal? The case of Artaud, which we have just discussed, is closely related too: how is it possible to fall away from sense, to lose the capacity to speak in an essential fashion?

The solutions to all of these questions will go by way of an extremely novel and dramatic, but also compact and difficult, deployment of psychoanalytic ideas over the final eight series of the book. He writes, for instance, that 'Psychoanalysis cannot content itself with the designation of cases, the manifestation of histories, or the signification of complexes. Psychoanalysis is the psychoanalysis of sense. It is geographical before it is historical'. (LS 92-3) This claim is amplified later on:

> [Freud's] *Totem and Taboo* is the great theory of the event, and, more generally, psychoanalysis is the science of the event, on the condition that the event is not treated as something whose sense is to be sought and disentangled. The event is sense itself, insofar as it is disengaged or distinguished from the states of affairs which produce it and in which it is actualised. (LS 211)

Such passages clearly indicate the foundational status of psychoanalysis for Deleuze in *Logic of Sense*, and for his own terminology. But it is important to be more specific too. Over and above endorsing—in Deleuze's view, at least—the ontological distinction at the heart of the book, what it provides him with is a family of developmental accounts that he will freely draw upon in answering the genetic question we have just posed. The three most important such accounts are those given in Freud, Lacan and, above all, Melanie Klein. It will be useful, therefore, to briefly review them before turning back to Deleuze.

Childhood sexuality and the Oedipus complex in Freud

We can summarise Sigmund Freud's main claims about childhood sexuality, and about the advent and resolution of the Oedipus complex for our purposes in eight main points. And though Deleuze's subsequent use of Freud's analysis is indifferent to the gender of the child, it is as always important to keep in mind that Freud takes the male child to be paradigmatic.

1. The first source of sexual pleasure in the life of the child involves the mouth. While the mouth functions first of all as the means by which the child receives nourishment, the sensations associated with oral stimulation—for example, thumb-sucking—become detached from the simple maintenance of life and become a source of pleasure.

2. For Freud the next major phase in childhood development—which he locates in the third or fourth year of life—involves, essentially, toilet training. Being able to *not* shit, to be able to determine when to do so, and to be able to conform (or not) to the demands of parents on this front, all of this is key, in addition to the pleasurable sensations that may be involved. Like sexuality in general for Freud, the anal phase is at once physical and social, as are the pleasures that it involves.

3. The third of Freud's famous phases is the genital phase, and with this we draw near to the Oedipus complex. As the name suggests, it concerns an increased focus of attention in the child's erotic life on the genital region:

> the anatomical situation of this region, the secretions in which it is bathed, the washing and rubbing to which it is subjected in the course of the child's toilet, as well as accidental stimulation, make it inevitable that the pleasurable feelings which this part of the body is capable of producing noticed by children in their earliest infancy. (Freud, 'Three Essays', 187-8)

4. But along with this dominant focus on the genital zone flourishes a new and complex social context in which the child's desires are played out. On the one hand, the child takes the mother to be the object of desire. For Freud, the mechanism of this attachment is what he calls identification: the child identifies with the father, and thinks of the mother as the fully satisfying love object.

5. On the other hand and as a result, the child's relationship to the father is profoundly ambiguous. The child *loves* the father (according to this model of identification; the child loves the father as they love themselves), but at the same time *hates* him, because it is he that the mother loves. Worse, as the child's desire for the mother strengthens, so too does child's *fear*, the fear that the father will take 'it' away, the source of pleasure. This is, of course, the famous Freudian notion of 'castration anxiety'.

6. This complicated social and libidinal situation—the Oedipus complex itself—is resolved for Freud when the child renounces and represses their desire for the mother and their aggression towards the father. This renunciation will take final, mature form in the attempt to find a *substitute* for the mother.

7. There is one other consequence of the passage through the complex, assuming that it more or less succeeds: 'The authority of the father or the parents is introjected into the ego, and there it forms the nucleus of the superego'. (Freud, 'Dissolution', 176) The superego for Freud is the internalised form of the 'severity of the father' ('Dissolution', 176): a self-critical, moral authority that judges the efforts of the ego in balancing the demands of unconscious drives and the pressures of the real world.

8. According to Freud, the advent of the superego involves a process that he calls *desexualisation*. In order for this new agency to have force in the psyche, it must obtain this force from elsewhere. As the child renounces the mother as the object of investment in the resolution of the Oedipus complex, a certain portion of libidinal charge becomes 'neutralised' and available for a new purpose. And it is this desexualised libido that, repurposed, makes the superego, in its force and inflexibility, possible.

Castration in Lacan

Now, while this Freudian account is of central importance to the genetic ambitions of *Logic of Sense*, Deleuze is in truth closer to Jacques Lacan's rendering of the same themes. This rendering, which displaces the significance of the biological register, relates childhood development much more closely to the social, symbolic character of the process rather than the biological register with which Freud props up his account. Here, even though there is a rich tissue of correspondence between Lacan's doctrine and the argument of *Logic of Sense*, five points will give us an adequate sense of what is at stake:

1. The early psychic life of the child is oriented by the attempt to understand what its significant others want. This 'Other' does not need to be the biological mother, or indeed anyone in particular, except that they constitute the most frequent encounters in the child's life.

2. The name that Lacan gives this 'what the Other wants' is the *phallus*. The phallus is, from the point of view of the child, an idealized 'fully satisfying object'. It is not the penis, or any other discrete physical object. The young child's goal to identify what this object is therefore dovetails with the desire to be this object for the Other.

3. It is at this point that the father intervenes—and once again, this need not be the biological father, but is instead the personage that the child fantasmatically takes to be the master, the source of authority, a personage Lacan calls the *imaginary father*. And the principal act of this figure is to rule out, for the child, their identification with the phallus, and thereby their position as the love object of the mother. The act by which this takes place is castration itself. So, for Lacan, unlike Freud, the event of castration is not just feared by the child but actually suffered. But this castration is for Lacan a symbolic rather than a physical event. It consists in the enunciation of *le non du père*— the 'no' of the father. The imaginary father as master and authority says the definitive word that rules out once and for all the child's desire.

4. Now, as Lacan's genius will indicate, the phrase *le non du père* is homonymous with another: *le nom du père*, the *name* of the father. Castration, therefore, has two facets, or faces in two directions. The first is the prohibition we have just seen. But this prohibition effectively comes down to informing the child that there exists a whole law-bound social world—embodied in the father's surname with all that this conveys. And it is this social world, rather than any terrifying Uranus-like figure of the imaginary father, that rules out the child's love for the mother. And like the child, the father is a part of this world, a father who is also transformed by castration into the *symbolic father*, just another individual who is caught up in the law of the social. The positive consequence of castration is therefore that it allows the child stable, rule-bound access to the world of other people, a world that is no longer (primarily) governed by the terrifying dramas of the pre-castration kingdom of the imaginary father.

The psychic life of the young child in Klein

Freud provides Deleuze with the foundation of his genetic account, and Lacan provides him with many of the materials he will make use of. But it is the work of Melanie Klein that Deleuze makes most extensive use in *Logic of Sense*.

Contrary to Freud, Klein will insist: on a primary role for the mother in the psychic development of the child; that the kernel of the crisis Freud calls the Oedipus complex takes place much earlier, by the age of two at the latest; and that fantasy plays a much more significant role in childhood development. Here is a final list, figuring the six elements of Klein's theory that will play an important role in Deleuze's account

1. The earliest moments of the psychic life of the child involve a libidinal investment in certain objects. These objects are most likely the first objects we routinely encounter: the mother's face and breast. But these objects are in no way simple. In fact, Klein will define them as *split, fragmented* or *partial*. The breast, to take the most characteristic of Klein's examples, is not one thing but two: the *good breast*, the one that feeds and comforts the child, and the *bad breast*, the breast that is absent, and whose absence the child experiences as persecutory.

2. Early personal identity—the earliest form of the ego—involves an identification with the good object, and a feeling of absolute hostility to the bad object. Such a situation, Klein emphasizes, is at once terrifying and exhausting for the child. Given this extremely polarized libidinal drama, it is easy to see why Klein will call it the *paranoid-schizoid position*, characteristic of the first six months of life.

3. The conflict that Freud identifies with the Oedipus complex is, for Klein, grounded in and preceded by this more primordial position of the child. As the child develops both physically and psychically, they begin to appreciate that the phantasmatic part objects are actually parts of a unified real object, the mother's body. In the light of this realization, the sadistic hatred and hostility towards the bad partial object engenders anxiety and guilt—what if that violence I felt towards the bad object *hurt* the mother? And what if it will make her go away for good? The ambivalence characteristic of the schizoid position doesn't evaporate, but is transformed by the introduction of an early form of the superego that turns the earlier aggression back on the child themselves. The child thus attains what Klein calls the *depressive position*.

4. In this position, in response to the anxiety and guilt, and under the gaze of the superego, the child begins to engage in a new genre of activities that Klein calls *reparation*—the whole suite of attempts to make what was 'broken' (*kaput*) in the paranoid-

schizoid position 'alright again' (*weider gut*). In a certain sense, reparation is the name for the entirety of the ego's attempts to reconcile desire and reality for Klein—so long as we keep in mind that the impulsion to engage in it springs from the earliest hostilities present in the psyche of the child. For Deleuze, as we will see, reparation is in fact a moment of unexpected, heartbreaking but inevitable disaster for the child, and marks the moment at which he will shift allegiances from Klein to Lacan.

5. The movement of integration characteristic of this shift to the depressive position is, in quite general terms, the signature of all mature psychic life. Every source of pleasure, the satisfaction of the drives, is also, at least potentially, a source of suffering and a well-spring of anxiety. Maturity consists in being able to manage this ambiguity. In other words, the depressive position is the mature position of the psyche, and it is characterized by a) a clear distinction between self and other as unified agencies, b) the operation of the superego, such that I take responsibility for my own actions, and c) the ability to deal with the pain and difficulty that is also found in all sources of pleasure. In a sense, then, the passage to the depressive position is one that has to be repeated throughout life whenever the fundamental disparate character of stable and unified objects flares up.

6. A final detail. Of primary importance in dealing with psychic tension, particularly in the depressive position, is *symbolization*: the use of symbols to stand in for what is absent. For Klein, these are primarily to be conceived in phantasmatic rather than linguistic terms—they are particular kinds of psychic objects. This point has a very great range in Klein's thought, much greater than it does for Freud. Symbols are phantasms, psychic stand-ins for unconscious drives. They are as a result a certain kind of intermediary between rational thought and the depths of the body's drives.

FIRST GENETIC MOMENT: SIMULACRA IN THE SCHIZOPHRENIC DEPTHS

Freely drawing from and modifying these different psychoanalytic accounts, Deleuze will fashion his own version of the passage from infancy to language use, thereby retracing 'the history which liberates sounds and makes them independent of bodies'. (LS 186) This genetic account has four moments or stages, and is punctuated by what constitutes in Deleuze's view the first events (in his full sense of this word) in the life of any human being: castration and murder.

He begins at the earliest moment of psychic life, prior to any understanding of a 'real, outside world'. At this moment, we are entirely within the unilluminated *depths* of the psyche, and 'The history of depths begins with what is most terrifying: it begins with the theatre of terror whose unforgettable picture Melanie Klein painted'. (LS 187) We already know why Deleuze will speak of depths here—at this stage, there is no access to the surface of sense at all. But then what is there? Deleuze's answer follows Klein: *partial objects*, paradigmatically the good and the bad breast. Now, these objects are not real things that the child encounters, as if they were explorers starting out on a journey into an unknown physical landscape. They are fantasmatic objects, produced by the child on the basis of encounters with the real that they have no way of directly grasping. Borrowing from Plato, Deleuze will call these objects *simulacra*—they are not mental copies of what is real, but objects confected without any reference to anything.

But now Deleuze will modify this picture in two ways. First, he insists that Klein was mistaken to indicate that any of the partial, fragmented objects could possibly be *good*—they are bad *by virtue of being partial*. The exact problem with the part objects is that, *being fragmented*, they are always vectors of suffering. If there are any good objects, they will both have to be *whole* objects, and will have to belong to a register other than the depths: 'every piece is bad in principle (that is, persecuting and persecutor), only what is wholesome and complete is good'. (LS 188)

This is to some degree a terminological issue—as Deleuze notes, Klein's depressive position is attained to the degree that the child is capable of integrating the part objects into a whole, which is to say that she doesn't in fact think that the 'good partial object' is good in any strong sense. Straightforward enough. Consequently, though—since the good object has been removed from any explanatory role for the moment—there must be another element that explains the violent dynamisms of the paranoid-schizoid position. Drawing on Artaud again, Deleuze will call this specific simulacrum the *body-without-organs*. Like the menacing part-objects, the body-without-organs is indeed a simulacrum, produced by the child in response to the terrifying, unpredictable character of mysterious bodily encounters in order to give them some purchase. But this object is characterized by being stable, silent and impassive. It gives the interior life of the infant a way to identify with a degree-zero of agitation. The satisfaction a baby feels when feeding, to take an important case, is not identified by the infant with the presence of something good, but instead with the temporary cessation of hostilities that characterizes the apparition and vanishing of the part-objects (when will I be fed again?)

In the depths, finally, there is no language at all—in fact, there is not even anything distinctly vocal in play. A baby's babbling is not a tentative attempt to speak, a grasping at the fringes of sense, but only senseless noise indistinguishable to the baby from the other simulacra. We are here in the presence of the schizophrenic nonsense of Artaud: *Ratara ratara ratara Atara tatara rana Otara otara katara.*

SECOND GENETIC MOMENT: THE ICON IN THE HEIGHTS

In sum, then, the schizophrenic depths are 'a universal cesspool', (LS 187) whose only discriminating feature is the oscillation between hostile part-objects and the dark impassivity of the organless body, and where there is no language but only noise. Now, for Deleuze as for Klein, the passage out of this moment requires the advent of a good, whole object. But, contra Klein, this object cannot belong to the bodily, schizoid depths.

The good object, or what Deleuze will call the *icon*, instead belongs to a new dimension, that of the heights. This is in keeping, first of all, with Freud's explanation of the advent of the superego, which originates in an encounter with a voice from 'on high'. The infant identifies a new element in its psychodrama in this iconic Voice, which is, at least at this point, unrelated to any of its particular drives. As a result, it has no part in the violent drama of the depths—it is not sullied by any such association, and appears to be whole, pure and good.

This new object nevertheless possesses a very strange profile in the psychic life of the child—it is experienced first of all as *having returned*, as having come back from being absent. As Deleuze puts it, 'The good object is by nature a lost object. It only shows itself and appears from the start as already lost, as *having been lost*'. (LS 191) The child, in effect, associates the positive moment of satisfaction with this object, and identifies with it, in an effort to extricate itself from the violent contingency of the depths. But what was the reason that the good object had gone away? The child knows the answer: the persecutory part objects must have made it withdraw into the heights. This will become an important factor in the third moment of genesis.

It is in this conjunction that Deleuze will endorse one of Klein's main theses, even if it is in his own, modified terms. This is the recognition of the profound tension, and even hostility, between the bad partial objects and the good object in the heights. The child, unfortunately, is caught between these two registers. Insofar as it identifies with the good whole object, trying to make peace with the world, it is the victim of the part objects: there is always a threat that the absence of the mother might provoke their hostility again. But insofar as the ego allies itself with the part objects—that is, grasps the world from this point of view, perhaps struggling again with the anxiety that the mother's breast won't return—it also becomes the target of the good object, which now adopts the hostile aspect of the superego (*how dare you doubt the existence of the good, nourishing breast!*) The good object is thus the kernel of the Freudian super-ego, that element of psychic organization that judges the dynamisms in the depths. It is clear, as a result, that this second moment, in which 'Everyone receives as many blows as he metes out', (LS 190) is just as fraught as the first.

Let's note, finally, that despite the fact that the noise of the depths has now been superseded by the sounding of a Voice, the child still remains outside of sense:

> For the child, the first approach to language consists in grasping it as the model of that which pre-exists, as referring to an entire domain of what is already there, and as the familial voice which conveys tradition, it affects the child as bearer of a name and demands his insertion even before the child begins to understand. [...] The voice, though, presents to us the dimensions of an organised language, without yet being able to grasp the organising principle according to which the voice itself would be a language. And so we are left outside sense, far from it, this time in a *pre-sense* of heights (LS 193-4)

THIRD GENETIC MOMENT: THE BODILY SURFACE AND THE IMAGE OF THE PHALLUS

At present, things look bad: 'The body of the infant is like a den full of introjected savage beasts which endeavour to snap up the good object; the good object, in turn, behaves in their presence like a pitiless bird of prey'. (LS 190) This difficult tension will be resolved to a significant degree through the production of an intermediary unity—*the body*. Of course, the complicated simulacrum-icon system is already for the child its (libidinal, phantasmatic) body, but this is a long way from being characterized as a unity of any kind. To escape from this situation, a new set of objects of desire that Deleuze calls *images* will first have to emerge that do not belong to either the depths or the heights, and, second, these images will need to somehow be systematically unified.

Deleuze describes the accomplishment of the first of these goals by recourse to Freud's account of childhood development. As we saw earlier, this involves the serial dominance of certain drives, each associated with a bodily zone: oral, anal, genital. In each moment, the child produces an image of what satisfies the local drives. For example, the pleasure that can be obtained through the oral zone is associated with the breast, the thumb, perhaps a certain spoon, perhaps a pacifier. By taking them together, the child forms a kind of sketch or schematism of what would be good to put in the mouth. Neither particular concrete objects nor concepts, these images are the primitive, habituated means of anticipating the satisfaction of particular drives.

But how do these images provide the child with a sense of *unity*, and a means of escape from the double persecution of the heights and the depths? What is required in order for the body to be unified is an *image of unity* with which the child can identify. And, Deleuze says, the child already has an object in relation to which it can produce such an image: the good object of the heights. Recall that, unlike the simulacra of the depths (for instance, the breast), this object has never let the child down—it has no downside, no persecutory double. So the next decisive moment in dynamic genesis consists in the infant's identification with an image of this good object. To be clear: the child does not think that it *has* the good object as such. It instead models itself on this object, producing for itself an image with which it can identify (Freud's *ideal ego*). In other words, the child begins to consider itself in terms of this object, rather than in terms of the chaos of the simulacra. Following Lacan, Deleuze calls this image the *phallus*.

The fully satisfying character that the child attributes to the good object is what explains the significant difference between the phallus-image and the other images associated with particular erogenous zones. Remember, the child identifies themselves *as a whole* with the image of the phallus. Consequently, 'the phallus, in this respect, does not play the role of an organ, but rather that of a particular image projected, in the case of the little girl as well as the little boy, onto this privileged (genital) zone', (LS 200) but the result is a transformation of the whole orientation of desire. In short, the phallus functions as a principle of integration, allowing for the various localized zones and their particular images to be interrelated. Deleuze uses a framework proposed by Serge Leclaire to illustrate how this works: we can see each local zone of the body as an isolated letter, and aggregated together, the body itself appears as 'an aggregate or sequence of letters'. (LS 231) The phallus, as it were, draws all the letters together, giving to them the coordination required to form a meaningful statement—a little like a spoon, by raising the letters out of the broth, can draw a sentence out of a bowl of alphabet soup.

This double movement of complete identification and bodily integration has a further, major consequence. Up until this point, the story of the ego of the child—their very sense of who they are—is the description of a struggle. The child is perpetually subject to two set of demands: 'to model itself after the good object or to identify itself with bad objects'. (LS 227). But now, the ego has a solid footing, a reliable identification with the phallus, which functions as what Freud calls the *ideal ego*. A new sense of self is therefore produced, one predicated on unity. We will return to the question of personal identity below, but what is already clear is that the ego-ideal ego complex is the first discrete and stable answer to the question 'who am I?' Unfortunately, as we are about to see, the child has chosen just about the worst possible moment to so strongly identify with the phallus …

Now, the key point that will allow us to move the argument forward is that—contrary to Freud's account of the Oedipus complex— the image of the phallus is *not* primarily deployed in a way laden with guilt and anxiety. Following the Kleinian account we saw above, Deleuze will insist that this guilt and anxiety comes from much earlier. It comes in fact from the violent and aggressive response the child adopted towards the mother in the schizoid position, one that is slowly undermined as the child comes to see that the mother is one person, and that both the good and the bad associations accrue to her.

The meaning of the complex is thus entirely transformed. The child, who identifies with the phallus as the image of the fully satisfying object, comes to believe that it finally has the means to rectify the two problems that dominate its young life: the damage inflicted on the mother, and the absence of the good object itself, which has always already been withdrawn into the heights, and which the child identifies with the father and the locus of an authority that might explain the oscillations of the mother's behavior. To summarise once again (because this is key): if the phallus is invoked, it is as an image of the good object that can *heal the damage inflicted on the mother* by the violent and terrified child in the schizoid position. And, in brandishing this image of the good object, the goal is to bring back the father who has withdrawn into the heights: 'The restoration of the mother and the summoning of the father are the targets: this is the true Oedipus complex'. (LS 205) Consequently, Deleuze insists that 'It is necessary therefore to imagine Oedipus not only as innocent, but as full of zeal and good intentions.' (LS 202)

CASTRATION AND THE PHANTASM

Things, unfortunately, do not go according to plan. The relevant series here, 'Twenty-Ninth Series. Good Intentions are Inevitably Punished', contains some of the most novel moves in the *Logic of Sense*. It also has some of its best lines. Here are some of the latter, which can serve as an introduction to the catastrophe about to occur:

> As for the wounded body of the mother, the child wishes to repair it, with this restorative phallus and make it unharmed. He wishes to recreate a surface to this body at the same time that he creates a surface for his own body. As for the withdrawn object, he wishes to bring about its return, to render it present with his evocative phallus [...] In the unconscious, everyone is the offspring of divorced parents, dreaming of restoring the mother and bringing about the return of the father, pulling him back from his retreat [...] Never has the child, in his narcissistic confidence, had better intentions, never again will he feel as good. (LS 204)

The fate of the mother and the father

The child executes the plan, an attempt at what Klein calls *reparation*. The mother's body, in the fantasy life of the child, was the object of violent attacks mounted from the schizoid position. Now in possession of the healing image of the phallus, the child can restore the mother: he or she can be at once the salve for the wounds, and the (incestuous) object of desire that will fully satisfy the mother's desires.

However, as Deleuze gnomically puts it, 'in his desire for incest-restoration, Oedipus saw'. What does the child see? That the mother is not just wounded by the child's previous aggression, but that the mother's body is also 'wounded like a castrated body'. (LS 205) In more prosaic terms: the child's very belief that he or she possesses an image-object that can satisfy the mother leads them to the realization that the mother herself is *lacking that object*: 'The phallus as a projected image [...] designates a lack in the mother'. (LS 205) For the child, though, this amounts to the belief that *they themselves have castrated the mother*. More prosaically again: despite everything the child invested in this image, and in the entire sequence surrounding it, the mother remains the person who goes on with her daily routines, seemingly unperturbed by the child's immense psycho-drama, and this heroic attempt at reparations for the terrifying violence that—as far as they know—they inflicted in the schizoid position.

Moreover, for the child, the consequences in relation to the father are just as grave. The phallus is an image of the father, in his guise as the good object withdrawn into the heights. The child's intention is to use the phallus to draw the father back from the heights—the only position the father has ever occupied in the child's experience (he was always already 'out for cigarettes'). The problem is that if the child has the phallus, and indeed now even identifies with the good object itself through it, then they can only have done so by usurping the father himself. In other words, the phallus with which the child identifies is the very thing that makes the father the father *as they imagined and identified with him*. In coopting the phallus, the child has unwittingly taken away what was essential to the father *as* the father. In the experience of the child, this amounts to nothing less than murder, and, tragically, 'by wishing to bring back the father, the child has betrayed and killed him'. (LS 205) The child, in attempting to lure back the father—identified with the good object retreated into the heights—with the phallus instead only manages to summon a part-time electrician called Greg.

The castration of the child and the access to sense

Now, in a preliminary sense the child is not initially castrated at all, but is instead a *castrator* and a *murderer*. In fact, though, the thing that the child is actually beginning to realise through all of this is that the real world is larger than their suite of simulacra, idols and images. The child's early years are effectively a cosmic drama playing out between a heaven and a hell that end up being clumsy dioramas painted *trompe l'oeil* on the inside of their experience. The fact that the phallus was not capable of achieving anything the child thought it would—based on its own identification—is the beginning of their coming to terms with the fact that there is no phallus at all, that there never was, and that they would never be or have it. Consequently, the castration of the mother is just the obverse of the child's own castration, as the murder of the father is the obverse of the child's own death, that is, the death of the ambitions of their profound infantile narcissism. The real outcome is 'dissipation of all the images'. (LS 218)

So what we have just seen is, in effect, Deleuze's own version of the Oedipus complex. While it does not follow Freud, Klein or Lacan strictly, it arrives at a terminus that would be familiar from all three perspectives. But Deleuze himself is not yet done. The genetic account of the *Logic of Sense* will only have been concluded when he has explained why this resolution of the Oedipus complex provides the child with access to the field of sense, and, furthermore, how this same resolution also explains the possibility of speculative thought. We will consider these points in turn.

Imbecilic criticisms of psychoanalysis often begin (and end) with embarrassing gestures of the kind: the child we've been discussing has no *real* blood on their hands; the father was not *really* murdered; the mother wasn't *really* castrated. But the nature of this reality—of psychic phenomena, of thought, of phantasy—is precisely what is in question. So then: in what sense is castration a real event? Fortunately, we already have the materials with which to fashion an answer. While the event of castration (and murder) involved in the Oedipus complex concern bodies, as events they are related to bodies not as material causes but as incorporeal attributes.

The first two acts of any child are not 'to walk' or 'to say "Dada"'. These are not actions in any meaningful sense, but reactions to stimuli—and so too are the more complicated reactions of imaginary identification with the simulacra and then the Idol. Their cause is found outside of the child, in, for instance, the presence of the mother, and while their effects are incorporeal attributes that both mother and the child will go on to actualize, the child's relationship to them is strictly as a patient rather than an agent. No, the first two acts of the child are 'to castrate' and 'to murder'.

To be more precise, we need to distinguish between two kinds of actions. The first action is the intended action of reparation. It pertains to the bodies of the father and the mother and, Deleuze notes, as an *intended* action, it also expresses the capacities of the child's body as a whole. The second action is the accomplished action of castration. The latter is 'produced and not willed', (LS 208) but it is produced with respect, no longer to the body, but to the surface of events. What is notable in all this is first, the fact that the agency of the child, as in agency in general, is split between intended bodily outcomes and produced incorporeal effects. But, second, by virtue of this splitting itself, the child has gained access to this second register, that of the sense-event. We thus arrive at the point we were looking for—the explanation for how the noisy body of a baby can gain access to the register of being which is able to provide these noises with sense.

Now, that the child possesses access to the dimension of sense does not mean that they are immediately masters of anything. What it does mean is that, now that access to sense has been established (and for as long as it holds), there is no restriction on what meanings can be expressed by the child. From the genetic point of view, the process is a gradual one, whereby the initial acts and their consequences are progressively investigated by the child, somewhat akin to the way a computer virus is introduced at one terminal and moves from link to link, constituting, in one particular fashion, the greater network.

Incidentally, we are now in a position to see why Deleuze claims that 'psychoanalysis is the science of events'. (LS 211) It is not at all concerned with bodies and their mixtures—an analyst could hardly care less who you actually sleep with, for instance—but only with the events that compose the incorporeal matrix condensed around your phantasms. 'What is psychoanalysis talking about with its grand trinity of murder-incest-castration [...] if not about pure events?' (LS 211) The only question the analyst is really interested in is 'what are your quasi-causes?' As such, all other things being equal, psychoanalysis is the true heir of Chaldean astrology.

The phantasm

Let's pause for a moment and note that the scope of Deleuze's concerns has significantly narrowed. We can no longer consider 'the tree greens' to be universally emblematic of this body-event pair. This is because a new element has been introduced: human subjectivity.

Indeed, the genetic account presented in the *Logic of Sense* is actually a story about how a certain kind of body develops a *different* relationship with sense than that which obtains for most bodies. It is a story about how human bodies gain access to the incorporeal surface insofar as it gives human speech its expressive capacity. Carroll's distinction between 'the multiplication table and the dinner table' (LS 64) is of course a distinction between the bodily depths and the metaphysical surface. But more than this, the pun itself is only possible because of our human capacity to engage with sense.

It is indeed important to recognize this. However, Deleuze is not an anthropocentric thinker, and the account that he has elaborated is in no way an attempt to present human subjectivity as what Spinoza labels a 'dominion within a dominion'. (*Ethics* III Pref) Above all, Deleuze is concerned to argue that while human existence is irreducible to the play of bodies in the depths, it does not for all this consist in a sovereign mastery of Nature or sense. It is therefore significant that the central concept he will use to advance the genetic account into its final stages, the *phantasm*, is a vision of human subjectivity that is neither personal, nor identifiable with conscious thought, nor possessing of free will in any traditional sense.

We have already encountered the notion of the phantasm in the brief sketch of Klein. For her, phantasy is the term for what Freud called primary process, our unconscious thought processes. What is notable about the functioning of phantasy, though, is that it is directly engaged with the use of symbols. While this is initially non-verbal and pre-conceptual—hence the emphasis Klein places on playing with toys in the analysis of young children—it develops into the capacity for meaningful speech. More precisely, it develops into a means whereby I can actively give meaning to my experience, rather than simply reacting to stimuli. For Klein, this is no small thing at all. As she points out, it is only by giving things symbolic meaning that the world becomes organized according to my investments: 'symbolism is the foundation of all sublimations and of every talent, since it is by way of symbolic equation that things, activities and interests become the subject of libidinal phantasies'. (Klein, 'The Importance of Symbol-Formation', 220) So we can see that, for Klein, symbols possess a double function: they provide the subject the means to manifest their phantasies, and thereby engage in intersubjective relations, but at the same time function to attach these phantasies to denoted objects in the real world.

But Deleuze also wants to invoke Pierre Klossowski in this context, a philologist, writer and artist for whom the phantasm holds an even more central role. Deleuze cites both his literary works, and his famous texts on Nietzsche which culminated in *Nietzsche and the Vicious Circle*, published in the same year as the *Logic of Sense* and dedicated to Deleuze himself.

Klossowski's thought revolves around three key ideas. First, there is (1) the interplay of *impulses*, unconscious and irrational dynamisms. My sense of myself as a sovereign agent is an inevitable misrecognition of this fact. Now, (2) the phantasm is an effect produced at the intersection of these impulses. It is an unconscious point of *condensation* of these impulses. Phantasms exercise a profound fascination—Klossowski often talks of them as *obsessional*—over life and thought. The third concept is (3) the *simulacrum*. Unlike Deleuze's concept of the same name in the *Logic of Sense*, Klossowski's simulacrum is any deliberate, chosen representation of the phantasm. Perhaps Klossowski's best definition of this relationship is the one cited in Daniel Smith's preface to *Nietzsche and the Vicious Circle*: 'The simulacrum, in its imitative sense, is the actualization of something in itself incommunicable and nonrepresentable: the phantasm in its obsessional constraint'. (Klossowski, *La ressemblance*, 76) At best, then, 'The simulacrum is not the product of the phantasm, but its skillful reproduction'. (*Nietzsche*, 133) At worst, simulacra effects nothing but dissemblance. Most often, we end up establishing some kind of normalized relationship to the phantasm that tamps down its talismanic, organizing power—and the conventional use of language is the main way in which this is done.

Klossowski's key example is Nietzsche's eternal return. If we begin by identifying it as a doctrine or conceptual claim, we would have entirely missed the point, Klossowski says: it was first of all a *lived experience*. That day in August 1881, walking through the woods near Lake Silvaplana in Sils-Maria, a certain confluence of (1) *impulses* coalesced in the person of Friedrich Nietzsche: 'the Eternal Return, at its inception, was not a representation, nor was it, strictly speaking, a postulate; it was a *lived fact*, and as a thought, it was a *sudden* thought'. (*Nietzsche*, 72) At the point of this intersection, (2) the *phantasm* of the eternal return was produced, an obsessional image around which his thought would turn from that point onwards. Nietzsche would of course try to develop certain doctrinal formulations or (3) *simulacra* of this image, which are explicitly included in his notes and published writings.

These comparative remarks are useful in illuminating Deleuze's own challenging presentation in the 'Thirtieth Series of the Phantasm' and the 'Thirty-First Series of Thought', which falls somewhere between these two accounts while drawing from both. In these chapters, Deleuze connects his account of the phantasm to the outcome of castration. The life of the child is now affected by their position in relation to the whole field of events, rather than their situation in relation to the various psychic objects of the depths, heights and bodily surface. They have a certain *position* on the surface—but what is the nature of this position?

As a body, I am composed of a particular set of other bodies engaged in causal relations. But as we saw when we were discussing the nature of the event, the structure of my body affects the degree to which particular events come into play—their particular weight or significance. Now we are in a position to be more precise: *my phantasm is the representative of my body in the field of sense*. As Foucault insightfully puts it: 'Phantasms [...] topologise the materiality of the body'. (Foucault, '*Theatrum Philosophicum*', 347) And if we reproduce the diagram from earlier, we are now in a position to see that this 'x' does not in fact indicate the position of the affected body, but the rather the position of the phantasm; the structure of events as they are organised around it is the result of the phantasm, and not of the body as such.

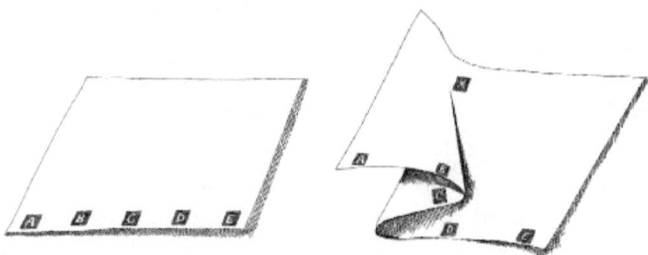

The other way to put this is to say that the phantasm itself expresses the entire field of events, and that each event takes on a specific weight or significance from its particular point of view, each one 'representing in the phantasm a variable combination of singular points'. (LS 215) The phantasm is thus like a telescope. Its lenses refract light from its aperture, which opens onto (for instance) the night sky, concentrating this light at the other end of the telescope *from its*

particular point of view. Another telescope, even one situated nearby, will gather together light from the same celestial phenomena, though not in precisely the same way—and the same would hold for a telescope whose lenses are differently organised. Now, note that the particular 'representation' of the cosmos is itself also composed of light. It is a very specific gathering of the visual spectrum of astral radiation that both preserves the disparate state of the stars and condenses them from a specific perspective. Leibniz already used this metaphor in a similar context when he wrote that 'each simple substance is a perpetual, living mirror of the universe'. (*Monadology* §56) These are the key features of the phantasm too: it belongs to the same register as the event (it is incorporeal, the result of causal relations between bodies, and so on), while functioning as a locus of condensation or resonance within this field.

The phantasm and the ego

So far we have seen that 'The phantasm is a surface phenomenon' (LS 216), that it *represents* the field of events as a whole, and that it is the incorporeal representative of the body. But there is a third object affected by the advent of the phantasm: the ego.

The ego in some sense attends every moment of the dynamic genesis. In the schizoid position, it is identified with the body without organs, whose indifference to the other part-objects allow it to be characterized in terms of a primary narcissism. In the depressive position, the ego becomes the object of conflict between the depths and the heights, suffering no matter which side it finds itself on. In the genital phase, the ego is straightforwardly identified with the phallus, and, given its new freedom from the dramas of the earlier moments, its narcissism is easy to understand. Now, it is true that this narcissistic ego is irrevocably shattered by castration, but for Deleuze, this is not the final word. On the one hand, the child's belief in their capacity to be an innocent healer and reconciler is destroyed forever. In the terms of Deleuze's account of events, the child has come to realise that they are never the master of either what occurs or what it might come to mean: it is a matter of grasping that they are always already the ex-president of the event (to quote Ashberry once more).

On the other hand, though, we must not forget what this disaster makes possible: the access to sense, and the correlative advent of the phantasm. Indeed, for Deleuze, 'the phantasm, properly speaking, finds its origin only in the ego of secondary narcissism, along *with* the narcissistic wound' (LS 216) The phantasm is then the successor of the ego, the incorporeal structure that issues from this corporeal wound; the ego 'merges with the event of the phantasm itself'. (LS 213) But what does this mean for who I am, who I feel myself to be? Alice knew that the answer is not an easy one:

> The Caterpillar and Alice looked at each other for some time in silence: at last the Caterpillar took the hookah out of its mouth, and addressed her in a languid, sleepy voice.
>
> 'Who are *you*?' said the Caterpillar.
>
> This was not an encouraging opening for a conversation. Alice replied, rather shyly, 'I—I hardly know, sir, just at present—at least I know who I WAS when I got up this morning, but I think I must have been changed several times since then.'
>
> 'What do you mean by that?' said the Caterpillar sternly. 'Explain yourself!'
>
> 'I can't explain *myself*, I'm afraid, sir' said Alice, 'because I'm not myself, you see.' (Carroll, *Alice in Wonderland*, 39)

Earlier, the name Alice^x was proposed as a kind of place-holder for the totality of the series of Alices. Now we can see that Alice^x does not refer to an indefinite series, but to Alice's phantasm. The upshot of the genetic account of the *Logic of Sense* is that, indeed, I am not myself—I am the 'process of the phantasm' (LS 226), which consists in the resonance of all of the events, weighted in terms of the structure of my body. In other words, who I am is certainly related to my bodily reality. After all, my body is all that *exists* of me. But what *subsists* is what makes of this collection of physical parts something singular in comparison to all other such collections. The field of the sense-event is anonymous; my body as a corporeal mixture is ubiquitous; the ego is only a 'dissolved ego' (LS 214) held together by social conventions and grammar. The one that is really my *self*, though this name does it no favours, is my phantasm, that singular locus around which the field of events is arrayed in a way particular to the history of my existence.

FOURTH GENETIC MOMENT: THOUGHT AND SENSE

We arrive now at the final moment in the process. Let's recapitulate. The child has gained access to sense, which is to say that the noises of the body are now caught up in the process of expressing events:

there is meaningful speech. In turn, what happens to the child from this point onwards plays itself out in and between the two registers we are familiar with from before. On the one hand, events are attributes of the various mixtures in the depths of the body; on the other, they affect the relative 'location' of the phantasm with respect to all the other events on the incorporeal surface.

Given this structurally complete *depths/incorporeal surface* set-up, what becomes of the first, bodily surface? Deleuze emphasizes a specific process involved in the transition from the first surface to the second, one first thematised by Freud: desexualisation.

Sexuality and desexualisation

Earlier we saw that according to Freud, any structural change in the psyche requires existing investments to be withdrawn before that libido is reinvested. More than this, he recognizes that a certain portion of uninvested 'displaceable and indifferent energy,' (Freud, *The Ego and the Id*, 44) is in play in the psyche. This is to say that desexualisation not only precedes the formation of new agencies (like the super-ego), but appears to be presupposed more generally: 'If thought-processes in the wider sense are to be included among these displacements, then the activity of thinking is also supplied from the sublimation of erotic motive forces'. (Freud, *The Ego and the Id*, 45)

Deleuze makes use of this account, even taking up Freud's use of the term sublimation, to describe what takes place in castration. The main investment that is withdrawn is the investment in the phallus itself. This desexualized energy is reinvested, through the phantasm, on the equally neutral incorporeal surface. So we can now say that castration thus involves: 1) an intention to perform certain (restorative) actions, 2) the accomplishment of other, unintended actions, 3) the renunciation of the investment in the phallus and a correlative desexualisation, and 4) the deployment of this newly desexualized energy on the surface of sense.

This little bit of argumentation is, perhaps surprisingly, the lynchpin around which the whole of the genetic account in the *Logic of Sense* turns. 'Had castration not transformed the narcissistic libido into desexualized energy', as Deleuze says, there would have been 'no "way out"' (LS 218) Without this transformation, there would be no passage to the metaphysical surface of the event. Of course, all of this does remain paradoxical, as Deleuze recognises: castration is the act which both constitutes the second surface, and cuts between the two *at the same time*. In other words, castration as an event has to give rise to the very register in which it will subsist as an event. This is a peculiar claim, not least because it seems to mean that the incorporeal surface in general—in which the event 'to green' subsists as the attribute of the tree—depends upon each infant's castration.

If we turn now to the phantasm from this new perspective, we will be able to ameliorate at least some of the concern that this paradoxical situation evokes. Since before it was born, the child was implicated sense-events. The meaning of its life was caught up in relations of quasi-causality well before it was itself a causal agent. Indeed, up until this point, the child had more in common with the tree that 'greens' than with their parents from the point of view of the event. But *their* phantasm is produced by their first, unintended acts—as we have seen. From the libidinal economic point of view, we can say that the phantasm is composed of the desexualized energy released through castration.

It is for this reason that I have repeatedly invoked the idea of *access* to the field of sense. The castration complex is what provides the child with this access *to* sense, but the phantasm is what is maintained *of* the child on the surface. The phantasm is first of all an obsessive organization of the obscurity of the whole field of events around the 'nuclear complex' of 'to kill' and 'to castrate'. All human beings share this kernel, even though the ways in which their phantasm will come to represent other events in relation to them, and the ways in which they will express them in their bodily existence, will differ.

So where does that leave the organized body, not to mention sex? Here's the key passage: 'Melanie Klein remarks that between symptoms and sublimations there must be an intermediary series corresponding to cases of *less successful sublimation*. But the whole of sexuality, in its own right, is a "less successful" sublimation'. (LS 224) In other words, the passage through the genital phase, and the unification of the body via the image of the phallus, this is necessary. But the sublimation in question—the attainment of the surface of sense—is not achieved at or by this moment. What is achieved, so long as we keep in mind that castration is first of all a result or event for the body of the child, is the formation of the rudimentary elements of adult sexuality. There is of course an implicit rebuke of certain psychoanalytic models here, those (like Freud's) which locate the sublimation related to the resolution of the Oedipus complex in the same biophysical register as the ego, or those (unlike Lacan's) who fail to see the productive character of castration. But beyond this, Deleuze's point is that sexuality itself, and the whole genital situation of the Oedipus complex *means nothing* and *explains nothing* by itself. Sexuality gains its meaning and its place as an organizational factor in subsequent life only insofar as the events of this stage are taken up *again* on the surface of sense. And, more generally, this is why Deleuze will describe the meaning that animates speech and is manifest in sexuality a retroactively constituted 'co-sense'. (LS 233)

Sense and thought

This leads us to the final moment of the genetic project of the *Logic of Sense*, and concerns the nature of *thought*. The main point can be put directly: the subject's access to sense is also the access to thought. But we should add: speech and thought are the two human capacities made possible by the access to sense, but they differ in kind.

We have just seen that the phantasm—the post-narcissistic self—is a kind of *open* ego. The passage through castration results in a kind of trepanning: a cracking-open of the self so that events pass through thought. It is because of this contact with sense-events that our bodily noises can be meaningful, to ourselves and others. Language use, in turn, expresses or actualizes sense; it involves a new kind of bodily relationship to events other than that which all causal interactions involves. Thought too involves the incorporeal, extra-causal field of events, but—and here is the key point—it does not involve actualization. Bodies express events as incorporeal attributes; speech is meaningful because it expresses the sense-event; but thought takes place entirely on the incorporeal surface. Thinking engages with events not insofar as they are actualized, but on their own terms, in their irreducibility to any present moment.

But what kind of idea does Deleuze have of thinking here, precisely? What does he mean when he invokes 'the obsessional paths by which the thinker passes. It is not a question of causality, but rather of geography and topology'? (LS 220) Here, Klossowski's notion of the phantasm is again useful. The thinker is the phantasm, and the phantasm for Klossowski is obsessional in character. It constitutes a locus of fixation or incorporeal circuit around which my every day self with its 'thoughts' circulates. The everyday use of language functions, for its part, to obscure the centrality of the phantasm, and to reinstate the ego of secondary narcissism—rational decision maker and conscientious, liberal consumer.

Deleuze has a related point in mind: we must distinguish between the 'thoughts' that I have as a person—as a habitual, bodily being engaged in a wide array of causal networks and who identifies themselves with the grammatical 'I'—and the process of the phantasm. It is the latter that is thinking as such: the condensation and resonance between events oriented around my singular point in the field of events. And indeed, this is what he says a little later on the same page: 'the phantasm is a machine [...] for the polarisation of the cerebral field'. (LS 220) The thoughts that I have as the person that I am result from the prior set of dispositions established and re-established (in the wake of new events) by the obsessional thought of the phantasm—an other, who is more me than I am, thinks in me.

Summary

One of the most striking definitions advanced by Deleuze in the *Logic of Sense* is this: 'It is thought which is the metamorphosis of sex'. (LS 220) Given that thought is made possible by the movement of psychogenesis, while being indifferent to it, differing in kind from it, we can see why Deleuze would make this claim. And yet, isn't the same true for speech itself, as the deliberate manifestation of sense? On the one hand, yes, sexuality is an intermediary moment on the way to speech. From this point of view, 'Sexuality exists only as an allusion, as vapour or dust, showing a path along which language has passed, but which it continues to jolt and to erase like so many extremely disturbing childhood memories'. (LS 242)

But on the other, speech and sex, the speaking body, only ever attain to a retroactive meaning, one that presupposes thought and the phantasm. However profoundly the meanings of our lives appear to be caught up in sex, they remain irreducible to it and in excess of it. From this point of view, as Deleuze puts it in an excellent phrase, 'There is nothing the sense of which is not *also* sexual'. (LS 233) He could also have said: there is nothing of sense which *will not have been* sexual. But the surface of sense itself is incorporeal and indifferent to its actualization, and it is at this level that thought exclusively operates. In turn, the thinker is not the embodied speaker, but the incorporeal phantasm, with its obsessional thought.

Putting all of these parts together, the genetic trajectory can be summarized in the following, bare-bones fashion:

Position	Dimension	Object(s)	Language
Schizoid	Depths	*Simulacra:* Persecuting part-objects; the body-without-organs	Infra-sense (noises of the body in the depths)
Depressive	Heights	*Icon:* the good object	Vocal pre-sense
Sexual-perverse	Integrated bodily surface	*Images*, including the phallus	Speech
Castration. Phantasm as agent.			
Ideal	Metaphysical surface	Thought	Non/sense

AN ETHICS OF THE EVENT

As the German army advanced towards Paris during the afternoon of May 27 in the Third Battle of Aisne, they passed through—after destroying with artillery—the town of Vailly. In this town was a twenty-one year old recruit by the name of Joë Bosquet, whose spinal cord was severed by a German bullet. Until he died in 1950 at the age of fifty-three, he lived in constant pain, bedbound and paralysed from the waist down. For Bousquet, the event of the battle lasted for the rest of his life. And yet he could write: 'My wound existed before me, I was born to embody it'. And: 'Become the man of your misfortunes; learn to embody their perfection and brilliance'. (LS 148; 149) The paradox of this affirmation is at the very heart of Deleuze's ethics of the event in the *Logic of Sense*. In turn, this ethics constitutes the third and last major strand of the book.

Stoic ethics

So far, we have seen that Deleuze relies on the Stoics for his theory of the event, and for his closely related theory of language. But

Deleuze will also draw on them one final time, if in passing, on the matter of ethics.

The very broad thesis of Stoic ethics is well-known: act in accordance with Nature. Do this because the course of nature is beyond your power to change, and the attempt to resist it is what will make you miserable. Deleuze does embrace this claim in a very broad sense, but to see the connection between what he writes in the *Logic of Sense* about ethics and what the Stoics had to say, we need to draw in a little closer. Epictetus can be our guide: 'Do not seek to have events happen as you want them to, but instead want them to happen as they do happen, and your life will go well. (*Handbook* §8) On the one hand, this sentiment could be translated in traditional, naturalist terms, or in the terms used by Spinoza in the *Ethics*: Nature follows its own set of rules; we are a part of Nature; fighting against these rules can only bring misery. But in the *Logic of Sense*, Deleuze very much does *not* want to relate ethics to Nature in this sense, and this is because events *do not* follow the rules of Nature, taken as the ensemble of bodily causes. When we read that 'Stoic ethics is concerned with the event; it consists in willing the event as such, that is, of willing that which occurs insofar as it does occur', (LS 143) we must be a little wary, not about the claim itself, but the degree to which it can be attributed to the Stoics. In effect, Deleuze will make use of Stoic ethics in much the same way that he does the Stoic philosophy of language—he takes the doctrine of the incorporeal event as the primary thesis, and then fits what the Stoics have to say about ethics back onto that. And beyond this, he very clearly situates Stoic ethics as the horizon of his own account: 'How much we have yet to learn from Stoicism ...' (LS 158)

This Stoic-inspired ethics turns around three main claims concerning, respectively, the *affirmation of the event*, the *counter-actualisation of the event*, and what, following Nietzsche, Deleuze will call 'the great Health'. (LS 161) In the course of discussing these three points, we will also stop to consider the importance of a particular event: the event of death.

The affirmation of the event

The first of these points is straightforward, astringent, absolute. Deleuze is not interested in presenting an elaborate set of ethical maxims. As it does for Kant, everything turns around a single point. Bousquet is Deleuze's emblem: 'My wound existed before me, I was born to embody it [...] Become the man of your misfortunes; learn to embody their perfection and brilliance'. (LS 148-9) As far as Deleuze is concerned, this is the full measure of what answers to the name 'ethics': 'Nothing more can be said; nothing more will ever have been said: to become worthy of what happens to us'. (LS 149)

Deleuze's admiration for Bousquet, and his astonishment at this remarkable capacity, are very clear here. But they are balanced by his awareness of the degree to which we fail to affirm the event, hence the following diagnosis:

> Either ethics makes no sense at all, or this is what it means and has nothing else to say: not to be unworthy of what happens to us. To grasp whatever happens as unjust and unwarranted (it is always someone else's fault) is, on the contrary, what renders our sores repugnant—veritable *ressentiment*, resentment of the event. (LS 149)

There are fundamentally only two responses to an event. Either I respond to events by affirming them, or I resent them for happening to me; I turn from affirmation to resentment and blame. Let's note in a preliminary fashion that these two alternatives each imply a temporal orientation. The affirmation of the event is oriented towards the future—by affirming the event, I affirm what it will make of me, *what it will make possible for me*. Resentment towards the event is allied with the immediate past, the time *before this was done to me*.

Counter-actualisation

Deleuze's position appears straightforwardly fatalistic, and, worse, trivial. What value is there in affirming what we can't do anything about? If Bousquet's wound was inevitable, a destiny, is there any significant difference between affirmation and resignation, affirmation and *ressentiment*? The first argument against this accusation is ontological in character. To charge Deleuze with fatalism is to confuse the event of Bousquet's wounding with the wound itself. Events are irreducible to causal 'happenings' at the level of bodily Nature, even if they are inseparable from what takes place. This is to say that, as Deleuze puts it, 'The event is not what occurs (an accident), it is rather inside what occurs, the purely expressed'. (LS 149) What matters is 'Not what happens to us in childhood, but what was inside what happened.' (Jack Gilbert, *Refusing Heaven*, 75) Bousquet does not, therefore, affirm his shattered spine itself, but the event expressed by his broken body whose meaning opens onto the future.

The second argument follows from this; it is also ontological, and concerns the nature of events themselves. As we have seen, no particular actualization of any event is exhaustive; events are always actualized in more than one way, and always mean more than one thing, and can always be actualized in a new and different way. This was Deleuze's point in identifying the temporality of the event: belonging to *Aion*, an event is always already past and always yet to come. The charge of fatalism forgets that the event always remains open to the future, and this means that it can be more than what it currently is: it's always 'a nice day to start again'.

But now, even if these two arguments are granted, what bearing do they have on Deleuze's ethical proposal? In short, the fact that events are open to being actualized differently is what gives us room to modify our relationship with them. Bousquet's wound is one way in which the event is actualized, but his poetry is another. Deleuze calls this work of modification *counter-actualisation*. Counter-actualisation consists in a *projection* (LS 207), in an act of the will that affirms the event in its excess over any given actualization. It wills 'not exactly what occurs, but something *in* that which occurs'. (LS 149) Deleuze gives the good example— one we've touched on above—of Nietzsche's sickness, one in which it is not hard to also see Deleuze himself, with his life-long experience of pulmonary illness. While he was still able to work, sickness provided Nietzsche with a unique vantage point from which to develop his philosophy and he affirms it as such. Deleuze quotes *Ecce Homo*: 'Looking from the perspective of the sick towards *healthier* concepts and values, and conversely looking down from the fullness and self-assuredness of *rich* life into the secret workings of the *décadence* instinct—this is what I practised longest, this was my true experience; if I became master of anything then it was of this'. ('Why I am so wise', §1) Whatever the event whose bodily actualization gave rise to such physical suffering, Nietzsche did not take it as a dead-end worthy of resentment. Instead, he found and affirmed something *in* that sickness that allowed him to live and work, not just despite, but in a way *because of* this event. Here is Deleuze: 'The eternal truth of the event is grasped only if the event is also inscribed in the flesh. But each time we must double this painful actualization by a counter-actualisation which limits, moves, and transfigures it'. (LS 161)

In trying to convey the practical reality of counter-actualisation, Deleuze makes use of the figure of the actor. While the playing of a role requires that an actor learn their lines, and the structure of the plot, they succeed only by playing the role in a way that is not presented in the script, or delimited by the demands of the director or the dramaturge. To play a role, the actor has to 'play the role differently', finding in Hamlet something that brings him close to a financial broker, a fisherman or a philosopher. This is what Deleuze is getting at when he writes that 'The role played is never that of a character; it is a theme (the complex theme or sense)'. (LS 150) He also notes that the actor is always anticipating what is yet to come in the play, while carrying forward everything that has already happened, such that the present moment of the performance contains the whole play in folded-up form. In the same way, every time I counter-actualise an event—play it differently, draw out different ways of living in relation to it—I draw upon the fact that the event can never be captured by any one present state of affairs.

Now, Deleuze does not conceive of counter-actualisation as a one-time deal. We really are dealing with an ethics here, and not an emergency response protocol only good for storms and riots. In other words, the ethics of the event is an ethical *orientation*. This is necessarily the case due to another feature of the event that we have already seen: its inter-expressive character. Strictly speaking, it is not possible to affirm *an* event, because to do so is to affirm all events at once, to affirm the evental character of human being. There is also a further reason why this is the case, and it concerns the nature of the phantasm. Who I am is not a fixed being to whom things happen, and which events modify from without, like a sculptor works on a block of marble. I am instead a body that expresses, through the specific location of my phantasm vis-à-vis the field of events, all events. In other words, the ethics of the event consists in an ongoing affirmation of the phantasmatic character of my being. Conversely, the resentful orientation would involve an attempt to reject—as if they were hostile biological entities—the influx of events and their manner of organizing what I am capable of, or of simply resigning oneself to the way the event is first actualized in us.

Deleuze summarises this argumentative trajectory in the following admittedly oracular, poetic terms:

> Nothing more can be said; nothing more will have ever be said: to become worthy of what happens to us, and thus to will and release the event, to become the children of our own events, to be reborn and again reborn, to break with our carnal birth. Children of our events and not our works, for the work itself is but the product of the event's children. (LS 149-50)

Thus, in an equally astonishing phrase, Deleuze will write that 'the *Amor fati* is one with the struggle of free men'. (LS 149) This struggle is the struggle *of* bodies, a material struggle. However, this struggle fails to be a struggle *for* anything unless it is an affirmation of events, and the plurality and openness of their meaning in our lives.

Deleuze defends a Stoic interpretation of astrology in these terms (LS 171). Astrology is not an extrapolation of the physics of bodies, and the Stoic sage is not Maxwell's demon in grease paint. It is instead an art of the quasi-cause, an attempt to divine the nature of the co-implication of incorporeal events for a given body. The sage is thus rather a species of water strider or jesus bug, an insect that moves across the incorporeal field of events, moving in accordance with their sensitivity to surface tension.

Interlude on death

It is at this point, following Deleuze himself, that we need to grasp this ethics of the event at the point where the stakes are immeasurably high, indeed, absolute. At issue is the event of death. Let's first register Deleuze's own passionate cry on this point: 'Better death than the health we are given'. (LS 160) He means by this, first, that what is called health has been misnamed. The contemporary cult of fitness, for instance, is not given over to health at all, but has exactly the same structure that Deleuze identifies in alcoholism: it is an affair of freezing time, of hardening the present such that the idealized past appears, crystalline, within it, a fly in amber. This is an act of preservation that disavows the future, or better, that fetishizes it as another past (one more opportunity to go to the gym and keep your high school figure). The stake of ethics for Deleuze is instead what Nietzsche calls 'the great Health', which consists in the practice of affirmative counter-actualisation itself.

The event of death itself constitutes an important moment in the argument of the *Logic of Sense*. Deleuze follows Maurice Blanchot in thinking about death in a way that goes beyond the perishing of a person. Here is the key passage:

> Death has an extreme and definite relation to me and my body and is grounded in me, but it also has no relation to me at all—it is incorporeal and infinitive, impersonal, grounded only in itself. On one side, there is the part of the event which is realized and accomplished; on the other, there is that 'part of the event which cannot realise its accomplishment,' There are thus two accomplishments,

which are like actualization and counter-actualisation. It is in this way that death and its wound are not simply events among other events. Every event is like death, double and impersonal. (LS 151-2)

The Stoics and Epicurean philosophers are justly well-known for their treatment of death. Death should remain a matter of strict indifference, if not because Socrates found it nothing to worry about (Epictetus, *Handbook* §5), then because it is a part of the order of Nature, and in any case, death 'is nothing to us; since when we exist, death is not yet present, and when death is present, then we do not exist'. (Epicurus, 'Letter to Menoeceus,' 29) The point that Deleuze is making, though, goes further than these points. It is not just that I cannot experience my own death, but that, *as an event*, death itself is inexhaustible in character. Like every event, it can always be actualised in other ways beyond the way in which it happens to be actualised in any given instance—what Blanchot calls 'the instant of my death' is the inexhaustible instant of the always past, always yet to come event.

But beyond this, Deleuze's invocation of death has a more general purpose. As Epicurus recognized, the fear of death is one of the most formidable challenges to a well-lived life. The ethical problem here concerns not the actual moment of my perishing, but the whole of my life before this happens. There is a very real chance—described by Deleuze in terms of *ressentiment*—that my whole life might be given over to an endless dying, *an undeath*. Is this why the spectre of the zombie can be so terrifying? Before shuffling off the mortal coil, I might have actualized the event of death over and over again in the same, deflating, venomous posture, poisoning the world around me.

What is at stake then is the affirmation and counter-actualisation of the event of my own death. The account of counter-actualisation already elaborated applies in this case, although the stakes are cast in the clearest possible light. By affirming the event of my death, I do more than this—I affirm the eventality of my existence, and affirm all other events into the bargain. But what does this mean other than the affirmation of *change as such*? If every event is, as Deleuze says, like death, this is not just because every event has an impersonal, impassive aspect, but because every event is the death of a present state of affairs and the birth of another. At this extreme point, where death, change and the event are united, the true nature of the affirmation Deleuze calls for becomes apparent—it is an affirmation of the transformation promised by every event, which is to say, *life*, in its ungoverned creativity. This is the sense of the following passage:

If willing the event is, primarily, to release its eternal truth, like the fire on which it is fed, this will would reach the point at which war is waged against war, the wound would be living trace and the scar of all wounds, and death turned on itself be willed against all deaths. (LS 149)

Deleuze quotes Bousquet in this context once more, invoking his amazing remark that we can 'assign to plagues, tyrannies, and the most frightful wars the comic possibility having reigned for nothing'. (LS 151) Plagues, tyrannies and wars—these cases exemplify a certain notion of the 'catastrophic' event, an event with one, definitive meaning. The tyrant wants to definitively and indelibly mark history with his name and his significance: to make history the story of his rule. General Erich Ludendorff, the architect of the Third Battle of Aisne espoused the idea that wars were won or lost in a single monumental battle. The comic aspect of the event, and the reason why counter-actualisation is humorous for Deleuze, is the fact that there is no single way for an event to be actualized, and certainly no one right way. There's nothing that anyone can ever do reduce the meaning of a word, an act, or a life, to just one thing—despite their seriousness, tyrants have only ever been clowns. The despots of the past don't require the melancholy counter-hagiography of Shelley's 'Ozymandias'—their lives and works are always already a joke.

We are now in a position to see why Deleuze's ethics of the event constitutes the *obverse of suicide*. Drawing again on Blanchot, Deleuze points out that the act of suicide is an attempt to make the two halves of this event—its ideality and its bodily actualization—correspond, as it were, on the side of the body. In other words, suicide is an attempt on my part to definitively *say the sense of my life*. Conversely, the affirmation and counter-actualisation of death as event requires that we valorize its evental character rather than its bodily actualisation, and this in turn means embracing the fact that our lives do not have *a* meaning, even when we so desperately want them to, even when they seem to only have one that we cannot escape. More: there is no one meaning of life, but only the ongoing series of contingent transformations in what it means to each of us to live. Bosquet once wrote that life is lived in a perpetual collaboration with death; here, death appears in the guise of the event itself, the anonymous inevitability of transformation.

We arrive back, then, where we started, with the two alternative responses to the event, this time grasped in their full generality. We can either remain attached to the present and the past we select for ourselves, only ever finding in each new event opportunities for resentment: 'If only ...' Ironically enough, this is to do nothing but to identify ourselves with some fixed state, and thereby with death in its material sense. On the other hand, we can affirm and counter-actualise the event of death. It is only by affirming death *as an event* that it becomes possible to 'play it otherwise', to counter-actualise the other, ideal, face of death—the inevitability of transformation—as something positive, even though this is necessarily to affirm that transformation that will also, on some particular day and at some particular time, be *my* death.

Health

The work of counter-actualisation constitutes the first, positive element of Deleuze's ethics of the event in the *Logic of Sense*. But a troubling question remains, one dealt with in the remarkable 'Twenty-Second Series—Porcelain and Volcano'. The question is as follows. Ethics involves affirming the event, and the Event as such, through counter-actualisation. It is an ethics of the incorporeal surface. But what kind of relationship should this ethical practice have in relation to *what happens to the body as a result?* As Deleuze will write, it's easy to theorise the distinction between body and event, but, really, how much of our *own* bodily existence should we be willing to put at stake in this work of affirmation? Consider the following astonishing sequence of questions:

> Well then, are we to go on speaking about Bousquet's wound, Fitzgerald and Lowry's alcoholism, Nietzsche and Artaud's madness, while remaining on the shore? Are we to become the professionals who give talks on these topics? Are we to wish only that those have been struck down do not abuse themselves too much? Are we to take up collections and create special journal issues? Or should we go a little further and see for ourselves—be a little alcoholic, a little crazy, a little suicidal, a little bit of a guerilla—just enough to extend the crack but not enough to deepen it irremediably? Wherever we turn, everything seems dismal. Indeed, how are we to stay at the surface without staying on the shore? How do we save ourselves by saving the surface and every surface organization, including language and life? How is this *politics*, this full *guerilla warfare* to be attained? (LS 157-8)

In the face of these question—and the howling of human suffering down through the ages, and the endlessly recrudescent stench of violence—how could 'the abstract thinker', and with him the entire canon of Western philosophy's dilettantish concern for the good life 'not be ridiculous?' (LS 156) There is no academic philosopher who should not feel the weight of this, and feel something akin to what André Gide felt after Artaud's last performance: 'We felt ashamed to go back to our places in a world where comfort consists of compromises'. (Caldart, 'Tête-à-tête', 17)

However important, this realisation hardly answers the question. And, at first, it does not seem that Deleuze will either. After posing this breath-taking sequence, he moves into the long discussion of alcoholism we touched on above. Some pages later, he returns to it just as abruptly, providing and an astonishing, unambiguous answer. How much should we put at stake in our affirmation of counter-actualisation? *Everything*:

> If one asks why health does not suffice, why the crack is desirable, it is perhaps because thought only occurs by means of the crack and at its edges, because everything good and great in humanity enters and exits through it, in people ready to destroy themselves—better death than the health we are given. (LS 160)

We arrive here at the pathetic kernel of the *Logic of Sense*, the point at which all of its themes resonate together, where life and death are at stake in the body. The text is analogous to Maria's cry 'Helfe' [Help!] in the first act of Berg's opera *Wozzeck* that so moved Deleuze.

According to Deleuze, the idea of counter-actualisation is not enough by itself unless it becomes much more than just an idea, a normative ideal, or a topic for a panel at a Deleuze studies conference. 'The eternal truth of the event is grasped only if the event is also inscribed in the flesh'. (LS 161) Certainly, ethics is concerned with the affirmation of the event, but it remains academic—and therefore risible, shameful, just as bad as treating counter-actualisation as an exercise in counterfactual wishes about *'what could have happened'* (LS 161)—so long as our bodies and their transformations, *our very selves*, are not at stake.

Works of Gilles Deleuze

Deleuze, Gilles, 'Quest-ce que fonder?', https://www.webdeleuze.com/textes/218, last accessed 7 April 2019.

Deleuze, Gilles, *Nietzsche and Philosophy*, trans. Hugh Tomlinson, New York: Columbia University Press, 1983. *Nietzsche et la philosophie*, Paris: Presses Universitaires de France, 1962.

Deleuze, Gilles, *Bergsonism*, trans. Hugh Tomlinson and Barbara Habberjam, New York: Zone Books, 1988. *Le Bergsonisme*, Paris: Presses Universitaires de France, 1966.

Deleuze, Gilles, *Difference and Repetition*, trans. Paul Patton, New York: Columbia University Press, 1994. *Différence et Répétition*, Paris: Presses Universitaires de France, 1968.

Deleuze, Gilles, *The Logic of Sense*, trans. Mark Lester with Charles Stivale, ed. Constantin Boundas, New York: Columbia University Press, 1990. *Logique du sens*, Paris: Editions du Minuit, 1969.

Deleuze, Gilles, *Kant's Critical Philosophy*, trans. Hugh Tomlinson and Barbara Habberjam, London: Althone Press, 1983.

Deleuze, Gilles, *Masochism*, trans. Jean McNeil, New York: Zone Books, 1989.

Deleuze, Gilles, *Empiricism and Subjectivity*, trans. Constantin Boundas, New York: Columbia University Press, 1991. *Empirisme et subjectivité*, Paris: Presses Universitaires de France, 1953.

Deleuze, Gilles, *Negotiations*, trans. Martin Joughin, New York: Columbia University Press, 1995. *Pourparlers*, Paris: Minuit, 1990.

Deleuze, Gilles. *Proust and Signs. The Complete Text*, trans. Richard Howard. Minneapolis: University of Minnesota Press, 2000. *Proust et les signes*, Paris: Presses Universitaires de Paris, 1973.

Deleuze, Gilles, *L'Ile Déserte et Autres Textes: textes et entretiens 1953-1974*, ed. David Lapoujade, Paris, Les Editions de Minuit, 2002.

Deleuze, Gilles, *Deux Régimes de Fous: textes et entretiens 1975-95*, ed. David Lapoujade, Paris: Minuit, 2003.

Deleuze, Gilles, *Lettres et autres textes*, ed. David Lapoujade, Paris: Minuit, 2015.

Other Works Cited

Aetius, 'Causation and Fate', in *The Hellenistic Philosophers*, volume 1, ed. and trans. AA. Long, A. A. and D.N Sedley, 1987, Cambridge: Cambridge University Press, 336.

American Psychiatric Association, *Diagnostic and Statistical Manuel of Mental Disorders*, fifth edition. Arlington, VA: American Psychiatric Publishing, 2018.

Aristotle, Categories, in Barnes, Jonathan (ed.) *The Complete Works of Aristotle: The Revised Oxford Translation*, Volume I, Princeton: Princeton University Press, 1984.

Aristotle, *Nicomachean Ethics*, trans. and ed. Roger Crisp, Cambridge: Cambridge University Press, 2004.

Aristotle, *Physics*, ed. David Bostock, trans. Robin Waterfield, Oxford: Oxford University Press, 2008.

Artaud, Antonin, *Antonin Artaud, Selected Writings*, ed. Susan Sontag, Berkeley: University of California Press, 1988.

Ashberry, John. *Three Books*, New York: Penguin, 1993.

Beckett, Samuel, *Proust*, New York: Grove Press, 1957.

Beiser, Friedrich, *The Fate of Reason: German Philosophy from Kant to Fichte*, Cambridge, MA.: Harvard University Press, 1987.

Berkeley, George, *De Motu and The Analyst*, ed. and trans. Douglas M. Jesseph, Dordrecht: Springer, 1992.

Bergson, Henri, *Mind-Energy*, trans. H. Wildon Carr. Westport, Conn.: Greenwood Press, 1920.

Bergson, Henri, *Matter and Memory*, trans. Nancy Margaret Paul and W. Scott Palmer, Mineola: Dover, 2004.

Bergson, Henri, *Creative Mind*, trans. Mabelle L. Andison, Mineola: Dover, 2007.

Bergson, Henri, 'Good Sense and Classical Studies'. In *Bergson: Key Writings*. Ed. Keith Ansell Pearson and John Mullarkey. London: Continuum, 2002, 345-53.

Bergson, Henri, 'The Possible and the Real'. In *Bergson: Key Writings*. Ed. Keith Ansell Pearson and John Mullarkey. London: Continuum, 2002, 223-32.

Bergson, Henri, *The Two Sources of Religion and Morality*, trans. R. Ashley Audra and C. Brereton, Notre Dame, University of Notre Dame Press, 1977.

Bonilla-Silva, Eduardo, *Racism without Racists*, Maryland: Rowman & Littlefield, 2018.

Borges, Jorge Luis, 'John Wilkins' Analytical Language'. In *Selected Non-Fictions*, ed. and trans. Eliot Weinberger, New York: Viking, 1999, 229-232.

Caldart, Elizabeth, '"Tête-à-tête avec Antonin Artaud:" On the Communicability of the Void', *Critical Theory and Social Justice Journal of Undergraduate Research* 5, 2015, 7-22.

Carroll, Lewis, *Through the Looking-Glass*, Mineola, NY: Dover, 1999.

Carroll, Lewis, *The Hunting of the Snark: An Agony in Eight Fits*, Plattsburg, NY: Tundra, 2012.

Carroll, Lewis, *Alice's Adventures in Wonderland*, New York: W.W. Norton, 2015.

Calvino, Italo, *Invisible Cities*, trans. William Weaver, London: Vintage, 1997.

Cohn, Ruby, *From* Desire *to* Godot: *Pocket Theater of Postwar Paris*, Berkeley: University of California Press, 1987.

Cowley, Robert, 'The Ludendorff Offensive', in *The Reader's Companion to Military History*, ed. Robert Cowley and Geoffrey Parker (Boston: Houghton Mifflin, 1996), 274.

Descartes, Rene, *Meditations on First Philosophy, with Selections from the Objections and Replies*. Trans. and Ed. John Cottingham. Cambridge: Cambridge University Press, 1996

Descartes, Rene, *Discourse on the Method for Conducting One's Reason Well and Seeking Truth in the Sciences*. New York: Hackett, 1998.

Duns Scotus, John, 'Concerning Metaphysics', in Wolter, Allan, ed. and trans., *Philosophical Writings*, Indianapolis and Cambridge: Hackett Publishing Company, 1987.

Epictetus, *The Handbook*, trans. Nicholas White, Indianapolis: Hackett, 1983.

Epicurus, 'Letter to Menoeceus,' in *The Epicurus Reader: Selected Writings and Testimonia*, ed. and trans. Brad Inwood, New York: Hackett, 1994, 28-31.

Foucault, Michel, 'Friendship as a way of life', in *Ethics*. Essential Works of Foucault, vol. 1, ed. Paul Rabinow, trans. Robert Hurley, New York: The New Press, 1997, 135-40

Foucault, Michel, *The History of Madness*, ed. Jean Khalfa, trans. Jonathan Murphy and Jean Khalfa. London: Routledge, 2006.

Foucault, Michel, 'Un plaisir si simple', *Gai Pied* 1 (1979), 1; 10.

Foucault, Michel, '*Theatrum Philosophicum*,' in *Aesthetics, Method, and Epistemology. Essential Works of Foucault*, vol.2, ed. James Faubion, trans. Robert Hurley, New York: The New Press, 1998, 343-68.

Freud, Sigmund, *Beyond the Pleasure Principle*, vol. 18, *The Standard Edition of the Complete Psychological Works of Sigmund Freud*, trans. and ed. James Strachey, London: The Hogarth Press, 1994.

Freud, Sigmund, 'The Dissolution of the Oedipus Complex', in *The Standard Edition of the Complete Psychological Works of Sigmund Freud*, vol. 21, trans. and ed. James Strachey, London: The Hogarth Press, 1961, 171-80.

Freud, Sigmund, *The Ego and the Id and Other Works*, in *The Standard Edition of the Complete Psychological Works of Sigmund Freud*, vol. 19, trans. and ed. James Strachey, London: The Hogarth Press, 1961.

Freud, Sigmund, *The Interpretation of Dreams*, trans. James Strachey, New York: Basic Books, 2010.

Freud, Sigmund, 'On Narcissism: An Introduction', in *Papers on Metapsychology*, vol. 14, *The Standard Edition of the Complete Psychological Works of Sigmund Freud*, trans. and ed. James Strachey, London: The Hogarth Press, 1994, 73-103.

Freud, Sigmund, 'Negation', in *The Ego and the Id and Other Works*, *The Standard Edition of the Complete Psychological Works of Sigmund Freud*, vol. 19, trans. and ed. James Strachey, London: The Hogarth Press, 1994, 233-40.

Freud, Sigmund, 'Repression', in *Papers on Metapsychology*, *The Standard Edition of the Complete Psychological Works of Sigmund Freud*, vol. 14, trans. and ed. James Strachey, London: The Hogarth Press, 1994, 146-57.

Freud, Sigmund, 'Three Essays on the Theory of Sexuality', *The Standard Edition of the Complete Psychological Works of Sigmund Freud*, vol. 7, trans. and ed. James Strachey, London: The Hogarth Press, 1994, 123-246

Gilbert, Jack, *Refusing Heaven*, New York: Alfred A. Knopf, 2005.

Hegel, GWF, *The Encyclopedia Logic*, trans. TF Geraets, WA Suchting, and HS Harris, Indianapolis: Hackett, 1991.

Hegel, GWF, *The Science of Logic*, trans. and ed. George Di Giovanni, Cambridge: Cambridge University Press, 2010.

Heidegger, Martin, *Being and Time*, trans. John Macquarie and Edward Robinson. Oxford: Blackwell, 1998.

Hölderlin, Friedrich, 'Remarks on *Oedipus*', in *Essays and Letters on Theory*, trans. Thomas Pfau, Albany: State University of New York Press, 1988, 101–108.

Hume, David, *An Enquiry concerning Human Understanding*, ed. Tom L. Beauchamp, Oxford: Oxford University Press, 2006.

Hume, David, 'On Suicide', *Selected Essays*, ed. Stephen Copley, Oxford: Oxford University Press, 1993, 315-24.

Hume, David, *A Treatise of Human Nature*, ed. David Fate Norton and Mary J. Norton. Oxford: Oxford University Press, 2011.

Jones, Graham, *Difference and Determination: Prolegomena concerning Deleuze's Early Metaphysic*, PhD thesis, 2002.

Kant, Immanuel, *Critique of Pure Reason*, trans. and ed. Paul Guyer and Allen Wood, Cambridge: Cambridge University Press, 1998.

Kant, Immanuel, *Critique of the Power of Judgment*, ed. Paul Guyer, trans. Paul Guyer and Eric Matthews, Cambridge: Cambridge University Press, 2000.

Kant, Immanuel, *Critique of Practical Reason*, trans. Werner Pluhar, Indianapolis: Hackett Publishing Company, 2002.

Kant, Immanuel, *Anthropology from a Pragmatic Point of View*, trans. Robert B. Louden, Cambridge: Cambridge University Press, 2006.

Klee, Paul, *On Modern Art*, trans. Paul Findlay, London: Faber and Faber, 1967.

Klein, Melanie, 'The Importance of Symbol-Formation in the Development of the Ego', *International Journal of Psycho-Analysis* 11 (1930), 24-39.

Klossowski, Pierre, *La Ressemblance*, Marseille: André Dimanche, 1984.

Klossowski, Pierre, *Nietzsche and the Vicious Circle*, trans. Daniel W. Smith, London: Athlone, 1997.

Lacan, Jacques, *The Seminar of Jacques Lacan, Book VII: The Ethics of Psychoanalysis 1959–1960*, trans. Dennis Porter, ed. Jacques-Alain Miller, New York: Norton, 1992.

Lacan, Jacques, *Le* Séminaire *Livre XVI: D'un Autre à l'autre*, Paris: Seuil, 2006.

Lacan, Jacques, *Seminar of Jacques Lacan, Book XIV: The Logic of Phantasy 1966–1967*, trans. Cormac Gallagher, http://www.lacaninireland.com/web/wp-content/uploads/2010/06/THE-SEMINAR-OF-JACQUES-LACAN-XIV.pdf

Leibniz, GWF, 'Preface to the New Essays', in Ariew, Roger and Daniel Garber, ed. and trans. *Philosophical Essays*, London: Hackett, 1989, 291-306

Leibniz, GWF, 'A New System of Nature and Communication of Substances, and of the Union of the Soul and Body', in Ariew, Roger and Daniel Garber, ed. and trans. *Philosophical Essays*, London: Hackett, 1989, 138-47.

Leibniz, GWF, 'The Principles of Philosophy, or, The Monadology', in Ariew, Roger and Daniel Garber, ed. and trans. *Philosophical Essays*, London: Hackett, 1989, 213-224.

Lyotard, Jean-François, 'Endurance and the Profession', in *Political Writings*, trans. Bill Readings with Kevin Paul Geiman, London: UCL Press, 1993, 70-76.

Maimon, Solomon, *Essay on Transcendental Philosophy*, trans. Nick Midgley, Henry Somers-Hall, Alistair Welchman and Merten Reglitz, London: Continuum, 2010.
Nietzsche, Friedrich, *Twilight of the Idols, or, How to philosophize with a hammer*, trans. Duncan Large, Oxford: Oxford University Press, 1998.
Nietzsche, Friedrich, *The Gay Science*, ed. Bernard Williams, trans. Josephine Nauckhoff, Cambridge: Cambridge University Press, 2001.
Nietzsche, Friedrich, *Beyond Good and Evil*, ed. Rolf-Peter Horstmann and Judith Norman, trans. Judith Norman, Cambridge: Cambridge University Press, 2002.
Nietzsche, Friedrich, *Ecce Homo. How To Become What You Are*, trans. Duncan Large, Oxford: Oxford University Press, 2007.
Nietzsche, Friedrich, *On the Genealogy of Morality*, ed. Keith Ansell-Pearson, trans. Carol Diethe, Cambridge: Cambridge University Press, 2007.
Paterson, Don, *The Book of Shadows*, London: Picador, 2005.
Paterson, Don, *Landing Light*, London: Faber, 2005.
Plato. *Phaedo*, in *Complete Works*, ed. John M. Cooper and D.S. Hutchinson, trans. G.M.A. Gruber, Indianapolis: Hackett, 1997, 49-100.
Plato. *Philebus*, in *Complete Works*, ed. John M. Cooper and D.S. Hutchinson, trans. Dorothea Frede, Indianapolis: Hackett, 1997, 398-456.
Proust, Marcel, *In Search of Lost Time: Sodom and Gommorah*, vol. 4, trans. C.K. Scott Moncreiff and Terence Kilmartin, revised D.J. Enright, New York: Random House, 1999.
Proust, Marcel, *In Search of Lost Time: Swann's Way*, vol. 1, trans. C.K. Scott Moncreiff and Terence Kilmartin, revised D.J. Enright, New York: Random House, 2003.

Rosset, Clément, *Faits divers*, Paris: PUF, 2013.

Russell, Bertrand, *The Philosophy of Leibniz*. London: Routledge, 2005.

Ruyer, Raymond, *La genèse des formes vivantes*. Paris: Flammarion, 1958.

Sade, Maquis de, *Justine, or the Misfortunes of Virtue*, trans. John Phillips, Oxford: Oxford University Press, 2013.

Sextus Empiricus, 'Causation and Fate', in *The Hellenistic Philosophers*, volume 1, ed. and trans. AA. Long, A. A. and D.N Sedley, 1987, Cambridge: Cambridge University Press, 333.

Shuttuck, Roger, *The Innocent Eye*, New York: Farrah Straus Giroux, 1984.

Spinoza, Benedict, *Ethics*, in *The Collected Works of Spinoza*, vol.1, ed. and trans. Edwin Curley, Princeton: Princeton University Press, 1985, 408-620.

Stoppard, Tom, *Rosencrantz and Guildenstern are Dead* (50th Anniversary Edition), New York: Grove Press, 2017.

Tranströmer, Tomas, 'Track', in *Selected Poems*, ed. Robert Hass, trans. Robert Bly, Hopewell, NJ: The Ecco Press, 1987, 35.

Postscript

A few books are written this way out of the weekly rumination. There was a horizon sketched, uncertain. You have made headway here and there for two, three, four years. Sometimes bits of analyses are already published as articles. Nevertheless, you collect all of those attempts and you publish them as a book. Producing such a book means only one thing: that you're fed up with this approach, this horizon, this tone, these readings. Of course the notes and even the parts already written don't exempt you from writing the book; that is, from rethinking almost everything. But you do it to get it over with. What makes you happy, gives you the sense of well-being you have with the book, is that you'll be done with the work. Whereas teaching is as endless as study itself. (Jean-François Lyotard, 'Endurance and the Profession').

www.ingramcontent.com/pod-product-compliance
Lightning Source LLC
Chambersburg PA
CBHW030102170426
43198CB00009B/455